D1565923

Fear of the Family

OXFORD STUDIES IN INTERNATIONAL HISTORY
James J. Sheehan, series advisor

THE WILSONIAN MOMENT
Self- Determination and the International Origins of Anticolonial Nationalism
Erez Manela

IN WAR'S WAKE
Europe's Displaced Persons in the Postwar Order
Gerard Daniel Cohen

GROUNDS OF JUDGMENT
Extraterritoriality and Imperial Power in Nineteenth-Century China and Japan
Pär Kristoffer Cassel

THE ACADIAN DIASPORA
An Eighteenth-Century History
Christopher Hodson

GORDIAN KNOT
Apartheid and the Unmaking of the Liberal World Order
Ryan Irwin

THE GLOBAL OFFENSIVE
The United States, the Palestine Liberation Organization, and the Making of the Post-Cold War Order
Paul Thomas Chamberlin

MECCA OF REVOLUTION
Algeria, Decolonization, and the Third World Order
Jeffrey James Byrne

SHARING THE BURDEN
The Armenian Question, Humanitarian Intervention, and Anglo-American Visions of Global Order
Charlie Laderman

THE WAR LORDS AND THE GALLIPOLI DISASTER
How Globalized Trade Led Britain to Its Worst Defeat of the First World War
Nicholas A. Lambert

FEAR OF THE FAMILY
Guest Workers and Family Migration in the Federal Republic of Germany
Lauren Stokes

Fear of the Family

Guest Workers and Family Migration in the Federal Republic of Germany

LAUREN STOKES

OXFORD
UNIVERSITY PRESS

OXFORD
UNIVERSITY PRESS

Oxford University Press is a department of the University of Oxford. It furthers the University's objective of excellence in research, scholarship, and education by publishing worldwide. Oxford is a registered trade mark of Oxford University Press in the UK and certain other countries.

Published in the United States of America by Oxford University Press
198 Madison Avenue, New York, NY 10016, United States of America.

CIP data is on file at the Library of Congress

ISBN 978–0–19–755841–6

DOI: 10.1093/oso/9780197558416.001.0001

1 3 5 7 9 8 6 4 2

Printed by Integrated Books International, United States of America

CONTENTS

ACKNOWLEDGMENTS

Writing acknowledgments feels fraught in a book about the value of social reproduction. While this book's existence in the world depends on many people who have never read a word of the manuscript, here, at least, I must resist the temptation to footnote that fact.

I am thankful to Pieter Judson and Timothy Burke for inspiring me to become a historian and to the entire German department at Swarthmore, but above all to Sunka Simon, for sparking an abiding love of the German language. At the University of Chicago, the initial idea for the project came in conversation with Tara Zahra, who has continued to be an unfailingly generous reader and interlocutor. Leora Auslander encouraged me to develop as a feminist scholar and helped me understand myself as somebody with multiple projects on the go. Finally, Michael Geyer informed my incoming class that "the book is dead" in the first seminar of graduate school. While I am somewhat sorry to have proved him wrong on that point, I deeply appreciate that he supported this project even when it took unexpected directions.

My experience in graduate school was also buoyed by friendship, commiseration, and support from people including Michaela Appeltová, Nicole Beckmann Tessel, Amanda Blair, Chris Dunlap, Kyle Gardner, Joachim Häberlen, Katya Motyl, Sarah Panzer, Eleanor Rivera, Basil Salem, Jake Smith, Jenna Timmons, and Michael Williams. Several friends were also members of the Transnational Approaches to Modern Europe workshop at the University of Chicago, which provided crucial feedback on several of the earliest iterations of this project. The Gender and Sexuality workshop at the University of Chicago and the German Historical Institute Transatlantic Doctoral Seminar also each workshopped one chapter. I also thank Cambridge University Press, which published an early version of chapter 3 as " 'An Invasion of Guest Worker Children': Welfare Reform and the Stigmatisation of Family Migration in West Germany," *Contemporary European History* 28 (2019): 372–389.

The book was also shaped by many fellow panelists, commentators, and audience members at multiple conferences of the German Studies Association, Labor and Race in Modern German History at Birkbeck, the Midwest German History Workshop, the International Conference of Europeanists, the Social Science History Association, and the American Historical Association. My deep gratitude especially to panel commentators including Emily Bruce, Rita Chin, Quinn Slobodian, and Lora Wildenthal and to all of those who braved 8:00 AM panels.

Thank you to every single archivist and staff member who patiently listened to my German, pointed me to useful sources, and accommodated my requests on short notice. While in the archives I also particularly benefited from the companionship of other researchers, including Jeremy Best, Adam Blackler, David Harrisville, Carla Heelan, Michelle Kahn, Stephen Lauritano, Brittany Lehmann, Jessica Plummer, Ned Richardson-Little, Alex Ruble, David Spreen, Sandra Vacca, and Matthew Yokell. Jane Freeland, Carla Heelan, Jessica Plummer, and David Spreen each went above and beyond, providing not just archival companionship but a roommate at one point or another. Larry Frohman and Mark Spicka each provided photographs of sources, while conversations with a host of kind and brilliant senior colleagues made their way into the book in convoluted fashion. May you all find something useful in the final product.

The training and archival research itself were possible because of financial support from the Jacob K. Javits Foundation, the Foreign Language and Area Studies Fellowship, the Critical Language Scholarship Program, the Council on European Studies, the German Historical Institute, the Central European History Society, and chiefly the German Chancellor Fellowship of the Alexander von Humboldt Foundation. Thank you to all of the 2013–2014 BUKAs, but especially to Natalia, Roman, and Kirill for the Russian lessons. The Alice Kaplan Institute for the Humanities at Northwestern funded the sabbatical that allowed me to complete the book, provided subvention funding for manuscript publication, and staged inspiring conversations with colleagues from across the university.

While completing the book, I was fortunate to have consistently secure employment as a College Fellow and later Assistant Professor in the History Department at Northwestern. I am grateful to every colleague organizing for said job security to be the norm rather than the exception, and also to colleagues at Northwestern who have made it a most supportive place to finish a book. The History and German departments provided the funding for a spirited manuscript workshop in 2019. Thank you to Lisa Heineman and Jordanna Bailkin for reading the entire manuscript and providing generous feedback. Ben Frommer, Tessie Liu, Deborah Cohen, and Gerry Cadava each read the manuscript and provided generative comments.

My writing group consistently reminded me about the existence of topic sentences but still somehow made me want to keep writing: I owe a lot to Julie Ault, Deborah Barton, Jennifer Lynn, Willeke Sandler, and Kira Thurman. Thank you to the two anonymous referees who provided generous reader reports at the beginning of an ongoing global pandemic, and thank you to the entire staff at Oxford University Press, above all my editor, Susan Ferber.

Finally, I am pleased to report that my own experiences with "the family" have been a source of love and support rather than fear. Thank you, Dana, Ken, Connor, and everyone else who sparked my interest in familial mobility and who showed interest in my work. This project would have been impossible without the person who agreed to be part of my family while I was in the middle of it. While my copy of *Risikogesellschaft* told me that "the market model of modernity implies a society *without* families . . . 'unhindered' by a relationship, marriage, or family," one might ask, what has the market model of modernity ever gotten right? Thank you, Robin, for outlining chapter four on a cocktail napkin—and for everything else.

ABBREVIATIONS

AAG	Ausländeraufenthaltsgesetz (Law on the Residence of Foreigners)
AfD	Alternative für Deutschland (Alternative for Germany)
AIG	Ausländerintegrationsgesetz (Law on the Integration of Foreigners)
AWO	Arbeiterwohlfahrt (Workers' Welfare)
BKA	Bundeskanzleramt (Federal Chancellor's Office)
BMA	Bundesministerium der Arbeit (Federal Labor Ministry)
BMI	Bundesministerium des Innern/Bundesinnenministerium (Federal Interior Ministry)
BMJ	Bundesministerium für Justiz (Federal Justice Ministry)
BMJFG	Bundesministerium für Jugend, Familie, und Gesundheit (Federal Ministry for Youth, Family, and Health)
BVerfGE	Bundesverfassungsgericht (Federal Constitutional Court)
BVerwG	Bundesverwaltungsgericht (Federal Administrative Court)
CDU	Christlich Demokratische Union Deutschlands (Christian Democratic Union of Germany)
CSU	Christlich-Soziale Union in Bayern (Christian Social Union in Bavaria)
DGB	Deutsche Gewerkschaftsbund (German Confederation of Trade Unions)
DST	Deutsche Städtetag (Association of German Cities)
EC	European Commission
ECJ	European Court of Justice
ECSC	European Coal and Steel Community
EEC	European Economic Community
EU	European Union
FDP	Freie Demokratische Partei (Free Democratic Party)

FİDEF	Federal Almanya İşçi Dernekleri Federasyonu (Federation of Turkish Workers' Associations in West Germany)
FRG	Federal Republic of Germany
IAF	Interessengemeinschaft der mit Ausländern verheirateten Frauen (Association of Women Married to Foreigners)
IM	Innenministerium (Interior Ministry)
NATO	North Atlantic Treaty Organization
RAF	Rote Armee Fraktion (Red Army Faction)
SPD	Sozialdemokratische Partei Deutschlands (Social Democratic Party)
ZDF	Zweites Deutsche Fernsehen (Second German Television)

Fear of the Family

Introduction

When Vera Rimski of Yugoslavia arrived at the Munich train station on March 8, 1972, she was celebrated as the two-millionth guest worker recruited to the Federal Republic of Germany (FRG). Rimski was joining her husband to work at a Siemens electronics factory in Munich. Although the couple would have to live in separate dormitories for the immediate future, a Siemens corporate recruiter at the welcoming ceremony promised to help them find an apartment "as soon as possible." Josef Stingl, president of the Federal Labor Office, presented Rimski with a bouquet of flowers and a portable television. He told her that he hoped it would help her to learn German.[1]

The image of Rimski following her husband to work at Siemens stands in sharp contrast to an earlier and more famous photograph capturing the arrival of the one millionth guest worker. When Armando Rodrigues de Sá of Portugal arrived at the Cologne train station in 1964, he was gifted with a moped. While both arrivals were staged for public consumption, the photograph of Sá and his moped has entered the public memory of labor migration, included in textbooks and academic works. The museum of national history in Bonn recovered the moped for its permanent exhibition.[2] Sá astride his moped is the image of the labor recruitment program that the German state wanted to project to the world. Sá was single, male, and highly mobile, a man who would sell his labor to West German employers before riding away with his savings. Rimski, by contrast, has been forgotten. No journalist followed up to discover whether Siemens secured an apartment for the couple. No curator went to Yugoslavia to recover the television.

Nonetheless, Rimski's arrival represents the fact that West Germany's "guest worker" migration was, from the beginning, simultaneously and purposefully family migration. Despite Rimski's status as both a family member and a worker, state officials frequently treated "family" and "labor" migration as separate categories. Chancellor Helmut Schmidt of the Social Democratic Party (SPD) did so in October 1978 when he called the president of the European

Fear of the Family. Lauren Stokes, Oxford University Press. © Oxford University Press 2022.
DOI: 10.1093/oso/9780197558416.003.0001

Figure I.1 Vera Rimski is celebrated as the two-millionth guest worker at the Munich train station on March 3, 1972. Picture alliance/Istvan Bajzat.

Commission (EC) to express his concerns about Greece's pending accession to the European Economic Community (EEC). At the time, negotiators had proposed a twelve-year transitional period to gradually lower barriers to freedom of movement between Greece and the EEC. Schmidt didn't think twelve years was long enough, arguing that it was "the kind of dodge thought up by Foreign Ministers who wanted to be nice to the Greeks." Schmidt did not think "that there should ever be totally free access," as "immigrants seemed to breed more quickly than Germans." He further specified that "he was not afraid of free movement of labor but of free movement of the families of labor."[3]

This book is about a political culture that turned fear of the family into a basis for making policy. Precisely because it took German fears of foreign families seriously, the West German state consistently implemented migration policies that produced fear within the foreign family. One divorced Turkish woman living in West Berlin with her two children told a reporter from her union in 1976 that "our hearts jump if we see a police officer in the street. When the door is knocked, we fear 'the police have come.'" Her family feared encounters with the state because they did not want to be deported and separated.[4] While their fears were based on their everyday experiences, the state rarely took their emotions into account as it made policy.[5]

The category of the family is important because at the time Schmidt articulated his fear of the family, the plurality of legal migrants in West Germany
and Western Europe more broadly had entered based on their status as "family
migrants." Scholars have tended to assume the contours of this "family migration" without investigating it. They have largely assumed that so-called family
migrants are dependents, that "dependents" are women and children, and that
their arrival changes migrant communities by making them more permanent
and settled.[6] This book argues that these assumptions are artifacts of a historical period and that presumptions about the "family migrant" changed over the
course of the 1970s. The West German state highly valued Vera Rimski's identity
as a "wife" in 1970—not only because Siemens was thrilled to have secured a
new employee who could be paid less than her husband, but also because the
state assumed that her presence would make her husband less likely to develop
long-term connections in Germany through relationships with local women and
thus more likely to leave at the end of his contract. The family was assumed to
be more mobile than the single man. Chancellor Schmidt's fear of the family in
1978, only eight years later, was based on the assumption that family members
are dependents who can only be burdensome to the economy and that their
presence led to unwanted permanence. Over the decade, the actual migratory
behavior of foreign families intersected with changing ideas about "family" and
"labor" to shape increasingly restrictive policies toward family migration.

The Federal Republic of Germany or West German state was never a sin-
gular actor with coherent intentions but a diverse set of actors chasing different
priorities. Local municipalities and federal institutions often clashed over the
proper way to regulate migration based on different interpretations of local and
national needs. The migration bureaucracy clashed with the independent judiciary and often sought to change practices on the ground in hopes of avoiding
binding court rulings. Different federal ministries took different perspectives on
migration. Most important, the Labor Ministry tended to see migration through
an economic lens and to resent the Interior and Foreign Ministries for using different priorities to make policy. West Germany was also caught up in the process
of European integration and the associated deregulation of movement, which
led to increasing limitations on the state's ability to unilaterally manage migration.[7] Policymakers' attempts to reconcile divergent interests led to halting and
conflicted policies that rarely succeeded even on their own terms.

State actors maintained persistent fantasies about their own capacity to control and regulate, but those were consistently undermined by the actual behavior of migrants. When Bavarian officials investigated a case of welfare fraud in
a Turkish family in 1976, they uncovered much more independent action than
they had anticipated. The investigation was sparked when two Turkish men were
claiming child allowances for daughters with the same birthdate and the same

mother. Were they trying to claim double allowances for one child? During the ensuing investigation, "Emine," the mother, explained that she had divorced her husband and father of her children in order to marry her step-uncle, a widower struggling to provide for his five children in Turkey. Her step-uncle used the marriage to migrate to the FRG in July 1973, and Emine had a daughter with her original husband while married to her step-uncle for migration purposes. Her step-uncle used the opportunity to register one of his daughters for welfare payments, and Emine subsequently divorced her step-uncle in order to re-marry the father of her children. The two men actually were claiming the benefit for two different children and had not committed welfare fraud. As the step-uncle told the investigators, "Our only goal was for me to be able to come to Germany as a guest worker." The police concluded that although the various manipulations of the family were indeed "morally dubious," they had not broken any laws.[8] This case is a striking example of the ways in which would-be migrants were continually seeking, and finding, loopholes. Scholars have theorized this kind of behavior as autonomous or *eigensinnig*.[9] The salient point is that the state was never fully able to control migration and turned the willful "family migrant" into a useful scapegoat.

Fear of the Family makes four interrelated arguments about family migration. First, it argues that the state used the category of the "family member" to enforce its own ideas about the appropriate gendered division of labor. Since the mid-1970s, most decisions about legal migration have also been decisions about what foreign families ought to look like, which helps to explain the fact that gender and sexuality have become primary categories for discussing difference in contemporary Europe. Second, the family has also been a key site for the production of ideas about racialized difference. In regulating family migration, West Germans thought in racialized categories without using the word "race," a process that led to the re-articulation of racial hierarchies in the wake of National Socialism. Using recent history to justify their policy, state officials invoked the Nazi past as a reductive cautionary tale about the way that "minority problems" could lead to popular violence. In this way, memories of the Nazi past produced fears for the future, fears that could be used just as easily to justify more restrictive migration policies as to justify liberal migration policies. Finally, the regulation of guest workers and family migrants contributed to the development of "market-conforming" and neoliberal governance within the West German state. Neoliberal states divest themselves of responsibility for social reproduction in order to place that responsibility on families. Foreign families' inclusion in the German welfare state depended on their willingness to conform to the market. Individuals whose families failed to meet the state's expectations of appropriate social reproduction found themselves cut off from social belonging and citizenship.

Guest Workers and the Gender of Labor

The history of labor migration has always simultaneously been the history of the family. In the early Federal Republic, officials from across the political spectrum idealized the nuclear family with a male breadwinner and a female homemaker, a supposedly "traditional" family form understood as "a repository of quintessentially German values that had survived the Third Reich."[10] This ideal was further legitimated by the new FRG within the context of the Cold War. Christian conservative politicians undermined attempts to reform family law in favor of working mothers by offering the counterexample of East Germany, where the communists purportedly forced married women into the full-time workforce and their children into institutional childcare.[11]

This ideal had consequences. In the 1950s, West Germany set new records for both the percentage of people who married and the percentage of married couples who had children.[12] The West German state institutionalized half-day school and invested only sparingly in childcare facilities, policies that made it difficult for married women to enter the full-time workforce. Although hundreds of thousands of married women began working on a part-time basis in the 1960s, the structural obstacles to full-time work ensured that women with children remained an under-utilized source of labor.[13]

In response, the state turned to a number of new sources of labor to meet employer demand, including the widespread recruitment of foreign workers in what became known as the "guest worker" program, starting in 1955. The so-called guest worker program was intended to attract foreign workers in their prime years of labor while assuming that the workers' childhood and old age would take place in another, cheaper, country. The guest worker model promised that "productive labor" could be shuffled around rapidly to meet the changing needs of employers, while the "reproductive labor" that went into those workers—the parenting, the education, the healthcare, the retirement—could be kept stationary and far from the national welfare state.[14]

However, West German labor recruiters undermined the intended division between productive and reproductive labor. They aggressively recruited foreign women, who composed between 15 percent and 30 percent of the workers who came to the FRG in each year between 1955 and 1973.[15] Some women entered as "guest workers," others as "family migrants," but labor recruiters implicitly understood the "family migrant" as a category that enabled the recruitment of women for factory jobs. Countries that were reluctant to approve the emigration of women "workers" were far more willing to approve the emigration of female "family members" following their husbands, fathers, or brothers, women who might happen to decide to work alongside male family members on arrival. The "family migration" category allowed women to work for wages without violating their roles as women, defined primarily in relation to male family members. The high percentage of foreign women in the West German workforce marks a significant departure from "guest worker" programs in the United States or other Western European countries, which have historically employed only men.[16]

The fact that hundreds of thousands of women entered as "guest workers" also raised the possibility that men would enter as their dependent "family members." Men were also able to enter the country as "family migrants," but every man who did so represented a kind of category crisis for the migration regime. Bureaucrats saw it as self-evident that men could not be primarily classified as dependents; men who tried to make use of a category intended for dependents were suspicious at best, actively attempting to defraud the German state at worst. Officials understood men who migrated using the category of the "family member" as deceitful "economic migrants," who used a category intended for dependents and caregivers as a cover for their true motive to work for wages. Migration policy was applied to keep foreign men from misusing the category.

The FRG further undermined its idealized split between "productive" and "reproductive" labor because it had no way to prevent foreign children from entering the country and no way to expel them once they arrived. When West Germany began the guest worker program, it did not require visas or residence permits for foreigners under the age of sixteen. Without a legal instrument to control or even count foreign children, the state was unable to react when foreign parents brought their children with them. These parents decided to move out of company dormitories and into private apartments, demanded childcare and education for their children, and insisted on making their own independent claims on the welfare state. Their actions violated the implicit assumption that "guest worker" programs outsourced reproductive labor and set in motion a long-term process with which the state needed to grapple.

"A Small Master Race": The Racialization of Guest Workers

In his essay about guest workers in Switzerland, Max Frisch observed of the guest worker program that "a small master race [*Herrenvolk*] feels itself in danger: labor was called for, and people came."[17] This sentence has become a truism of the migration literature, but scholars almost always quote only the second half of the aphorism—"labor was called for, and people came." In so doing, they omit Frisch's sly remark about the "small master race," a reference that points the reader to the unavoidable persistence of racial thinking after

National Socialism.[18] The failure to quote the first half of the aphorism is indicative of the way that race and racism have been marginal within migration scholarship to date. The full aphorism brings the function of hegemonic whiteness within West German migration policy back into view.

German historians have long been extremely reluctant to use the category of "race" for the period after 1945 and have tended to explain discrimination and social exclusion using the category of "xenophobia, which is what Germans of the postwar era themselves used."[19] When German sociologist Helma Lutz interviewed Turkish social workers in the Netherlands and in West Germany in the 1980s, she found that all of her interviewees mentioned "xenophobia—that is what the informants in the Federal Republic called it—and racism—according to the women in the Netherlands."[20] This German avoidance of the language of "race" stemmed from an unwillingness to countenance the possibility that there could be racial thinking after Nazism.[21]

Relying on "xenophobia" to explain discrimination against people considered to be "foreign" works to keep these people outside of the polity.[22] The category of "xenophobia" does not just fail to explain the experiences of groups like Afro-Germans, Jewish Germans, and migrants and their descendants, but it also naturalizes the false assumption that to be German is to be white. In the case of migrants and their descendants, by the second or third generation, many consider themselves to be German—they have never lived anywhere else and do not speak any other language—but they are denied social recognition as such. Racism is a far more accurate explanation for this denial of social recognition for people who are not "foreign" by birth, and increasingly not by citizenship, but who are judged by many of their fellow citizens to "look foreign." This racialization is premised on the idea that "races" are not biologically determined but that the experience of racism is a social fact reproduced in everyday experience.[23]

The rap group "Advanced Chemistry" highlighted this point about German society in their 1992 song "Foreigner in My Own Country." In the first stanza, Afro-German rapper Linguist holds up his German passport and asks why he is always asked to show it when crossing the border: "Is it so strange/when an Afro-German speaks his language/without having a pale face? /The problem is the ideas in the system/A proper German must also look properly German." Cem Özdemir, the Green Party representative who became the first Turkish-German elected into the Bundestag, also referred to this experience in 1999 when trying to persuade his colleagues to vote for comprehensive citizenship reform. Özdemir asked his colleagues: "How will we deal with the fact, that the skin color and hair color will not change? . . . We will have German citizens, who have somewhat more sun than the average citizen of this Republic."[24] Although taboos prevent the use of the language of "racism," Linguist and Özdemir call out the codification of observable physical difference as an ongoing barrier to their social recognition as fully German.

The boundaries between groups, however, can be drawn and redrawn over time. Most studies of "guest workers" have focused on particular national groups—particularly the three most populous: Italian, Yugoslav, and Turkish citizens—and have shown that attitudes toward each national group fluctuated over time. Germans commonly held negative stereotypes about Italians when migration began in the 1950s and 1960s, and memories of Italians as forced laborers under the Nazi regime shaped the early treatment of Italian guest workers.[25] Germany's changing understandings of its own past and the Cold War shaped attitudes toward Yugoslav migrants.[26] Scholars who have focused on Turkish migration have shown, counterintuitively, that ideas about Islam initially played a relatively minor role in negative stereotypes about guest workers, but that this changed in the late 1970s and early 1980s, coinciding with the Iranian Revolution and broader global awareness of political Islam.[27]

This book tracks the process of racialization by focusing on how white Germans evaluated the behavior of the "migrant family" across multiple national groups. Guest worker families were originally categorized only as "Mediterranean" or "Southern," a descriptor that broadly homogenized ideas about "guest workers" from Portugal to Turkey. These early generalizations about the backward and illiberal "Mediterranean family" reappeared and were applied to the "Turkish family" and the "Muslim family" in later decades. One of the most consistent generalizations about the "foreign family" is about its supposed inferior treatment of women. In the 1960s, the "Southern patriarch" allegedly oppressed women and kept them in the household against their will; in the 1980s the "Muslim patriarch" oppressed women and forced them to wear a headscarf as the supposed mark of their essential remove from the public sphere. Upholding the German family as the norm, both notions said more about West German political ideologies than about the actual experience of immigrant families.

Historians and scholars who have analyzed these stereotypes about foreign families have argued that Germans and other Europeans increasingly "turned to gender" as a prime marker of difference beginning in the 1980s.[28] The fact that most legal migration occurs through kinship ties has reinforced this turn. Politicians who want to limit legal migration can do so by casting doubt on the legitimacy of the category—the family—that enables said legal migration, for example, by insinuating that the "foreign family" is an oppressive, excessively patriarchal institution.[29] However, politicians who complain that foreigners have negative attitudes toward homosexuality rarely address the fact that, for decades, Western migration regimes rigorously enforced compulsory heterosexuality for foreign families, actively excluding foreigners who desired to enter into same-sex partnerships with Germans or with other foreigners.[30] German ideas about gender and German family law both changed more rapidly than migration law, ensuring that migrant families would always appear to lag behind processes of liberalization.

Frustrated by their inability to control the behavior of migrant families, state officials resorted to racialized categories as a way to make sense of unpredictable behavior. Stereotypes about the "foreign family" positioned it as out of step with German emotional regimes. According to the records of the migration bureaucrats, foreign families were overly emotional, irrational, and illiberal in their dependence on each other. They consistently made the wrong decisions about migration. Foreign spouses who wanted to live together were "irrationally attached," foreign parents who brought their children to West Germany were delusional, and anything a Turkish family did to secure a residence permit was probably a form of elaborate deception. These families also passed down the wrong values to their children and grandchildren. In pedagogy and social work, the "foreign family" and the individual's attachment to it presented obstacles that had to be overcome to create proper liberal subjectivities and citizens.

The term "family reunification" also has codified racial categories. The West German state sought to enable "family reunification" for ethnic German expellees and refugees who had left family members in Eastern Europe. Officials never wrote a restrictive legal definition of the family into law in part because such a definition would have limited their own ability to act across the Iron Curtain. Instead, the German language developed two separate words for "family reunification" so as to maintain different kinds of family migration morally and lexicographically. *Familiennachzug* and *Familienzusammenführung* both describe the phenomenon of spouses and children migrating to join a settled partner, but the former roughly translates as "chain migration" and the latter as "family reunification." *Familienzusammenführung* is self-evidently humanitarian and emphasizes intimacy and reunion after a period of painful separation, while *Familiennachzug* lacks the emotional connotation of the primary term. Sociologists first used the latter term to describe family reunion of guest workers in Switzerland in the 1960s, and it seems that West Germans borrowed the term to distinguish this kind of migration from the family reunion of ethnic Germans.[31]

While my sources often used both words seemingly interchangeably, over time they drifted toward the exclusive use of *Familiennachzug* to describe the family migration of guest workers and asylum seekers. The deliberate use of the term became more consequential after the 1975 Helsinki Accords included a promise to facilitate "family reunification" across the Iron Curtain, translated as *Familienzusammenführung*. The German translation of this international human rights instrument made it important to maintain the distinction between the two terms. The Foreign Office often corrected colleagues in other ministries about inappropriate usage of *Familienzusammenführung* in draft statements about new restrictions, replacing it with *Familiennachzug* and citing the Helsinki Accords.[32] Activists would accuse the state of hypocrisy despite this linguistic splitting, but having two distinct words for the process of family reunion was one strategy that the FRG used to defend the fact that it only applied the human rights instrument to some kinds of families.[33] This book will translate both terms as "family reunification" or "family migration," but will often specify the word used in the German original because of its strong political implications.[34]

"Our History Means": The National Socialist Past in the Migration Regime

Nazi Germany relied on foreign forced labor to fuel its economic growth, enslaving populations in occupied territory and forcing them to work alongside Germans in sectors including agriculture, munition manufacturing, and mining.[35] As the "guest worker" regime followed the defeat of the Nazi regime by only ten years, many scholars have assumed that restrictive West German migration and citizenship policies were a "lingering deficit" from the Nazi period.[36] Historians of migration have also shown that the West German state sought to self-consciously distance itself from the recent past. Officials abandoned the Nazi term for "foreign worker" [*Fremdarbeiter*] for the more neutral term "foreign employee" [*ausländische Arbeitnehmer*], choreographed the workers' train journeys from the sending country to Germany, and included foreign workers in the welfare state to make it clear that the new arrivals were not "forced laborers."[37]

Fear of the Family argues that the Nazi past also served as a kind of cautionary tale for policymakers about the inevitability of violence, a recent memory that kept alive fears of the consequences of diversity. State officials believed that within the court of international public opinion, it would be easier for them to defend harsh migration restrictions than to defend widespread popular violence against foreigners. When the Labor Minister announced a set of new restrictions on family migration in 1981, for example, the speech prepared for the occasion originally included the statement that "our history means that we cannot afford a domestic political situation that is marked by open xenophobia and related unrest."[38] While the phrase "our history," with its implicit reference to National Socialism, was ultimately omitted from the final draft, the speech retained the same logic: "It ought to be easier to defend restrictions on family reunification, than to defend the circumstances that will inevitably unfold when the foreign population continues to grow. It's better to act now with the motto 'as far as possible, no more foreigners,' than to be forced later to make policy under the slogan 'Foreigners out!' "[39] The gesture to public opinion and to the inevitability of popular violence allowed policymakers to disavow their own racist attitudes while enacting racist policies. The state's restrictive policies were preemptively justified against criticism when presented as safeguards against pogroms.

West German officials invoked a coming outbreak of racist violence in no small part because a vocal minority of their constituents told them it was coming. State archives about migration policy include hundreds of racist letters and right-wing tracts amid files marked "Foreigner Policy" or even "Foreigners' Rights."[40] Many letter writers were influenced by radical right texts. For example, Wolfgang Seeger, a police chief inspector in Stuttgart and active member of the right-wing Ludendorff movement, sent his 1980 pamphlet "The Integration of Foreigners Is Genocide" to dozens of municipal authorities.[41] The pamphlet argued that a shadowy cabal of elites had failed to completely destroy the "German people" in 1945. In their frustration, the group had worked with the United States in order to destroy Germans over the long term through the methods of "'refined' geno-cide," which meant flooding the state with foreigners who would out-breed and inter-breed with the German people: "Those who reject the over-foreignization of our land are not fascist—the fascists are those who support a policy of mixing the peoples!"[42] The publisher sent out hundreds of free copies, including to schools and kindergartens. Attempts to have the pamphlet classified as "dangerous to youth" failed.[43] Seeger in his own obituary said he had not been demoralized by the "capitulation of the *Wehrmacht* [the armed forces of the Third Reich]" but had continued to defend Nazi principles for the rest of his life.

Figure I.2 A man walks with a child in front of "Turks Out!" graffiti in the Kreuzberg neighborhood of West Berlin in 1980. Picture alliance/ZB/Paul Glaser.

Many letter writers picked up on parts of Seeger's argument in the 1980s, including one man who wrote to protest giving Turks citizenship, lamenting that sometimes he wished he lived in East Germany because at least their politicians were protecting the German people from their ongoing genocide by safeguarding them behind the Iron Curtain.[44] While many writers expressed such noxious views anonymously, others signed their names. Racist letter writers also commonly invoke their academic credentials or high-status jobs as part of the reason that the government should listen to them. The state did not move to prosecute their authors for "incitement of hatred," and policymakers appear to have understood these views as background noise.

Restrictive migration policies were not an aberration but an integral part of West German "liberalization" and "Westernization," precisely because they were intended to quell discontent and thus to keep these views marginal. While popular violence committed by Germans would provoke comparisons to Nazi violence, migration restriction was an accepted feature of liberal statecraft across Western Europe. Compared to other Western European nations, the FRG had a relatively de-regulated migration regime, one that became more restrictive as it borrowed features from more explicitly post-colonial migration regimes. These post-colonial regimes confronted the question of family migration earlier and with more restrictions. France suspended family reunification entirely from July 1974 to June 1975 and again in 1977, and the United Kingdom effectively banned husbands from migrating to join their wives for most of the period between 1969 and 1982.[45]

While the West German state was undeniably invested in maintaining a homogeneous German population, it also recognized that fascism and biological racism were no longer acceptable ways to enforce hierarchies of race and gender. The state borrowed from its Western European neighbors in order to learn how to describe and enforce these hierarchies through liberalism. The migration regime increasingly described and enforced these hierarchies through the ideology of market conformity. The regulation of foreign workers and their families became a key site for the development of a specifically German strain of neoliberalism.

"The Market-Conforming Family": Family Migration and Neoliberal Paternalism

Ludwig Erhard, West Germany's first minister of economics and the self-proclaimed architect of the "economic miracle," believed that all state interventions into the economy needed to be "market conforming," to promote the competitive market order and not to interfere with its internal logic. The state needed to produce subjects capable of competing within it and to secure that market order from the threat of democracy—specifically from the threat that popular political demands might interfere with market mechanisms.[46] For the first decades of its existence, the FRG staked its legitimacy, and thus the legitimacy of its migration policy, on its ability to continue to provide economic growth. In his 1979 Collège de France lectures, Michel Foucault observed that "in contemporary Germany, the economy, economic development and economic growth, produces sovereignty. . . . It produces a permanent consensus of all those who may appear as agents within these economic processes, as investors, workers, employers, and trade unions."[47] Foreigners became part of this "permanent consensus" through labor.

Neoliberal logic influenced the institutions of the welfare state through the assumption that "economic policies are the best social policies."[48] The state consistently approached migration policy as a form of economic policy. As employers struggled to find labor in a context of full employment, Labor Minister Anton Storch proposed that the state respond either by encouraging employers to relocate to rural areas or by trying to bring women into the labor market. Erhard saw both as unacceptable interventions in the economy and instead favored labor recruitment abroad. Erhard was able to win over Chancellor Adenauer, leading to the first bilateral labor agreement with Italy in 1955.[49] Foreign workers appeared to be a source of labor that did not require the state to intervene in the market or to invest in their reproduction.

Families are central institutions for neoliberal states because they are the central institutions of reproduction. Contrary to common understandings, neoliberal economists and policymakers understand the competitive market order as not exclusively a collection of individuals but assume that "the self-sufficient family" that cares for its members is the basic unit of the free market.[50] Neoliberal states use individualism to disavow responsibility for care work and place the burden of social reproduction onto non-state actors. Such states tacitly assume the existence of a group of individuals who are not market maximizers—principally, but not exclusively, women—who are always already available to do the work of social reproduction in lieu of establishing state social welfare programs. The retreat of the postwar welfare state has made the family even more important, as it is required to take up the slack and to continue the social reproduction without which the economy would no longer function.[51]

The assumption that women's unremunerated care work will always exist and the disavowal of responsibility for social reproduction that this assumption enables arguably open the possibility for alliances between neoliberals and social conservatives. Where neoliberals implicitly presume that the family will be the central institution of social welfare provision, religious conservatives celebrate the family as sacred.[52] Many thinkers drew on the social Catholic principle of "subsidiarity," whereby "the state shall only interfere in 'private life' when the capacity of smaller social units, such as the family or the business, to guarantee their members' social security has been reached."[53] For Catholics, this principle protected divinely ordained Christian families from the intervention of the secular state; for neoliberals, this principle protected the state from paying the cost of social reproduction. Neoliberals and Catholics frequently clashed about specific measures, but their overlapping interests in producing self-sufficient families shaped the first decades of West German politics.[54]

The FRG initially took a deregulated approach to family migration in part because it believed that such migration could help workers make fewer claims on the welfare state since female migrants would perform the role of caretaker. This kind of migration made married women available for full-time work and prevented the welfare state from having to perform care work. The state also expected foreign women to perform sexual labor; with their presence, state officials believed, foreign men would be less likely to sleep with German women and produce illegitimate children, as well as less likely to marry German women. But as the economic boom receded in the 1970s, and foreign families continued to stay and to make additional claims on the welfare state, this positive attitude toward the migrant family eroded. No longer a self-contained and self-deporting unit, these families were seen as threats to German society and to the welfare state. Accordingly, new restrictions on family migration sought to ensure that foreign families could care for themselves. Today the state authorizes the migration of only family members who can demonstrate that they are part of a "market-conforming family," one that delivers cheap labor for difficult jobs without creating additional costs for the welfare state.

The West German migration regime was also shaped by a paternalist attitude toward those it governed, that is, the substitution of its judgment for migrants' on the grounds that it is in the latter's best interests or welfare and that they are incapable of making proper decisions.[55] West German officials continually argued that migration restrictions were in the interest of migrants themselves, foreign families who inexplicably continued to arrive even after Germany no longer had a use for them. Officials rarely consulted migrants about their own understanding of the situation. The state simply enacted new restrictions to keep foreigners from making bad choices and harming themselves and their families in the process.

The state was quickest to use the language of paternalism when it could claim that migration restrictions worked to protect foreign women and children from the poor decisions of foreign men. By denying migrants and would-be migrants the capacity to rationally evaluate their own situation, it furthered a profoundly unequal relationship between the state and the foreigners who live there.

Officials assumed that foreigners would make poor decisions when left to their own devices, no matter how long they had already lived in West Germany. They consistently accused foreign adults of making poor decisions: breaking labor contracts in order to live with their spouses, deliberately choosing poor housing conditions, bringing their children to Germany without regard for their educational needs, and failing to inculcate their children with the appropriate values of democracy and market conformity.

The state's repeated insistence that "Germany is not an immigration country" functioned as a warning that migration was an individual project that the state did not support. It announced that the nation refused to take any responsibility for its new residents. Foreigners' lives in Germany might indeed turn out poorly, but they would never be able to say that the state had not warned them. This attitude furthered neoliberal governance by removing the responsibility for ameliorating inequality from the welfare state and putting the onus on the foreign family, whose purported deficiency and deviance were blamed for social inequality. The continued social exclusion of these families was not understood as evidence of enduring structural racism but as evidence that foreigners repeatedly made the same poor choices. Their personal failures became a justification for the continued implementation of racist policies in a polity that prided itself on having historically transcended the category of race.

Fear of the Family contends that migrant families continually challenged the state's initial conception of the guest worker as a self-sufficient unit of labor, and the state responded by seeking to discipline their families into market conformity. The first chapter analyzes the conventional periodization of "labor migration" between 1955 and 1973 to show that the process of "labor recruitment" actively encouraged "family migration." The state's belief that family migration accomplished socially valuable ends depended on the idea that "family migrants" were women. The federal administrative court recognized family migration rights in May 1973, basing its ruling on the idea that the state had a responsibility to protect not just any families but specifically self-sufficient families, and thus a responsibility to authorize the migration of those family members who performed reproductive labor.

Nearly from the moment that the court issued this decision, the migration bureaucracy sought to limit its significance in practice. Officials spent the rest of the 1970s and 1980s trying to rebut the court's argument that these migrants could perform valuable labor and to replace it with a narrative of the family as a threat. The second chapter examines attempts to regulate the migrant family through housing restrictions. Another way to undermine the court's reasoning was to depict "family migration" as a cover for some more nefarious purpose, such as illegitimate access to the welfare state or to the labor market. Chapter 3 shows how a welfare reform that created a two-tiered system of child allowance payments inadvertently created a plausible narrative of family migrants as "welfare migrants" moving to Germany for higher child allowance payments. Chapter 4 reveals that male family migrants called the entire idea of "family migration" into question, as local administrators resented the fact that the "family migrant" was formally gender neutral and sought to enforce their own ideas about gender roles in practice.

Although the state had recognized the foreign family's reproductive labor as a way to unburden the welfare state during the 1960s, over the course of the 1970s and 1980s the same reproductive labor came to be recognized as a source of threatening foreign values, a process chronicled in chapters 5 and 6. Migrants often arrived through channels that explicitly promoted "traditional" family values and family roles, but the gendered division of labor and self-containment of the foreign family that migration policy had actively promoted were instead taken to be unchanging characteristics of those same families. Officials identified these newly undesirable characteristics not as artifacts of their own policy but as values emanating from the old country that were wrongfully imposed in the FRG.

When the state introduced new restrictions on family migration in the 1980s, it claimed that the new policies would "protect" the weaker members of the foreign family—women and children—from their oppressive foreign fathers and husbands. During these debates, officials claimed that the migrant family was held together not by love but by instrumental relationships toward the welfare state. They also charged that the migrant family was a coercive institution that oppressed and tyrannized its members, arguing that the "Southern family" or increasingly the "Muslim family" prevented its members from developing properly. The repetition of these messages made the foreign family appear ever more foreign.

The state posed as a paternalist protector throughout the 1980s, arguing that restrictive migration policies could "save" foreign women and children from foreign men who made bad decisions. The seventh and final chapter argues that the 1990 Law on Foreigners and the 1999 citizenship reform were the next logical steps in this family romance. In 1990 the state reformed the Law on Foreigners so as to require residence permits for children under sixteen, a reform that brought child migration under state control for the first time. The 1999 citizenship reform introduced the idea of *jus soli* within German citizenship but failed to significantly open access to naturalization for those who had not been born in Germany. The paternalist state finally claimed a kind of paternity over a generation of "foreign" children.

The state had begun to invoke the "excessive family sense" of migrants to excuse its bureaucracy's persistent failure to understand the population it was supposed to be managing. When a husband left his job in order to live closer to his wife, or when parents brought their child to live with them even though it would presumably be cheaper for that child to grow up elsewhere, the values of the putatively "Mediterranean family" became a reason that migrants were deviating from the imagined life trajectories of the rational "market-conforming" individual. "Family" was an institution that state officials suspected and stigmatized, one that racialized the people within it. The German family was ascribed different human motivations than the foreign family.

Reforms to migration law since the 2000s have insisted that families must be functional in order to constitute themselves in Germany. Their reproduction is ever more tightly monitored, and the "ability to integrate" is increasingly understood as an individual project that requires a break from the family of origin. The racialization of "foreign" families—including those in which all members were born in Germany—contributes to a strategy of neoliberal governance in which the governed must continually prove their worthiness by overcoming the unintended consequences of government policies. If they fail, they are deemed unworthy of the full privileges of citizenship, placing them in a category of the native born but existentially foreign.

The "Market-Conforming Family" in the Era of Labor Recruitment

In November 1972, a group of Spanish and Italian women brought their children to a demonstration calling for a "multinational kindergarten" in Frankfurt. The multilingual flyer announcing the protest was addressed to "German women, female colleagues and neighbors. . . . [M]any of us are forced to leave our children with relatives in the South of Italy, but we have to be here and work, otherwise we would starve. We are separated from our children *as mothers*, and we suffer from this just as our children do." Two weeks later, the women wrote a letter to the mayor detailing the costs of labor migration for the most vulnerable members of the family: "Our children have already paid far too much for this situation. They have become nervous and neurotic. . . . [O]ne of our daughters was struck dumb after the shock of separation from her parents who had to send her back home to her grandmother: the parents had to work and there was no kindergarten that the child could go to."[1] Their individual decisions to migrate were inseparable from their roles as mothers and financial providers. In demanding that the mayor build a kindergarten in Frankfurt in order to help them balance these two roles, they refused to accept the tacit assumption of the guest worker program that they should work for wages in Germany while agreeing to offshore their reproductive labor.

The state had no control over whether guest workers brought their children with them; until the 1990s, children under sixteen did not require residence permits to live in the FRG. Foreign families did more than just bring children with them: they also organized political protests for kindergartens, brought childcare demands to labor strikes, and petitioned state officials for residence permits to sponsor additional extended family members. When those applications for residence permits were denied, migrants filed suit in court, basing their claims to family life on Article 6 of the West German Basic Law, which states that "Marriage and the family shall enjoy the special protection of

Fear of the Family. Lauren Stokes, Oxford University Press. © Oxford University Press 2022.
DOI: 10.1093/oso/9780197558416.003.0002

Figure 1.1 Spanish-language flyer announcing the November 1972 kindergarten protest in Frankfurt. DOMiD-Archiv, Köln FL0023.

the state." As this chapter argues, one of these court cases led to a limited toleration of the migration of extended family members who could prevent foreign workers from making further demands on the welfare state.

Within the state bureaucracy, representations of the "Southern" or "Mediterranean" family were used to contain the unsettling implications of the fact that many guest workers refused to leave their families at home. Experts argued that these guest workers migrated with their family members because they were pathologically dependent on said families. They contended that close-knit "Southern" families safely prevented their members from entanglement with German society and thus ensured that these families could be sent away without long-term implications when employers no longer needed them. This semiofficial doctrine of the "excessive family sense" of the guest worker meant that migrants who brought their families to West Germany were not recognized as agents making conscious decisions about their family lives and their futures. It thus de-politicized and de-emphasized migrants' actions in this period of active labor recruitment. The idea of the "Southern family" consistently worked to promote policies that were extremely favorable for family reunion while ironically blinding officials to the fact that family migration also had the potential to be the first step in a process of long-term or permanent settlement.

Guest Worker Recruitment and Family Reunification

During the period of active labor recruitment, foreigners from the primary "guest worker" countries could enter without a visa and try to find a job on their own, bypassing the entire selection process. To encourage would-be migrants to use official channels, official bilateral recruitment agreements promised a variety of benefits for workers who went through the official selection process, including inclusion in the West German welfare state. These foreign workers received health insurance and pension contributions as well as family allowances even for their children who remained outside Germany.

Each of the bilateral recruitment agreements also contained provisions guiding family reunification. The original 1955 agreement with Italy promised that local Foreigners' Offices would "favorably consider" applications for residence permits for family members who did not work. At the time, the *Frankfurter Allgemeine Zeitung* praised the "model contract" for this promise to allow family reunification, arguing that it was a positive step in breaking with "earlier images of foreign workers [*Fremdarbeiter*]" from the Nazi era.[2] The first agreement with Turkey, signed in 1961, was originally the only agreement that did not include such a provision, but the second agreement with Turkey, signed in 1964, incorporated the language about family migration.[3]

The FRG did not require people from any of the sending countries to have a visa to enter the country, which meant that family reunification in the period of active labor recruitment was almost always legalized after it had occurred. Spouses or teenage children could visit for up to three months before having to apply for a residence permit, and according to the labor recruitment treaties, local Foreigners' Offices had to "favorably consider" such applications. Local employers also pressured Foreigners' Offices to grant residence permits to family members liberally, fearing that refusal of a permit might lead to the loss of a trained worker.

In 1965, the federal government rewrote the Law on Foreigners [*Ausländergesetz*] in response to long-standing local demands for a law that would make it easier to control and to expel foreigners. The new law did so by making an individual foreigner's residence in West Germany dependent on a single factor: whether the residence of the foreigner in question harmed "the interests of the Federal Republic."[4] This formulation gave local Foreigners' Offices a great deal of discretion in interpreting those "interests." The Interior Ministry, at this time controlled by the CDU/CSU (Christian Democratic Union of Germany and the Christian Social Union in Bavaria), wanted to strive

Figure 1.2 1965 Federal Labor Office map of the official routes from Portugal, Spain, Italy, Greece, and Turkey to Germany. Statistik der Bundesagentur für Arbeit.

for a consistent practice nationally and consequently drafted national guidelines for administering the law. The new guidelines were intended to further restrict existing practice, which was primarily oriented to the needs of employers. The Interior Ministry hoped that they would give Foreigners' Offices more support in refusing employers' requests to interpret the law in favor of their employees.[5]

The Interior Ministry's new guidelines rested on four basic principles. The first was to refuse to grant residence to citizens of the Soviet bloc, a principle that primarily impacted unrecognized asylum seekers and displaced persons. The second was to refuse to grant residence to non-Europeans. This principle reflected the racism of the bureaucracy, which worried about the "growing discomfort of wide segments of the population, who feel threatened by the different mentality of workers from outside of Europe."[6] It did not impact citizens of Turkey, who were at the time unambiguously European within bureaucratic categories.[7]

The next two principles would have a greater impact on guest workers already present in the FRG. The third was that Foreigners' Offices should always refuse to grant residence permits to those foreigners who had entered the country without prior authorization—not only a common way to enter the country and look for work outside of official channels but also the single most common way to achieve family reunification. The final principle stipulated that the state should require foreign workers to be resident and employed in West Germany for at least three years before they could have non-working family members join them.

The Interior Ministry insisted that these new principles did not violate the clauses in the recruitment agreements, which only promised to "consider favorably" applications for family reunification.[8] It argued that the Foreigners' Offices should approve family residence permits only when the primary employee— always imagined as the husband—had secured a long-term job and actively planned to integrate into West German life. For anyone who did not plan to stay for a long period, "the inclination to return to the home country and the actual ability to return are decisively impaired through family settlement in the Federal Republic," so family settlement should be discouraged. The Economics Ministry did not see the need for the guideline on family migration and suggested that the Interior Ministry was overreacting: "It is hardly to be expected that foreigners will bring their family members in a worrying quantity if we continue the current practice, which did not have a three-year limit."[9] Most officials simply could not imagine that guest workers would choose to bring their families as a precursor to a long-term settlement.

The Labor Ministry was even more strongly opposed to the guidelines. It forced the Interior Ministry to reduce the residence and employment requirement from three years to one year. This was not a party dispute—both ministries were headed by the CDU; rather, it was a dispute about interministerial jurisdiction and about the goals that each ministry was pursuing with its foreigner policy. The national guidelines were eventually distributed with a lengthy catalog of exceptions attached. Most were oriented to the needs of employers— for example, an exception for skilled employees or in cases where both partners intended to work for wages. These "market-conforming" exceptions completely hollowed out the Interior Ministry's original intention to give Foreigners' Offices more support in standing up to employers.[10]

As the dispute over the 1965 guidelines reveals, during the period of active labor recruitment the Labor Ministry was in fact the greatest official proponent of family migration. When it formed its own working group on foreigners in December 1965, it counted as one of its most important goals "promotion of family reunification despite the 'principles' of the Conference of Interior Ministers."[11]

Labor Migration and the "Southern" Family

The Labor Ministry actively supported family migration in large part because it was hungry for female labor. The FRG was wedded to an ideal of a male breadwinner and female homemaker and chose not to provide the childcare infrastructure essential for mothers to enter the full-time workforce in large numbers.[12] The state's decision not to mobilize the labor of married German women for the factory floor encouraged the recruitment of foreign labor.[13] West Berlin was investing heavily in the microelectronics and textile industries, both of which produced huge numbers of "women's jobs" whose low salaries did not incentivize women to relocate from other parts of the country. Canning companies in the suburbs of Hamburg and in the northern federal state of Schleswig-Holstein had similar problems. Foreign women with no pre-existing ties to Germany were attractive because they could be sent anywhere.

This need for hyper-mobile female labor drove the FRG to sign new labor recruitment contracts. Italy was the first country to sign a bilateral recruitment agreement with West Germany in 1955—an agreement that leading industry journal *Industriekurier* described as necessary "from the standpoint of family policy." Recruiters in Italy had an exceptionally difficult time finding women, in part because Italy restricted the emigration of single women between eighteen and twenty-one, a situation the Federal Labor Office attributed to the "strong family ties" of the Italians.[14] Spain and Portugal also both restricted female emigration. The Spanish Emigration Law stipulated that that single women under twenty-five required parental permission, while married women of any age required their husbands' permission. Portugal allowed women to be recruited only with male family members.[15] Greece and Turkey did not restrict female emigration, which meant that Greek women became the largest group of foreign women working in Germany in 1962, a position they held until it was overtaken by Turkish women in 1967.[16] The state's decision to sign a labor recruitment contract with communist Yugoslavia in 1968 was also partially inspired by the desire to access more female labor.[17] When Italy tried to convince the FRG to reject the Yugoslavian agreement in order to improve the position of their own citizens, the FRG replied that the contract was needed to access the female labor that Italy was unwilling to relinquish.[18]

Experts from welfare organizations, state officials, and employers all believed that the successful employment of female labor required family reunification. One vocal advocate was Giacomo Maturi, a law student from Italy at a German university who saw guest worker migration as an opportunity to re-invent himself as a native expert on Italians, first for welfare organizations and later for the Ford Motor Company. He later became editor of the state's magazine for guest workers, *Workplace Germany*.[19] At a 1960 conference, Maturi laid out a vision of the "Southern" family that he would return to throughout his long career, explaining that "Southerners . . . both married and single, are more closely tied to the family. . . . [T]aking care of the home and preparing food is an exclusively female affair. The southern man is far more inept at these household tasks than the German." Maturi also understood family reunification as a way to save German girls from being harassed by foreign men, alluding to "problems" regarding "the Southerner's attitude to women and the consequences in relation to German girls and women, and in relation to the leisure time of these workers who live alone."[20] Maturi's arguments resembled those made elsewhere in Western Europe about the positive impact of wives on male workers—ideal prophylactics to prevent both sexual aggression and political activism.[21]

The hunger for female workers gave the argument for family reunification an added urgency in the context of the FRG. As Maturi explained, "In the South it is a generally recognized principle, that the woman thinks, feels, and must comport herself completely differently from the man."[22] As a result, "she always feels herself in need of protection, she feels and she is looked after and controlled by her family and her environment."[23] West German social workers who believed that foreign women were "ordinary girls" were deceiving themselves: "These girls and women . . . find themselves in a completely new world, and without special supervision they are exposed to many dangers that can have negative effects. Successful employment of foreign women will only be possible through the *reunification of families*."[24]

Social workers from both Catholic and Protestant organizations also promoted these arguments as they worked to preserve the foreign family. The Catholic organization Caritas frequently invoked ideas of Catholic womanhood, arguing that foreign women needed close supervision to ensure that they could reintegrate upon return: "In Italy, Spain, Portugal and Greece girls have a completely different familial and religious tie than they do for us."[25] In April 1960, the Catholic Office in Bonn wrote to the Federal Labor Office asking for lists of Italians, explaining that "foreigners from Romance countries with their own strong family attachments" would be unable to function without equally strong pastoral care.[26] Anton Sabel, president of the Federal Labor Office, a devout Catholic, and a CDU member, proved highly receptive to such arguments.[27] The image of the foreign woman in need of protection was not limited to Catholic circles. To prove the need for its services, Protestant welfare organization Diakonie invoked similar ideas when it argued that Greek women abroad were subject to "moral decline" and in need of strong supervision, citing the example of a woman who had purportedly had sex with six Greek and three German men within ten days of her arrival.[28]

Diakonie also spent a great deal of effort trying to find adoptive families for children born to Greek women out of wedlock. Social workers believed that most of the fathers of these children were Greek men who refused to recognize their own children. They petitioned the state to create a solution whereby women could obtain identity documents for children born in Germany without having to inform their mothers' hometowns and thus potentially to ruin their reputations. The Interior Ministry agreed to allow German authorities to issue "foreigner passports" for these children so that they could be adopted by foreigners without the knowledge of authorities in the woman's home country. Although initially developed for Greek women, the policy was extended to all female guest workers in 1967.[29]

Advocates of family migration often argued that guest workers came from cultures where the family was particularly important. A representative from the Italian Embassy stated that "the Italian woman only leaves her family, when she is forced to out of urgent necessity,"[30] while the trade attaché from the Greek embassy argued that "women from the Greek peasantry . . . can only with difficulty leave the family, under whose special protection they stand. The Greek woman is difficult to separate from her husband and especially from her children."[31] Employers in Baden-Württemberg promoted family reunification because of the "specific mentality and pronounced sense of family of the foreigners, especially the Italians."[32] Throughout the first decade of labor migration, families consistently appeared as a solution rather than as a problem.

The constant repetition of these arguments had an unanticipated consequence: foreign workers' relationships to their family members were continually described as what distinguished them from Germans rather than a trait they shared. In 1966, Maturi was commissioned to write a booklet for newly recruited foreign workers to read on their way to the FRG.[33] *Hello Günther! The*

Foreign Worker Speaks to His German Colleagues describes the "foreign family" as an obstacle to mutual understanding:

> We live far from our families, which is hard for us, but strengthens the bonds with our relatives even more. The German can hardly imagine, dear friend, what the family means for us. . . . We are astonished by the freedom and independence that the individual enjoys in the family in Germany. It seems to us that the family has lost too much of its meaning for the old and the young. The family's ability to stick together seems weak to us. The German for his part would find our family ties unbearable, even irrational. Family ties and the norms that come out of them have their roots in the blood and in the heart—for that reason they are not always as rational as they should be and as we would like them.[34]

Maturi draws a sharp distinction between two cultures depicted as static by pitting the rational against emotional, modern against traditional, and family against individual.[35] Germans are depicted as rational, independent individuals, while Southern Europeans are depicted as emotionally, even inexplicably, devoted to their families.

The sharp distinction might be read as a kind of disavowal of the continued central role of the family within West German society. The FRG was recruiting foreign women to maintain its own conservative familial welfare state, which depended on the German woman's ability to stay with her family and to not have to work outside the home. The FRG arguably also had "irrational" attachments to its specific family model, and yet discussions about family migration consistently focused on the "Southern" family as a deviation from the norm.

The case for liberal family reunion policies did not come from abstract ideas about the right to family life or, for that matter, from foreigners' own actions. It rested on the unique familial dependence of "Southerners" and particularly of Southern women. These arguments were extremely effective in promoting liberal policies, but the belief that migrants were pathologically dependent and excessively family-oriented influenced how officials interpreted the resulting family migration. Those who tried to keep their families together in West Germany were interpreted as part of a Mediterranean cultural pattern that made migrants incapable of functioning outside of the family. While the idea that German and Southern families were mutually incomprehensible might appear benign when used to promote policies favorable for family unity, the pervasive assumption of different family values was a form of racialization that could be turned against the best interests of migrants.

Employers Demand Foreign Families

Throughout the period of active labor recruitment, the Labor Ministry consistently objected to more stringent requirements for family reunification precisely because it used the category of the family to meet employers' demands for foreign women. However, when a foreign woman invoked the same category of the family in her own actions—for example, by quitting a job in order to find a job that would let her live with her husband—her desire to unite her family was understood as a cultural pathology of Southerners.

Because the Greek Labor Office had actively recruited married couples to work in Germany, the Federal Labor Office sent out a circular in July 1962 asking regional labor offices about their experience with these couples, specifically the women. The circular asked whether the regional labor offices had a problem with contract breach by married women, as well as whether Greek women should be required to sign a document stating that they understood that they might be sent to a different city from their husbands and that contract breach might lead to deportation.[36] Every single regional office reported that contract breach was indeed a problem, but most were skeptical that such a document would help. The women already did not take their labor contracts seriously, so why would an additional document make any difference? Officials repeatedly described the women's actions as typical of their cultural background: Baden-Württemberg and North Rhine-Westphalia both singled out Greeks for their "exceptional feeling of togetherness,"[37] while the Labor Office in Cologne used the opportunity to criticize Italian women, explaining that "because of the close family ties that are normal for them, the demand that women fulfill a work contract that requires them to live apart from their husband seems unintelligible to the women."[38] The Labor Office in Northern Bavaria blamed the "pronounced sense of family of the Southerner."[39] Seen through the lens of labor recruitment, the idea that a couple might want to live together became understood as a problem specific to those foreign cultures that placed family ties over contractual ties.

Officials also held very strong assumptions about which members of the family ought to be placing family above contract. In the discussion about Greek couples, many offices reported with evident surprise that men were also breaking contracts to be close to their wives.[40] The recruitment commission in Turkey made an even more shocking discovery in 1963. The insatiable demand for female labor meant that recruited women were usually placed in a position in Germany almost immediately, while men often had to wait several months before receiving a work assignment. According to the recruitment commission in Turkey, Turkish women were frequently going to Germany and then trying to use either named recruitment or family migration in order to "bring their husbands in reverse." The official who read this report at the Federal Labor Office penciled an exclamation point in the margins.[41] The idea that men might leave their jobs to follow women appeared to violate the gender order of male breadwinners and female dependents. The number of couples who subverted officials' expectations about appropriate gendered behavior only increased over time. The number of Turkish men on the waitlist for West Germany reached 600,000 in 1965 and over 1 million in 1971, whereas Turkish women continued to be called up immediately.[42] By the early 1970s these men who followed women became a full-blown category crisis for the migration regime.

The specific practice of assigning married couples to different cities came under scrutiny in 1964, when the president of the Federal Labor Office reportedly witnessed an unhappy scene at the Munich train station: a Turkish man, bound for Braunschweig, putting his eight-year-old daughter on a train to Darmstadt all by herself. Following his wife to Germany, the man had brought his daughter with him because he assumed that they would live together until he discovered that the cities were more than 200 miles apart.[43] Anton Sabel, president of the Federal Labor Office, was furious: "The attempt to place spouses in the same district is not made often enough. . . . [U]nder these circumstances one of the two will try to relocate to the place where the other spouse is located. That leads to failure to observe the work contracts that have been agreed upon. In recruitment the reunification of family members is an important point, that is to be valued higher than other goals."[44] The Federal Labor Office responded by sending a circular to the recruitment offices abroad with the instruction to send spouses to the same location. The office in Turkey responded by blaming those newly recruited workers who lied to recruiters and hid the fact that their spouses already worked in Germany.[45] In practice, workers who concealed information about their family relationships from recruiters were often responding to rumors that recruiters preferred single workers to married ones—rumors that were based in fact.

Another possible solution for spouses who were trying to live in the same city was "named recruitment," whereby workers could name a specific person to be recruited directly to the same factory. This form of recruitment was continually contested in ways that reveal the divergent interests of migrants, employers, and states. Migrants highly valued named recruitment as a way to reconstitute their social networks—including not just spouses but also siblings, cousins, and even friends and neighbors. Married women, especially from Turkey, often went to West Germany by themselves with the intention to use named recruitment to help their husbands "jump the line." Migrants' desire to use named recruitment consistently outpaced the availability of the measure, creating secondary markets where migrants would pay massive sums for the ability to put a name on the list. Translators could reportedly demand and receive up to 1,000 deutsche marks (DM) for providing this service—a price reported everywhere from a cheese factory in rural Bavaria, to the Pierburg automobile factory in Neuss, to the Siemens factory in West Berlin.[46] The last city was particularly difficult for married couples because of the existing imbalance between jobs for women and men: one woman who worked in West Berlin recalled that she paid first to get her husband to Ulm and then a much larger sum to get him a job in West Berlin.[47] Husbands often did not understand why the process took so long. One Turkish woman's husband "was furious that he had to take care of the children. As if I were the one who wanted to come here! As if I told the German authorities, 'Have my husband come two years later!'" Another recalled that her husband "wrote to me, 'if you don't make me come, I'll kill your parents.' He was so angry, he always screamed.... [H]e felt guilty, it was as if he wasn't a man."[48] The FRG's desperation for foreign female workers upset traditional divisions of gendered labor and forced married couples to renegotiate their roles.

The sending countries continually tried to limit the kinds of relatives eligible for named recruitment against pressure from the Federal Labor Office. They worried that relying on the family networks of migrants to organize the movement of people would lead to an uneven distribution of the benefits of emigration and to perceptions that the state was allowing some families to become rich at the expense of others.[49] Their concerns about domestic unrest led to continual adjustment of the rules about named recruitment. Conflict began in early 1969 when both Greece and Turkey decided that recruited siblings and their spouses could no longer proceed to Germany at the same time. Instead, the named recruitment of couples would have to proceed in stages—first, a worker who was already in the FRG could recruit a sibling, but only once said sibling had arrived could the sibling then recruit his or her spouse. In Greece, these restrictions applied in both directions. Turkish citizens could recruit a sister and her spouse at the same time, but not a brother and his spouse at the same time, perhaps in deference to the idea that women were in special need of male protection and should not be left alone.[50]

Employers were incensed by these new restrictions. They had supported named recruitment because they believed that it stabilized the workforce by offering "a certain guarantee for good morale at work" and "lesser difficulties of integration."[51] Even before the new restrictions, employers had been asking the Federal Labor Office to extend the circles of people eligible for named recruitment, arguing that their refusal to do so "contradicts the social order in Turkey, in which the togetherness of the extended family and clan has a certain meaning, so that already from this viewpoint the Turkish worker does not understand why only spouses and siblings can be recruited."[52] When the Greek and Turkish states tried to slow down the use of named recruitment, employers once again cited the timeless "Southern family" to protest a measure that put brakes on their access to labor: "In view of the distinctive sense of family of the Southerner one cannot expect that they will understand named recruitment in stages."[53] West German employers were so eager to tap the foreign family as a resource that they saw no contradiction in lecturing "Southern" states about the "family sense" of their own citizens.

The Turkish state continued to hope that limiting named recruitment would lead to an increase in the number of "anonymous" recruitments and thus reduce the waiting time for the many hopeful émigrés. After months of asking Germany to refrain from recruiting siblings, Turkey banned named recruitment for all male relatives in September 1969.[54] By this time more than 900,000 Turkish citizens were on the waitlist for the FRG, while some 800 to 1,000 siblings were entering per month. The German Embassy in Ankara begged German employers to comply with the Turkish ban, claiming that the continued recruitment of siblings was leading to "growing social unrest" in many villages.[55] After receiving this letter from Ankara, the Interior Ministry sent a circular instructing local Foreigners' Offices not to approve the residence and labor permits of siblings who had arrived on tourist visas because it was "against the declared will of the Turkish authorities."[56]

Employers' support of named recruitment met its limits when migrants used the practice to circumvent employers' restrictions. Men who had more than four children or who were older than the age limit were banned from the normal recruiting procedure but not from named recruitment.[57] Named recruits were also exempt from medical screening procedures. Some women migrated to the FRG explicitly after their husbands had been rejected for poor health, intending to use connections on the ground to land jobs for their husbands.[58]

In 1972, officials began to worry that women were coming to work in Germany with the plan to import their sick or elderly husbands. Although the Law on Foreigners allowed the state to deport somebody with an infectious disease, in practice a man whose wife worked in Germany could often get a doctor's note explaining that he was too sick to be deported, and "the trailing husbands . . . committed to sanatoriums" burdened the welfare state.[59] The Labor Ministry passed guidelines in February 1973 stating that women should not be recruited for work in West Germany if their husbands were incapable of working, although, even as these guidelines were passed, officials suspected that they would be "hardly legally possible" to enforce.[60]

This spike in concern about sick husbands shows that the Labor Ministry's support for family reunion had always been conditional. When named recruitment of family members was the most efficient way to access labor, employers and officials were more than happy to appeal to the Southerners' "family sense," but as soon as migrant actions on behalf of those same families began to hinder their most efficient distribution as labor power, employers were equally quick to complain about their "Southern" disposition to prioritize the family above the labor contract. "Family ties" were a valuable resource for the West German employer only insofar as the extended family was also able to conform to the demands of the labor market.

Avoiding Entanglements

Officials, social workers, and a wide variety of experts also argued that family reunification was a way to protect West German women from foreign men, not just from unwanted sexual advances but also from ill-advised relationships.[61] The highest circulation newspaper in Germany, *BILD*, in 1966 published a series of sensational stories that depicted Southern European men as irresistible to German women—but also as unable to form long-term relationships and particularly likely to skip out on pregnant women. The authors of the series recommended "social-hygienic prophylaxis in the form of increased family reunification."[62] The argument in favor of family reunification was not confined to the tabloid press. After foreign workers committed nineteen violent crimes in Cologne in 1966, the city paid a group of psychoanalysts to research the phenomenon of guest worker criminality. Karl Bingemeier and his colleagues concluded that foreign men who were cut off from most German women tended to find sexual relief in older women on the margins of society and subsequently to commit violence against these women.[63] They had only one recommendation: "The families should be brought together as liberally and as quickly as possible."[64]

Municipal authorities made similar arguments behind the scenes.[65] Cities worried about German women having children out of wedlock. The Association of German Cities (DST) worried that "the differences between our legal principles and those of the Roman lands" meant that cities were more likely to have to foot the bill for a German woman's illegitimate child with a foreign man than with a German man.[66] Single mothers in the FRG were allowed to file a suit for child support even if the father had not recognized the child, but foreign workers mostly came from countries that did not allow mothers to ask fathers for child support unless the father had already recognized the child as his own. These foreign men could easily flee the country without acknowledging their responsibilities, leaving the German mother with no recourse to appeal for child support.[67] The expansion of foreign labor recruitment also happened to coincide with a reform in the way that the state treated single mothers. Before 1961, a child born out of wedlock was automatically assigned a legal guardian from the local Youth Office, a state guardian who had more power over the child than the birth mother did. After 1961, a single mother could apply to receive legal guardianship over her own child, but she had to testify about her relationship with the father for judges to rule on whether she was capable of performing the duties of a legal guardian.[68] Because this reform increased the amount of discussion about the responsibilities of single mothers, it may also have contributed to city administrators paying closer attention to those men deemed to threaten the family.

Municipal authorities advocated family migration as one way to protect the state from having to support single mothers. The mayor of Stuttgart wrote to the DST in 1962 demanding action to solve "the problem of illegitimate children . . . because many of the fathers [of illegitimate children] are already married and have a family in their homeland, it is clear that the endangerment of German girls through the many foreign men separated from their families . . . is closely connected to the crucial issue of family reunification."[69] Leverkusen and Frankfurt both argued in favor of family migration for the same reason.[70] When the DST conducted a survey of its members about their experiences with guest workers in January 1964, every single city administrator responded that they were in favor of family reunion, and many were explicit about its role in containing the consequences of sexual activity. Bielefeld worried about "the problem that foreign workers will link up with German women," while Hamburg specified that it did not want foreign workers to have relationships with German girls whom they had no intention of marrying.[71] Reutlingen hoped that family migration would "transfer the foreigners' private lives from the waiting room in the train station and the street into apartments"[72] while Bayreuth stressed its positive effects on the crime rate and insisted that "above all, many marriages will be preserved."[73] Duisburg insisted that when men came to Germany without their wives, the story could end in one of two ways, both unfortunate: "Either the married foreign worker who is already well trained will return home, or he will develop illegitimate relationships with German girls and women, with all of their undesirable side effects (negligence of his own family, disturbance of other marriages, alimony suits)."[74] Municipal authorities consistently linked family migration to social stability.

Social workers were concerned not just about the possibility of sexual relationships but also about the possibility of binational marriages between German women and foreign men. They employed diverse arguments against intermarriage. Sometimes they used the language of biological difference, drawing from medical texts like the 1965 study that speculated that intermarriage would produce "asocial" children.[75] They also frequently racialized the population of foreign workers through analogy—for example, comparing the danger purportedly posed by foreign workers to the danger posed by Black GIs.[76] Throughout the 1950s, German officials and social scientists had reformulated their notions of race as they debated the appropriate way to treat the 3,000 biracial children of

German women and African American soldiers.[77] One sociologist wrote in 1973 that women who used to have relationships with Black men now had relationships with Italians: "The illegitimate children who were named James, William or Beth-Ann before 1960 are now named Massimo, Marcello or Manuela."[78] The logic of racialization transferred from one group of men to another while the focus on the sexual behavior of German women remained constant.

Social workers expended a great deal of effort convincing German women not to enter relationships with male guest workers. The head of social services for Italians in the Rhineland-Palatinate advocated introducing a unit about the lower status of women in the Mediterranean into the school curriculum in order to warn German girls away from guest workers.[79] Other social workers urged German families to be vigilant about their daughters' contact with foreign workers—for example, by keeping them from going to dance halls where the men were known to congregate.[80] The Youth Office of the Rhineland reported in 1966 that 5 percent of all marriages in their region were between Germans and foreigners and that "the long-term survival of these marriages is complicated by the fact that the status of women is very different here than it is in the home countries of the guest workers."[81]

Official warnings against intermarriage were frequently linked to an image of the patriarchal Southern European. Having attended a 1965 conference on the legal problems of intermarriage, a journalist for the *Süddeutsche Zeitung* opened his report with a warning for female readers: "The young men often begin a very patriarchal family life, according to their native customs. . . . The first acquaintance with the family members in Sicily, on a Greek island or in a Spanish village is often sobering. Many a once happy bride soon thinks of divorce."[82] In a striking turn of phrase, Maria Begliatti, a social welfare expert at the Italian consulate in Munich, told *Stern* that even though only one in twelve marriages between German women and Italian men failed, "Even most of the marriages that have not failed yet are unhappy." She warned German girls: "The Italian man, especially the one from Southern Italy, enjoys the role of pasha. He is used to being the boss in the house."[83] Her use of the Ottoman term "pasha" for Italians underscores the fact that the stereotype of the oppressive male partner was applied across the entire Mediterranean. While religious authorities were undoubtedly concerned about Christian women entering into marriages with Muslim men, at this time descriptions of Muslims were similar to descriptions of "Southern" men. Social workers at a 1966 conference warned that, for Muslims, "the relationship between man and woman is no longer a private relationship as it is for us. There is no intimate sphere, as it exists for us, rather everything is in the clan or the extended family."[84] Muslim families differed from "Southern" ones in degree rather than in kind.

The patriarchal foreign man was implicitly juxtaposed against a progressive German man, the extended foreign family against a nuclear German family. In 1966, the National Initiative for the Protection of Youth published *Marriage with Foreigners,* a pamphlet with "tips for parents and tips for daughters who want to marry a foreigner."[85] While the pamphlet primarily focused on the dangers of marrying exchange students from the Middle East—a category understood as separate from Turkey—it also included information about marriage law in Spain, Italy, Greece, and Turkey.[86] The author depicted the difference between German and "Southern" families in stark terms: "For us the woman is responsible for herself and has the same rights as the husband. But in many Southern countries she is a dependent creature, who must leave all decisions to the husband." The extended family of the "Southerner" was a vestigial institution that German girls would find oppressive: "For us the extended family has almost no more meaning. The nuclear family has replaced it. But in the southern countries ... the near and far family members stick close together." The different meaning of the extended family was linked to the modern welfare state: "We have public social welfare.... [T]here, the extended family has to take care of the sick grandfather or the crippled aunt because of family unity."[87] Like *Hello Günther!*, *Marriage with Foreigners* depicts modern German families and "Southern" families as completely different institutions, failing to recognize the fact that the family had not exactly disappeared from West German life. The West German state also needed women to perform care work, and a woman considering marriage and children was going to be expected to care for them in Stuttgart, just as she would be in Sicily.

Youth advisors who counseled West German women against marrying foreigners were in one sense performing a real service in advising women about the legal risks inherent in binational marriages. The sexism in family law in both the FRG and abroad made intermarriage a risky choice for a woman who hoped to continue her family life in the FRG. Although West German men who married foreign women could easily sponsor their wives for citizenship and residence permits, marriage to a West German woman did not give a man an automatic right even to remain in the country, much less become a citizen. Some foreign men married to German women found that marriage actually hurt their legal status, since, once marriage proved their intent to remain in the country, the local Foreigners' Office would refuse to grant them further residence permits. A child of a German woman and a foreign man also received the man's citizenship status. A woman who had a child with her foreign husband might abruptly find herself the only member of her family who could live in the FRG.

Women who wanted to marry Spanish and Greek men also found themselves navigating significant hurdles to get married in the first place. Spain and Greece recognized only religious marriages as legal, and Spanish family law under Franco was based on a conservative interpretation of Catholicism that did not recognize divorce.[88] A Spanish-German couple married in a Protestant church would be legally married in West Germany but not in Spain, while a divorced German woman who married a Spanish man might later discover that Spain considered the couple unmarried and her children illegitimate.

Letters to the Federal Ministry of the Family testify to the stress that many women experienced on discovering that their children were considered illegitimate and had to carry their mothers' last name, creating an unanticipated social stigma. One man whose daughter had married a Spaniard wrote to the Family Ministry on behalf of "German girls and women" who "can be seen as 'fair game' by all Greeks and Spaniards, men who can return to their home country as 'free and single,' in order to seek another wife as soon as they have become weary of their wives or are struck by homesickness, which has already happened many times. . . . What an unhappy situation for the woman who has been robbed of all of her rights and possibly left with a child who carries neither his father's name nor that of his mother!"[89] One civil registrar refused to give at least two children born to Spanish men and divorced German women any surname at all, a bureaucratic anomaly that caused a minor diplomatic incident.[90]

Many civil registrars responded to the "Spanish marriage problem" by refusing to marry Germans to Spaniards if they knew that Spain would not recognize the marriage. In the summer of 1965, a Protestant lawyer from Berlin decided to travel to Tondern, a small town on the other side of the German-Danish border, to wed his Spanish wife. By the end of 1968, approximately 250 German-Spanish couples had married in Tondern as civil registrars in Germany continued to debate whether these marriages should be recognized.[91] The *Stuttgarter Zeitung* published an article depicting the town as "a last refuge for people treated badly by laws that are practically prehistoric." Couples who traveled to Tondern had to petition the king of Denmark for permission to wed. While waiting for royal consent, which usually took about a week, they could plan an anticipatory honeymoon at a Danish hotel.[92]

Some men who dealt with binational marriages in a professional context felt strongly that the "Spanish marriage problem" was proof of national weakness. An Evangelical pastor from Bavaria argued that when a German Protestant had to go to a Catholic church to marry a Spaniard, this was a violation of the German's rights to religious freedom and further proof that "since the German collapse, the Federal Republic has resigned full sovereign rights over German territory."[93] One civil registrar felt that in enforcing Spanish marriage law he was being forced to bow to a country "ruled by clergy from the Middle Ages," accusing his own state of "throwing its own citizens upon the laws of clerical dictatorships just as if there were no Basic Law!"[94] A comic in a weekly Evangelical magazine illustrated this complaint with a Spanish inquisitor leaving a castle with a 1966 calendar on the wall: "Look here, *caballeros*, they are doing the most unbelievable things outside!"[95] The discussion of the "Spanish marriage problem" arguably contains residual anti-Catholic sentiment at a time when West Germans boasted about their progressive and modern family law.

Binational marriages turned questions about the intimate sphere into questions of national sovereignty. In 1971, the Federal Constitutional Court finally heard the case of a Protestant woman who had been previously divorced and consequently denied the ability to marry a Spanish man in the FRG because Spain would not recognize their marriage.[96] The court agreed with her lawyers that this infringed on the woman's right to choose her own spouse as guaranteed by Article 6 of the Basic Law. The Spanish groom could indeed abandon the German woman, leaving her without recourse in Spanish courts, but "the state should not force the fiancée into such protection against her will; it has to be left to the fiancée, to decide if she wants to take the risk of a marriage that is not recognized by Spain."[97] This decision explicitly refused state paternalism toward German citizens, and *Die Zeit* greeted it with the headline: "No longer bound for Tondern."[98] West German citizens could in fact make their own decisions about who to marry, but some choices would continue to leave them without state protection.

The social workers who warned German women about intermarriage during the 1960s and early 1970s were arguably successful in making women think twice about getting involved with guest worker men. While the absolute numbers of marriages between West German women and men from the six primary guest worker countries did increase in this period, the rate of intermarriage did not increase nearly as quickly as the absolute numbers of single male guest workers. The probability that a single male guest worker would marry a West German woman decreased during the first decade of labor recruitment: men from each of the six primary national groups of guest workers—Spaniards, Portuguese, Greeks, Italians, Yugoslavs, and Turks—were more likely to marry a West German in 1961 than in 1970. In 1980, only intermarriage for Spaniards had rebounded above its 1961 levels, while the rate of intermarriage had remained flat or decreased even further for the other groups.[99] These statistics must be read against the increase in family migration, which had evidently had the intended effect of discouraging entanglements between foreign men and German women.

Childcare and the "Grandmother Solution"

Just as they had been early to register the problems caused by illegitimate children, municipal governments also recognized the challenge of providing childcare for foreign children. In the January 1964 DST survey, most cities wrote that they supported family reunion not just to avoid undesirable relationships between foreign men and German women, but also because foreign women were willing to take jobs in the service sector that were difficult to fill otherwise. The cities also identified a closely related problem: when both members of a married couple intended to work in the FRG, what happened to their children? Because children under sixteen did not require residence permits, the federal state had no practical way to keep these children out—but local municipalities certainly noticed that they were there.

The presence of foreign children was particularly challenging for municipalities because the FRG officially expected mothers to be full-time homemakers. Indeed, the decision to draw on foreign labor in the first place had centered around keeping married German women in the home, and because the labor market did not rely on the labor of married women, the state had not treated childcare as a priority.[100] During the 1960s there were only enough places in institutionalized childcare for roughly one-third of all children in the FRG.[101] Half of all working women in the FRG in 1962 relied on grandparents for childcare while they were at work, a proportion that remained largely unchanged through the 1980s.[102] West German women on waitlists for kindergartens relied on their extended family to help them balance domestic responsibilities with jobs outside the home. Migrant women were at the bottom of these waitlists, and their social networks in the FRG were composed primarily of other full-time workers. What options did they have when they were looking for childcare?

City administrators wrote dozens of letters to the German Council on Municipalities about the burdens foreign children placed on local welfare services. Ludwigshafen am Rhein complained about the foreign children who were taking up spaces in childcare facilities,[103] while in Munich the municipal Youth Office rejected all applications for childcare facilities from foreigners "because otherwise an uncontrollable flood of such applications will rush in, creating massive costs for the city."[104] In Kassel, "young women with children, who make do with the most primitive housing in order to save money and avoid family separation" found that their husbands did not make enough money to support the family in Germany. "The wives are therefore forced to take a job and allow their children to be watched by relatives whom they have brought in. In some cases, public support has been granted for the care of foreign families."[105] Wilhelmshaven was reliant on female labor for its textile industry but hoped that the women it recruited would remain single while they were in Germany and constantly worried about the possibility that they might bring husbands along with them: "If they were to bring their husbands, their wives' companies could not find jobs for them. . . . With multiple small children the housing of the family would become difficult, the working mother would have to look after the children, and her labor assignment would be put into question. . . . [T]he family would become needy and would revert to public welfare."[106] As these letters make clear, foreign women were valuable as workers only as long as they did not make claims on the welfare state. Once they began to raise families in West Germany, the assumptions of the guest worker program would no longer hold and the program itself would no longer be tenable.

Several cities reported that although they promoted family reunification to stabilize male workers, they would give trailing wives work permits only if the women could prove that their children were being looked after without the help of the state.[107] In practice, foreign women who worked and could not find childcare options outside the home often relied on older children to look after younger siblings. One social worker in Frankfurt reported on the human costs of this policy. She had worked with a family where an older daughter brought to look after her younger sister while the parents were at work attempted suicide "because she can no longer stand the loneliness that she has gotten into." She had also counseled a thirteen-year-old who became pregnant when she was visited "by an acquaintance of the family" while her parents were at work.[108] At a 1968 meeting in the Interior Ministry, social workers complained that "unfortunately the trend . . . is that [foreign women] give their children to other people during the day. . . . Every now and then the children are also left to their own devices." At this meeting, some social workers suggested that the state ought to consider whether there was any legal way for it to deport minor children with negligent parents, since this could be a "more humane solution" than allowing the child to live in Germany.[109] This passing aside is an early example of how purported concern for child welfare could be used to justify anti-migrant policies, up to and including child deportation.

The cold language of bureaucrats obscured wrenching decisions for individual families. A Turkish woman who came to the FRG in 1971 remembered that after her daughter was born, a German woman took the girl to her home, and the Turkish mother and her husband saw their child only once a week. One day they discovered multiple wounds on their daughter's body. They suspected that the woman was not paying enough attention to their child, so they decided to send her back to Turkey, to be cared for by an aunt. The woman later decided to quit her job at Siemens so that she would be able to bring all of her children to Germany and look after them. She did not return to work until her oldest daughter was old enough to look after the younger two children.[110] Other women actively chose to work illegally—for example, as cleaning women—precisely because under-the-table jobs enabled them to bring children along or to send a substitute when a child's illness required them to stay home.[111]

Migrant women also demanded that the welfare state meet their needs. When a branch of Caritas in Essen announced plans to build a new kindergarten for Spanish and German children, local parents were initially excited. But when they discovered that the half-day kindergarten would only open two hours after most women went to work and would send the children home without lunch, 600 Spaniards entered the aisles of the local Catholic church during the German-language mass. Three hundred of them remained there for an entire day and night, refusing to leave until they secured a promise from the local bishop that the kindergarten would look after children all day, enabling their mothers to work full-time.[112] Foreign women who called for childcare facilities were at the cutting edge of the German women's movement, as women in the German Confederation of Trade Unions called for an expansion of kindergartens and the contemporaneous "mother's movement" created autonomous childcare collectives.[113]

Grandparents were the classic solution that West German women deployed to manage their childcare needs, and many migrants tried to make the same solution work for them. Sometimes this was explicitly political: a group of Greek migrants in Baden-Württemberg submitted a petition to their Interior Ministry suggesting that guest workers be allowed to bring parents with them to look after children.[114] Migrants also often brought their parents with them and then asked for permission after the fact. Responding to these demands, Baden-Württemberg began to let in grandparents on a case-by-case basis in 1968, although it tried to ensure that their residence remained the exception rather than the rule.[115] North Rhine-Westphalia issued a circular allowing for the residence of grandparents in January 1970.[116] West Berlin had the highest proportion of female guest workers of any city in the country because of its electronics and textile industries.[117] Alert to these women's childcare needs, West Berlin began in the 1970s to issue visas to grandparents that would allow them to stay to look after children for up to six or nine months at a time instead of the standard three months.[118] City officials suggested that other states should follow their lead and allow extended stays for grandmothers, explaining "we should accept the foreigners' different definition of the family and, for example, allow the grandmother to stay, when she can be used to look after the unattended children."[119] Such language promotes the idea of a distinctive "foreign family" in order to argue for an inclusive policy, but the disingenuous suggestion that a grandmother represents a distinctive form of the family enables West Berlin officials to see themselves as uniquely generous.

By early 1970, all three of the major social work agencies had issued a statement in support of what was called the "grandparent solution." Hans Apel, an SPD representative from Hamburg, asked the Bundestag about this recommendation in April 1970, pointing out that there were at least 500,000 foreign children in need of supervision. The Interior Ministry replied that the "grandparent solution" would lead to the "resettlement of extended families and entire clans" and thus cause more problems than it solved.[120] The use of the word "clan" subtly exoticizes the foreign family. In August 1970, social workers and representatives from the sending countries met with Federal President Gustav Heinemann to make the case for grandparents. The Turkish representative claimed that half of the approximately 100,000 Turkish children in Germany were prevented from going to school "because the children have to look after younger siblings. . . . It would be a great help, when the grandmothers of these children could enter the Federal Republic." The Federal president rejected the idea out of hand.[121]

When Foreigners' Offices rejected residence permits for grandmothers, migrant families could appeal those cases in court. In one case, a widowed Greek woman with two sons in the FRG and two daughters in Greece wanted to stay in Sindelfingen—at the time the site of the largest Mercedes-Benz plant in Germany—to look after her grandchildren so that her daughter-in-law, who brought in 45 percent of the family's income, could continue to work. Both of her daughters in Greece already had mothers-in-law who lived with them, so she would prefer to live with her sons in the FRG. The local Foreigners' Office refused to give her a residence permit, a decision upheld in court in December 1971.[122] The same court ruled in April 1972 that a forty-eight-year-old woman from Greece could not stay with her son, his wife, and their three children. Her lawyer argued that it was in the public interest for the woman to stay and look after the children so that the foreign workers would not be "fully isolated and without support, but would lead an orderly family life," but this argument did not persuade the judge:

> In light of the well-known fact that particularly for Southern and Southeastern Europeans, who compose the largest portion of guest workers in the Federal Republic, the extended family has an especially pronounced cohesion, we can expect that if it were allowed, migration of further family members would also occur. It is clear that if we were to relinquish the principle of only allowing family migration for the nuclear family, this would lead to a severe additional burden on the internal order in the Federal Republic and its social and economic structure.[123]

The widespread presumption that Southerners had a "different definition of the family" functioned as a double-edged sword. West Berlin officials had invoked the stereotype in favor of generous policies, but federal officials and judges also used it to make arguments for exclusion. Furthermore, once German officials presumed that foreigners had a "different definition of the family," they understood foreigners' requests for residence permits as a form of special treatment and the state's willingness to provide those residence permits as an act of generosity. The presumption created a context in which migrant actions on behalf of their own families no longer appeared to be political activism—not even when their demands for family reunification took conventionally political forms like protests and petitions. Such activism could be dismissed as another sign of the "excessive family sense" of the Southerner.[124]

Foreigners who brought grandparents to care for children were in fact demonstrating an exceptional level of integration into the German welfare state and its pre-existing assumptions about working motherhood. West German women were also only able to manage waged labor through reliance on their extended families. One of every two West German mothers who worked for wages relied on their own parents to look after their children while the mothers were at work. In other words, foreign women had not exactly invented the "grandparent solution"; they just needed residence permits to make use of it. When West German officials criticized the "Southern family" and its excessive dependence, they remained curiously unable to admit that German mothers were able to manage part-time labor only because of their own extended families. When foreign women demanded the same conditions as West German women—the promotion of extended families to meet their childcare needs—their demand for family reunification was interpreted as an expression of their inherent Southern mentality rather than as a political demand related to West Germany's continued failure to invest in public childcare facilities.

The "grandparent solution" made its way to the Federal Administrative Court in 1973. In this case, a Spanish woman had come to West Germany in 1961 and married a Spanish man in 1965. The couple had three children, all born in Germany, and the mother tried to bring her own mother in 1968 to look after the children. The local Foreigners' Office denied the grandmother's residence permit, claiming that, if it gave her a permit, the consequence would be "an unlimited migration of family members."[125] The chief federal attorney made the same argument in court. He also pointed out that the grandmother could become sick at any time, a situation that could quickly become an expensive problem for the state: "If the plaintiff were to become sick and no longer be able to take care of the grandchildren, the daughter would have to give up her job. Then her insurance would also be cancelled." One bad bet on a grandmother might lead to the state supporting an entire family of sick Spaniards.[126]

The Federal Administrative Court rejected these arguments on the principle that foreigners were also protected by Article 6 of the West German Basic Law: "Marriage and the family shall enjoy the special protection of the state." The court argued that Article 6 created a "duty of care towards the family" of the guest worker. Drawing on the principle of subsidiarity, whereby social tasks should be performed by the smallest possible social unit, the court reasoned that the state was responsible for helping this social unit achieve self-sufficiency.

In the court's judgment, the grandmother had the potential to help the family care for itself and in so doing to unburden the German welfare state. Normally families with sick children "can only cope through breaking off work, giving up income and endangering the mother's job," but for this family, the grandmother would be able to look after the sick children. Her presence also meant that the children would not cause problems for the state, as "they will not increase the number of so-called 'latch-key children.' They can be crossed off the waiting list for kindergarten spots, already inadequate for the German population. When the children get sick they will not need to be brought to hospitals that are already overcrowded for the sole reason that they do not have someone to look after them, and prevent the acceptance of those children who truly need hospitals."[127] As long as grandmother remained healthy, the state would be unburdened.

This ruling is embedded in several assumptions about the family's relationship to German society and to the welfare state. First, her care work gains value in part because her daughter and son-in-law both already work full-time. If the parents needed to spend more time on childcare it might "endanger the mother's job." By enabling the mother to focus on work, the grandmother enables the state to extract as much labor as possible from its recruited workers. Second, she gains value because the court assumes that the family will remain in the FRG only temporarily. The court posited that the family would leave more quickly if they had grandmother with them, as "they bought their own apartment in Madrid at the beginning of 1968 and have to pay off their debts."[128] If the mother had to reduce her hours at work for any reason, the couple would have to remain in the FRG for a longer time to repay their debt. Finally, she gains value because the family is disciplined by debt. Debt means the mother is not a flight risk at work—she is motivated to make money. Grandmother enables two adults to work and to save to leave quickly and make few claims on the welfare state. She enables the family to be a welfare state unto itself.

As the first court case to establish that the Basic Law also guaranteed rights to foreigners, this case provided migrants with an important precedent in future legal battles. This precedent was not grounded in an abstract ideal about family life as a human right but on a concrete understanding of the role of reproductive labor within the West German welfare state. The grandmother's entire claim to residence is based on the fact that she is a "market-conforming" solution to the problem of childcare. She frees the mother up for more obviously "productive" labor and is cheaper than a kindergarten. If the children grew up, if the mother lost her job, if the grandmother became ill, or perhaps even if the family finally paid off its debts on its distant apartment, the state's case for the grandmother's residence permit would evaporate, and she would become a burden rather than an asset.

The limited understanding of the utility of the grandmother's reproductive labor is clear from the March 1974 meeting where the federal meeting of Foreigners' Offices discussed how to put the court's ruling into practice. The representatives closely followed the court's reasoning that the grandmother's claim to stay was based on her utility for her family and for the state. They issued an administrative circular stating that a residence permit should be granted to only "one grandmother who is healthy, who enhances the functioning of the family, and who is not a burden on the public sector of the Federal Republic." Bavaria and Hamburg both wanted additional specifications that permits be granted for a limited period of time only, so that the grandmothers would have to go home as soon as the children were old enough to look after themselves, although they did not define the precise age at which children became self-sufficient.[129] The circular also specified a "grandmother" rather than a "grandparent"—a significant change from the original demands of foreigners and social workers, who had consistently described residence permits for extended family members as the "grandparent solution." In the bureaucratic imagination, only women could perform care work, and in practice only women would be granted residence permits on this basis. The entire argument for family reunion assumed that "family members" were women devoted to the work of social reproduction. Women made male workers less likely to enter romantic and political entanglements and performed the kind of reproductive labor that kept workers from burdening the West German welfare state.

The "Spanish grandmother" case proved difficult to use as a precedent for caretakers who were not healthy older women looking after the children of dual-income couples. Seven years later, a teenage girl from Turkey used this case to argue for a right to stay in Germany because she looked after the children of her aunt and uncle. Her case was rejected by the Federal Administrative Court, which argued that, because of her age, the teenage girl could be expected to try to access the labor market after caring for the children. The uncle and aunt were also deemed not to be dependent on the dual income—in this case, the wife's smaller income was deemed inessential, so that the court ordered her to return home to care for her children.[130] A grandmother in West Berlin who brought her case in front of the same court in 1983 was rejected because the court deemed that her labor was unnecessary. Her son-in-law had been unemployed since September 1981 and "it is not probable, that he will have a job again in the foreseeable future." Despite the seeming violation of gender norms, an unemployable father could be expected to look after his own children, making the grandmother's reproductive labor nonessential.[131] In both cases, families were required to rearrange their reproductive labor in order to conform to the demands of the market. A dual-income couple in which the husband made more than the wife was not allowed to leverage their niece for care work and the mother was forced back into the home. A single-income couple whose wife was the breadwinner was not allowed to bring her mother to perform care work; the father was forced into the home for the first time. Following the Spanish grandmother precedent, care work within the family was primarily valuable insofar as it enabled employers to extract waged labor from that family.

The grandmother precedent also eroded because the West German attitude toward grandmothers as caretakers changed as foreign children began to be discussed as potential long-term residents of West Germany. In 1973 the grandmother was seen as a cheap source of childcare delivery that would enable the family to return home more quickly. By 1983, the Labor Ministry would justify a new blanket exclusion on the entry of foreign parents of German citizens by arguing that foreign grandparents endangered the "integration" of their grandchildren.[132] The 1973 case had recognized that families are sites of essential reproductive labor, labor that the state would have to perform if the family failed to do so. By the early 1980s, foreign families were coded as sites of excessive and deviant reproductive labor that failed to socialize their members into German norms and culture. As expert attention turned increasingly to the socialization of foreign children and to another set of welfare state institutions, grandmothers who might teach their children to speak Spanish or Turkish began to be seen as a threat rather than an asset. Whereas the grandmother's care had once been understood as a way to keep her grandchildren out of kindergartens and hospitals, the same care had become seen as more likely to bring them into the juvenile justice system.

* * *

The foreign family was an indispensable resource for the West German state in both recruiting and maintaining a workforce, puncturing claims that German officials were unaware of family settlement in the period of active labor recruitment. State officials actively promoted the migration of married women so as to access female labor and to discourage intermarriage, fought sending countries so the receiving country could use extended family relationships to facilitate named recruitment, and sometimes even supported the migration of grandparents to save scarce kindergarten spots and hospital beds for German children. While using the foreign family as a resource, the West German state also consistently disavowed its own reliance on foreign family ties to avoid creating a long-term social responsibility to those same families.

Migrants who went to extraordinary lengths to keep their families together in West Germany were denied the status of political actors when their actions were interpreted through the widely held assumption that German families and "Southern" families were different in nature. Men and women left their jobs to find jobs closer to their spouses, petitioned the state to bring grandparents to help with childcare, and staged protests demanding kindergartens. Officials consistently registered these actions not as political demands or even as conscious choices, but merely as confirmation that foreigners had a distinctive dependence on their own family. The stereotype of the "Mediterranean" family inadvertently made it easier for officials to choose to ignore the glaring contradictions of labor recruitment. The decision to hire foreign women was intended to support economic growth without pulling West German women away from their reproductive role, but that decision became costly once foreign families also insisted on their roles as families. In part because officials consistently chose to understand family settlement in terms of containment and dependency rather than in terms of purposeful behavior, it would take those same officials a long time to understand the process of long-term settlement that had been set in motion.

The evidence mounted that families were not quite as self-sufficient as state officials had fantasized in their account of the market-conforming grandmother and her provision of care. In 1972, the same year that the Federal Constitutional Court supported the residence of the grandmother who "enhanced the function of the family," other officials were discovering that family migration created the new problem of the "second generation." The city of Munich commissioned a report on the consequences of guest worker migration for municipal politics that circulated widely among other city administrations and on the federal level.[133] In a passage that contradicted the previous ten years of policy, the authors of the report warned that family migration did not solve problems but compounded them:

> Highlighting this situation reveals the following case: a school in Swabia needed three Turkish teachers. The Turkish consulate named three teachers, two of whom had four children apiece, one of whom had three children. That means almost an additional half-classroom just for the teachers' children. This effect grows exponentially. A larger population—through the migration of foreigners—causes further migration of foreigners in foreigner-intensive sectors (nursing, public maintenance, the service sector, etc.). . . . Family reunification fundamentally changes the problem of foreign workers.[134]

In Munich and elsewhere, the state was caught in the contradiction of reproductive labor on two levels. The first contradiction was that foreigners were in fact already largely segmented into parts of the economy where they did the kinds of feminized jobs that reproduced German living conditions rather than creating new products for export. Hans-Jochen Vogel, then the mayor of Munich, was himself working on an essay about the indispensability of foreigners to city services, reflecting that without foreigners "some public services, such as garbage collection, street cleaning or the sewage system would . . . become inoperable."[135] Relying on foreigners to do the "dirty work" was only creating more such work, as the workers who performed this labor themselves needed to be reproduced—and thus required more garbage collectors, more hospital beds, and more seats in kindergartens and classrooms. Family reunification fundamentally changed the problem of foreign workers because it meant that the reproduction of the labor force could no longer be outsourced. It was happening on German soil and required German support.

The state reacted to this possibility not by facing the contradiction its own actions had created but by reinforcing the fantasy that foreign families could be made "market-conforming." Specifically, officials imagined that they could use the tight housing market as a regulatory factor for the entire problem of social reproduction. The 1965 guidelines for family reunification issued by the Interior Ministry had included the stipulation that foreigners were required to show proof of "sufficient housing" before their family members could receive residence permits. Officials hoped that this "sufficient housing" requirement would place a market-determined limit on the growth of the foreign population, since foreigners could receive permission to reproduce their families in the FRG only after they first found their own space within which to do it.

The Racialization of Space

Family Housing and Anti-Ghettoization Policy

Finding housing for children was a persistent problem, as one Turkish woman in Rüsselsheim with an eight-year-old son learned when her landlord told her that he did not rent to families with children: "So we had to hide my son. The toilet was not in the apartment, but in the staircase. When the child wanted to go to the bathroom, I had to bring [him] there secretly and then hide him immediately again in the room. When the doorbell rang, I had to hide him again." Although the landlord never discovered the boy, this woman was ultimately kicked out of her apartment because one of her husband's female relatives came to live with the family and they did not turn her away. An adult woman was harder to hide than a child. The landlord threw them out.[1] A Greek woman who came to live with her parents as a child lived in a building in Nürnberg where the toilet was in the courtyard. Her mother instructed her and her sister that they were not allowed to go to the toilet while both parents were at work "because there were so many strangers. My mother was afraid, we were girls, little girls . . ."[2] She later married another Greek citizen who had come to live with his parents when he was fourteen. His parents had wanted to bring him earlier but had been unable to find an apartment large enough. They finally brought him in 1974, after the Turkish invasion of Cyprus, as they feared that he might be drafted into the army and sent to war. He had to sleep on a couch rather than a bed, and he and his younger brother had to go to the city pool to shower because they did not have running water at home.[3]

These visceral experiences of living in poor housing conditions reflect the many difficulties that migrant families experienced while looking for a home in Germany. Federal officials seeking to regulate family reunion tried to exploit existing housing shortages as a tool for reducing family migration. Instead of investing in areas with a shortage of suitable housing units, the officials who devised housing policy repeatedly argued that "migrant workers' practices of

Fear of the Family. Lauren Stokes, Oxford University Press. © Oxford University Press 2022.
DOI: 10.1093/oso/9780197558416.003.0003

housing [were] the cause for urban problems and crises."⁴ Because migrant
workers were understood to cause housing problems, responsibility for solving
said problems was shifted onto foreign workers—a responsibility that many experienced as a daily ordeal.

This chapter examines two different policies that developed from this underlying logic of holding foreigners responsible for urban problems. First, it
examines the long-standing policy requiring migrants to prove that they had
"adequate housing" to sponsor family members to come to the FRG. The requirement was understood as a "market-conforming" policy that protected
foreigners from making bad choices to live in tiny or decrepit apartments while
at the same time not requiring the state to intervene in the housing market that
provided these apartments. The same logic of protecting foreigners from themselves also underlay the second policy in which the state sought to dissolve
existing concentrations of foreigners by banning foreigners from settling in
"overburdened" areas. This measure restricted foreigners' ability to find housing
and to move internally as a way to keep them from living together and thus from
being perceived as a threat by their German neighbors.

In practice, both forms of housing restriction—one targeted at the level of the
individual housing unit, one at the level of the neighborhood—failed to be as
"market conforming" as officials had imagined. Both effectively pushed migrants
into precarious living situations. Many migrants who had entered the country legally and who were working legally were unable to find housing defined as "adequate" for their families, particularly when that "adequate" housing needed to be
outside of a restricted area. The disjuncture between entry permits, work permits,
and residence permits produced a situation in which migrants who entered and
worked legally might reside illegally by falsifying a rental contract to make it look
as if their apartment were larger or as if they lived at a different address. These
restrictions produced a new form of "undocumented" migrant who held a legal
residence permit but not the housing that the residence permit implied.⁵ Some
migrants publicly claimed housing as a social right when they participated in
housing squats, rent strikes, and other struggles for better conditions. Migrants
were frequently blamed for their poor housing conditions but largely ignored
when they attempted to change those conditions. State housing policies consistently encouraged perceptions of the migrant population as a threatening mass
that would alienate Germans from their own spaces.

Migrant Housing as Family Policy

When foreign labor recruitment began in 1955, 400,000 West Germans were
still living in wartime relief camps. To preempt concerns that foreign workers

would take up the scarce resource of housing, initial bilateral labor contracts stipulated that employers were required to provide housing for foreign workers. While extended families had proven to be an excellent recruiting tool, employers consistently rejected proposals that those who hired these workers take on the responsibility for providing family housing, and most met their obligations to provide housing through dormitories that housed men and women separately and that had no room for children.[6]

Local and municipal governments were often unhappy about the decision to rely on institutional housing. Such housing brought up memories of National Socialism and of the immediate postwar period, when Germans and foreigners had lived in barracks, in forced labor camps, and in displaced persons camps. Officials worried that dormitories for foreign workers would be incubators of disease and magnets for social unrest. The Association of German Cities (DST), which represented the views of local governments on the federal level, spearheaded a campaign against constructing "new German barracks." The DST argued that dormitories could be an international embarrassment that "would also stimulate the feelings of social superiority—people are already speaking about forced foreign laborers [*Fremdarbeiter*] again—and damage Germany's reputation abroad."[7] The Italian press used housing conditions to draw comparisons to Italians' previous experience as forced foreign laborers on German soil, publishing headlines such as "The Italians in Germany have returned to the *Lager*."[8] When a communist newspaper in Italy published a 1965 article accusing the Germans of housing workers in former concentration camps, the ensuing investigation confirmed how thoroughly "encamped" German society had been over the previous thirty years. The dormitory in question had never been used as a concentration camp, but it had been used as a dormitory for telecommunications specialists in the Air Force, as an emergency camp for civilians bombed out of their homes in 1943, and finally as a prisoner of war (POW) camp for German soldiers captured by the Americans.[9]

The DST found an ally for its anti-barracks campaign in the minister of housing, CDU member Paul Lücke, who the organization praised in October 1960 for "freeing the cities from their isolated resistance against new 'German barracks.' "[10] A devout Catholic and founding member of the "Family Association of German Catholics," Lücke admired the "Southern family," seeing it as an institution that preserved religious values and parental authority against the corrosive influences of mass culture and women's work outside of the home.[11] He argued that employers should be required to provide not just housing but explicitly family housing to insulate Southern families from corrupting German influence and thus to ensure their orderly return home.[12] He promoted the construction of closed settlements in rural areas where foreigners could live under the supervision of Catholic social workers.[13]

Lücke worried that the "economic miracle" had become the new source of
ultimate authority, displacing religious sources of authority. Most employers did
not share Lücke's concern. The German Chamber of Commerce and Industry
wrote an angry letter about his proposal to require employers to invest in
housing: "this command undoes measures that industry undertook at a great
deal of effort and cost. After all, the foreigners were not brought to Germany for
pleasure, but exclusively and only because they were urgently needed as workers."
Reading this letter, Lücke underlined the phrase "for pleasure," writing in the
margins: "We should forbid ourselves the tone taken here! Here it becomes apparent that industry takes the economic boom as Gospel, and openly does not
think about doing anything to absorb it!"[14] He continued to insist on the need
to build family housing to counter the ongoing "dissolution of the family by
the modern economy," a point that he made in meetings with the Federal president, the Labor Recruitment Commission in Rome, the Italian ambassador,
Chancellor Ludwig Erhard, Cardinal Bafile in his capacity as Apostolic Nuncio
to Germany, and even Pope Paul VI.[15]

The Family Association of German Catholics gradually lost influence over
the government's family policy during the Erhard chancellorship, and Paul
Lücke's project to preserve foreign families from the corrosive effects of the
economic miracle also fell out of favor.[16] In late 1964, the other ministries
unanimously rejected his proposal to construct closed settlements for guest
worker families.[17] They only agreed to make funding available to help construct new housing intended for the temporary residence of foreign families.
The Finance Ministry wanted to explicitly limit this funding to the construction of apartments and to exclude single-family housing; the ministry worried
that if it started to use taxpayer funds for housing, "the construction of schools,
kindergartens, hospitals and so on for foreigners would follow."[18] Lücke pushed
back, and after nearly a year of back and forth, the state finally approved a
compromise funding package in November 1965. Employers could apply for
funding to build "family housing units" for married foreign workers who had
been in the FRG for at least two years. Lücke had advocated the term "family
housing units" because it technically allowed the funding to be used for either
apartment buildings or single-family homes.[19] Employers largely failed to use
the program. By 1973, the state had provided 450 million DM for dormitories
and only 40 million DM for "family housing," almost all of which went to apartment buildings.[20] Lücke was unable to use his position as housing minister to
preserve what he saw as the traditional Catholic family. That family would instead have to fend for itself on the market, along with the many other foreign
families who would not have fit into his ideal.

The "Adequate Housing" Requirement in Practice

Each bilateral labor recruitment agreement included the stipulation that the ability to bring family members to the FRG would depend on the individual worker's ability to secure "adequate housing" for said family members. When the Interior Ministry issued national guidelines for interpreting the new Law on Foreigners in 1965, it had wanted to increase the period required before people could bring their families from one year to three, but it was prevented from doing so by the rest of the ministries, all of which wanted to preserve the possibility of family migration. The other ministries, particularly the Economics Ministry, further insisted that the housing requirement was a sufficient brake on family migration, one that would ensure that it did not grow to troubling dimensions.[21] The housing requirement aligned with the neoliberal fantasy of a "market-conforming" social policy. By limiting the number of new migrants to the availability of "adequate housing" units, it ensured that the housing market would function to regulate migration without requiring additional government intervention.[22]

Local Foreigners' Offices were only supposed to approve residence permits for foreigners who had apartments that met "the normal standards of comparable German workers," but those standards were never defined in the law. After a flurry of national press reporting on the poor housing conditions of guest workers at the end of the 1960s, the federal Interior Ministry finally discussed setting national guidelines on "adequate housing."[23] Several of the regional ministries supported this proposal, including the Saarland, which welcomed it as a way to prevent "Sicilian living conditions" in the FRG.[24] The Interior Ministry of North Rhine-Westphalia made the first concrete suggestion for an enforceable standard—five square meters per person—but this was rejected by the federal Housing Ministry, subsequently led by SPD politician Lauritz Lauritzen, which refused to set its own definition of "adequate housing."[25]

Because the federal government refused to define "adequate housing," each federal state was free to set its own standards. Most set far more restrictive ones than that first proposed by North Rhine-Westphalia. Rhineland-Palatinate required the apartment to have twelve square meters per adult and eight square meters per child under six, but also counted children who lived abroad as residents of the apartment unless the couple was willing to sign a written promise never to bring the other children to West Germany.[26] In Bavaria, the standard for foreigners was higher than the standard for native Germans. The Bavarian Housing Supervision Law required residents to have only a minimum of six square meters per person, but foreigners applying for residence permits needed to prove that they had twelve square meters per person over the age of six and nine square meters per person under the age of six.[27]

In practice, the "adequate housing" requirement was often invoked but rarely enforced. The Labor Ministry and other federal officials repeatedly urged local officials to do their part to curb foreign migration by enforcing the "adequate housing" requirement, but they lacked the staff to do so.[28] Because local officials did not have the capacity to inspect the physical space of every apartment, they relied on leases instead, and families often showed officials leases that did not match their living conditions in order to obtain their residence permits. The state's reliance on a paper trail created a black market in false leases.[29] Schleswig-Holstein specifically feared that foreign families with large apartments were selling their address to multiple additional families, who registered in the large apartment while living in smaller apartments.[30] Families with false leases not only presented false documentation to the authorities, but they also lived in violation of the "adequate housing" requirement on which their residence depended. They were vulnerable to deportation if either fact were discovered.

The fantasy that the housing market could regulate migration was also disrupted by the belief of many German officials that foreigners were not educated consumers of "adequate housing." Officials lamented in 1970 that "foreigners are often inclined to see apartments as adequate that do not in any way meet the minimum requirements for an apartment. . . . The danger of the emergence of slums is not just theoretical, but is becoming increasingly real."[31] These officials studiously ignored the fact that foreigners were navigating a different housing market than German citizens. Social science studies consistently showed that foreigners paid more for the same housing as Germans, in part because landlords believed that foreign workers were short-term residents willing to pay more money for worse apartments than natives. A study conducted across eight cities in 1978 revealed that on average foreigners paid 13 percent more than Germans for a square meter of housing.[32] A 1979 study showed that Turkish families were on average willing to pay twice the amount they already paid to obtain an apartment with more space and better facilities—but they struggled to find landlords willing to take their money.[33] These studies repeatedly confirmed that families with children had a much more difficult time finding housing than those without.[34]

From the perspective of foreigners, the relevant point of comparison was not the "comparable German worker" invoked in the "adequate housing" requirement but the dormitory housing where many had spent their first months in Germany. One Italian man who worked at the Volkswagen plant in Wolfsburg was excited to find an apartment in the city, assuming that he could bring his wife and child. His wife's application for a residence permit, however, was denied on the basis that a three-person family had only secured a two-room apartment. Forced to continue living in the company dormitory, the man wrote an angry letter to the union newspaper: "Now I ask myself, how I can believe in this joke, when here in the 'Berlin Bridge' dormitory, three people are allowed to sleep and eat in 12 square meters, including cupboard, table and chairs. Perhaps the Health Office doesn't look so closely here, or perhaps we live in a different Republic."[35] He experienced a housing requirement meant to protect him from exploitation primarily as an obstacle to his leaving the overcrowded dormitory.

Social workers for Diakonie in Baden-Württemberg documented dozens of punitive uses of housing requirements against families with children.[36] Foreign children had to apply for an independent residence permit for the first time when they turned sixteen. At this point the state could reject their application, claiming that their continued presence in the neighborhood was a danger to social welfare because "if foreigners make use of apartments that are much too small and defective for the purpose of family reunion, this necessarily leads to the creation of slum-like foreigner ghettos and all of the known social, hygienic and criminal consequences."[37] This explanation surely did not comfort a Turkish teenager whose application for a residence permit was rejected when he turned sixteen because the apartment he shared with his father was twenty-three square meters instead of twenty-four.[38] Some families ran into problems well before their children turned sixteen. One Spanish couple that had been deemed to have sufficient space when they had two teenage children received a letter ten days

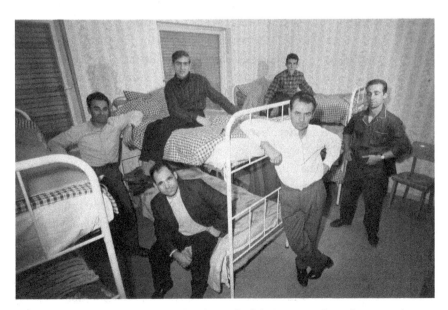

Figure 2.1 Dormitory room in the "Berlin Bridge" dormitory at the Volkswagen plant in Wolfsburg in 1966. Max Scheler/Süddeutsche Zeitung Photo/Alamy Stock Photo.

after the birth of their third child informing them that the residence permits of the wife and the two children had been limited until the end of the year and would expire unless the family found a larger apartment.[39]

Punitive housing requirements often led to the temporary division of families. One Turkish teenager left Germany at both thirteen and sixteen, in both cases because the residence permit of a family member had been denied because the apartment was too small. The family finally secured a larger apartment when he was seventeen, allowing him to return.[40] A Turkish couple with four children in Frankfurt was threatened with deportation because they had a 43.78 square meter apartment and needed a 54 square meter apartment. The second warning letter from the Foreigners' Office explicitly chastised the family because the husband had recently traveled to Turkey but had failed to bring his children with him. According to German officials, the husband should have used the trip as an opportunity to relocate two of his children and thus to make the German apartment livable. In response to this second warning letter, the couple decided to send the two eldest children back to Turkey. While their parents looked for a larger apartment, the children had their education and family life completely disrupted.[41]

Other families found that even temporary separation was insufficient for local authorities, who required them to account for an entire transnational family in their living space in Germany. A father and son in Stuttgart were informed that their apartment needed to be large enough to also house the mother and remaining children in Turkey. Had the father and son been counted as two individuals, they would have needed a twenty-four square meter apartment, but with the family members in Turkey counted, they needed to prove that they had a sixty square meter apartment—a nearly impossible task, particularly as the men were sending most of their earnings home to the mother and other children.[42] This family's transnational structure was held against them. In another case, a Greek family of two adults and three children ran into problems when their eldest son turned sixteen. At the time the family was living in a forty-two square meter apartment that had been provided through the local housing office. Despite the fact that the housing office had already tried and failed to find "adequate housing" for this family, the responsibility devolved to the family, who were told that the residence permits of both parents and the eldest son would all be rescinded unless they could find a sixty square meter apartment within the next five months. The family proposed a creative solution that drew on their extended family in Germany as a resource. Perhaps the teenage boy could live with other relatives in the city and continue going to school while the parents looked for a larger apartment. The Foreigners' Office rejected their solution, insisting once again that the family either find a larger apartment or send the boy back to Greece.[43] Family members seemed to appear when they could be used as a means of restriction and to disappear when they could be used as a resource.

Foreigners lived with the constant threat of having their housing inspected and declared inadequate. In the 1980s, anti-census activists recognized that the planned West German census might pose a danger to foreigners living in violation of the housing ordinances, because information about "residentially illegal" foreigners could theoretically be used to open deportation proceedings.[44] The census boycott movement did not advise foreigners to take part in the boycott because the personal risks were too great, but it did distribute multilingual flyers to inform them about the census.[45] One group of Evangelical students in Munich distributed bilingual flyers assuring foreigners that "the apartment is inviolable!" and informed them that, based on Article 13 of the Basic Law, they could refuse officials entry: "In Munich officials from the housing office are going to be coming around in order to measure guest worker apartments. When an official comes to measure your apartment, tell him unambiguously: 'YOU ARE NOT MY GUEST!' 'YOU CANNOT COME IN!' Show the official this flyer and tell him: 'I am against you entering my apartment.'" The flyer continued: "ADMINISTRATIVE DECREES ARE NOT LAWS. BASIC RIGHTS HAVE PRIORITY. USE YOUR RIGHTS," and presented migrants with a telephone number to contact in case they needed legal assistance.[46] Another flyer distributed in West Berlin informed foreigners that "the 'census' is not just *dangerous snooping*, it is also an insult to foreigners. . . . They say that we don't belong to the people. But when it is time to count and snoop, suddenly we do belong to the people!"[47]

Foreigners, particularly uncountable foreign children, did in fact pose a major challenge to the state's knowledge of its own population. The additional value of information about foreigners was made explicit in Munich's promise to pay census enumerators 2.5 DM for any German who had not previously been registered and 5 DM for any foreigner who had not previously been registered. Neo-Nazis subsequently volunteered to be enumerators, proudly telling the media that they hoped to help reveal the true number of foreigners living in the FRG.[48] Green Party representative Dirk Schneider denounced what he called Munich's "head bounty" in the Bundestag, warning that the data might be used to determine "whether foreigners have violated the different provisions, for example if they live in the areas where they are supposed to live, or whether they have reported all the children that they really have."[49] The unreported foreign child was an image that could evoke either sympathy or fear.

"Adequate housing" requirements claimed to protect foreigners from poor housing conditions, but in practice they created new obstacles for foreigners to navigate. Some foreign families suffered periods of separation and disruption as they sought to find apartments that would satisfy the authorities, while others spent their money in order to obtain a better piece of paper rather than a marginally better apartment. Families living in violation of housing requirements were made "illegal" and potentially vulnerable to police action and deportation. Other migrants actively chose to become "residentially illegal" by deciding not to register. One husband who had followed his wife to Germany on a tourist visa recalled that housing requirements forced him not to register. "Our apartment was just a hole, and the square meter requirement alone meant that our situation was hopeless. Besides looking for work, we looked constantly for a better apartment. But everything was connected: We looked for a 'normal' apartment. But we couldn't have paid for it, because I couldn't work. In order to work, I had to have a normal apartment. How does one get out of this cursed situation?"[50] Like thousands of other foreigners, he experienced housing requirements as a means of exclusion rather than as an effective instrument for protecting his interests.

Foreign Families Become Foreign Communities

In early 1971, Hans-Jochen Vogel, mayor of Munich and SPD politician, drafted an essay titled "Where Is Harlem?"[51] In the essay, Vogel reflects on the existence of a neighborhood where "colored people" lived in a "social ghetto . . . as if behind walls. They feel themselves shut out of the community, exploited, abandoned and without rights. They pay high rents for bad apartments. In case of recession they are the first to lose their jobs." He warned that this set of problems was hardly unique to the United States:

> We already have our own little Harlems. I mean the Turkish blocks and the Greek quarters, the Italian streets and the mass quarters for so-called guest workers from all corners of the globe. . . . They press themselves ever more tightly into the areas of old housing stock on the outskirts of the inner cities. Or more honestly: they are herded there, even penned up. And much of what I say about Harlem is also true of them. . . . As seismographs of coming social shocks, the cities can already feel it. Do we want to wait, until the big Harlems are also in Germany?[52]

Vogel was one of many politicians and journalists to invoke the American analogy to draw attention to the problems faced by foreign workers and underscore the existence of discrimination. Journalist Ernst Klee titled his book about discrimination against foreign workers Die N***** Europas, while Die Zeit warned against "laying the ground for a future 'German Negro problem.'"[53] The labor minister of North Rhine-Westphalia also called for new policy to ensure "that the guest workers do not become the Negroes of our Nation."[54] The specific urban analogy was also common. The State Criminal Police Office of Bremen identified the "danger that developments will occur, as they have been observed in the slum-areas of large American cities."[55] The famous 1973 *Spiegel* cover story titled "The Turks Are Coming" echoed Vogel when it worried that in Kreuzberg "the first Harlem symptoms can already be detected."[56]

Vogel was tapped to be the next head of the federal Ministry for Regional Planning, Building and Urban Development in 1972, at the moment when the ministry had just dropped the word "Housing" from its name and added the word "Regional Planning." The changing name reflected a shift in scale that was mirrored by discussions about housing for foreigners. Whereas the "adequate housing" requirements were meant to address the threat of overcrowded and unhygienic homes, in the early 1970s the fact that foreign families clustered in specific neighborhoods would come to be seen as problem in need of a solution.

In this context, the constant invocation of the "Harlem" analogy placed the emphasis on racial difference rather than national difference or a difference of citizenship status. If these commentators wanted to use the American analogy to talk about the challenges stemming from migration and the associated xeno-phobia, it might have been more appropriate to draw a comparison to "Little Italy" or "Chinatown." New migrants to the United States, like new migrants to the FRG, did not speak the dominant language of the country and lacked citizen-ship. But commentators consistently spoke of the danger of "Harlem," a neigh-borhood associated with African Americans and Puerto Ricans, US citizens whose racialization as foreign prevented them from accessing the full benefits of citizenship. When elected officials, urban planning experts, and journalists invoked the Harlem analogy, they racialized foreign populations without explic-itly using the morally delegitimized language of biological racism.

In 1972 urban planners in both West Berlin and Munich published reports on urban development that described the "ghettoization" of the foreign com-munity as a particular threat.[57] The Munich report explicitly stated that its goal was to prevent both "minority problems after the example of the USA" and cases of social conflict after the example of Switzerland "and particularly the United States."[58] Both reports explicitly rejected allocating more funding to improve the infrastructure of these neighborhoods. West Berlin's report explained that if measures were taken to improve living conditions in foreigners' neighborhoods, more foreigners might want to move in, thus accelerating ghettoization.[59] The Munich report explained that "when a certain proportion of foreign workers is reached, a complex bundle of social problems arises, the dimensions of which will first become clear in a period of crisis."[60] The "ghetto" in these reports is not a threat to public health, but a threat to social order, with the underlying as-sumption that there is a "tipping point" or "threshold" at which a concentration of foreigners becomes a threat.

The discourse on urban housing consistently framed the "urban ghetto" using the American analogy and thus subtly suggested that the problem of racial difference was an import rather than a legacy from the recent German past. That past was inescapable, however, as Labor Ministry officials recognized when they warned that "for political reasons we cannot allow conditions to break out that have occurred in other countries."[61] Any outbreak of popular violence against foreigners would be interpreted as an upsurge of Nazi sentiment, but, at the same time, officials worried that an excessive use of police power against concentrations of foreigners would be interpreted as a return to a Nazi police state. One Labor Ministry report discussed the potential adoption of the "Swiss model" in 1973, which would have meant imposing a global cap on the percentage of foreigners in West Germany. The original memorandum about the "Swiss model" rejected it for two reasons. The first reason was neoliberal. Imposing a global cap would represent a "problematic administrative intervention into the operation of the market." The second reason was the Nazi past. Imposing a global cap would remind foreign observers of "the past use of forced foreign laborers [Fremdarbeitereinsatz]." The final draft of the report definitively rejected the "Swiss model" but removed the sensitive term Fremdarbeiter.[62]

The Nazi past was something that the FRG did not want to revive but could not fully escape. At another March 1972 meeting in the Federal Labor Office, attendees worried that using "liberal methods" to combat ghettoization, measures such as constructing housing specifically for foreign families, would only exacerbate what officials perceived as the larger problem of the growth of the foreign population. This insight is communicated in the meeting report as follows: "Creating space [Lebensraum] for the foreign workers who stay would mean limiting the space [Lebensraum] of the other people who live in the Federal Republic."[63] This startling reappearance of a National Socialist term reflected an understanding of the allocation of living space as a zero-sum game in which creating space for foreign workers and their families could only come at the cost of space for West Germans.

Anti-Ghettoization Measures in West Germany

Federal officials eventually decided to impose regional limits on foreign settlement to disperse foreigners across the country. The Federal Labor Office began in 1972 to consider telling municipal officials that they could deny residence permits to foreigners when the municipality was already having difficulties with the "social infrastructure." The Federal Labor Office's primary concern about this plan was initially the fact that it represented an unacceptable intervention into the labor market. Foreigners clustered together mainly because they were coming to the FRG to work at specific firms, so the fact that they lived close to those firms was normal.[64] Reflecting this close attention to the needs of employers, the Labor Ministry initially described the areas of concern as "dense economic agglomerations," until September 1973, when it instead defined them as "overburdened regions of settlement." The shift in the language used to describe the spaces that needed regulation also reflected a shift in the target of the measure. The Labor Ministry discussed and rejected the idea of limiting the percentage of foreigners in the local workforce by requiring employers to pay for housing or to pay higher fees to recruit workers. It decided instead to limit the percentage of foreign residents living in a particular city by barring them from registering as residents in places that were determined to already have too many foreigners. In other words, the state imposed "market conformity" in a one-sided fashion. The employers whose dependence on foreign labor had created "dense economic agglomerations" would not have to change their behavior. The foreign workers who had moved to "overburdened regions of settlement" because that was where they had been recruited to work would have to make changes. New arrivals would be required to live far away from the factories where the jobs were.[65]

In November 1973, only one month after the planned measure had been reworked to target settlement rather than employment, the state imposed a ban on new labor migration. The state was increasingly concerned about the long-term social consequences of migration, although the oil crisis and the "wild strikes" of guest workers in the summer of 1973 both helped to create the "crisis conditions" that enabled the decision.[66] Officials continued to work on their plan for regional limits after the recruitment stop was announced because they assumed that the ban would be lifted in the near future. The Labor Ministry hoped to better align foreign labor recruitment with the needs of the market, or, as the interior minister of Bavaria put it, "to build in concrete limits that will function automatically and irreversibly in the next economic upswing."[67] By May 1974 the Labor Ministry had settled on several principles for future recruitment. These included the idea that, when possible, companies should seek to recruit unemployed foreign workers from elsewhere in Germany rather than recruiting new workers from abroad, and second, the idea that if they did recruit new foreign workers, they should try to recruit only single workers.[68] It never had the chance to implement these principles because the November 1973 ban on labor recruitment was never lifted. The ban did not lead to the dramatic decrease in foreign population that officials had anticipated. Because family migration became the only realistic way to enter the FRG, the pre-existing concentrations of foreign population became only more pronounced as new arrivals moved to be with their family members.

The Interior Ministry finally issued an administrative circular banning foreign settlement into "overburdened regions" in April 1975. The circular defined
an "overburdened region" as one with over 12 percent foreign nationals in the
local population. Districts with a foreign population of between 8 and 12 percent could decide for themselves whether they wished to ban further foreign
settlement, but districts where the foreign population was more than 12 percent
had no choice.[69] Although the decisive percentage of foreigners in the local population was determined by counting all foreigners in an area, the ensuing ban
applied to only a subset of those foreigners. Citizens of the European Economic
Community were exempted, as well as foreigners for whom "no integration
problems existed," which meant the United States, Canada, Australia, the UK,
Switzerland, Austria, and Japan. Critics of the measure pointed out that this was
a discriminatory regulation because it targeted only some concentrations of
foreigners. The Foreigners' Committee of West Berlin, initially formed to protest
a deportation, pointed out that the measure did not target the Allied occupying
forces, groups who "live in their own housing developments entirely for themselves—the highest form of the 'ghetto.' "[70] American, British, and French families
counted toward the 12 percent cap at which a district became "overburdened,"
but these groups would never be confronted with the consequences.[71]

In terms of implementation, foreign nationals who went to the Foreigners'
Office to apply for or renew their residence permits received stamps in their
passport stating that they were "Not eligible for settlement in overburdened
areas." If foreigners with this stamp subsequently tried to register their address in
an "overburdened area," their registration would be refused, and they would be
unable to apply for a residence permit based on residence in that location. There
was an exemption for nuclear family members—spouses and children under sixteen—that did not apply to adult children or to any extended family members.

Because the ban was implemented at the point of registration for a new residence permit, and because there was virtually no press reporting on the ban,
it often took months or even years before affected foreigners found out about
this new restriction.[72] On discovering it, some affected foreigners filed suit
against the ban in court, while others wrote to politicians in protest. The Turkish
workers of Opel addressed one such petition to Chancellor Helmut Schmidt in
March 1976. Rüsselsheim, home of the Opel factory, had been declared "off-
limits" to further foreign settlement, which had created problems for men who
had gotten jobs there after April 1975. Hasan and Mehmet were a father and
son who both worked at Opel but who were unable to live together. Mehmet
had already lived in Rüsselsheim before April 1975, which meant that he could
continue living there once he got a new job in November. His father Hasan got
a job alongside his son shortly afterward, but he could not move in to his son's
apartment because he had previously lived outside of Rüsselsheim. Instead, he

was forced to rent a second apartment outside of city limits to comply with the regulations on settlement. The father and son could work together to improve Opel's profits, but they could not live together to improve the family's profits. Another man wanted to rent a room in the Opel company dormitory, but he was prevented from doing so by the settlement ban. Instead he had to rent his own apartment in neighboring Wiesbaden and commute to work, which meant that he could send less money home to his wife and eight children, which in turn meant that he had to extend his stay in the FRG in order to save money for his children's education.[73] The state's answer to the petition cited the standard justification: the measure was "in the interest of the foreigners themselves," because if the state did not prevent the foreigners from living together "all of the efforts for integration and improvement of living conditions would be for nothing."[74] The response ignored the many specific ways in which the men had explained that the policy failed to serve their interests.

The experiences of the Opel workers demonstrate that the ban on settlement had been designed in order not to inconvenience employers. The Labor Ministry had considered and rejected the idea of fining employers who contributed to "dense economic agglomerations" of foreigners. It had opted instead to prevent employees from living in "overburdened regions of settlement." Employers still complained about the existing ban because it increased their difficulty in hiring foreign workers, who could no longer move into the towns where the jobs were, and whose lengthy commutes made them late to work more often.[75] The ban was also remarkably unpopular with the city authorities who enforced it, as the DST found in an August 1975 survey.[76] The federal state had claimed that the ban would alleviate the pressure on "social infrastructure," which included institutions like schools and hospitals, but city governments argued that it did exactly the opposite, since they could no longer easily hire foreigners for jobs like cleaning those same schools and hospitals. Several cities also mentioned that dependent family members—spouses and minor children—were still moving into their cities, but that those new arrivals were unable to get work permits because of a new policy of excluding family members from the labor market. As Nürnberg explained, "On the one hand the claims on city infrastructure (especially on the kindergartens, primary schools and secondary schools) have increased, while on the other hand the gains for city management, that ensued through the offer of mobile foreign workers, can no longer be fully realized."[77] Because newly arrived family members were barred from entering the labor market, the cities had to support a larger population but could not treat that population as part of the labor force.

When the DST conducted a follow-up survey about the effects of the ban on settlement in 1976, most cities were still unhappy about the measure. It was true that most cities did report small decreases in the foreign population. In Frankfurt,

for example, the foreign population had decreased from 120,000 to 115,000 between April 1975 and 1976. However, cities that were not subject to the ban on
settlement had experienced similar decreases, leaving city governments skeptical
about whether the measure had produced the effect. Cities also continued to
complain about the fact that the measure allowed family migration to continue
while barring newly arrived family members from the workforce. However, only
Augsburg believed in 1976 that the correct solution was to ban family reunification. All other cities continued to support family reunification for a combination
of humanitarian and pragmatic reasons.[78]

The federal state suspended the ban on settlement in overburdened areas
abruptly in April 1977 after only two years in effect. The immediate cause for
the suspension was that the ban could no longer apply to Turkish citizens. In
December 1976, as part of the ongoing process of Turkish association with
the European Economic Community, Turkish citizens received the right to
free movement within member countries after five years of paid employment
there. This meant that the regulation officially ceased to have legal standing
for the overwhelming majority of Turkish citizens, who composed the largest
group of foreigners in the FRG. In the summer of 1977, the federal interior minister polled the interior ministers of the federal states, all of whom agreed that a
measure that applied only to citizens of Portugal and Yugoslavia was no longer
very useful.[79] The Labor Ministry also worried that at this point Yugoslavia and
Portugal might claim discrimination against their citizens. It is unclear why a
measure considered reasonable when it applied to Turkish, Yugoslavian, and
Portuguese citizens suddenly became "discriminatory" when it applied to only
two of those groups.[80] The settlement ban was suspended not because of a prin-
cipled decision that the measure was incompatible with German liberalism but
because the external process of European integration imposed new restrictions
on the ban that would make it ineffective at dissolving concentrations of Turkish
families.

Anti-Ghettoization Measures in West Berlin

West Berlin's internal ban on foreign movement would be in effect for much
longer than the national ban—from January 1, 1975, through the fall of the
Berlin Wall and German unification. West Berlin functioned as a "third
Germany" where the sovereign power was not with Bonn or East Berlin but
with the three Western Allies.[81] Many aspects of its legal status were kept pur-
posely ambiguous in order not to enflame tensions with the Soviet Union. For
example, West Berlin was part of the European Economic Community only insofar as this did not conflict with the Allied authority, so an open question was

whether EEC law applied there.[82] West Berlin also had a particularly high percentage of foreign residents because the 1961 construction of the Berlin Wall had cut employers off from access to the labor force that commuted from East Berlin. Employers responded by recruiting foreign workers. West Berlin also did not impose border control with East Berlin, which meant that foreigners from Turkey and elsewhere could and did enter West Berlin via East Berlin without proper authorization.[83] The combination of an unclear legal status and an effectively open border made West Berlin a frequent innovator in policies intended to curb migration.

West Berlin maintained a localized restriction on foreign settlement longer than anywhere else in the FRG. The city began its internal restriction on January 1, 1975, three months before the similar federal restriction went into effect. Foreigners moving to West Berlin after this date had their residence permits stamped with the announcement "Not valid for residence in Wedding, Tiergarten and Kreuzberg."[84]

The targeted neighborhoods were the three "inner-city" districts that abutted the Berlin Wall, all increasingly undesirable locations after 1961. As West Berlin residents chose to move away, private investors had little incentive to improve the housing stock in these neighborhoods, and foreigners moved into deteriorating housing with cheap rents. As architect Cihan Arın told the Berlin Senate at a hearing on the settlement ban in 1983, it might have made more sense to speak of a "settlement ban" enforced by landlords, because it was virtually impossible for a foreigner to rent an apartment in most of the other neighborhoods in West Berlin.[85]

Just as on the national level, the measure was intended to prevent the creation of "American-style" ghettos, with local newspapers explaining that without the ban, "within a few years Kreuzberg would almost certainly have conditions such as those in Harlem or other large American cities."[86] The West Berlin ban was far stricter than the national policy because it applied not just to extended family members but also to spouses and minor children within the nuclear family.[87] Officials hoped that the extension of the ban to nuclear family members would discourage foreigners' migration plans altogether.[88] In practice, married couples who had lived in West Berlin for years found that husbands who went to Turkey or Greece to complete their required military service could not re-register in the same apartment as their wives when they returned. Turkish and Yugoslavian teenagers also had to apply to continue living with their parents in the apartment they had grown up in upon turning sixteen. Many received a dismal birthday present in the form of a letter informing them that "your private interests in living with your parents in the same apartment . . . cannot prevail over the public interest in decreasing the number of foreigners in Tiergarten, Wedding, and Kreuzberg."[89] The assumption that preventing nuclear families from living

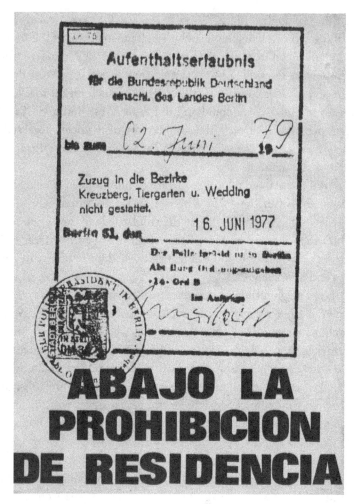

Figure 2.2 This flyer shows an image of the residence ban stamp in a passport and makes the demand "Down with the Prohibition on Residence!". DOMiD-Archiv, Köln FL0042.

together could ever be in "the public interest" reveals that the city government considered only some residents to be part of the "public" in question.

The measure arguably failed even on its own terms because it did not reduce the concentration of foreigners living in the inner city. By 1978, the percentage of foreigners in Berlin who lived in the three barred districts had decreased from 46.3 percent to 38 percent, but the percentage registered in the neighboring districts of Charlottenburg, Spandau, Schöneberg, and Neukölln increased from 33.5 percent to 40.3 percent. Pre-existing spatial concentrations of foreigners had only shifted slightly, as the vast majority of this growth had occurred directly along the borders of the restricted districts.[90] Neukölln politicians from

Figure 2.3 Women gathering in front of the Berlin Wall. Picture alliance/zb/Paul Glaser.

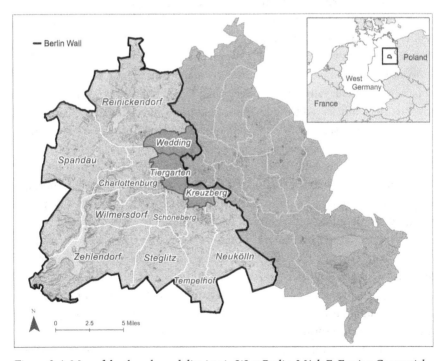

Figure 2.4 Map of the three barred districts in West Berlin. Méch E. Frazier, Geospatial Specialist, Northwestern University Libraries.

both the CDU and the SPD repeatedly asked to extend the restriction to the northern part of their district throughout the 1980s, but the city administration repeatedly rejected their requests because it did not relish the additional administrative burden of imposing restrictions on the more granular level of the post code.[91]

The city of Hamburg studied West Berlin's use of a residential ban in 1976 but rejected the possibility of deploying something similar because it concluded that it was not working very well and that the city struggled to impose appropriate sanctions on those violating the ban.[92] Foreign residents of Hamburg had a more pointed critique when they organized a letter-writing campaign demanding that their city take an active stand against Berlin-style measures, which would only "achieve what they presuppose: the so-called unwillingness and inability to integrate of the Turks." The letter suggested that Hamburg should instead create opportunities for foreigners to participate in local decision-making, such as granting communal voting rights.[93]

The foreign activists in Hamburg correctly recognized that even as the measure failed at the official goal of dissolving concentrations of foreigners, it succeeded in making it much more difficult to be a foreigner living in West Berlin. The ban made many family members residentially "illegal" in the places where they were already living. Faced with the difficulty of finding an apartment outside of the banned areas, many foreigners lived in their apartments without bothering to register with the police, registered addresses using false rental contracts, or paid bribes to get their papers in order.[94] Families with false rental contracts also had to work to maintain an official address separate from their actual living space. A family living "illegally" in Kreuzberg had to regularly send someone across town to their "official" address in Charlottenburg to check the mail.[95]

Migrants protested the ban on settlement not only through everyday defiance but also by organizing explicit political campaigns against the ban. The Foreigners' Committee of West Berlin referred to the long history of Jewish ghettos in European cities, explaining that Jews "were not without rights because they lived in the ghettos: they lived there because they had no rights."[96] Architect Cihan Arın worked with this committee and others as he documented the ban's effects and proposed better solutions. In one policy paper, he asked, "Why don't these men and women have the idea to impose a settlement ban on Zehlendorf for those who, let's say, make more than 3.000 DM a month?" Zehlendorf was an affluent neighborhood of single-family homes and the primary location of the US occupation forces, a concentration of foreigners who did not receive the same kind of scrutiny.[97] The Turkish Cultural Center labeled the measure an example of "Prussian imperatives" and demanded that 20 percent of the public housing units be given to foreigners, "because that is the percentage of foreigners in the population, and because when they look for apartments, they run into the prejudices and rejection of Germans."[98] The city of West Berlin had recommended that 10 percent of the public housing stock should be rented to foreigners in 1978, and it raised this recommendation to 15 percent in 1982, but these had virtually no effect. Many housing authorities chose to use recommendations not as a minimum but as a quota and thus excluded foreigners from buildings where 10 percent of the units were already rented to foreigners. These guidelines were also ineffective because they included no stipulation about which foreigners counted. A building that rented 10 percent of its units to US and EEC citizens could claim that it was fulfilling the recommendation even though it was doing nothing to alleviate the situation of the specific foreigners who were forced to navigate the ban on settlement.[99]

Migrants also challenged the settlement ban in court. A Turkish woman who tried to move in with her husband in February 1975, in the second month of the settlement ban, had her application for a residence permit denied for two reasons. First, the Foreigners' Office argued that her husband's apartment did not fulfill the "adequate housing" requirement. It was large enough for two people, but the couple also had five children living in Turkey, and the apartment was not large enough for all seven. Second, her husband's apartment was in Wedding, which meant that no other foreigner could move into his apartment, not even his spouse. The first court to hear this case overturned the decision of the Foreigners' Office, arguing that the decision violated Article 6 of the Basic Law—"Marriage and the family shall enjoy the special protection of the state"— by preventing the couple from living together.[100] The city appealed the decision, arguing that it had to count the family as a seven-person family for the purpose of "adequate space," noting that because the couple's minor children would not be required to have residence permits, there would be no way to prevent them from moving in. The city's only line of defense against the children was to deny their mother's residence permit. More fundamentally, the city argued that Article 6 and its protection of the family did not have absolute priority, but that it had to be weighed against other guarantees in the Basic Law, such as Article 20, the welfare state principle, which meant that "the administration is obliged to hold the foreigners who live here to a humane social standard. This includes the responsibility of fostering the integration of foreigners . . . and discouraging an excessive concentration of foreigners in certain neighborhoods in order to prevent the creation of ghettos and sources of social tension."[101] The city argued that to allow the wife to move in with her husband would mean that the state was failing to guarantee a "humane social standard" for the entire city. The "adequate housing" requirement had supposedly protected foreigners from living in apartments that were too small, but the "anti-ghettoization" restrictions quite literally protected foreigners from living with their family members so that society would not see them as a threatening mass.

The city administration interpreted this duty to hold foreigners to a "humane social standard" in a very narrow fashion. In another court case, the husband had moved to West Berlin in 1962 and his wife had followed him in 1965. The couple subsequently had five children, all of whom lived with them in West Berlin. The family had lived in Kreuzberg between 1967 and 1974, at which point—shortly before the settlement ban went into effect on January 1, 1975—the entire family had moved to Wedding. Less than a year after their move, the eldest son became ill and required an extended inpatient hospital treatment. The family doctor advised that the family return to Kreuzberg where the son's treatment would take place, but the chief of police refused to make an exception to the settlement ban.[102] The first court to hear this case agreed with the family. How precisely did forcing a family to live far away from their sick child uphold a "humane social standard"? The city appealed the decision.

As these cases made their way through the justice system, city administrators worried that the settlement ban would be struck down by a higher court. Starting in early 1977, the Berlin senator of the interior and the three district mayors decided to defend themselves from this possibility by directing their own district offices to grant more exceptions to the ban, particularly in cases where a married couple was trying to move in together. As one internal memorandum explained, the city administration hoped to avoid an "emotionally charged public discussion that will be conducted under the slogan, 'the Federal Republic does not integrate foreigners, but defends itself from them.'"[103] The widespread use of administrative circulars enabled restrictive measures to be introduced without public fanfare, but when migrants responded by taking the city to court, the city struggled to defend its measures.

The city's effort to hold on to the measure by granting more exceptions did not succeed. By June 1978, administrative courts in Berlin had ruled five times that the settlement ban was illegal, not just because it infringed on Article 6 of the Basic Law but also because it violated Protocol 4 of the European Convention for the Protection of Human Rights and Fundamental Freedoms, which states, "Everyone lawfully within the territory of a State shall, within that territory, have the right to liberty of movement and freedom to choose his residence."[104] In July 1979 the Superior Administrative Court of Berlin made a fundamental decision that the measure was unconstitutional.[105] The court cited the city's last-ditch practice of granting exceptions to particular couples as an additional problem that violated Article 3 of the Basic Law, "all persons shall be equal before the law," because those foreigners who knew to ask the district office for an exception would receive individualized consideration of their case, but foreigners who did not know to ask for an exception or who mistakenly asked the city Foreigners' Office for an exception would not receive such consideration.[106]

The Senator of the Interior responded to this fundamental decision not by repealing the regulation entirely but by formalizing a very long catalog of exceptions, including exceptions that allowed nuclear family members and asylum applicants to live in the restricted districts starting in February 1980.[107] This decision weakened the practical effects of the measure considerably and meant that far fewer migrants would come into contact with it over the next decade, but the city still refused to drop the measure from the books entirely. The measure reinforced the nuclear and heterosexual family as a form by continuing to prevent unmarried couples, adult children, and extended family members from moving in with people who already lived in the three barred districts. It also continued to prevent new migrants from even considering these three neighborhoods as a site for legal settlement. By keeping the measure on the books, the city administration held on to its official position that concentrations of foreigners threatened the "public interest" and undermined social welfare. Much like the "adequate housing" requirement that was invoked more often than it was enforced, the ban on settlement had become a powerful symbol of the social order that the state fantasized about enforcing, a symbol worth retaining despite massive resistance.

Migrant Struggles for Reproductive Space

The state attempted to use a tight housing market to restrict migration—and thus to make migration conform to the market—but migrants refused to accept these restrictions. They lived in unauthorized housing arrangements, challenged settlement bans in court, and became involved in social movements that argued for housing as a social right that should be guaranteed by the state rather than left to market forces. Although the scholarship on struggles for housing in the FRG has tended to downplay their involvement, foreigners participated in rent strikes, squatted in unoccupied housing, and renovated their own apartments in urban renewal projects.[108] Italian guest workers sparked this movement when they brought the "rent strike" to Frankfurt, where nearly 18 percent of the total residents were foreigners.[109] Between August 1971 and May 1973 the "Renters' Union" had organized a rent strike with at least thirty houses inhabited primarily by foreigners, including Italians, Turks, Spaniards, and Yugoslavians.[110] The Renters' Union staged multilingual and multigenerational protests where people carried signs with slogans like "the largest apartments for the largest families," "our children want to play—we want a house," and for the children in attendance, "I am small and don't want any more loan sharks."[111]

The image of a protesting child underscores the different role that the family played for Germans and migrants involved in the squatting movement.

Foreigners needed to have access to a unit of "adequate housing" to live with their family and to avoid deportation, a fact that shaped their engagement with wider struggles for housing. While migrants were often seeking to find space for family life in a legal structure that sought to make such family life impossible, many of the West Germans who joined them were trying to live outside of the family or to create radically new family forms. As a result, migrant participants tended to place great value on the possibility of legalizing the squat, which many Germans saw as a betrayal of the movement.[112]

The autonomous left was interested in guest workers as a potential revolutionary vanguard, but when West German squatters mentioned their migrant counterparts, they were often quick to dismiss those same workers for reinforcing traditional family norms. A West German student squatting in Frankfurt criticized Italian squatters who tried to prevent their wives from leaving the house: "Of course, their basic approach is smothered by their culture but also by all of the emigrant bullshit. (By that I mean all of the reactionary clerical educational ideals and the practices in the family, especially the way the family patron relates to the wife . . . and the repressive situation in the houses, marked by the work conditions, living conditions, the ghetto situation and racism: as a result, they oppress each other and can't fight against their real enemies!)"[113] Another group of university students who squatted alongside Turkish families in Frankfurt decided that teaching the children how to speak German would be a good project in order to reduce tensions. The book they wrote about the experience shows that the students started with a set of problematic assumptions, such as the idea that when extended family members migrated to Germany "surely this happens less for emotional than for financial reasons—the number of breadwinners is higher that way."[114] The students gave up on radicalizing the Turkish parents after a single meeting with them. They also struggled to relate to the Turkish children, who suffered from "bourgeois attitudes" and "struggled to renounce [their] authoritarian-patriarchal upbringing."[115] The students do not appear to have looked within to consider whether their own attitudes might have hindered their work with the Turkish squatters.

Paying closer attention to migrant activism reveals a focus on creating spaces for children to learn and play. Turkish children from the squatted home in Frankfurt made signs that said "WE WANT A KINDERGARTEN" in Turkish to carry at a May Day demonstration, and one of the squatted homes in West Berlin where Turkish and German squatters clashed over legalization later became an intercultural kindergarten.[116] Italians in Wolfsburg complained that the district where most of them lived had no playgrounds for their children, Turks in West Berlin demanded that parks and playgrounds be part of any urban renewal project, and in Frankfurt a multinational coalition of women drew attention to the fact that "children forced to play on the streets have been run over more than once" as they demanded a kindergarten and a playground.[117]

One group of squatters in Frankfurt circulated a flyer with the arresting title "CHILD MURDERED" that drew connections between economic policy, housing policy, and family life as it used a traffic accident to make a broader critique of West German society. A country that had recruited labor with no consideration for its reproductive costs was a country that would build an entire city with no space for children to play.

ON SATURDAY, MARCH 31st ONE OF OUR CHILDREN WAS RUN OVER WHILE PLAYING ON THE STREET. For all children of foreign workers, as well as for all children of "little people," there is insufficient space to play. For us only the traffic-filled streets are left. . . . It is not the first time that proletarian children have been killed on the middle of the street. THIS IS NOT AN ACCIDENT OR BAD LUCK BUT MURDER! The only people who are responsible are the SPECULATORS AND THE MAYOR, who force us to live under these conditions, who build us high-rise buildings and office palaces instead of decent, affordable apartments and kindergartens. YOU ARE GUILTY OF THE DEATH OF THIS TURKISH CHILD![118]

The flyer reflected a distressing reality: by 1983, foreign children were the victims of 40 percent of pedestrian traffic accidents, meaning that they were two to three times more likely to be hit by a car than native-born children.[119] Social workers responded by organizing special classes about traffic safety for foreign children.[120] They also used this fact as an indictment of the priorities of city planners when they compared the cost of a spot in kindergarten to the cost of rehabilitating a severely injured child.[121] One Kreuzberg resident who witnessed a Turkish couple slap a child who had run in front of a car was upset to see the parents use physical punishment but argued that it was surely more important to consider the context: "Who will punish those who place the child, the wife, the husband under such pressures?"[122] A 1981 exhibition of photographs of Kreuzberg featured dozens of pictures of children playing in the street, including children playing in a vacant lot next to a graffiti tag: "Finally a new PLAYGROUND is here!"[123] In the images, children play under the specter of the ambient threat of traffic. The graffiti tagger, the photographer, and the book editor arguably all shared the same critique of city planners' failure to design for children and families and of the city administrators' failure to anticipate the very human needs of its foreign labor force.

The state had held on to a persistent fantasy that making adequate housing outside of a restricted district a requirement for a residence permit was a

Figure 2.5 Graffiti tag "Finally a new playground is here!" written on the side of a parking structure in Kreuzberg circa 1972. The image was later reprinted in the 1981 catalog of the *mornings Germany, evenings Turkey* photo exhibition. Picture alliance/ pepego/Timeline Images | pepego.

"market-conforming" solution that would manage to keep foreign settlement within appropriate limits without the need for state intervention. In fact, these requirements created new illegal markets in false rental contracts and drove migrants toward survival strategies like rent strikes and squatting. The state initially refused to put money into building family housing and renovating foreign neighborhoods, believing that this would prevent the further growth of precisely those foreign neighborhoods. Migrants refused to accept these restrictions: they circumvented registration requirements and turned streets into playgrounds, making lives in the neighborhood despite state obstacles.

* * *

The federal state enacted policies premised on the idea that concentrations of migrants in specific neighborhoods were a racialized threat to German national space. The "adequate housing" policy and the restriction on settlement in "overburdened" areas both failed to achieve their stated goals while succeeding in pushing migrants into quasi-legal living situations that left them vulnerable to punishment and to deportation. Regulations surrounding migrant housing

Figure 2.6 A child promises "I'll throw the cars out and make a playground!" in this 1983 flyer inviting Kreuzberg residents to come to a meeting about redesigning their neighborhood as part of the International Building Exhibition in West Berlin. S.T.E.R.N. Gesellschaft der behutsamen Stadterneuerung/FHXB Friedrichshain/Kreuzberg Museum.

also continually failed to address the ways in which the migrant ghetto was also partially created by West Germans. Restrictions on "adequate housing" hurt foreigners who could not find apartments rather than landlords who refused to rent to them, and settlement bans on specific areas penalized foreigners who wanted to live close to their workplaces rather than employers who aggressively recruited workers but failed to provide them with adequate housing.

The fear of crossing a "tipping point" at which a concentration of foreigners became a "ghetto" was shared broadly across Europe and the United States in this period, so these practices of restricting urban space were not necessarily exclusive to the FRG. In the Netherlands, Rotterdam officials decided in 1972 that migrants could not get housing permits for districts that already had over 5 percent of migrants in the population, although this policy was discontinued by 1974.[124] Rotterdam implemented a second dispersal policy in 1979, but this was suspended in 1983 after migrant protest.[125] Belgium adopted policies modeled on the West Berlin settlement ban in 1981 that were also struck down by the courts, a fact that did not stop Brussels from considering an updated version of the policy in 1984.[126]

Restrictive policies against "ghettoization" were resounding failures wherever they were implemented, functioning to racialize and stigmatize migrant communities rather than to address real needs, whether those needs were for safe playgrounds or for adequately sized apartments. Struggles over housing were also struggles over the space for reproduction. Foreigners demanded that authorities see them as full members of the urban community who were entitled to a say in their living conditions rather than workers to be packed up and shipped off as soon as they were no longer valuable. These isolated protests about housing laid the groundwork for a national protest movement in 1974 against a state reform to welfare benefits.

3

Trickles of Money, Floods of Children

The 1974 Child Allowance Reform and the Birth of the "Welfare Migrant"

The Turkish Workers' Choir of West Berlin released the *"Kindergeld* epic" as a single in the summer of 1974. Sung to the tune of "Santa Claus Comes Tomorrow," the song responded to a recently announced reform to the child allowance system.[1] One aspect of the reform meant that parents would receive a smaller child allowance [*Kindergeld*] for children who lived outside of the European Economic Community (EEC). The song suggested one potential solution:

> When the children in Turkey
> No longer receive *Kindergeld*
> What is left for us to do?
> Don't wait, send the money
> Let us bring the children here!
> Every day the airplane flies
> Flies with many children
> The children who live here
> What will become of them?[2]

The song suggested that the state's plan to cut costs on children living abroad might backfire when airplanes full of those same children arrived in West Germany. The line "What will become of them?" and the first line of the next verse, "The back courtyard is dark/there are too many in one room" introduce a note of anxiety: was the state in fact prepared to assume the reproductive costs of guest worker families? The cover of the single, an image of a child in front of a worker dormitory, reminded viewers that the answer to the question was

Fear of the Family. Lauren Stokes, Oxford University Press. © Oxford University Press 2022.
DOI: 10.1093/oso/9780197558416.003.0004

Figure 3.1 The cover of the "Child Allowance Epic" single by the Turkish Workers' Choir features a photograph of a child standing in front of a workers' dormitory. Record in author's personal collection.

currently a resounding no. The state had repeatedly chosen not to invest in infrastructure for families.

In 1974, the FRG announced a significant overhaul of the entire child allowance system. The state took on the responsibility of providing a child allowance for every child, regardless of the parents' employment status. It simultaneously eliminated tax credits for families with children so that all children could receive a larger child allowance benefit. The 1974 reform also turned child allowances from a corporatist benefit, one funded by employers, into a benefit funded fully by the state.[3] Once this benefit was understood as part of the state-citizen relationship rather than the employer-employee relationship, the rationale for giving the same amount to foreign workers was undermined, since their children would presumably not become German taxpayers when they grew up. The state also argued that children in countries where the cost of living was presumed to be lower did not actually need the full "family wage" paid out to children living in Germany. The protest song's image of an airplane full of children insinuated that the state's calculation would backfire. Placing a lower value on children who lived abroad would only result in a mass migration of children to the FRG, forcing the state into the position of having to pay for them after all. Opponents of the reform argued that it would lead to foreign children crowding into their parents' tiny apartments and overwhelming schools in working-class neighborhoods.

The architects of the child benefit reform had not intended to influence migration patterns. They had proposed a compromise that they hoped would not change the migration behavior of guest worker families. It is unclear whether they were successful. Because children under sixteen did not require residence permits to live in the FRG, there are no reliable numbers about where foreign children lived prior to 1975. With no baseline to work with, measuring whether the reform produced an increase in the migration rate of children is not possible. The reform did create a new imperative to accurately track the position of foreigners' children. Data from child allowance payments after 1975 would become the statistical information about the location of children that politicians and officials used to understand the potential for family migration.

Despite the lack of reliable information about migration patterns, the decision to create two-tiered child allowances for children who lived abroad offered contemporaries a deceptively simple and wildly popular explanation for post-1974 family migration. After the 1974 reform, family migration was persistently seen as a form of selfish "welfare migration" in which foreign families sought increased child allowances while pretending to move their children for more justifiable reasons. Flexible movement of productive labor had been useful while the economy was growing, but the similarly flexible movement of child dependents was experienced as a threat. Narratives that cast foreign children as "invaders" of German national space reflected the fear that the state had unleashed a development it could no longer control, fusing anxieties about the long-term social impacts of migration with those about dependence on the welfare state.

The idea that child migrants were in fact "welfare migrants" produced an active disinterest in interrogating other causes of family migration, ultimately obscuring the longer history of family migration and erasing the multiple, highly individual reasons that families decided to migrate. By continually insinuating that foreign families were held together by welfare rather than by emotional bonds, state officials suggested that "family reunification" was being pursued for illegitimate reasons. Because of the child benefit reform, foreign parents who brought their children to the Federal Republic after 1974 had to defend themselves against accusations of welfare seeking. The image of the "child benefit migrant" and his grasping parents became a key plank in the case for increasingly restrictive migration policies throughout the late 1970s and 1980s.

Child Allowances for Foreign Workers

The FRG first introduced child allowances in 1954. While all major political parties agreed that child allowances were a good idea, they disagreed over the kind of family that they ought to support. The governing CDU/CSU understood child allowances as a supplement to the male wage that would ensure that the decision to have a large family and thus to "secure the existence of the community in the future" would not lead to downward social mobility.[4] Following this vision, child allowances were first introduced as an employer-funded benefit that began with the third child and was linked tightly to the place of employment. Families with children also benefited from tax credits, although these credits benefited only higher-income families. By the end of the 1950s, over 70 percent of all families with two or more children were exempt from income tax altogether and thus received no benefit from these tax credits.[5]

The European Coal and Steel Community (ECSC) first discussed the problem of child allowances for cross-border workers in 1955: should employers pay the benefits that corresponded to the place where the waged work of the male breadwinner was being performed, or the benefits that corresponded to where the child was actually being raised? France, Belgium, and Luxembourg, all countries with comparatively higher allowances, voted for paying child benefit based on the child's place of residence. France had a particular interest in this "residence principle" because it wanted to continue the policy of paying smaller child allowances to Algerians who worked in France and raised their children in Algeria.[6] The FRG joined the Netherlands and Italy—countries with comparatively lower allowances—in voting for child benefit based on the place of employment.[7] The FRG had higher wages than other European countries and a lower child benefit, and officials worried that a child benefit based on place of residence would disadvantage those West Germans who worked abroad. For instance, German citizens who worked across the border in France would receive not just the lower wages of France but also the lower child benefit of Germany. This preference also reflected the fact that, in the FRG, child allowances were understood as a benefit linked primarily to the father's employment status and only secondarily to the mother's reproductive labor.

The FRG first put this "employment principle" into practice in 1955 when it negotiated a labor contract with Italy that included child allowance payments for Italians in Germany.[8] Within a context of competition over labor within Europe, German employers worried that it would be difficult to attract workers without a full program of benefits, so subsequent labor recruitment agreements with countries outside of the EEC also included family allowances. The Spanish and Greek governments both wanted to promote family stability, and their initial agreements stipulated that child allowances would be paid for children living outside of Germany only for two years. In practice, these limits were dropped almost as soon as they were reached, as officials and employers agreed that persistent housing shortages meant that workers should not have to justify their failure to reunite in order to continue to receive child allowances.[9] This decision to drop the two-year limit was a tacit acceptance of the split between production and reproduction that characterized the "guest worker" regime: employers were happy to pay full child allowances so long as those children were not contributing to housing pressures in the FRG.

During the same decade when increasing numbers of non-citizens were receiving child allowances for their non-citizen children, the responsibility for those payments was gradually shifting from employers to the state. In April 1961, the state extended child allowances to the second child—25 DM per month for the second child and 40 DM per month for subsequent children—and began sharing the cost of the measure with employers. In April 1964, the state raised payments to 50 DM for the third child, 60 DM for the fourth, and 70 DM for every subsequent child. The state also assumed full responsibility for these higher payments.[10]

With this shift from a corporatist employer-provided benefit to a state-provided benefit, the Labor Ministry began to reconsider the earlier agreements to grant equivalent child benefits to children living abroad and to consider ways in which it could divest itself of the full responsibility for paying child allowances to children of foreigners.[11] In 1968 it calculated that every two months it paid a total 13.55 million DM in benefits for all the children who lived outside the EEC.[12] That year it began negotiations to renew the labor recruitment treaty with Turkey in 1968. The bureaucrats in the Labor Ministry knew that although Turkish workers composed just one-seventh of the foreign workforce, they received half of all child benefits paid to foreigners. Based on these statistics, they proposed limiting to four the number of children for whom Turkish workers could claim benefits. Perhaps unsurprisingly, Turkey did not accept the proposal.[13] That same year, the Labor Ministry made a proposal to Yugoslavian diplomats not to pay any child benefits to children in Yugoslavia.[14] Yugoslavia also paid child benefits to parents based on a state-citizen relationship so that parents received child benefits for their children no matter where they worked, thus creating situations where Yugoslavian workers in the FRG could receive benefits from both states. Equally unsurprisingly, the Yugoslavian government refused the offer, and the final agreement stipulated that Yugoslavians would also receive full benefits for children who lived outside the FRG.

Officials consistently feared that Morocco and Tunisia would request the benefit for their workers. Although there were fewer than 20,000 workers from these two countries in the FRG in 1967, the Labor Ministry argued that allowing their workers to access child benefits was "undesirable, because these countries have plural marriage and possibilities for monitoring are even worse than in the treaties with Turkey and Greece."[15] In 1977 the Foreign Ministry asked the Finance and Labor Ministries to consider extending the benefit to citizens of these two states as a small concession that could be used to gain an advantage in a different set of negotiations. The Labor Ministry responded with the proposal that had previously been offered to Turkey: perhaps they could limit Maghreb citizens to receiving child benefit only for the first four children using a "tiered principle." The memorandum proposing this idea also described it as the "Southern European solution."[16] Although the idea of paying child allowances to citizens of Morocco and Tunisia was eventually dropped, this phrasing reveals both the malleability of European borders and the persistent association of "Southern Europe" with large families.

Officials regularly lamented the difficulty of translating German concepts of the family for "Southern" audiences. An internal memorandum about translating the "certificate of household membership" into Italian stated that it was especially important to make sure that the translation clarified the difference between children who belonged to a family and children who belonged to a household and for whose maintenance parents were chiefly responsible, since Italians were prone to conceive of the family as a larger category than the household and thus to claim child allowances for the children of their siblings or cousins.[17] Turkish families also posed a problem for the bureaucracy because although bigamy was legally prohibited, many Turkish citizens from rural areas had both a civil wife and a second customary wife. The illegitimate children by this second wife were regularly legitimated after the fact—which in turn made them eligible for child allowances within the West German system.[18]

The money intended to create a "family wage" did not reliably flow into the pockets of the family members who were still living in the home country. Family members abandoned by emigrants undeniably experienced significant emotional and financial distress. An Italian woman whose husband had gone to Germany and stopped communicating with her wrote of receiving a money order from a social work organization that "my children kissed the letter believing it was from their father, and crying, I told them he is not sending us anything anymore because he has abandoned us to our cruel fate. . . . When the children cried, if not for a friend of mine I would have gone and thrown myself into the sea to avoid suffering anymore."[19] Several of the sending countries tried to prevent situations like these by asking Germany to directly remit child allowances to the children's guardians, arguing that it was necessary to preserve the family.[20] This request was not just intended to relieve distress; it would also have increased cash remittances to the home country and relieved the state of the need to support women and children who had been abandoned by their breadwinners. Despite repeated requests, the FRG never agreed to directly remit child allowances, seeing it as a massive bureaucratic project that would only anger workers without producing benefits for the FRG.

The 1974 Family Allowance Reform and Its Impact on Foreigners

In 1974 West Germany eliminated tax credits for families with children in favor of giving all children a higher direct cash payment. Reflecting a move from a corporatist welfare benefit to a state welfare benefit, the state took on the responsibility of providing a child allowance for every child, independent of their parents' employment status. When employers had been partially responsible for funding child allowances, child benefits and the associated tax credits were understood to be part of the labor contract whereby employers and the state cooperated to equalize the burden of raising children. However, after 1974 the state promised to provide a "family wage" to every family, funded by taxation and independent of the labor market.[21] Parents would receive 50 DM per month for the first child, 70 DM per month for the second, and 120 DM per month for the third and beyond. This new structure significantly increased the financial burden for the state, which had paid 3 billion DM in child allowances in 1974 but was projected to pay 14.6 billion DM in 1975.[22] By de-emphasizing the role of the labor relationship and employer contributions in favor of the state-citizen relationship and taxpayer contributions, the reform arguably transformed child allowances from part of the labor contract to part of the social contract. How foreigners would fit into this vision would be financially significant. Foreign workers comprised 11 percent of the work force in 1973, but because they had larger families than West Germans on average, they were already receiving 20 percent of all child allowances.[23] While the parents had undeniably signed labor contracts, it was unclear whether the children could be considered part of the social contract that the new child allowances implied, as the state did not expect them to grow up and become German taxpayers.

The question of what to do with foreign children under the planned child allowance reform was first raised between the Family Ministry and the Labor Ministry in 1971. The Labor Ministry believed that public opinion already opposed any child allowances being paid to foreign children and that paying more money to those children would only "sharpen this criticism" and lead to "domestic unrest."[24] The Labor Ministry also argued that the higher child allowances would have undesirable effects by stimulating further reproduction in countries that were already trying to export surplus population.[25] One official projected this argument far into the future, writing that high payments "would fuel a further population explosion in Turkey, with the consequence that the pressure on the German labor market would become even greater."[26] The Labor Ministry consequently preferred a solution that did not involve paying higher benefits to foreign children.

The Family Ministry worried that it would be unfair to revoke tax credits for foreign children but not pay them the higher child allowances. In making this argument it invoked Article 6 of the Basic Law, "Marriage and the family shall enjoy the special protection of the state." At this point in the debate, the Interior and Justice Ministries both stepped in to explain that they believed that Article 6 applied to foreigners only in a negative sense, which is to say that it protected them from "state encroachment" but did not oblige the state to offer positive support in the form of child allowances.[27] This interministerial debate took place in 1971, before the May 1973 "Spanish grandmother" decision, which would establish that Article 6 did in fact oblige the state to provide positive support for foreign families. Nevertheless, with the constitutional question temporarily clarified in 1971, the Family Ministry and the Economics Ministry both came to agree with the Labor Ministry that paying higher allowances for children who lived abroad would be a form of "false development policy."[28]

The Labor Ministry also feared that if they failed to pay anything to children who lived abroad, "one would have to expect an unstoppable flow of particularly Turkish children into the Federal Republic."[29] To solve this problem, the Labor Ministry's preferred solution was for the FRG to create a two-tiered system of child allowances, with parents receiving different amounts based on the location of their children. The Labor Ministry never explicitly claimed to be adopting a "French model," but, because child allowances had previously been discussed at the EEC level, it would have known about France's staunch support for two-tiered child allowances. Algerian nationalists had vocally protested the existence of a lower "Algerian rate" in the 1950s, a policy measure that "simultaneously exposed the colonial regime's antinatalist goals and the fissures in the French state's approach to the Algerian problem."[30] The FRG took a similarly anti-natalist approach to its foreign population when it decided to introduce two-tiered child allowances in the 1970s. Its willingness to adopt a colonial policy—without considering the significant backlash to the policy in France—shows that the state's model for managing migrant populations was becoming more racialized over time.

The Finance and Labor Ministries both argued that paying a partial child allowance for children who lived abroad would place a partial brake on child migration, but their position was not entirely uncontested. The Federal Labor Office warned that two-tiered allowances would create a permanent threat of fraud by inspiring foreign workers to bring their children for a short period to register them as residents in the FRG before sending the children back home.[31] The Foreign Ministry opposed the two-tiered plan from the outset, asking the Labor Ministry: "whether the cost savings that you evidently expect . . . will be realized" since the proposal would inevitably cause child migration, such that "in the end no savings will be achieved" and in fact there would be "additional costs on our already strained social infrastructure."[32]

When the Labor Ministry finally presented the new plan to the public in the spring of 1974, it described two-tiered child allowances as a necessary corrective to an "exceedingly generous" previous policy.[33] Although foreign workers paid income tax in the FRG, the child allowance payments that went to support children living in Spain, Turkey, or Yugoslavia were not also subject to indirect German taxes on consumption, so that foreigners with children abroad already got more value from their child allowances than West Germans with children. Furthermore, the Labor Ministry argued that family allowances were intended to "minimize," but not to "eliminate," the extra costs of raising a child. If the larger amounts were sent to "countries with a lower standard of living . . . the child-related economic burdens on foreign parents would be completely lifted from their shoulders."[34] Had these new higher child allowances been implemented equally among children at home and abroad, "one would have been able to speak of discrimination against those who raised their children in Germany."[35]

To further bolster their claim that this was a fair solution, the Labor Ministry commissioned an opinion poll through the Wickert Institute to ask West Germans whether children living abroad and children living in the FRG should receive comparable child allowances. The slight majority of respondents— 52 percent—thought that foreign children should receive smaller allowances, while 40 percent thought that foreign children should receive the same amount. Despite the overall support for their position, the Labor Ministry forbade the publication of these poll results because the number who disagreed was considered too high.[36]

The other ministries followed the Labor Ministry's lead in supporting the reform. Family Minister and SPD politician Katharina Focke wrote an article for the newsletter of the German Confederation of Trade Unions arguing that the solution was fair and the Economics Ministry assured concerned social workers that the change was "only the partial dismantling of a privilege."[37] Sociologist Margret Kuhn had previously used the official SPD party magazine to warn that child allowances for foreigners were encouraging the FRG to become "Mediterraneanized." She greeted the reform in the same magazine, explaining that equal child allowances would be "probably unconstitutional. . . . The Germans would have every reason to protest."[38] The article announcing the child allowance reform in the *Federal Labor Gazette* ended with a warning against child migration. The economy would continue to depend on foreign workers, but the German "capacity for integration" would make it impossible for those workers to bring their families "in the numbers in which they desire."[39] The article did not speculate further on the measures that might be necessary to thwart those desires.

Negotiating the Reform with Foreign States

Child allowances for foreign workers were regulated by Social Security Agreements that the FRG had previously negotiated with each of the sending countries. The Labor Ministry had been the most influential in devising the new policy of two-tiered child allowances, which it calculated should save the state close to 1 billion DM every year.[40] Although the Foreign Ministry had always been skeptical of the cost savings and thus the utility of the new measure, it was the ministry that would be responsible for re-negotiating the bilateral agreements, which regulated not just child allowances but also a variety of other welfare benefits, including health insurance, unemployment insurance, and pension payments.

The Spanish government was the first to sign a new agreement in June 1974. According to the new agreement, children who lived in Germany were to be paid 50 DM for the first child, 70 DM for the second child, and 120 DM for the third child and beyond, while children who lived in Spain would be paid 10 DM for the first child, 25 DM for the second, 60 for the third and fourth, and 70 for the fifth child and beyond. Officials settled on the cheapest possible solution for families whose children lived in both locations. Children in Germany and abroad were both counted starting as 'the first child'; four children, two in each place, would earn 50 and 70 DM for the two in Germany and 10 and 25 DM for the two abroad. This policy disincentivized the maintenance of transnational families.[41] The payments for children abroad were almost identical to those before the reform, but, because tax credits for children were disappearing at the same time, workers with large families who lived abroad would in fact experience a reduction in their take-home pay.[42] Spain exacted the concession that foreigners who had worked in Germany for at least fifteen years could receive the higher child allowances for children living abroad.[43]

During the negotiations with Yugoslavia, the Yugoslavian Confederation of Trade Unions feared that the new policy was meant to promote the assimilation of Yugoslavian workers in Germany, while the Yugoslavian ambassador argued that the change was intended to create a wave of child migration. The national press service even originally claimed that the reform applied only to Yugoslavia, inaccurately arguing that Germans only wanted to force the assimilation of Yugoslavian children.[44] Workers picked up on these arguments in a 1979 petition protesting that the FRG was attempting to reverse its own declining birth rate through the "Germanization" of Yugoslavian children.[45] The argument that child allowances were a weapon of assimilation likely found fertile ground in Yugoslavia because of memories of the campaign for the forced Germanization of Yugoslavian children during World War II.[46]

Greece and Turkey did not interpret the reform through the "Germanization" lens in the same way as Yugoslavia did, but both used the Turkish military invasion of Cyprus in July 1974 as a reason to cancel the initial meetings scheduled for the negotiations. The Schmidt cabinet subsequently voted to cancel the social security agreements despite the Foreign Ministry's warning that Greece and Turkey would interpret this unilateral cancellation as an act of aggression. Unilateral cancellation forced the two countries to accept the terms that had been given to Spain in order to prevent the broader agreement from expiring, which would have disrupted not only child benefits but also a range of other social welfare provisions.[47]

The bilateral negotiation between Turkey and the FRG was particularly tense because, among foreign workers, Turkish citizens were the most likely to have their children living in their home country. The FRG estimated that Turkish children were responsible for two-thirds of all child allowances paid to children living abroad. In this negotiation, the Foreign Ministry stuck to the official framing of the policy, arguing that that the true victims of the current policy were those German workers unable to outsource reproduction by sending their children to grow up in cheaper countries. Diplomats also presented the current regulation as a source of "discrimination" for children living in Turkey "depending on whether their father works in the Federal Republic or in the homeland."[48]

Turkish diplomats countered by adopting the language of "strained infrastructure" that had been used to justify the end of German labor recruitment less than a year earlier. They informed the FRG that, if the proposed two-tiered allowances were implemented, "the Turkish government must give advance warning of adverse consequences for German infrastructure, since the planned reform would lead to Turks working in Germany bringing their children to the Federal Republic." FRG diplomats replied that they did not plan to take responsibility for those children:

> Turkey cannot be indifferent to the fate of Turkish children brought to Germany only in the expectation of a higher net income. The Federal Republic is not an immigration country and will therefore not raise these children to be Germans. A good portion of these children will therefore return to Turkey at some point. Furthermore, the German side must, if necessary, defend itself with the measures that stand

at our disposal against the strain on infrastructure that is no longer sustainable.[49]

In this negotiation, both sides implicitly accepted the idea that the FRG was "not an immigration country" and therefore not a good place for Turkish children. West German diplomats argued that foreign parents ought to know that their children had no future in Germany and that they ought to act accordingly by leaving their children in Turkey, the place where they would eventually have to return. Given the dismal prospects that their children would face in Germany, those Turkish parents who brought their children with them could only be acting out of a selfish desire for "a higher net income." Their individual desires to both live with and provide for their families were characterized as careless and irresponsible.

Diplomats who argued that foreign parents were acting without regard for their children's futures shifted attention away from their own state's failure to anticipate consequences to foreign families' failure to do so. The FRG had granted work permits to millions of foreigners without thinking through the possible long-term consequences. In the negotiations over child allowances, the state made it clear that it did not intend to take responsibility for this failure and for the associated challenges of integrating foreign children into German schools. Instead, it intended to blame the existence of those challenges on the irresponsible actions of their parents. Turkish workers who had responded to economic incentives by taking jobs in West German factories had once been lauded, but when those same Turkish workers responded to economic incentives by moving their children to the place where they received higher benefits, they were blamed for their short-sightedness, their selfishness, and their poor parenting skills. The moralizing tone of German officials underlined the fact that the "guest worker" regime had never been about the harmonious overlap of the economic interests of West German employers and foreign employees. The "guest worker" program was always a form of migration intended to keep the national community closed to foreigners except as a source of waged labor. Foreign workers who chose to reproduce on German soil broke the implicit contract.

Migrant Responses to the Child Allowance Reform

Foreign families vehemently disagreed that the new law "equalized burdens" between foreigners and West Germans. As one Spanish-language flyer aptly put it, "It is shameful to pretend that having to live separately from our children is an 'advantage.'"[50] After the reform was announced, migrants organized "child allowance committees" in at least nineteen different cities across the country to protest the proposed two-tiered child allowances.[51] The Spanish Center in Essen appears to have been the national coordination center of these multinational demonstrations. Founded as a workers' self-organization in 1969, the Spanish Center, according to its own publications, sought to educate German workers about the labor movement in Spain and to show that the problems of foreign workers were in fact problems of the entire working class.[52] The prominence of Spaniards within the movement demonstrates that they could "depend on a level of state solidarity that no other guest worker movement came close to attaining." Both the SPD and the DGB (German Trade Union Confederation) lent logistical aid to Spanish socialist organizations within Germany, and this support from German organizations also meant that the ban on political activity by foreigners was interpreted more flexibly for Spanish migrants than for any other national group.[53] Spanish activists made good use of that additional security to coordinate multinational protests.

In 1974, the "National Committee of Spaniards against Child Allowances" funded buses to bring a multinational group of 3,500 guest workers to Frankfurt to protest the reform. The march was advertised as a demonstration of the "international working class," with flyers announcing that the date of November 17 had been chosen to coincide with the first democratic elections in Greece since the establishment of the military junta in 1967. The Spanish-language version of this flyer further explained that the Greek elections were "particularly interesting for the Spaniards and for all who struggle with dictatorship" and explained that "our German comrades have told us that in Germany there is also a form of dictatorship because a political prisoner was murdered in the German prison in Wittlich"—a reference to Holger Meins, the RAF (Rote Armee Fraktion—Red Army Faction) member who had starved to death while on hunger strike earlier that month.[54] Another Spanish-language flyer featured a translation of a Turkish worker's letter to Prime Minister Bülent Ecevit.[55] These multinational protests often confounded officials who assumed that migrants were unable to organize across national lines. One Labor Ministry official interpreted a call for "international solidarity of the working class" at a July protest as evidence that East Germany had to be the driving force behind the protest.[56] The official assumption that migrants were incapable of independent political activity was used to de-legitimize their demands.

Protests replicated similar arguments in multiple locations. Part of the state's argument in favor of two-tiered child allowances was that child allowances were no longer funded by employers, but by taxes, and "tax revenue must be used according to necessity."[57] Migrant activists protested that they also paid taxes and that while tax credits had been eliminated for all children, it was unfair that only children in Germany were being compensated with higher child allowances.

As one Spanish flyer declared, "When we pay taxes we are Germans, but when we receive income we are foreigners."[58] Protest slogans also included "We resist because we pay the same taxes and do not get the same rights" and "Are our taxes worth less than German taxes?"[59] The editor of the newsletter of the Spanish Parents' Association worried that this might be the first step toward cutting other welfare benefits, writing "We demand the same child allowances for children living at home today in order to prevent our pensions being cut once we return home tomorrow, using the argument that life is cheaper there than it would be here."[60] Activists also heard popular versions of the argument that foreign children cost less to raise. Members of the committee in Wiesbaden had to rebut arguments like "Foreigners have eating habits that are cheaper than those of Germans—Italians eat spaghetti every day."[61] Migrants who organized against the cuts to child benefits protested this implicit devaluation of migrant needs and, with them, migrant lives.

The "child allowance committees" also criticized the expectation of family separation inherent in the "guest worker" regime and demanded better conditions for families in the FRG. Labor migration enabled migrants to provide for their children in a way that was impossible at home, but the state's failure to provide appropriate infrastructure for their needs in the FRG, particularly family housing, forced them to live apart from their families. When faced with housing shortages, the state had opted to impose punitive housing requirements rather than to build additional housing. The child allowance protests became a venue at which migrants could criticize this failure to respond to their needs. To quote a speaker at the rally in Frankfurt, "We want to bring our children, but there is no housing. There is no space in the schools."[62] A flyer for the demonstration in Bonn asked "Where are the houses, the places in kindergartens and schools? How much more will the German state have to spend on these facilities than on child allowances? What will the Germans do later with two million inadequately educated children? . . . The lawmaker is taking back rights that already existed! But does that create schools?"[63] Gerhard Braun, a Bundestag representative for the CDU, attended a protest in his district of Remscheid at which "over 100 guest workers declared that they would bring their families from Spain to Germany." He wrote to the Labor Ministry to ask whether they were aware of this threat, explaining that it would "create not insignificant difficulties for the municipalities, because kindergartens and schools cannot be created overnight."[64] The Nürnberg Foreigners' Council organized a letter-writing campaign with the question: "Is the state able to guarantee that all of the children of foreign workers who are currently living abroad can be brought through family reunification, and is it ready to prepare the additional social institutions that will be necessary?" The Spanish Parents' Association used a similar argument in its organized letter-writing campaign, which was explicitly linked to the problem of education.[65]

Finally, migrant activists argued that the state did not understand the true cost of a transnational family. The Labor Ministry argued that it was cheaper to raise children outside of Germany, but its only evidence for this fact was a table of comparative GDP per capita.[66] The Labor Ministry's claim that it was an "advantage" to raise children abroad utterly ignored the emotional pain of separation—a clear example of German policymakers deeming the emotional lives of foreigners irrelevant. The Labor Ministry also underestimated the financial costs of maintaining two households and traveling between two locations. Parents from most of the sending countries also had to pay for their children's education in the home country, and the vast majority sent remittances to the people who cared for their children at home.[67] This last fact raised particular ire among migrant activists, who argued that "nobody, not even a relative, looks after the children of the 'rich ones from Germany' for free."[68] One Turkish man explained, "They don't believe us or they don't want to believe us. Instead they repeat like PARROTS that our family relationships are so close that an uncle can support his nephews without a problem."[69] The state had assumed that guest workers could rely on the unpaid care work of the extended family and had failed to recognize that those relatives might expect compensation.

Activism around the issue of child allowances also became a way to criticize the unions for failing to represent their foreign members.[70] By 1973, roughly 30 percent of all migrants were union members, but most unions were slow to actively represent the interests of migrants.[71] A Turkish-language flyer linked the unions' failure to fight for equal child allowances with the failure of unions to organize workers at Ford before the "wild strikes" in 1976, while a Spanish communist newspaper argued that the entire episode was "a lesson for the comrades who believe and say that we can rely on the aid of the unions."[72] Italian communists condemned the policy for "trying to divide the Germans and the Italians from the Turkish, Spanish, Greek and Yugoslavian emigrants" and argued that "with this attack the bosses want to let us know that we are here in Germany *only* as manpower . . . and that we have to renounce our rights to life, to residing in decent houses and not in barracks, to having schools for our children."[73] In Hamburg, members of the metalworkers' union signed a resolution to protest their union's passive stance.[74] Union officials found themselves in the position of needing to respond, as they realized that their neglect of "a problem that allows the emotions of our foreign workers to be easily aroused" might well "expand the sphere of action for subversive political groups."[75]

The German Confederation of Trade Unions responded by passing a resolution condemning the reform at its 1975 national congress. Union representatives criticized the state's failure to invest in working-class neighborhoods. One speaker warned that working-class children would shortly find their classrooms overwhelmed by foreign children for whom schools had made only minimal provisions.[76] This point was sometimes repeated by educators protesting the reform, such as the school principal in Hamburg who thought that child migrants would create a "new proletariat" and represent a "threat to our free democratic state order."[77] The metalworkers' union newsletter declared that the anticipated migration would not represent such a threat "if only the responsible parties . . . had listened to the demands of the unions, for example, if they had not introduced the difference in the child allowances, or if only they had taken care of creating the necessary infrastructure—housing, schools, kindergartens, etc.—before calling foreigners to serve capitalist interests for greater profits."[78] Unions argued that the guest worker program had been designed for the needs of employers who hoped to temporarily extract more labor without having to cut into their profits by also paying for the reproduction of that labor.

The experience of multinational organizing catalyzed new forms of migrant political engagement, as child allowance committees brought together religious groups, communists, and a wide variety of migrant-led groups that were usually more oriented to homeland politics. Despite this unprecedented degree of engagement, migrant activists and their allies ultimately failed to change the policy of two-tiered child allowances. Bonn even reneged on its prior commitments in 1979, when it canceled the agreement that it had previously made to pay equal child allowances for those children whose parents had worked in the Federal Republic for fifteen years. This decision led to the revival of many previous child allowance committees.[79]

The FRG reiterated its commitment to two-tiered child allowances during negotiations over new countries wishing to join the EEC, seeking to use the accession negotiations to enforce a "residence principle" that would enable the state to continue to pay smaller amounts to children who lived outside the FRG.[80] In 1975, the Labor Ministry's internal calculations had shown that the FRG would save 58 million DM a year on Italian workers alone if the EEC switched to the "residence principle"— calculations that inexplicably continued to ignore the possibility that foreigners might move their children in response to welfare reform.[81] During the accession negotiations with Greece in 1978, FRG representatives repeatedly raised the issue but found themselves isolated in their desire to impose two-tiered child allowances. Most of the other EEC countries and the European Commission "found the German proposals clearly discriminatory," and the Greek representative believed that the proposal showed that the FRG "wanted to create second-class citizens in the Community."[82] The Germans were so stubborn on this point that it was not officially settled until the final meeting before the Treaty of Association was signed—at which point it was one of only two outstanding issues, the other being Greek contributions to the EEC budget during the transitional period.[83] At this meeting, German representatives begrudgingly agreed to a "transitional period" of three years during which foreign workers with children in Greece would continue to receive lower child allowances for children before they would be entitled to the full child allowances. Even then, they insisted that their opposition to the compromise be recorded in the official minutes.[84] German diplomats wanted to ensure that the solution found for Greece would not set a precedent for future accessions to the EEC. They worried about the future accession of Spain and Portugal as well as the potential accession of Turkey.[85] This stubborn insistence on two-tiered child allowances might be seen as an early articulation of the concept of a "two-speed Europe," here based on the costs of reproduction.

The earlier argument about taxes proved prophetic, as the 1987 tax reform further penalized transnational families by no longer recognizing children who lived outside the EEC. Once Greece, Portugal, and Spain were part of the EEC, the change only penalized Yugoslavian and Turkish workers. If their children lived in Yugoslavia or Turkey, they no longer existed for the purposes of the tax code. A group of Turkish men in West Berlin formed "TISPJG"—an acronym of the six primary guest worker countries (Turkey, Italy, Spain, Portugal, Yugoslavia and Greece)—to protest the changes in the tax code. They published a pamphlet "For Tax Justice. Do workers' children who live abroad no longer exist for the federal government?"[86] TISPJG members connected all of these issues in their letter campaign, which argued that they should be able to count their children who lived abroad as dependents and that they should receive the full child allowances for those children. They also demanded that the state go even further in recognizing the particular needs of men who supported transnational families, demanding both additional paid vacation days when their wives gave birth to children in the home country and unpaid "moral vacation" days that would allow a worker in the FRG to visit his or her family "when it is important for the family."[87] A comic in the pamphlet depicted the German state as a magician casting a spell on a foreign family that made the children invisible. Guest workers and their families felt that the state made their families appear and disappear when it was convenient for the state—counting them as resident when it came time to apply housing regulations, but then "disappearing" those same families when it came time to apply for child allowances and tax breaks.

Depictions of Child Migration as a Threat

The introduction of two-tiered child allowances encouraged policymakers and the general public to see the policy as the sole cause of child migration. Many media outlets depicted child migrants as threats to West German society. The

Figure 3.2 Demonstrators carry signs with slogans including "Same work, same wages" and "We want equality in child allowances!" at a protest in Munich. DOMiD-Archiv, Köln B 000071.

center-left *Süddeutsche Zeitung* used the headline "An Invasion of Guest-Worker Children?" and worried about "the announced Turkish invasion."[88] The center-right *Frankfurter Allgemeine Zeitung* protested, "Nothing against the dear small Turkish children, but our representatives surely did not want an invasion of child-allowance-Turks."[89] *Der Spiegel* reported that "Ankara threatens to send the children to Germany, where the men in Bonn would have to produce kindergartens, living space and schools for them."[90] The language used in all of these stories cast child migrants as military combatants.

The "child allowance migrant" entered the national stage at a moment of significant concern about West German fertility, which in 1972 had fallen below replacement level for the first time.[91] In response to this perceived demographic threat, the state founded the Federal Institute for Demographic Research in 1973.[92] One of the institute's stated aims was to produce knowledge about foreign families that could be used in the service of migration policy.[93] *Der Spiegel* began a 1975 cover story about declining fertility with the sentence: "Nowhere in the world are so few children born as in the Federal Republic. Only guest workers are creating a surplus of babies." The article explained that in Frankfurt "the number of guest worker children grew at nearly the rate at which the number of German children shrank" and warned that many cities had experienced an "invasion of guest worker children" into kindergartens.[94] A political cartoon included in the article showed a doctor opting for a national reveal rather than a gender reveal as he held up a baby to announce "It's a German!" The doctor's waiting room has one "German" couple and is otherwise entirely full of visibly "foreign" couples, so that the comic provides a visual representation of the argument that guest worker families had "invaded" the social infrastructure.

Child allowances were introduced at least partially as a pro-natalist measure, but when foreign parents claimed the same benefits as German parents, they were suspected of taking unfair advantage of the welfare state. In 1976, a widely reprinted article from the German Press Agency news service described foreign children as "ticking time bombs" and went on to explain that there were two reasons for the growing number of foreign children. First, guest workers did not use hormonal contraceptives, and second, the child allowance reform had incentivized them to "let their offspring come from the home country."[95] Foreign women's comparatively high fertility once living in the FRG was also frequently interpreted as a response to child allowances. When a group of social workers noticed an increase in abortions among Turkish women, they speculated privately that perhaps this population was "increasingly realizing that progress comes not through child allowances, but through a reduction in the number of children."[96] Migrants were incensed by this innuendo. One child allowance committee asked: "Do they think that we're animals, or that we have children in order to do business?"[97]

Media in foreign countries also narrated the child allowance reform as a driver of child migration, placing the blame for emigration squarely on the "pull" of German welfare rather than the possibility of "push" conditions elsewhere.[98] The Turkish press was obsessed with the topic. *Tercüman*, the center-right Turkish-language newspaper that published an FRG edition, featured twenty-two articles about *Kindergeld* in October 1974 alone. In an article titled "The Flow of Children from Turkey Begins!" a father of seven was quoted as saying, "I am bringing my children, whom I miss very much, to Germany because the German state will pay a lot of money." Two weeks later, "The Flow of Children from Turkey Continues!" featured pictures of unaccompanied children on airplanes.[99] *Milliyet*, a Turkish-language newspaper that supported the SPD, also published twelve articles about the topic in October 1974, including one editorial that implored Germans to think about how they would justify this reform to one of the Turkish soldiers who had helped to defend the Germans from Russia during World War I.[100]

The people who read these stories might have wondered who to blame for this unfortunate situation. Was the West German state at fault for creating an incentive for child migration, or were the foreign parents irresponsible for taking them up on that incentive? The Labor Ministry actively promoted an interpretation that placed the blame on parents, as it continually defended itself against public criticism by insisting that foreign parents who brought their children were irrational. They were parents "to whom it has not been made clear, that the higher child benefits for children in Germany will be consumed by the higher cost of living."[101] In response to a previously mentioned critical article in *Der Spiegel,* the Labor Ministry circulated a memorandum explaining that Ankara's "possible threat 'to send the children to Germany' is of no avail. The Ministry of Finance has calculated that bringing the family to Germany will normally not be worth it."[102]

Perhaps aware that families rarely consult finance ministries before making decisions, the Labor Ministry in December 1974 went on the offensive in Turkey when it prepared a packet of information for the Turkish press intended to discourage families from moving their children.[103] Fifty Turkish publications published over 120 articles and editorials on the topic that month. The report singled out a *Milliyet* article by young adult novelist Gülten Dayioğlu for particular praise because it represented "a more objective discussion of the situation."[104] Her article instructed parents to leave their children in Turkey: "If children are brought to Germany because of child allowances the situation will become worse." Children "torn out of school for a few cents, shouldered like a bundle," would "fall into a pitiable situation" because children were not " 'goods' to be transported haphazardly from place to place."[105]

Dayioğlu continued to use child allowances as a motif in her later work. One of her young adult novels is about Atil, a young boy who leaves his grandmother's care to join his parents in the FRG, where he gradually loses his ability to speak Turkish. Throughout the novel, child allowances are repeatedly used to characterize the decision of the parents to bring their son to the FRG as selfish. At one point, Atil's father shouts at him: "I didn't bring you here for your own private amusement, but because of the tax rebate and child allowances!"[106] By the end, the entire family returns to Turkey, realizing that the pursuit of financial gain in the FRG has come at an unacceptably high cost.

In 1986, Dayioğlu published a collection of interviews with Turkish migrants to Germany that took up similar themes about the "lost generation" of Turkish children.[107] A full decade after the reform, a Turkish teacher working in Germany told the interviewer:

> When I think about child allowances, I still feel sick. People took their children helter-skelter to Germany in order to earn Deutschmarks. They didn't think about school or think about whether they could settle in here. In this way hundreds of thousands of children were thrown to the dogs! If one thinks about it rationally, the great German state also failed! In order to cut child allowance payments, it didn't just burden itself with hundreds of thousands of children, but also with their problems.[108]

The teacher was hardly alone in "feeling sick" when thinking about the impact of child allowances on the sending countries. Yugoslavian officials had argued that two-tiered child allowances were a form of "Germanization" policy, but Turkish officials also worried about their nation's demographic future. Prime Minister Bülent Ecevit used a 1979 meeting with the head of the SPD in the Bundestag to complain that the policy was the primary reason that 450,000 Turkish children lived in Germany.[109] The idea of two-tiered child allowances sometimes had a face-saving function, enabling Turkish officials to blame German policy for a wide variety of problems. In 1982, a reporter from *Tercüman* asked Deputy Prime Minister Turgut Özal about his failure to increase employment opportunities in Turkey in order to enable workers to return from Germany. Özal dodged the question with the statement that child allowances were the primary cause of child migration and therefore of "foreigners' problems in general."[110]

Migrants had argued that families made decisions about migration on highly personal timelines. Parents brought their children to the FRG when they were able to secure a larger apartment, when relatives at home grew older or passed away, when children completed primary school in the home country, or simply when their parents could no longer bear to be without them. Two-tiered child allowances were certainly one factor in making this decision, but the media and state narrative emphasizing the money as the most important factor failed to acknowledge the difficulty of the decision. Officials who wanted more restrictions on family reunion seized on the narrative of two-tiered child allowances as the sole driver of child migration in part because it depicted foreigners as bad parents, seduced by Deutschmarks into neglecting the psychological well-being of their children.

Counting and Controlling Foreign Children

To what extent did the common narrative of two-tiered child allowances as the cause of child migration reflect reality? Were contemporary observers correct when they interpreted them as the primary stimulus for child migration? Because the child allowance reform was announced only shortly after the November 1973 decision to stop labor recruitment, it is impossible to fully disentangle these two factors in the decisions of individual families. Demographer Amparo González-Ferrer's analysis of self-reported data about family migration suggests that the reform was more important than the recruitment stop for accelerating the decision to bring children, while historians Ulrich Herbert and Karin Hunn speculate that the decision to bring children was more often motivated by fear that new restrictions on family reunion were imminent.[111]

The question is difficult to answer because the reform created the information necessary to measure its own effects. There are no reliable records about where foreign children lived before the introduction of two-tiered child allowances because children under sixteen were not required to have residence permits before the 1990s. Two-tiered child allowances created a new need to accurately track the location of foreigners' children in order to limit the possibility of welfare fraud. Data from these claims quickly became the most accurate way to count and to locate foreign children. At a meeting on the topic in 1976, German diplomats lectured their Turkish colleagues that their demands for accurate data did not come from "mere bureaucratic perfectionism" but were intended to stop "great quantities of wrongful payments."[112] Welfare reform turned the location of children into a matter of foreign relations.

Officials themselves were unsure how to interpret new data about child allowance claims. The border police believed that the new regulation would lead to more children entering Germany and began to count the number of Turkish children crossing the border in November 1974 "in order to determine how accurate these assumptions are." While the border police described the entry of 2,352 children between November 8, 1974, and December 1, 1974, as "extraordinarily high," they also had no data from before the welfare reform that would have allowed for systematic comparison. The border police continued to count Turkish children for one year before they were ordered to stop in November 1975.[113]

Scattered pieces of data suggesting that larger numbers of foreign children were being registered with the police in 1975 could be interpreted in multiple ways. Some contemporary observers believed that the reform had resulted in many children who had already been living in Germany being registered with the police for the first time. Officials at the Labor Ministry speculated that foreign parents had already lived with their children before the reform but had previously failed to register those children because they feared having their residence permits revoked for having too many people in the apartment. After the reform, the prospect of higher child allowances had convinced them that the potential risk was worth it. In other words, the parents had previously committed housing fraud, but the prospect of financial gain had convinced them to come clean.[114] After 130 children registered as new residents within two weeks in November 1974, the city administration of Bielefeld wrote to their Bundestag representative explaining that their source—a "Turkish informant"—had told them that "there are already Turkish profiteers who have specialized in relocating children from Turkey. . . . [I]n order to avoid problems at border control, the escorts represent themselves as relatives." The same letter claimed that these parents were renting "demonstration apartments" when they registered their larger family with the police, but that they planned to downsize and return to inadequately-sized apartments once their registrations were accepted.[115]

A competing narrative argued that parents were committing not housing fraud but welfare fraud on a massive scale. They were falsely registering children as residents of the FRG so they could claim higher child allowance payments while their children actually lived abroad. The German Embassy in Ankara even worried that Turks might undergo false adoptions in order to claim more child allowance money.[116] Heinz Richter, head of the Foreigner Section in the German Confederation of Unions, told a radio journalist in October 1974: "About 14 days ago at the airport in Munich, I saw with my own eyes that approximately two-thirds of the family members traveling to Germany on that day were clearly in the Federal Republic for the first time. That is apparently already a consequence of these alleged child allowance disadvantages."[117] Richter later speculated that families were organizing airplanes full of children to visit for two weeks in order to register for child allowances before returning to Turkey, and he argued that any fathers found guilty of this practice should be deported.[118]

Discrepancies in the data about foreign children rapidly turned into fraud accusations. In October 1975, several parliamentary representatives sent the Labor Ministry a clipping from BILD titled "1068 Children of Guest Workers Are Missing from School—Where Are They?"[119] According to the article, 1,068 foreign children were registered as residents in the town of Mönchengladbach but were not going to school. Local school officials blamed guest worker parents, who were either keeping their children at home or falsely registering their children as residents of the FRG for the purpose of claiming child allowances. The Labor Ministry launched its own investigation and discovered that there were only 78 false claims. The apparent discrepancy came from the fact that the British Armed Forces were headquartered in the region, creating a large population of British soldiers who had registered their children as residents but who did not send their children to German school. British occupiers, not "child invaders," were at fault, but the correction never made headline news.[120]

Although this particular case turned out to be a false alarm, officials continued to use concern about children attending school as a pretext to require foreigners to provide additional documentation to prove that their children lived in Germany.[121] In 1977 the Federal Labor Office instructed foreign parents registering for child allowances to bring not just proof of residence but also proof of school attendance.[122] A lawyer for the German Trade Union Confederation believed that this was an illegal measure, one that violated the principle of equal treatment by creating a burden of proof for foreign workers that was greater than that which German workers had to provide. He won a court case in which he defended a member of the metalworkers' union who refused to provide additional documentation.[123] The Federal Labor Office claimed that requiring such documentation would improve school attendance among foreign children, but the requirement also reflected the widespread presumption that foreigners were likely to commit welfare fraud.

Statistics about the number of children receiving child allowances at each rate became the primary data set at the disposal of officials who wanted to know more about where foreign children lived. In 1982, the Federal Constitutional Court asked the Interior Ministry to calculate "the migration potential of foreign children" as it sought to determine the threat that family migration posed for the second and third generations. The Interior Ministry informed the Federal Constitutional Court that unfortunately the Central Register of Foreigners still only recorded the foreigners "as single people" rather than tracking their family relationships.[124] The best available data about foreign families were based on child allowance payments. Although these data included the nationality of the children, it did not record information about which "generation" the parents came from or whether both parents lived in the FRG. This made the data useless for calculating the numbers that the Federal Constitutional Court had requested.[125]

In the decade after the child allowance reform, both the Schmidt cabinet and the Kohl cabinet would discuss several proposals for limiting child migration. In December 1981, the Schmidt cabinet briefly considered not paying any child allowances to children who arrived in the FRG after the age of six. The memorandum introducing the idea explained that it would harness child allowances to the "goal of timely relocation for integration.... The denial of child allowances would balance the higher expenditures in the areas of school, education, and vocational training that would have to be made on children and teenagers who relocated later."[126] This proposal did not make it beyond its first cabinet meeting, but its existence reveals both the enduring power of the fantasy that child allowances could be used to direct migration flows and the consistent linking of discussions about family migration to anxieties about the capacity of the welfare state. The child migration panic exposed the underlying logic of the "guest worker" regime: workers needed to be flexible for the needs of the "economic miracle," but their families needed to be stationary and predictable. Waged labor needed to be mobile because the movement of productive labor was understood as a spur to economic growth, but the labor that accompanied producing new workers— particularly in the areas of childcare and education—was persistently understood exclusively as an unexpected and unwanted drain on the welfare state. As long as foreign families were not envisioned as part of the social contract between German generations, their participation in its institutions could only be illegitimate.

* * *

The continuation of family migration after the end of labor recruitment in the FRG was consistently narrated through the figure of the "child allowance migrant" and thus as a transition from "labor migration" to "welfare migration." Almost everyone who weighed in on the 1974 child allowance reform connected it to the specter of increased family reunion, although the figure of the "child allowance migrant" had different purposes depending on who invoked it. The Turkish Workers' Choir sang about airplanes full of children to convince the state to change its mind, while the bureaucrats at the Labor Ministry used the same image to criticize parents who failed to leave their children at home. The German, the Yugoslavian, and the Turkish press agreed on one point: the reform was an embarrassing failure.

German officials expressed frustration that parents failed to heed their warnings about their children's dismal futures. The FRG had insisted that it was unwilling to take any responsibility for guest worker children, such as when the diplomats had informed Turkey that "Germany is not an immigration country and therefore will not educate these children to be Germans." The only way to explain child migration was to harp on the irrationality and irresponsibility of their parents. One Labor Ministry working group wrote in 1981 that for foreigners, "the illusion of financial gain (interpreting the nominal difference between German and foreign child allowances as a real difference) can cause foreigners to bring their families."[127] Economic rationality was cast as irrationality as the state accused parents of irresponsibly responding to an economic incentive that the state had created. The Labor Ministry's blinkered insistence that parents should know better than to bring children was one of the "moral notions partly disguised as economic doctrines" that characterize neoliberal governance.[128] Their unshakable position that children should remain in Turkey was not based on an assessment of the budget of the foreign family but on a deeply held position that such a family did not belong in the FRG.

The architects of the 1974 child allowance reform had not intended to change either migration patterns or migration policy. In fact, the Labor Ministry had purposefully chosen the solution that it hoped would disrupt migration patterns the least. Despite its intentions, contemporaries found that the reform offered a plausible narrative for explaining the persistence of family migration. Foreign parents who brought their children to the Federal Republic after 1974 had to defend their motives, while officials seeking to legitimize new restrictions could refer to the existence of "child allowance migrants" to imply that these parents acted out of short-sighted desire for financial gain rather than genuine emotional attachment. Was "family migration" really legitimate if the "family" was a welfare-seeking machine? The close association of child allowances and fertility also made an even more offensive claim plausible—the idea that foreign families had children explicitly to take advantage of the welfare state. It cemented a narrative whereby guest workers were irresponsible parents and their children victims.

The figure of the "child allowance migrant" directed public attention to both the purported "threat" of family migration and to the state's lack of tools with which to regulate child migration, and thus set the stage for the discussion of new restrictions. The narrative was pervasive enough that even in April 1982— nearly a decade after the reform—a public opinion survey discovered that 76 percent of West Germans "see the high German child allowances as the primary cause for the influx of foreign children."[129] Later that year, many Germans would have read, and likely found plausible, a December 1982 editorial in the *Frankfurter Allgemeine Zeitung* which began with the statement "There are always more foreigners, who only want to benefit from social welfare (starting with child allowances): this is indefensible."[130]

Are Men Family Members?

Husbands, Teenagers, and "False Family Reunification"

In a study of foreign women working in West Berlin in the early 1980s, several women at one firm complained about the same co-worker, who always arrived at the factory an hour early in order to make her piecework quota. Her colleagues did not appreciate her lengthening the workday, but she refused to relent. One of the interviewees recalled: "Her husband was here as a family member. When I told her 'You shouldn't do that!' she said 'Your husband works. . . . I have no security, I have to work.' "[1] Considered out of context, the statement "her husband was here as a family member" appears to be tautological: husbands, much like wives, are necessarily always also members of families. But within the context of migration law, "her husband was here as a family member" indicates an unusual and even unnatural situation: this woman's husband was a dependent. Within the German migration bureaucracy, "family member" was assumed to mean "dependent woman" and never "man."

Guided by the same questionable assumptions, scholars continue to describe "family migration" as a form of migration that involves women and children and have largely ignored the existence of the "trailing husband."[2] In so doing, they inadvertently omit one of the most important aspects of migration after the 1973 recruitment stop in West Germany: although the proportion of women among all new migrants did increase, the majority of people who entered using the category of "family migrant" were adult men.

Roughly 14 million people entered the FRG as "guest workers" and roughly 11 million of those left. Statistics suggest that the decision to remain was gendered. Foreign men were more likely to leave the FRG for good after 1973, while foreign women who were already in the country at the time of the recruitment stop were more likely to remain and to bring their husbands to join them. Women were not the majority of new arrivals in any year. The single most "feminized" year was 1975—also the year of the "child allowance migrant"—but

Fear of the Family. Lauren Stokes, Oxford University Press. © Oxford University Press 2022.
DOI: 10.1093/oso/9780197558416.003.0005

even in that year almost 54 percent of new adult migrants were men.[3] The Labor Ministry itself estimated in 1978 that 340,000 spouses—190,000 men and 150,000 women—as well as 190,000 teenage children had come to West Germany as "family migrants" since 1974.[4] The popular image of family migration as husbands sending for wives is simply inaccurate. The "trailing husband" was statistically more common than the "trailing wife."

Trailing spouses found themselves caught in a dispute between the Labor Ministry and Interior Ministry about how best to regulate ongoing family migration. During the period of active labor recruitment, the Labor Ministry—under both CDU and SPD leadership—favored a permissive stance toward family migration. The Labor Ministry believed that family members made workers not just more productive by supplying care work for free but also more likely to leave the country in the future because workers who lived alone were more likely to marry Germans. In contrast, the Interior Ministry—under both CDU and FDP leadership—had always favored more regulation and was more comfortable with pushing back on employer demands for more labor in order to prevent long-term settlement.[5] After the 1973 recruitment stop, the two ministries shifted position relative to each other. The Interior Ministry, under the FDP, rejected imposing new restrictions on family migration, while the Labor Ministry, led by the SPD, began to see family migration as an existential threat that demanded regulation. Interministerial conflict, not interparty conflict, shaped migration policy.

This reevaluation of "family migration" as a threat occurred at a time of increasing insecurity for the entire West German workforce. The FRG lost over 1.2 million jobs in heavy industry, such as steel and iron production and ship construction, between 1972 and 1982.[6] After remaining at 1 percent or below for years, the official unemployment rate jumped to 2.5 percent in 1974 and 4.6 percent in 1975, where it would remain for the rest of the decade.[7] The German Trade Union Confederation supported the recruitment stop, and during the precarious 1970s, the German unions generally supported a very restrictive use of the principle that foreigners should not be hired unless no German could be found for the job.[8]

Discussions about the best way to steer the FRG through the economic crisis were also discussions about the existing breadwinner model. The SPD continued to see itself chiefly as the representative of the organized working class, particularly of skilled native-born male workers. The CDU attacked this position when it introduced the "new social question" into public debate at its 1975 party conference. The CDU argued that the existing welfare state was oriented exclusively to the needs of organized male workers while leaving behind the "unorganized" segments of society, including single mothers, large families with many children, and the elderly.[9] As the political parties debated the role of the welfare state, no party understood migrants as part of its constituency. In a 1976 book he titled *The New Social Question*, CDU politician Heiner Geißler specifically criticized the fertility of foreign women and argued that labor migrants had cost the state more than the value they had brought.[10]

The governing SPD also displayed its lack of concern for the migrant population through Labor Ministry policies on family migration during the second half of the 1970s. The Labor Ministry believed that most male family migrants were "false" family migrants. Isolated cases where migrants falsified their family relationships to secure papers undoubtedly stoked paranoia about family migration, but the label primarily functioned to suggest that real relationships were being exploited for illegitimate purposes. The Interior Ministry continued to grant residence permits to newly arrived family members, but the Labor Ministry called for a kind of affective investigation of the new arrivals as it suggested that the majority of them were not intending to live as a family but were only there to collect welfare payments for their children and to access the shrinking labor market. Hoping to discourage a form of migration that it deemed illegitimate, the Labor Ministry imposed a blanket ban on work permits for "family migrants"—men, women, and children—who entered the FRG after November 30, 1974.

The blunt instrument of denying work permits to all new migrants created a large population of family members who were authorized to live in the FRG by the Interior Ministry but completely excluded from its legal labor market by the Labor Ministry. This disjuncture between residence and work permits created precisely the disadvantaged underclass that organized labor had tried to avoid through its earlier insistence that employers incorporate "guest workers" into the welfare state. By 1980, a full 42 percent of "non-working" foreign men had never worked legally in West Germany.[11] Those who had arrived in the previous six years had never been allowed to. The men and women who continued to migrate legally in this period were primed to engage in illegal work—work outside of the welfare state and the wage contracts struck by the unions—because it was all that was available to them.[12]

By the end of the decade, public concern about the social and economic impacts of the work permit ban led to the "Waiting Period Law," whereby foreigners could obtain a work permit after a waiting period that could be shortened if they entered vocational training or took particularly undesirable jobs. Politicians framed the law as an "integration measure" that would motivate unemployed foreigners to make themselves more employable. While historians have argued that the Federal Republic fully embraced neoliberal workforce reforms only in the 1990s and 2000s in the wake of German unification,[13] the treatment of "guest workers" and their family members shows that the logic of requiring individuals to prove their own willingness for work existed well before German unification. It also highlights the action of the SPD as the primary party responsible for writing this logic into the law in the 1970s, making the SPD's

introduction of workfare principles in 2003 less of a rupture than it has sometimes seemed.

From 1974 to the present day, the ill-fated policy of the work permit ban has
consistently been erased from public discussion, removing the state's responsibility for ameliorating the situation it created. Social scientists and bureaucrats
tasked with thinking about foreigners stressed the ways in which the cultural
values of foreigners led them to engage in conduct that the state deemed undesirable: petty criminality, illegal work, and, in the case of women, taking up the
role of the housewife. When officials suggested that foreigners should work to
achieve "integration" into the labor market and into society, they held foreigners
themselves accountable for the risks they had assumed in migrating to a country
that had declared itself "not an immigration country," and forced them to take
full responsibility for their own futures.[14] The Labor Ministry barred foreigners
from the legal labor market for years on end, but "integrated" foreigners would
manage to produce seamless work biographies despite this external obstacle.

"False Family Migration" and Male Dependents

The federal government's discussions about family migration relied on a deceptive binary between the family as economic unit and the family as affective
unit. The SPD-controlled Labor Ministry insisted that its ban on work permits
for family members was "the price paid for maintaining the liberal—for humanitarian reasons—regulation of family reunification for spouses and single
underage children of foreign workers."[15] As this quote suggests, the ban was expected to act as a filter that would ensure access for those coming for "humanitarian" reasons—pre-existing relationships of dependency—while ensuring
that those coming for illegitimate "economic" reasons would give up and stay
away. This desire to filter the motives behind migration built on over a decade
of anxiety about men who exploited the category of "family member" to access
the labor market. The label of "false family migrant" was applied almost exclusively to husbands following their wives or to male teenagers. The latter were
considered somewhat less suspect when they were following both parents and
far more suspicious when they were following only their fathers, creating a per-
verse all-male family unit.

Employers' desire for cheap female labor—cheap because women were
assumed to be primarily family members and only secondarily wage workers—
inadvertently placed hundreds of thousands of men in the position of the dependent. By 1971, an unskilled male worker from Turkey had to wait an average
of six to seven years to be called to work in the FRG, while an unskilled female
worker had to wait only three to six months. Employers recruited single women

almost instantaneously, pleased that there was no danger of such a woman trying to reunite with her husband. The preference for single women was so marked that the German Embassy in Ankara suspected Turkish women of routinely getting divorced in order to move up the waitlist and then re-marrying their husbands after securing a job.[16]

Married women recruited to work in Germany often hoped to use their position to help their husbands move closer to the front of the migration line, but many local Foreigners' Offices thwarted such plans by using their administrative discretion to systematically discriminate against trailing husbands. During the 1960s and early 1970s, most Foreigners' Offices were willing to recognize "trailing wives" as "family migrants" and to grant them residence and work permits. The same Foreigners' Offices routinely denied the applications of "trailing husbands," arguing that men did not qualify as "family migrants" because they came as family members only to achieve their true goal of working in Germany. The consequences of this policy could be devastating for families that had already spent time apart. One man recalled that his wife had left Turkey to work in a cannery near Hamburg because "women had better chances then. The waiting period was relatively short for her." His wife tried and failed to facilitate a named recruitment for her husband for ten months. He finally came to join her on a tourist visa, but his application for a residence permit was denied. With one child in Turkey and another on the way he "was determined to keep my family together at any price" and decided that living and working illegally in the FRG was the best option.[17]

Press reports about an apparent increase in unauthorized Turkish male migrants at the beginning of the 1970s suggested that many of these men had wives who lived in Germany legally.[18] When the crime procedural *Tatort* first featured guest workers in an episode in 1975, the main character was the unauthorized "trailing husband" of an authorized guest worker wife. According to the script, "the wife received a work permit more easily than her husband, because as a female guest worker she is in a lower wage group than married guest worker men." The first draft of the script also included the unauthorized brother of an authorized sister and an unauthorized grandfather who looked after his grandchildren but who hid in a closet every time the doorbell rang to avoid being discovered.[19] In the episode, the unauthorized men are drawn into a criminal conspiracy as they try to escape their desperate situation. While fictional, the episode reflected the fact that the gendered policies of Foreigners' Offices encouraged men to migrate illegally.

In 1971, the interior minister of Schleswig-Holstein sparked a discussion about the practice of not granting work permits to "trailing husbands." He worried that the existing practice was vulnerable to court challenges because it violated the Basic Law's guarantee of gender equality. He suggested that instead of using gender as the basis for making decisions, perhaps Foreigners' Offices could grant work permits based on whether the applicant for the work permit had worked for wages in the home country. Counterintuitively, applicants who had worked for wages would be ineligible for a work permit in Germany while applicants who had not worked for wages would be eligible for a work permit in Germany. According to Schleswig-Holstein, such a policy would be formally gender-neutral and thus able to withstand a court challenge, but in practice it would allow most trailing wives to work while excluding virtually all trailing husbands.[20]

The West Berlin and Bavarian Interior Ministries both wrote lengthy responses rejecting this suggestion. West Berlin was a center of female employment due to its textile and microelectronics industries. As a result, the West Berlin Foreigners' Office frequently received applications from "trailing husbands" and had decided that common sense dictated a policy of systematically giving work permits to "trailing wives" while denying them to "trailing husbands." West Berlin's explanation drew on an existing construct of women as "consumer-citizens."[21] They argued that a wife in the home country would believe that her husband was making a lot of money because his remittances allowed her to buy everything she wanted at home. She would then come to West Germany intending only to "run the household for her family," but discover that the prices were higher than she had expected, which meant that she also needed to work to maintain her home at her accustomed standard. Her application for a work permit was a way for her to complete her primary, gendered duty of running the household. When a husband who had followed his wife applied for a work permit, however, it could be assumed that he had entered the country under false pretenses and had "intended to work from the beginning. Assertions to the contrary are usually unreliable."[22] West Berlin's practice punished women who had migrated independently. When a man migrated first, followed by his wife, it was fine to have two working adults in one household, but when a woman migrated first, followed by her husband, the disturbance in the gender order demanded state correction.[23]

The Bavarian Interior Ministry's argument was far more essentialist than West Berlin's complicated story about the "trailing wife" as a disillusioned consumer-homemaker. For Bavaria, the abstract legal principle of gender equality could not override the inherent differences between men and women. "Family migration" was for wives and children, and under no circumstances for adult men. Bavaria argued that the idea of a male "family migrant" was "not compatible with Western beliefs about the man's duty to the family and is also highly problematic from a sociopolitical standpoint." Bavaria explained that among native-born, white West Germans, wives often stopped working to take care of their children, but "for the opposite case [men] there are hardly any examples." For Bavaria, a man's primary identity was as a breadwinner. A foreign man who had sent his wife ahead of him to Germany was exploiting her as a kind of "billeting officer" so that he could come as a family migrant and circumvent the requirements of labor recruitment. Perhaps he was too old to work in Germany, or perhaps he had tuberculosis.[24] This public health concern was acutely gendered. Dozens of officials worried about the possibility that women would import sick husbands, but no official worried about sick wives, who presumably would have transmitted the same disease and taken up the same hospital bed. Their obsessive focus on sick men and comparative lack of interest in sick women shows that their purported concern with public health was more fundamentally about the gender order.

The federal Interior Ministry sided with West Berlin and Bavaria in December 1971, ordering that "trailing husbands" should not receive work permits. Although the Baden-Württemberg Interior Ministry had not entered the initial debate, it reflected that debate in the administrative circular announcing the new policy. The first draft of the Baden-Württemberg circular explained that foreign men were not to be trusted when they claimed that they had not intended to work in Germany. Such a claim "runs contrary to Western beliefs about the husband's position and duties, and also does not accord with general life experience." Over the course of the drafting process, officials eventually deleted the reference to "Western beliefs" but made the same point by appealing to a putatively shared common sense about family values: "It is also uncommon in the native countries of the people in question for the wife to be the sole breadwinner and to support the family while the husband does nothing—except help out around the house."[25] Crucially, this appeal to common sense had never been invoked to prevent West German employers from recruiting married foreign women who wanted to work full-time jobs. The insistence on shared family values came into play only to keep foreign men out of the legal labor force once their wives had already undertaken waged work in West Germany.

In fact, just as Schleswig-Holstein had predicted, the policy of not granting husbands work permits had already been challenged in court. In one case, a Turkish woman had begun working in West Berlin in September 1969. Her husband followed in January 1970 and brought their three children with him. When he applied simultaneously for a work and a residence permit at the Foreigners' Office, he was denied both, following the secret discretionary practice of denying all "trailing husbands." He subsequently applied for a residence permit alone, but was denied by bureaucrats who believed that his previous application for a work permit meant that he intended to use his residence permit to work illegally. When he went to court, he argued that he had a right to a residence permit based on his interest in family life. He also pointed out that he could perform useful labor by providing childcare while his wife worked. The West Berlin Foreigners' Office countered: "It is unnatural that, as in the case before us, the plaintiff, that is, the husband, takes care of the household and the child. When the wife takes care of the household and the husband earns a livelihood, this corresponds better to the societal conception of a sensible division of labor within marriage." The judge ruled against the state in November 1971, pointing out that the state did not have the right to decree how a marriage should work.[26]

This ruling and a remarkably similar one in North Rhine-Westphalia both threatened the status quo of allowing "trailing wives" while excluding "trailing husbands." The May 1973 national meeting of the Interior Ministries' Experts on Foreigners discussed an appropriate response. Looking at existing court decisions, the delegates at the meeting worried that the existing practice of granting permits to trailing wives while denying them to trailing husbands could not be maintained for much longer. Were such a case to make it to a federal court, naïve judges guided by the abstract ideal of gender equality in the Basic Law would probably "assume that the primary motive [of the trailing husband] is the resumption of the marital relationship" and were likely to rule that the practice of denying residence permits to husbands constituted a form of unconstitutional gender discrimination.[27]

The representatives at the meeting agreed that they should change their policies preemptively before a federal court forced their hand. Several representatives, including Bavaria, wanted to move in a more restrictive direction and to deny both trailing wives and trailing husbands work permits. The representative from Schleswig-Holstein agreed with this position, referencing the "Spanish grandmother" ruling from earlier that month when he added that one advantage of denying work permits to all trailing wives was that "because the wife would be able to take care of the children, the grandmother would not have to receive a residence permit." The representative of Rhineland-Palatinate also wanted to move in a more restrictive direction because he was worried about having to give work permits to the husbands of the Korean and Filipina nurses who staffed the hospitals in his state. Other representatives argued in favor of a more liberal practice. The representative of crowded West Berlin was happy to grant work permits liberally when one apartment could fill two jobs, while the representative of bustling North Rhine-Westphalia worried that employers would be angry if the government stopped granting work permits to wives. The representatives at this meeting ultimately agreed to liberalize their practice: in the future they would extend work permits to both "trailing husbands" and "trailing wives," but only after the spouse in question had lived in Germany for a period of at least nine months.[28] They reasoned that a period of nine months was long enough for a consuming wife to come to the realization that her family needed more money for her to run the household successfully, but also long enough to discourage a breadwinning husband, who would hopefully give up in frustration and return home.

Despite the formal instruction that Foreigners' Offices should act in a gender-neutral fashion when granting residence permits to spouses, the assumption that "trailing wives" were natural while "trailing husbands" were necessarily trying to gain illegitimate access to the labor market continued to shape practice on the ground. A 1976 circular on family reunion issued in Bavaria expressed a common sentiment when it specified: "The reunifying spouse, especially in the case of a trailing husband, must provide proof that the partner who is working in Germany can support the family. If proof is not provided, the residence permit is to be denied."[29] This circular and the practice it tacitly approved created a difficult situation for foreign women. Foreign women were valuable to employers precisely because they were imagined to be secondary wage earners who could be paid less than men—and that same status could be used to exclude dependent husbands from the Federal Republic, so the secondary wage earner would in practice always have to be primary.

The Contested Link Between Family Reunion and Labor Market Exclusion

After the November 1973 recruitment stop, the SPD-controlled Labor Ministry and the FDP-controlled Interior Ministry reached a stalemate over how best to regulate family migration. The Labor Ministry desperately wanted to impose new restrictions to protect the labor market, but the Interior Ministry, responsible for granting residence permits, refused to consider any further restrictions, arguing that family members had to be given residence permits as long as they could bring proof of "adequate housing." The Interior Ministry believed that the Labor Ministry's demands for tighter regulation were unrealistic. Most family members entered the country without visas and stayed for weeks or months before applying for residence permits, at which point, according to the Interior Ministry, "it appears unrealistic to forcibly remove family members from the FRG in large numbers." The state would need to require visas for entry to regulate family migration, and "such a rule would make the FRG the least generous state in the free world in terms of foreigner law." Even if the state decided to damage its international reputation by introducing visa requirements, Article 6 of the Basic Law still made it impossible to deny visas to nuclear family members, so that "family migration would be 'controllable,' but not—as the Labor Ministry now demands—reducible."[30] The Interior Ministry wanted to accept the situation and to gradually make it easier for family migrants to obtain residence permits.

In the context of an ongoing economic downturn and alarming unemployment statistics, the Labor Ministry was frustrated by the Interior Ministry's refusal to impose new migration restrictions. So it turned to the administrative measure that it controlled: the work permit. On November 13, 1974, the Labor Ministry issued a circular preventing all family migrants who entered West Germany after November 30, 1974, regardless of gender or age, from ever receiving a work permit.[31] The ban also applied to those family members who had previously lived in Germany but had left for a period of more than three months and returned after November 30, 1974. This stipulation particularly impacted young men who had left temporarily to perform their required term of military service in Turkey or Greece.[32]

The Labor Ministry believed that the work permit ban would discourage any family migrants who intended to enter the labor market. They proceeded from the same assumptions as the Foreigners' Offices that had granted residence permits to trailing wives and denied them to trailing husbands before 1973. The Labor Ministry hoped that family members who intended to enter Germany to care for the household—particularly wives—would continue to enter, while family members planning to perform waged labor—particularly husbands and male teenagers—would abandon their migration plans. While it is certainly possible that more migration would have occurred without the work permit ban, migration continued regardless. During the mid-1970s, hundreds of thousands of family members were granted residence permits but denied work permits, able to live in Germany but unable to work. The Labor Ministry's attempt to protect the legal labor market for Germans inadvertently nourished the market for illegal labor.

Although the ban on work permits was applied without regard for gender, the unspoken but widely shared assumption that "family migration" was the migration of women and children ensured that the impact on adult men went largely unmentioned in the press. For example, in January 1975, *Der Spiegel* published an article about the SPD's efforts to get rid of guest workers which described the work permit ban as follows: "Guest worker children over the age of 16 who have entered since December 1 of last year, no longer receive work permits. Wives are no longer placed in jobs." Husbands were also no longer placed in jobs, but the article did not mention this fact. A journalist from *Bild* who interviewed the Labor Ministry in the same month asked, "Are wives of guest workers still being placed in jobs?" The spokesperson did not correct the journalist's incorrect assumption: "First-time work permits are not being issued on principle. This rule impacts wives above all. . . . This course of action is justified by above-average female unemployment."[33] The Labor Ministry even stressed the measure's impact on women in its own publications, for example, explaining that it affected "trailing wives above all" in an informational sheet in August 1975.[34] The Labor Ministry's own figures showed that the measure affected more trailing husbands than trailing wives, but it consistently elided this fact in its public relations strategy.

The *Frankfurter Rundschau* exposed the existing disagreement between the Interior and Labor Ministries to the public when it published excerpts from a confidential draft of "seventeen theses on foreigner policy" that the ministries had voted on at a meeting of the Chancellor's Office in October 1975. The "seventeen theses" draft revealed that the SPD-controlled Labor Ministry was isolated in its hardline policies: it was the only ministry to support introducing new restrictions on unemployment benefits for foreigners, the only ministry to categorically oppose any changes that would make it easier for foreigners to receive permanent residency, and the only ministry categorically opposed to family migration. Every other ministry had voted for a version of the "seventeen theses" that included the sentence, "The federal government does not intend to make family migration more difficult." The Labor Ministry, by contrast, had voted to raise the requirement for family migration from one to three years of employment and to introduce a complete ban on family migration to "overburdened regions of settlement."[35]

Social work organizations had never been consulted about the "seventeen theses," and their representatives were furious on reading the leaked draft. At the first meeting of the Coordination Committee on Foreign Workers after the article was published, it "burst like a targeted bomb," with a representative from Diakonie reportedly screaming at the Labor Ministry representative "Why weren't we informed? We were duped! Now we look like idiots in front of the foreigners and especially in front of our own counselors!" The Diakonie representative reported that the Labor Ministry representative sat "pale and speechless" throughout the meeting, unable to defend himself.[36] The social work agencies left the meeting to issue an open letter strongly criticizing the "seventeen theses." In it, they accused the Chancellor's Office and the Labor Ministry of "increasing the insecurity of the foreigners and strengthening their suspicion of German offices, authorities, and institutions."[37]

The state responded to the social workers' criticism in the summer of 1976 by creating a new decision-making body on foreigner policy, the first such body to include representatives from the social work agencies as voting members.[38] The "Federal Government-Federal States Commission for the Further Development of a Comprehensive Foreigner Policy" was charged with crafting a "comprehensive" migration policy that would include a unified national regulation about family migration.

During the commission's deliberations, the Interior Ministry and Foreign Ministry both wanted to protect family migration. The Interior Ministry argued that Article 6 of the Basic Law protected foreign families, while the Foreign Ministry took the stance that the FRG could not afford to fall behind international standards for family reunification. For example, the FRG could not have more restrictive policies than Switzerland, which had recently reduced the required waiting period for family reunification from three years to one.[39] The Foreign Ministry worried that new restrictions would open the FRG up to the charge of violating the human rights provisions of the 1975 Helsinki Accords, which included the promise to "deal in a positive and humanitarian spirit" with applications for "family reunification [Familienzusammenführung]." The Foreign Ministry worried that writing a more restrictive definition of "family migration [Familiennachzug]" into law might jeopardize their work facilitating "family reunification [Familienzusammenführung] across the Iron Curtain," using both forms of the word in the same sentence in order to distinguish between foreign and German families.[40]

In contrast to the Interior and Foreign Ministries, the SPD-controlled Labor Ministry consistently advocated the "most extensive restriction possible" of family members.[41] Its arguments stemmed from its fundamental belief that foreigners were misusing family reunion to circumvent labor market restrictions. To prevent this misuse, the ministry would consider granting foreign family members work permits only if the Interior Ministry would agree to "a satisfactory restriction" of family members.

The Labor Ministry devised several new arguments in support of its position. While all of these arguments would become associated with the CDU/CSU during the 1980s, they were actually introduced by the SPD in the 1970s. First, the Labor Ministry countered the claim that restriction was unconstitutional by insisting that the foreign workers' "right to family life" was sufficiently secure as long as they could return to their family in their home country. Second, it argued that foreign parents who brought their children to Germany were potentially abusing their children's rights, as "there is often an abuse of the parental right, when the foreign worker tears his children from their native environment and transplants them into a foreign society."[42] Third, it insisted that extensive restriction of child migration was necessary to protect "youth integration into the labor market . . . over the long term." Integration could succeed only as long as the population to be integrated remained small.[43] Finally, the Labor Ministry used the commission to introduce the possibility that the 807,000 single foreigners between the age of 18 and 45 would go on to marry yet more foreigners ("secondary family reunion") who would then proceed to have another generation of foreign children ("tertiary family formation").[44] Family migration might become a never-ending challenge for the FRG.

The FDP-controlled Interior Ministry criticized the behavior of the SPD-controlled Labor Ministry, which it worried was using the commission to "legitimate the package deal between lifting the work permit ban for foreign youth and the restriction on family reunion for this group."[45] By getting the commission to confirm that the two issues were necessarily connected, the Labor Ministry would be able to make the case that the Interior Ministry was responsible for the unpopular work permit ban. The Interior Ministry also believed that the Labor Ministry was directing a covert press campaign to turn public opinion against family migration by "constantly stress[ing] the negative side of family reunion (the future 'subproletariat,' 'American conditions')," suggesting that migration would inevitably lead to ghettoization and race riots. The Interior Ministry was particularly incensed that "the Labor Ministry . . . uses misleading figures in order to exaggerate the magnitude of family reunion." The Labor Ministry constantly told reporters that 550,000 family members had entered West Germany in 1974 and 1975 without mentioning that 500,000 family members had left during the same period. This omission made the increase in the foreign population appear substantially larger than it actually was.[46]

The most controversial issue for the Federal Government-Federal States Commission was whether they should restrict the migration of "young foreigners of working age," specifically sixteen- and seventeen-year-olds. In the FRG, compulsory schooling ends at fifteen, at which time a substantial percentage of children, particularly working-class children, start either an apprenticeship or a vocational training program in preparation for the labor market. Child migrants who first entered at sixteen or seventeen would not be subject to compulsory schooling and could theoretically enter the labor market immediately. The status quo was to grant these minor children residence permits but to deny them work permits. The commission discussed several alternative models, including denying residence permits to them or giving them residence permits only if they had already secured jobs. The commission also discussed creating a new category of residence permit exclusively for these young people, one that would specify that they would never be eligible for a work permit and that they would have to leave on turning eighteen. Although proponents of this new residence permit category believed that it might reduce the number of teenage migrants for whom "the intention of employment . . . is in the foreground," the administratively unwieldy proposal was not pursued further.[47]

The commission eventually voted on the proposal to deny residence permits for all sixteen- and seventeen-year-olds, since the members believed that a categorical ban was the only solution that would not immediately lead to a cascade of exceptions. The Labor Ministry supported the proposal, arguing that an age limit of sixteen would in fact conform to Article 6—"Marriage and the family shall enjoy the special protection of the state"—because for older teenagers "the dominant motive for entry is the desired employment and not family reunion."[48] The final vote was close. Seventeen members were in favor of the Labor Ministry's preferred solution—ending the residence permits—while fourteen members were in favor of the Interior Ministry's preferred solution of maintaining the status quo.[49] The majority in favor of banning teenage migrants was too slim for the commission to make an official recommendation in its final report.[50] Frustrated by the Federal Government-Federal States Commission's inability to pass new restrictions on family migration, the Labor Ministry responded to growing pressure to move the cutoff date for access to the labor market for foreign youth, issuing a June 1977 circular allowing youth who had entered between November 30, 1974, and December 31, 1976, to receive work permits. Spouses received no such concession and continued to be shut out of the legal labor market.[51]

Each ministry left the commission with its own narrative about what had occurred. The Labor Ministry told the press that "the work permit ban was implemented because the Interior Ministry was not ready to restrict family reunion for foreign workers."[52] Meanwhile the Interior Ministry continued to catalog examples of what it believed to be the Labor Ministry's organized press campaign. When the *Frankfurter Allgemeine Zeitung* published an article in February 1978 titled "A new sub-proletariat is forming," an Interior Ministry official filed the clipping with the handwritten note "Labor Ministry. Here they go again! Against family reunion?"[53]

Officials at the Labor Ministry were pessimistic about their ability to retain the upper hand in migration policy. In a July 1978 Labor Ministry report, the author complained that the Interior Ministry continued to argue "that a measure that is questionable from a humanitarian and constitutional standpoint cannot be justified by 'mere' labor market policy." For the Labor Ministry economic policy, in this case "labor market policy," is always the most important social policy. The author suggests making an appeal to Chancellor Schmidt to use his emergency powers to circumvent the obstructive Interior Ministry and ban the migration of sixteen- and seventeen-year-olds "for whom the motivation to earn, not the desire to live with the family, is as a rule the decisive motive for their relocation." He laments that even a ban on teenage migration is inadequate to manage the problem, as parents would likely react by bringing their children to the FRG at fifteen, still too late for the children to integrate. Because the Law on Foreigners required residence permits only for those over sixteen, it was impossible to ban the migration of younger children.[54]

The Labor Ministry was under significant pressure to get rid of the work permit ban, particularly from the three social work agencies, all of which experienced its effects in their work with foreign families. The Protestant social work agency Diakonie funded lawyers to bring cases against the work permit ban. It also encouraged social workers to read local newspapers for stories about criminal foreign youth and to send letters to the editor to clarify the fact that the work permit ban forced youth into socially undesirable activity: "some of these youth work illegally under poor work conditions and as underpaid labor, others sell themselves in the form of prostitution or make income illegally through criminal activity."[55] Diakonie also collaborated with the other two social work agencies, AWO and Caritas, to gather signatures for a petition against the ban.[56] Unable to actually vote on the state's migration policy, the social work agencies tried to exert influence over public opinion.

Scholars who analyzed criminal behavior among foreign youth in the late 1970s also realized that the work permit ban was a causal factor. Criminologists Peter-Alexis Albrecht and Christian Pfeiffer began their 1979 study on criminal foreign youth with the sentence "If a social problem was ever foreseeable, then it is the one in this study."[57] This particular study was based on interviews with social workers and not with the affected youth themselves. Although the social workers described the "highly patriarchal structure" and "authoritarian educational style" of foreign families as aggravating factors, they all made the same recommendation to the state: foreign youth needed to be able to enter the legal labor market.[58] Two years later, another group of researchers interviewed 100 foreign teenage boys about youth criminality. They were so shocked by the difficulties that the boys experienced in West Germany that by the end of their study they believed that they had been working on the wrong research question. If they could design a study again from the ground up, they wrote, they would pose the research question the other way around: "Why are *so few* foreign youth criminals?"[59] The 1981 researchers were particularly impressed by youth resilience, including a group of young men in Munich who had organized a petition campaign to argue that the restrictions on work permits were against West German law.[60] They concluded that the best way to fight youth crime was to "open the skilled labor market for foreign youth."[61] On this point, foreign youth, social workers, and social scientists all agreed.

Despite pressure from multiple stakeholders, the Labor Ministry clung to the work permit ban because it insisted on understanding migration through the lens of the labor market. Having previously depicted child allowances as the sole cause for a mass wave of child migration, the Labor Ministry now pivoted to depict the labor market as the sole cause for teenage and spousal migration. It believed that responding to pressure to move the cutoff date for access to the labor market a second time—having already shifted from November 30, 1974, to December 31, 1977—would destroy any remaining "deterrent effect" for family migrants, while lifting it for specific jobs or industries might "sink the psychological threshold for family reunion."[62] The Labor Ministry feared that any relaxation of its tough stance on work permits would lead to a quantitative increase in foreign migration.

Introducing the Waiting Period

The courts broke the stalemate between the Labor and Interior Ministries as they began to rule on the hundreds of lawsuits that migrants filed against the work permit ban. Some courts upheld the ban. In one such case, a Turkish man in Hamburg filed suit because local authorities refused to give him a work permit for a job as a dishwasher at a restaurant. His lawyer argued that the refusal to grant a work permit violated Article 6 of the Basic Law because his wife's wages of 1,000 DM per month were not sufficient for the couple to live in Germany and also support their two children in Turkey. Every month the couple sent 300 DM to the grandparents in Turkey, who raised both of the children, leaving them with only 700 DM per month. At the time, a West German family qualified for social assistance when it made no more than 806 DM per month for a two-person family or 1,251 per month for a four-person family. After remittances for the children, the couple's income was significantly below this threshold.[63] The court disagreed. It ruled that the children who lived in Turkey could not be considered part of the family. Once the couple was treated as childless, the wife's 1,000 DM salary was in fact nearly 200 DM more than the threshold of social assistance. According to the court, the couple was not experiencing hardship because they "can even divert 300 DM to the grandparents in Turkey, who raise both of the children." The court saw the couple's remittances to their own children as an optional expense rather than the central reason for the couple's migration to the FRG.[64] As in the housing and child allowance debates, state authorities recognized transnational family members when convenient, but "disappeared" them from the family as soon as inconvenient.

Other courts struck down the ban on work permits. A Greek man who had followed his wife to North Rhine-Westphalia in 1975 had found a position preparing and packaging fish for sale with a firm that had been trying and failing to fill the job for two years. Yet the local authorities refused to give him a work permit for what was evidently an undesirable job. The court in Essen ruled in the man's favor, arguing that the work permit ban was illegal because it was inconsistent with the Employment Promotion Law, according to which work permits had to be granted based on the circumstances of the individual case. According to the court, an employer's interest in filling a particular job could in fact be compelling enough to justify giving a foreign worker a work permit despite the ban.[65]

The Labor Ministry, always pessimistic about liberal jurisprudence, expected that when one of these cases finally reached the highest court, the court would rule against the work permit ban. As a preemptive measure, the ministry began to develop a plan whereby an individual migrant who entered the FRG would begin a "dynamized" or "flexible" waiting period to be eligible for a work permit.[66] Spouses would have to wait four years and teenagers two years to access the labor market, but they could shorten that waiting period if they were willing to take vocational courses for specific segments of the labor market or take jobs in specific branches or locations. Some voices within the Labor Ministry worried that shortening the waiting period only for undesirable jobs "could lead to the reproach of 'our Negroes,' " but officials hoped to counter that impression by describing the waiting period as an "integration measure."[67] According to the Labor Ministry, a "flexible" waiting period would encourage foreign youth to take more responsibility for developing their own skills and would thus help them "integrate" better into the West German labor market. This was a neoliberal definition of integration, one where conforming to market demands is the most important form of belonging.

The CDU/CSU attacked the work permit ban in late 1978 when it introduced a parliamentary petition to eliminate the ban for foreign youth "condemned to idleness," forcing them onto the black market and into criminal activity. The petition argued that this was an untenable situation. These youth needed the opportunity to enter vocational training and the labor market.[68] The SPD and FDP countered in early 1979 with the proposal that the Labor Ministry had been developing, a flexible "waiting period" that could be shortened for youth who had participated in language classes and vocational training, which world create an "incentive towards their own efforts to integrate."[69]

In the ensuing debate, both sides argued that their policy was better for foreign youth and mentioned spouses only in passing. The CDU/CSU stressed the family as the central institution of society and argued that the idle youth were burdening their families, while the SPD and FDP focused on the waiting period as a measure that would turn youth into "market conforming" citizens. Gerhard Braun, a CDU member from Remscheid, gave a speech in which he opposed the SPD-FDP proposal for a waiting period as "half-hearted" and "completely arbitrary." He cited the president of Diakonie to bolster his argument that the youth should be allowed to work immediately. A waiting period would only perpetuate a situation in which "youth who are capable of work and willing to be educated, but who are condemned to idleness, burden their own families" and "fall into the fingers of sub-contractors who place them in the black market."[70] Albrecht Hasinger, a CDU representative from Leverkusen, insisted that "we cannot have family policy for Germans and a no-family-policy for foreigners" and chastised the SPD for failing to realize that "foreigner policy should not just be labor market policy, but is also essentially family and youth policy."[71] SPD and FDP representatives responded to the CDU/CSU criticisms by framing the waiting period as an "integration" measure that would help foreign youth in the long run by encouraging them to take more responsibility. Hermann Buschfort, SPD member and secretary of the Labor Ministry, insisted that the waiting period would motivate youth to educate themselves and learn German "through their own integration efforts."[72] Friedrich Hölscher, an FDP representative from Stuttgart, explained that, while he would personally prefer to abolish the waiting period, he agreed with the SPD that it would incentivize individual efforts to integrate by teaching youth that "he who *himself* makes efforts for a faster integration, will also obtain an apprenticeship training position earlier, and will also be able to be incorporated into occupational life earlier."[73] The SPD and FDP representatives consistently argued for using market policy as social policy, using the reward of labor market access to teach youth what it meant to conform to the labor market.

The Labor Ministry implemented the waiting period by administrative circular in March 1979, and, following the arguments presented in parliament, the circular described the waiting period as an "integration measure" that served the interests of foreign youth. The circular defined "integration" almost exclusively as the ability to flexibly adapt to the needs of the economy. The guest worker program had already divorced labor power from other forms of social belonging. The "flexible waiting period" policy not only carried this logic into the period of family migration, but it also introduced the logic of workfare into the FRG two decades before the Hartz reforms. Legal access to the labor market was turned into a reward for those foreigners willing to prepare themselves for that labor market. The unemployed had to make themselves employable.

Competing Definitions of Integration

The waiting period circular defined "integration" almost exclusively as a labor market matter, and it faced criticism from within the SPD. Chancellor Helmut Schmidt appointed fellow SPD politician Heinz Kühn, former president of North Rhine-Westphalia, as the first "Federal Commissioner for the Promotion of Integration among Foreign Workers and Their Family Members" in 1979, the same year as the introduction of the "flexible waiting period." The SPD initially proposed a budget of 300,000 DM a year for the office, but the CDU rejected this budget, leaving Kühn with a total of 6,000 DM a year. This was not really a problem for Kühn, who always understood the position as a kind of stopgap in his career. He intended to run in the first direct elections for European Parliament in June 1979, and he and Schmidt agreed that he would write the report and then move on to work in Brussels.[74]

After nine months of research Kühn completed his report. The September 1979 report proposed a set of solutions geared toward the long-term integration of the foreign population, including communal voting rights and liberalized citizenship access for the second and third generations.[75] It met with a chilly reception, which previous scholars have attributed to Kühn's ambitious proposal for "citizenship by post," to his poor timing with regard to an emerging asylum crisis, and to his controversial statement that West Germany had become an "immigration country." CDU/CSU politicians publicly declared their opposition to the report and have received most of the blame for the failure to implement its recommendations.[76]

Although the governing SPD was Kühn's own party, it also reacted negatively to the report because Kühn had dared to criticize the idea that the labor market should frame foreigner policy.[77] The Labor Ministry tried to influence Kühn's recommendations while he was writing, such as asking Kühn to focus on labor market participation among youth and not broach the topic of labor market participation for adults.[78] While Kühn complied with that recommendation, his final report criticized the Labor Ministry and the recent report of the Federal Government-Federal States Commission for being "influenced by a basic philosophy oriented to the labor market."[79] One of Kühn's many recommendations was that the Labor Ministry drop the "flexible waiting period" so that foreign youth could receive work permits immediately. The Labor Ministry rejected this proposal, insisting once again that their waiting period allowed foreign youth to provide "proof of their capacity for integration" and thus that it was a good social policy.[80]

Although Chancellor Schmidt had commissioned Kühn's report, on reading the final product, he canceled the cabinet meeting scheduled to discuss it.[81] The Coordinating Committee on Foreign Workers in the Labor Ministry, still the primary discussion group for migration policy, did not put the Kühn report on its agenda until February 1980, five months after it had been issued. On that day, however, the committee ran out of time to discuss the report, prompting the social worker representatives at the meeting to walk out in protest. Caritas and Diakonie later issued a press release criticizing the Labor Ministry for its refusal to discuss the report. For the welfare agencies, this was just the latest in a string of incidents confirming that the Labor Ministry wanted their humanitarian credentials but not their expertise. They accused the Labor Ministry of secretly consulting with the German Trade Union Confederation to produce migration policy and only then inviting welfare agencies after the fact, effectively using them to "rubber stamp" policies prepared without their input.[82]

After Kühn left to take up his new position at the European Parliament, Chancellor Schmidt appointed Liselotte Funcke of the FDP as the next federal commissioner for the Promotion of Integration among Foreign Workers and Their Family Members. Funcke had previously been the first woman to serve as minister for economics in North Rhine-Westphalia. Like her predecessor, she began to clash with the Labor Ministry and its insistence on framing all foreigner policy as labor market policy before she even took up the position. She asked for her office to be moved from the Labor Ministry to the Chancellor's Office, arguing that integration was a "cross-sectional problem," but her request was denied. Chancellor Schmidt also took the opportunity to remind her that she was not allowed to comment on asylum policy.[83] After beginning her job, she petitioned Chancellor Schmidt to change her title to "Commissioner for Foreigner Issues," but his office rejected this idea because the phrase "foreigner issues" was far too broad and would encourage her to address issues beyond her portfolio, including asylum policy and the granting of residence and work permits. Her office was intended to work exclusively on behalf of foreign workers and "family members," whoever those might be.[84] These early exchanges set a pattern whereby the Chancellor and the Labor Ministry would continually criticize Funcke for overstepping her role. Kühn and Funcke both took their role as federal commissioner for the Promotion of Integration seriously, and both used it to push forward much broader understandings of the concept of "integration" than those envisioned by the Labor Ministry. Meanwhile, the Labor Ministry sought to ensure that the labor market would remain the primary frame for migration policy. It maintained control first by burying the Kühn report and later by consistently blocking Funcke's attempts to intervene in debates on foreigners' problems.

Turning the Waiting Period into Law

Even after introducing the "flexible waiting period," the Labor Ministry remained resolutely pessimistic about its ability to achieve the results that it wanted. Eighteen months after issuing the circular, local Foreigners' Offices had granted new work permits to a total of 11,800 spouses—a statistic that was not further broken down by gender—and 10,500 children. It had rejected another 900 applications for new work permits. These numbers were significantly lower than those the Ministry had projected, but this fact hardly comforted officials, who worried that the number was low only because "a portion of the potential was already illegally employed."[85] The Labor Ministry felt it necessary to remind Foreigners' Offices that every single decision to issue a work permit had "negative consequences for *the integration of foreigners*, because it would presumably stimulate family migration so that the magnitude of integration problems would quantitatively increase."[86] Despite publicly claiming that the "flexible waiting period" would encourage individual integration, in internal memorandums the Labor Ministry appeared to operate from the assumption that integration was impossible.

The Labor Ministry was also pessimistic because it had identified two imminent threats to the waiting period—the domestic judiciary and the ongoing process of European integration. Only fifteen months after the ministry had issued the circular, a total of 686 people had initiated cases about whether the circular was legal in domestic courts, 190 of which had reached a final ruling. Of these, 146 had concluded that the waiting period was illegal because it failed to consider the individual circumstances of prospective employers and employees.[87] Different courts emphasized different parts of that equation. While most stressed the circumstances of the employer who could not find an employee, a handful stressed the circumstances of foreigners who ought to be allowed to work given their pre-existing obligations to family members.[88] European integration was also eroding the legal basis for the waiting period circular, similar to its erosion of the legal basis for the settlement bans. Greece would enter the EEC in 1981, giving its citizens the right to an automatic work permit, while the Turkish Accession Agreement meant that after December 1, 1980, Turkish citizens could not be required to wait more than three years to obtain a work permit.[89]

The Labor Ministry decided to prepare a Waiting Period Law to put its preferred policy on a more secure legal footing in the face of court challenges and European integration. It also hoped that such a law would deter the "false asylum seekers" who were purportedly filing frivolous asylum applications to access the German labor market. The perception that people who applied for asylum were driven by economic motives had existed from the beginning of the FRG, but this narrative was further fueled in the 1970s not just by an increase in the number of asylum seekers but also by a series of specific policy changes.[90] The number of asylum seekers increased from slightly under 10,000 in 1975 to over 100,000 in 1980. Most of the new arrivals in this period came from Pakistan—which had a coup in 1977; Afghanistan—which had a coup in 1978; and Turkey—which had a coup in 1980.[91] The FRG interpreted the rise in asylum seekers not primarily as a response to the political unrest in these countries but as a response to Germany's changing policy toward asylum seekers. Beginning in 1974, asylum seekers had been divided among the federal states rather than housed in a single centralized location. After federal states complained about the new financial burden, the policy was changed the following year to allow asylum seekers to work while waiting for the outcome of their application. In June 1980, the state decided that it had made a mistake and introduced an "Emergency Program to Limit the Entrance of 'False' Asylum Seekers," to be revisited in three years. The "emergency" measures, the majority of which were never repealed, included a visa requirement for Turkish citizens and the creation of a new "waiting period" for asylum seekers to work.[92]

Within the context of public anxiety about asylum seekers, the Labor Ministry was able to pass the Waiting Period Law with almost no public debate in August 1981. The new law required adult family migrants and asylum seekers to wait for four years before they could apply for a work permit and required teenage family migrants to wait for two years before they could apply for a work permit. As with the circular, the waiting period could be shortened for migrants who were willing to work in specific sectors of the labor market. While some politicians objected that it was unfair to assume that all "family members" were in fact "economic migrants," all three of the major parties agreed that the law was a good idea for the purpose of deterring "economic refugees."[93] Funcke also encouraged the Labor Ministry to describe the law primarily in terms of its consequences for asylum seekers rather than family members.[94] The speech announcing the new law went through several drafts, each of which further emphasized the law's ability to deter asylum seekers and de-emphasized its intention to deter family members.[95] The final speech described the law as a measure that protected foreign youth because "without the waiting period these youth would overwhelmingly immediately rush into unskilled jobs," while the law gave them an "incentive to participate in vocational courses and language courses."[96] The speech did not mention the adult family members who were also impacted by the law. The passage of the Waiting Period Law appeared to affirm the Labor Ministry's position that integration policy was primarily labor market policy and that work permits could be used as a tool to encourage foreigners into responsible labor market behavior.

The Waiting Period Law began as a policy intended to protect the German labor market from foreign family members and only became a law intended to deter "economic refugees" relatively late in the process. The Labor Ministry's long-standing suspicion of husbands and children had turned family members into a specific subcategory of the deceitful "economic migrant." For the Labor Ministry, family members, particularly male family members, were falsely claiming that their migration was motivated by affective ties, while asylum seekers were falsely claiming political persecution. Both groups, in their view, were primarily motivated by the labor market.

This pervasive assumption placed both groups of migrants in an existential dilemma. When they expressed a desire to work legally, the state implied that they were in Germany for the wrong reasons, but legal work was also the only role that policymakers could envision for them. "Integrated" foreign youth would take vocational courses and train themselves for a future job while acting as if the job was not their reason for coming to Germany, and "integrated" foreign spouses would accept that they could never be breadwinners and that they were supposed to access only specific sectors of the labor market. Foreign family members and asylum seekers both needed to "integrate" seamlessly into the labor market while at the same time disavowing their personal interest in doing so, resolving the contradictions of state policy through their individual actions. In the neoliberal Federal Republic, the right to work was a reward for foreigners who expressed a desire to integrate, and integration was defined as a willingness to work.

Non-Working Wives and the Turn Toward Culture

The Labor Ministry pushed for the waiting period and in so doing promoted a narrow definition of "integration" as a form of self-actualization on the labor market. At the same time, other parts of the state increasingly turned their attention to the "cultural" sources of migrant problems. Officials were particularly seduced by the idea that migrant women did not work in West Germany because patriarchs in their own family prevented them from working, not because of state exclusion. Rhetoric about migrant culture allowed the state to disavow any responsibility for the problem it had created and to place the blame for the problem, and thus the responsibility for solving it, squarely on the foreign family.

The federal Ministry for Youth, the Family and Health commissioned a study on the "non-working wives of foreign workers" in 1977 that exemplifies this tendency to blame the foreign family. At the time, two-thirds of the "wives of foreign workers" did in fact work for wages, but sociologist Franz Brandt chose to construct the study as if the remaining one-third posed a unique problem that demanded an explanation. The study proceeded from the hypothesis that the reason one-third of foreign wives did not work could be found in "the general perception of the role of the sexes in the Mediterranean countries."[97]

This hypothesis was questionable. German wives had obtained the right to work outside the home without a husband's consent only in 1976. The Civil Code had previously stated that a wife "had the right to be employed outside the household only insofar as this was consistent with her duties in the marriage and the family."[98] In 1977, just one-third of married German mothers worked outside the home.[99] In other words, despite the additional challenges of obtaining a work permit and finding childcare without having ready access to the extended family, married foreign mothers still worked twice as often as married German mothers.

The researchers chose to focus on the minority of foreign women who did not work, and their research questions sought to reveal the foreign family's deficits rather than its strengths. For the study, Brandt and his research assistants interviewed 100 women, twenty-five each from Italy, Greece, Yugoslavia, and Turkey, to find out what kept them from working. According to the study, over half of the interviewees had to "limit themselves to the role of the housewife against their will," with women explaining that they struggled to find jobs, childcare, and work permits. Roughly one-quarter of the women in the study had arrived in Germany after November 30, 1974, and thus were officially ineligible for work permits, but the state policy of work permit denial was mentioned only once in the entire 209-page study.[100]

The final product obsessively circles around a single unproven idea: foreign women's husbands did not allow them to work. Yet it did not quote a single woman who says that her husband does not allow her to work. The majority of women who are directly quoted state that their husbands wish that they could work. Many even specify that their husbands are angry and upset that they cannot work because it meant that the family was saving money more slowly, which was delaying their return to the home country.[101] Only one of the women quoted says anything about her husband not allowing her to work, and she says that her husband does not allow her to do so because somebody needs to look after their children. One imagines that many of the two-thirds of West German married mothers who did not work could have made similar statements.[102] The researchers did not ask about illegal work, but if they had, they might well have found that some women were in fact opting for illegal work because they were able to more easily combine illegal work and domestic responsibilities, for example, by bringing children to their jobs as cleaners or by sending someone in their place if a child was sick—both strategies that were impossible in more formal working arrangements.[103]

The study drew similar conclusions about foreign women's low participation in language courses. The study cited a single social worker in support of the thesis that husbands do not allow their wives to go to language courses but was unable to produce a single quote from a woman who said anything about her husband in connection with language courses. Every single woman directly quoted stated that the difficulty of finding childcare was the largest barrier to attending language courses.[104] West German women also felt frustrated by their inability to pursue education without readily accessible childcare and had made it a central demand of feminist activism for the previous decade.[105]

Brandt and the other researchers consistently failed to listen to what the women were telling them. In one example, a Turkish woman who had previously worked in a factory said that she did not visit West German advice centers because "the advice that is given there cannot be practiced in everyday life in this society." She explained that she had once visited an advice center where a social worker told her to get her children vaccinated and schedule them regularly for checkups. However, "what comes after putting this into practice? The working mother is let go because of frequent unexcused absences." Brandt described this statement as "a typical rationalization . . . that is to say, an attempt to give a rational reason for behavior whose cause is actually to be found in a psychological disposition perhaps unknown to the women."[106] The woman had offered a clear explanation for her behavior: if she fulfilled what social workers saw as the duties of a "good mother," she would lose her job and potentially no longer be able to provide for her children. Brandt ignored what the woman actually said in order to diagnose her with a psychological problem rooted in her foreign culture.

Brandt concluded that "the non-working wife of the foreign worker can only, as paradoxical as it may sound, emancipate herself with the permission of the husband."[107] Despite the multiple interviews where women had talked about migrating before their husbands, making exceptional efforts to obtain work permits, attending or wanting to attend language courses, and supporting the education of their children, the study argued that "individual efforts at emancipation are hardly visible" and that "these women see the different position of the sexes and recognize its effects, but they do not rebel against it."[108] The women cited in the study repeatedly state that access to legal work permits and to childcare would improve their lives, but the final text does not suggest either opening the labor market to spousal migrants or increasing funding for childcare. Instead, it concludes that "sociopolitical initiatives in the Federal Republic can only have a small chance of success in addressing the specific problems of these women."[109] The study had just once mentioned the policy of refusing to give foreign spouses work permits. It had completely ignored policies that made it difficult to balance motherhood and paid labor—policies that also forced German women out of the paid workforce every single day.

The study's conclusion would have shocked the tens of thousands of women who worked while their husbands could not receive a work permit, those women whose husbands were put in the unnatural position of the "family member."[110] The researchers clearly didn't talk to Kadriye Demir, who had come to West Germany as a guest worker in 1969. Demir wrote to the Labor Ministry in 1978 asking why her husband, who had joined her in 1975, could not have a work permit. "We don't live very well from my small salary. But it's still better than in our home country, where both of us were unemployed. Here in Kahlgrund it is still possible to find a job for us, because the wages are . . . out of the question for many Germans. So why is my husband not allowed to work?"[111] Sezen Aydın would also have objected to the study's conclusion. She wrote to the Labor Ministry in June 1980 explaining that she had lived in Germany for ten years and had recently married a man from Turkey. She wanted to know why her husband had to wait for four years to receive a work permit.[112] The Labor Ministry told her, and other women, that it could make exceptions to the four-year-waiting period for spousal migrants only if the current breadwinner gave up her work permit for good—for example, if she became pregnant and stopped working in order to care for her children.[113] By suggesting pregnancy as a solution, the Labor Ministry reinforced the gender order whereby men were breadwinners and women family members. These women's husbands could work only if the women accepted their natural roles as mothers and "non-working" housewives.

Women who struggled to balance childcare and work would also have objected to the study's conclusions. One Turkish woman interviewed in the 1980s remembered lying about her marital status to secure a spot in a kindergarten for her son. Although her husband also worked in Germany, she had represented herself as single in order to secure childcare and keep her job.[114] Another Turkish woman, a union representative at her factory, told the interviewer that she was always defending working mothers to her employers: "Sometimes when I have to support a foreign woman in a meeting because of her 'frequent absences,' I can't explain her situation correctly. Well, I can explain it, but a German colleague can't understand it. . . . The employer says 'you have three children. Why don't you stay home and take care of your children?' But that is a personal matter for the woman."[115] German expectations about good motherhood, not "Mediterranean" values, restricted these women's access to waged labor.

Because it was the first state-sponsored study to focus on foreign women, the "Analysis of the Situation of Non-Working Wives of Foreign Workers in the FRG" had an outsized impact on the expert knowledge that would be produced in the future. The study argued that foreign women's culture was the key factor keeping them out of the workforce, while ignoring the lack of childcare, the structural sexism of the labor market, and the work permit ban for newly arrived "family migrants." This blinkered focus on culture and exclusion of state policy would be replicated in dozens, perhaps hundreds, of future policy documents and social scientific studies. The Ministry for Youth, Women and the Family cited "Non-Working Wives" in order to push for language about how women were particularly "stuck" in their "Mediterranean values" in future statements about foreigner policy.[116] North Rhine-Westphalia's 1980 report on integration was hailed as progressive because it explicitly acknowledged the unique needs of women. It did so by foregrounding Brandt's argument that "true vocational integration will only be possible for [foreign women], when the social environment, primarily the family, allows a change in the model of the woman's role."[117] The Labor Ministry commissioned a follow-up study on "non-working women" in 1980 that proceeded from the assumption that cultural difference was a stumbling block, posing the question of "to what degree women with children . . . are at all in a condition to accept the model of working despite having children and being imprisoned in their families."[118] The results showed that foreign women were actually far more committed to the "model of working despite having children" than the Labor Ministry had ever been. Two-thirds of the women interviewed for the 1980 study said that they wanted to work full-time, an increase over the Brandt study, where over half of the women wanted to work full-time.[119] Fewer than one in ten women in the 1980 study said that their husband, or in some cases their parents, did not want them to work. Many of those women qualified their statement by mentioning the difficulty of finding childcare, once again suggesting that "my husband does not want me to work" may have been closely linked to this practical problem.[120]

When the fact that two-thirds of foreign women worked despite these obstacles is taken into account, the only possible conclusion is that foreign women were already "emancipating themselves" from the passive role they were prescribed by bureaucratic logic. Why did studies about their families so consistently start from the premise that foreign housewives represented a unique problem? German state officials had insisted for years that the very idea of a female breadwinner violated common sense and had even penalized women who were the first members of their families to work in the FRG. West German men had also been able to prevent their wives from working until the 1976 reform of marriage law. The idea that women belonged in the home was a West German idea just as much as it was a "Mediterranean" idea, and it was an idea that the West German women's movement was actively trying to dismantle while these studies were conducted. Brandt's study on non-working wives and the studies that followed its lead missed the opportunity to connect the situation of foreign women to the situation of West German women. Both groups shared the experience of struggling to combine work and family in the context of a welfare state that assumed that women would stay at home. By 1977, foreign women who did not work were officially understood as the visible sign of a traditional culture that oppressed the undifferentiated "Mediterranean woman."[121] In the process, the fact that most of these women could not legally work was ignored. If a "foreign woman" could only emancipate herself with her husband's permission, the state could no longer be held responsible for solving a problem entirely of its own making. Foreign families were held responsible for solving the problem, and the supposed intractability of their foreign culture proved a convenient alibi for state inaction.

* * *

Even before the 1973 recruitment stop, assumptions about the proper gendered division of labor within the family shaped work permit policy and, with it, migrant strategies for survival. After 1973, as mass unemployment became a durable part of West German life, the right to legally enter the economy became harder to obtain than the right to legally enter the territory.[122] The Labor Ministry redistributed unemployment by making foreigners unemployable and in so doing ensured that the labor market would remain the primary lens for making migration policy.

The excluded family members—along with the excluded "economic refugees" who became an increasing topic of debate in this period—were caught in a double bind: if they expressed a desire to work, they were clearly in Germany for the wrong reason, but once forced out of legal work, they created other kinds of problems for the welfare state and its labor markets. The 1981 Waiting Period Law reincorporated them into the labor market by demanding that foreigners prove their willingness to be employable to earn the right to employment. By framing the "waiting period" as an "integration measure," the SPD used labor market policy to induce foreigners to take more responsibility. Individuals could prove their willingness to "integrate" into German society by taking undesirable jobs.

While the Hartz IV reforms of 2003 have been recognized as an example of a neoliberal turn in German labor market and welfare policy, the center-left SPD had already insisted on the logic of workfare for foreigners a full two decades earlier. In the 1970s, the CDU/CSU had wanted to drop the work permit ban for foreign youth entirely, but the FDP and especially the SPD insisted on linking work permits to proof of integration. The Waiting Period Law was a neoliberal labor policy that sought to "activate" misguided foreigners into better market conformity. Foreigners earned the right to participate in the market by first accepting their responsibility to meet its demands.

The understanding of "integration" as labor market integration was further bolstered by arguments about the intractable culture of foreign families. The work permit ban and later the Waiting Period Law created lengthy absences from the labor market and irregular employment histories for every single member of the foreign family. These biographies were not seen as a product of state policy but instead were blamed on a purportedly backward, potentially unalterable foreign culture. Policymakers fixated on the proverbial foreign patriarch as the domineering figure who prevented his wife from going to work and his daughter from getting an education. This composite character functioned as the scapegoat who allowed the state to avoid facing the consequences of its own policies. The "integration measures" for helping foreigners enter the labor market that developed during the 1980s rarely focused on non-working men— the single largest group affected by the policy of work permit denial, according to the Labor Ministry's own data. Instead, projects of state intervention targeted women and youth as the members of the family who needed support to emancipate themselves from the husbands and fathers who were supposedly holding the rest of their families back with their purported "refusal to integrate."[123] In the early 1980s the Interior Ministry drew on this concept of cultural deficiency as it finally came to agree with the Labor Ministry's position that restrictions on family migration were the best way to preserve the foreign family.

"Foreign Parents Violate the Rights of the Children"

Restricting Child Migration in the Name of Child Welfare

On November 28, 1981, more than 10,000 people marched from Neukölln to Wilmersdorf in West Berlin in the largest demonstrations that had ever been organized to criticize policy toward foreigners in West Germany.[1] Media coverage of the protest marches—twice the size of the largest single demonstration against the child allowance reforms—showed clearly that they were multinational and that they included multiple groups of Turks, Greeks, and Spaniards who were usually more oriented toward homeland politics.[2] At least one group carried a banner stating "We do not want to be the Jews of tomorrow."

The protesters opposed a new administrative decree in West Berlin that limited family migration to dependent children under sixteen, banned children migrating to a single parent, and imposed a new "integration test" for foreign children who were applying for their first adult residence permit on turning eighteen. The Alternative List of West Berlin, a collection of left-wing groups that also functioned as a local affiliate of the new national Green Party, co-sponsored the demonstration and actively encouraged the historical analogy to the Holocaust when it issued a press release titled "Are the Turks the 'Jews' of Tomorrow?"[3] Party members also wore Star of David badges with the words "Turk" and "Foreigner" to the press conference.[4] At least one Jewish member of the Alternative List criticized what he saw as the casual use of the Holocaust analogy, particularly given the party's unwillingness to address ongoing antisemitic behavior within its own ranks.[5] In a context where popular racist jokes frequently linked the fate of Jews to the future fate of Turks, the decision to invoke the same analogy for protest purposes was an early example of migrants engaging with Holocaust memory on their own terms.[6]

Fear of the Family. Lauren Stokes, Oxford University Press. © Oxford University Press 2022.
DOI: 10.1093/oso/9780197558416.003.0006

Figure 5.1 Protesters carry a banner with the slogan "We do not want to be the Jews of tomorrow" at the November 28, 1981, protest against new residency restrictions in West Berlin. Picture alliance/zb/Paul Glaser.

Figure 5.2 Politicians from the Alternative List at a November 28, 1981, press conference against the new residency restrictions in West Berlin. They wear Star of David badges with the words "Foreigner" and "Turk" on them. Picture alliance/zb/Paul Glaser.

The protest occurred during a period of increased interest in the German past and heightened debates over German national identity. After the *Holocaust* miniseries aired on West German television in 1979, it inspired a kind of "history boom" of local interest in grappling with the legacies of National Socialism.[7] At the same time, Chancellor Schmidt and the SPD-controlled Labor Ministry were drafting new policies to reduce the number of migrants in the country. Schmidt lost a vote of confidence in October 1982. His junior coalition partners, the FDP, withdrew their support and transferred it to CDU politician Helmut Kohl. Chancellor Kohl and other conservative politicians explicitly sought to promote a positive national identity and an interpretation of postwar German history as a success story. They did so while continuing their predecessors' policies of encouraging foreigners to leave and discouraging new arrivals.[8]

While Kohl was pursuing projects of national renewal, the newly formed "anti-party," the Green Party—associated with the West Berlin Alternative List—emerged as an electoral force determined to upset politics as usual. The Green Party had begun as a loose coalition of politically diverse environmentalist groups and initially lacked a coherent position on immigration. Some early members even argued that immigration led to the ecological degeneration of Germany.[9] However, the Greens rapidly embraced a non-ethnic conception of German identity, and nationalist environmentalists abandoned the party.[10] By the middle of the 1980s, the national Green Party became the first party in the FRG to consistently advocate the rights of foreigners. The Green Party archives in fact use the subject heading of "immigrant" rather than "migrant" or "foreigner," reflecting the party's long-standing commitment to seeing foreigners as full members of German society rather than temporary and contingent presences.

During this decade, foreign residents were both active participants and implicit objects in an ongoing debate on the nature of German identity. Was German identity inherently linked to blood, as citizenship law continued to suggest, or could it be acquired? If German identity could be acquired, should it be acquired? Cem Özdemir became a German citizen in 1983, at which point he was already an environmental activist and member of the Green Party. In his 1997 memoir reflecting on his parliamentary career, he wrote that many of his activist friends were bewildered that he had had a party to celebrate his new German citizenship. "They thought it was horrible: everybody in the enlightened left-liberal spectrum was ashamed of being German, and this guy is happy about it!"[11] Was German identity too tainted to be worth acquiring, as Özdemir's leftist friends believed, or was it in fact a "normal" national identity that foreigners might actively want to acquire for themselves?

These debates about the nature of German national identity circled around the children of guest workers, a group that included Özdemir, as the federal state began to propose and implement measures to limit the migration of children. These measures built on over a decade of negative portrayals of foreign children. State officials had repeatedly depicted child migration as a form of "welfare migration" driven by access to child allowances and also as a form of deceptive "labor migration."[12] At the same time, a rapidly expanding body of social scientific research on this "second generation" contended that children who migrated to Germany would have a dismal future no matter where they ended up. State officials could and did point to these studies to support their position that new restrictions on child migration were not cruel measures but in fact humanitarian measures to protect children.

While officials proposed new restrictions, the larger context of European integration also meant that these new restrictions could apply to fewer and fewer prospective migrants. By 1981, Italy and Greece were both EEC members whose citizens had the right to move in and out of the FRG freely, while Spain and Portugal were both actively negotiating their accession to the EEC. Some parents used this legal privilege to pursue consciously chosen strategies of cosmopolitan childrearing and to encourage their children to develop hybrid identities. While socialist Yugoslavia remained definitively outside of European institutions, NATO ally Turkey was firmly on the road to membership. In 1963 Turkey and the EEC had signed an Association Agreement promising that the signatories would jointly pursue a number of goals, including freedom of movement for workers. In 1970, Turkey and the EEC signed an additional protocol that designated December 1, 1986, as a deadline by which "freedom of movement for workers between Member States of the Community and Turkey shall be secured by progressive stages."[13] Throughout the 1970s and first half of the 1980s, Turkish families believed that they might also be able to move freely in the near future.

Unfortunately for Turkish citizens in the FRG, West German leaders appeared to have regretted this agreement almost as soon as the recruitment stop went into effect in 1973 and subsequently began to discuss Turkish freedom of movement informally with their counterparts in other EEC countries.[14] Throughout the 1980s, German diplomats worked behind the scenes to make sure that other EEC members would support their interpretation of the Association Agreement—which was that no promise about freedom of movement had been made. West German diplomats prioritized keeping the regulation of "family migration" on the national level and not allowing it to move to the European level. German negotiators worried that their European partners did not take their concerns about family migration seriously and that "because the other member states are less impacted by family migration than we are, they pressure us to be more liberal."[15] As Chancellor Kohl told his party in October 1983, his most important task when it came to foreigners was to stop the Association Agreement from coming into effect "because everything we are doing now will be marginal if the great floodgate opens. We won't be able to free ourselves."[16] Like Schmidt before him, Kohl also feared the foreign family. He and other politicians from his party repeatedly argued that it was necessary to impose new restrictions on child migration so as to exclude Turkish, and to a lesser degree Yugoslavian, children who, they insisted, could not develop hybrid identities and become productive members of society.

The intense focus on Turkish difference was accompanied by a new concern about the role of Islam in Turkish culture. As late as 1977, the year of the "non-working wives" study, it was possible for researchers to write more than 200 pages about oppressive husbands without mentioning Islam once. The study repeatedly identified patriarchal ideas about gender as either "Mediterranean" or "Southern" values. The mainstream media and the German bureaucracy began to pay sustained attention to Islam only after the 1979 Iranian Revolution.[17] Politicians and officials who discussed Turkish families in the 1980s increasingly emphasized the intractability of their patriarchal values as a specifically "Turkish" or "Islamic" problem. As they dropped "Southern" and "Mediterranean" from their vocabulary, they largely ignored having used almost the same arguments about Spanish and Italian families only a few years earlier. German society was increasingly able to imagine integrating Spanish, Italian, Greek, and Portuguese families through a shared "European" identity, while Turkish and Yugoslavian families were increasingly singled out.

Restricting Teenage Migrants

The rights of foreign youth to migrate to the FRG eroded as West German observers began to question whether they were really the "youth" they claimed to be. The border control authorities at Frankfurt airport registered a significant increase in the number of birthdate changes visible on passports in the months after the new visa requirement for Turks was introduced in June 1980. The border police wrote to the federal Interior Ministry asking whether they could refuse to accept birthdate changes that they believed to be fraudulent. Reflecting the structural similarity of these categories in the bureaucratic imagination, the border police reasoned that they were allowed to reject those foreigners who falsely claimed to be tourists but were actually labor migrants, so surely foreign teenagers who could be shown to have lied about being teenagers could also be rejected on the same principle.[18] Their proposed course of action was legally problematic because the changes in question had been verified by Turkish courts, and the Foreign Ministry knew that there was a high potential for a public relations scandal if German authorities began to refuse to recognize Turkish identity documents.[19] In comparison to the FRG, the Turkish state made it fairly easy for people to change their birthdates. Turkish authorities wanted to preserve flexibility because birth registration in rural parts of Turkey was still inconsistent, and many rural children were originally registered long after their births. This policy also accommodated Turkish women who were in plural marriages that

were not officially recognized by the state. These plural wives had officially illegitimate children who could be retrospectively legitimated through birth registration during specific grace periods.[20]

Some Turkish migrants did falsely represent their age to be able to enter the
FRG as dependent family members, and a handful of cases rapidly engendered
an atmosphere of suspicion toward all teenage migrants. State archives make it
extremely difficult to discern how common birthdate changes actually were as
well as how many of these birthdate changes were truly fraudulent. In January
1981, the Labor Ministry issued a report claiming that it had found 908 cases
in which teenage migrants had changed their birthdates, of which it suspected
that 555 were fraudulent. The report included no information about how large
the total sample was.[21] The Labor Ministry was not above presenting statistics in a misleading fashion to get its way. Recall that during the debate about
work permits it had consistently focused on how many migrants *had entered
the country* without ever mentioning how many had left in the same period.
Reporters once again drew on the Labor Ministry's incomplete data as the
basis for stories about Turks using "imaginative tricks" to enter the FRG.[22]
Under public pressure, the Interior Ministry decided in May 1981 that the potential for friction with Turkey was worth it. From then on, if a Turkish court
did not officially inform the FRG about a birthdate change when it occurred,
German officials could reject Turkish documents if they had reason to assume
that the birthdate change had been made to circumvent the upper age limit
on migration.[23] In practice, applications that parents had made for child allowance payments became the most important source for German officials to
cross-check birthdates on passports and thus to uncover the deception of "suspiciously young Turks," tightening the existing link between welfare provision
and policing.

The Interior Minister of Baden-Württemberg established a commission
on "false family reunion" in 1982 which recommended that border control
authorities also be permitted to X-ray the wrists of foreign teenagers to determine
their real age.[24] This may have been another example of FRG officials officially
borrowing a practice from a state with a postcolonial migration regime, as the
British newspaper *The Guardian* had broken a story about the United Kingdom
using wrist X-rays to verify the age of migrants from the Indian subcontinent
in 1979.[25] WDR television journalists who read the Baden-Württemberg proposal aired a program implying that the practice seemed inhumane, and civil society organizations including the Society for Threatened Peoples insinuated that
the practice was reminiscent of Nazi medicine.[26] In a flurry of correspondence
after the TV program aired and the story hit the headlines, West Berlin, always
at the forefront of migration restriction, confessed that it had already begun X-
raying the wrists of teenage migrants. The federal Interior Ministry insisted that

West Berlin abandon the practice, informing it that this was potentially unconstitutional. It was not clear that doubt about the age of a person counted as the kind of fundamental "doubt about the person" that would justify the use of an X-ray.[27] Despite this concern, Germany began once again to use X-rays for age verification in the early 1990s and continues to do so to process claims of asylum seekers.[28]

Forensic age estimation supposedly produces accurate knowledge about minors, but the controversy over the practice is not really about the biological markers of aging. With both family migrants and asylum seekers, the presumption that migrants are not telling the truth about their age is linked to the suspicion that migrants are not telling the truth about their motives. Following the gendered logic of the migration regime, young women did not come under nearly as much suspicion as young men. Officials suspected that teenage boys were not really dependent "family migrants" but were would-be labor migrants taking advantage of the state. Even when the "suspiciously young Turks" did in fact turn out to be biological children, they were increasingly denied the presumption of vulnerability and innocence that the legal category of the "minor" is intended to protect.

Protecting the Children

At the same time that border guards were challenging the age of Turkish children, the Interior Ministry was changing its mind about whether restricting teenage migration would be constitutional. Central to this shift was Gerhart Baum of the FDP, appointed interior minister in 1978. Baum was a trained lawyer and founding member of the Freiburger Circle, a center-left discussion group that sought to expand the FDP's definition of "liberalism" to include broad civil and social rights. Baum initially held firm to the position that family migration was protected by Article 6, Paragraph 1 of the Basic Law, which states "Marriage and the family shall enjoy the special protection of the state."[29] Article 6 also has two additional paragraphs that focus on the relationship between children and parents:

(2) The care and upbringing of children is the natural right of parents and a duty primarily incumbent upon them. The state shall watch over them in the performance of this duty.

(3) Children may be separated from their families against the will of their parents or guardians only pursuant to a law, and only if the parents or guardians fail in their duties or the children are otherwise in danger of serious neglect.[30]

These paragraphs recognize that parental authority is not absolute and that the state may sometimes have a duty to protect children from their parents. Many areas of German family law, including illegitimacy law and custody law, were becoming more concerned with the promotion of "child welfare" during the 1970s.[31] In a 1979 article, Helmut Rittstieg, Professor of Public Law at the University of Hamburg and a leading expert on foreigner law, examined what this new emphasis on "child welfare" might mean for the state's relationship to foreign families. He speculated that German authorities would have the right to intervene if a foreign father wanted to send his daughter, who had grown up here, back to "strict relatives" in the home country.[32] He also suggested that German authorities might want to "consider child welfare more strongly in family migration in the future"—for example, by requiring parents to bring foreign children at an age when they could complete their entire schooling in Germany.[33]

Baum wrote a 1981 article in which he argued that the "child welfare" argument might apply to teenage migrants.[34] It was possible that by allowing sixteen- and seventeen-year-olds to move to the FRG, the state was "supporting not family reunification but the establishment of a new generation of foreign workers under false colors." Because this group of foreign youth were "pre-programmed" for a dismal fate, their migration hurt not just the FRG but also the youth as it "stands in contradiction to the interests of the affected themselves."[35] Baum worried that parental indecision damaged "the children and teenagers, who are overstrained from growing up in two languages and two cultures. The danger exists that an entire generation will become illiterate in two languages and no longer be able to get along in either culture."[36] Finally, Baum signaled that he was open to discussing new restrictions on child migration, specifically to consider "whether and to what extent it is possible within the limits of our liberal order to persuade the parents to make a decision about staying or returning in a timely manner."[37] The article reflected the new thinking about child welfare within German liberal thought. The paternalist state was tasked with overseeing foreign parents and ensuring that those parents were making the most responsible decisions for their children.

An internal Interior Ministry memorandum from November 1981 further develops the legal basis for the "child welfare" argument. The memorandum cited the second paragraph of Article 6 along with the welfare state imperative (Article 28, Paragraph 1) to argue that limiting the migration of sixteen- to eighteen-year-olds might not just be permissible but might actually be a constitutional imperative: "Because the regulation does not just obligate the state to protect marriage and family, but also explicitly child welfare, the state is not barred from taking into account the different developmental and educational levels of foreign children from the perspective of larger or smaller chances for integration when it defines family reunion." If children came to Germany too late, they would have lower chances of integration and thus could be prevented from migrating. It went on to explain that teenagers "choose to move to their parents overwhelmingly not for familial but for economic reasons. The expectations they hold in this respect cannot be fulfilled or can only be fulfilled inadequately.... The family reunion restriction ... is not just oriented to community interests and to the interests of the foreigners who already live here, but also to the interests of the affected group of people themselves."[38] Family migration was intended to protect the family life of a breadwinner father and his dependents but was not intended to protect those dependents' connections to German society. Because teenage migrants were necessarily doomed, the state's responsibility to guarantee child welfare could take precedence over its responsibility to protect marriage and family from state incursion.

Using the Basic Law's guarantee to protect child welfare along with marriage and the family, the Interior Ministry under Baum's leadership moved from a position that restrictions on family reunion were unconstitutional to a position that the constitution required such restrictions.[39] It increasingly saw family migration as a privilege linked to the individual family's "capacity and willingness to integrate."[40] The Interior Ministry's new position shared its logic with the Labor Ministry's justification for work permits as a form of "integration measure." Both policies argued that new restrictions on foreign families were necessary to ensure that those families would make more responsible individual choices. Both substantially shifted the responsibility for the success or failure of "integration" from the state to the family and the individuals within it. With the Labor Ministry and Interior Ministry finally in agreement about the need to restrict family migration, the most important obstacle to new restrictions was the Foreign Ministry, which was concerned about the impact that new restrictions might have on the attempt to get out of the EEC's earlier agreement to grant freedom of movement to Turkish workers by 1986.[41]

Restricting Child Migration to Protect Children from Parents

West Berlin would cut short ongoing discussions about family migration between the Labor and Interior Ministries when it pioneered new restrictions on teenage migration and settlement. Heinrich Lummer, a CDU politician and the West Berlin Senator of the Interior, issued an administrative decree in November 1981 that banned the migration of sixteen- and seventeen-year-olds. It also banned child migration to a single parent, so that children could enter the country only if both of their parents already lived in Germany.[42] The second measure was targeted at teenage boys who supposedly migrated to their single fathers for the sole purpose of accessing the labor market.

West Berlin argued that it was not in violation of the Basic Law because the new regulations did not target "family *reunion* [Familien*zusammenführung*]," a word that it took to mean the entire family coming together in a single move. In this matter, West Berlin was following French practice. Since 1976, France had banned "partial regrouping," a movement in which some family members resettled in France while other members stayed in the country of origin. The French state required the entire family to live in one location.[43] Banning transnational families made migration flows more predictable. Dirk Oncken, West German Ambassador to Turkey since 1979, also supported this policy, arguing that most children still in Turkey already lived in functional extended families and did not necessarily suffer from the absence of their parents. "A potential decrease in the age limit for the migration of children would *not* mean that children remaining in Turkey had to live alone or in defective family relationships. For older children, migrating means that they are giving up a functional family structure for an uncertain future."[44] He did not consider how parents might feel.

West Berlin's press release announcing the new measure also proposed that the Law on Foreigners should be revised to specify that foreigners who were not obviously threats when considered as individuals could be considered threats when considered as part of a larger group. Residence permits were currently granted based on the merits of the "*individual* foreigner" in relationship to "the interests of the FRG," but West Berlin wanted the 1965 Law on Foreigners to be rewritten to state that "the interests of the FRG are also compromised, when the total number of foreigners or the number of foreigners of a specific nationality or a specific social group grows greater than the integrative capacity of the Federal Republic."[45] This proposal extended the logic of the ban on settlement in "overburdened areas" to the initial decision to grant a residence permit. Without using the word "race," it would have introduced a racist logic into the law, as once a group was determined to be a threat to social cohesion, the rights of individual members of that group could be curtailed in the name of not allowing the group to grow. Individuals would be entirely subsumed by their group identity, the passport they carried overriding any other consideration of their individual merits or claims to belonging.

The most controversial part of the "emergency measures" was a new "integration test" for foreign teenagers. West Berlin announced that in the future, foreign children who turned eighteen would have to meet three conditions to have their residence permits renewed: having lived in Germany since they were thirteen, being able to prove that they could speak German, and being in a job or educational program. West Berlin could not deny entry to teenagers from the age of thirteen to sixteen because children under sixteen did not require residence permits under federal law, but the decree back-handedly introduced an "age limit" whereby teenagers could certainly enter after thirteen but would not be able to stay for more than five years before being forced to leave. Those who had entered before age thirteen had to prove that they could speak German and either had a job or were training for a job before their residence permits could be renewed. This "integration test" for continued residence was similar to the logic of using the work permit ban as an "integration measure." If youth could be required to do vocational training in order to receive a work permit, surely they could be required to migrate early, learn German, and do vocational training so as not to be deported on their eighteenth birthday.

West Berlin may have heard about the practice in Gelsenkirchen, a city of over 300,000 people in North Rhine-Westphalia where the mining industry had relied on guest workers in the 1960s. As the mining industry shrank, the Foreigners' Office in Gelsenkirchen began to require migrant teenagers to sign promises that they would leave the country when they turned eighteen. A Turkish teenager in Gelsenkirchen who fought his deportation order in court in the summer of 1980 lost his case. The court recommended that the deportation be carried out because "experts argue that an integration of foreigners of Turkish origin can first be hoped for in the third generation." Unfortunately for the applicant, he was in the "second generation," and the court argued that "the willingness to integrate especially for foreigners of Turkish origin is low, because their large number allows them to live in an environment which allows them to maintain Turkish morals and customs. For this reason, it must also be feared that the applicant's willingness to integrate is endangered."[46] This judge followed the same logic as the West Berlin proposal to write "specific social groups" into the Foreigner Law. Individual rights evaporated as soon as the individual could be identified as part of a larger group. The "third generation" of foreigners might be able to integrate, but the hopeless "second generation" needed to be pruned from the population while possible. Although local courts unanimously upheld the legality of enforcing the deportation contracts that the teenagers had signed under duress, the Interior Minister of North Rhine-Westphalia successfully prevailed on the mayor of Gelsenkirchen to drop the practice and grant the teenagers residence permits so as to avoid bad press.[47]

The Foreigners' Committee of West Berlin staffed an office for documenting and advising youth about the new decree; it encouraged the teenagers who visited them to apply for unrestricted residence permits before turning eighteen.[48] The office found that perhaps a third of the teenagers who applied for unrestricted residence permits were turned down for reasons that did not actually exist in the law on unrestricted residence permits. Language tests proved to be a particular obstacle. Although the Foreigners' Office was supposed to accept a certificate from an adult education center or from one of the certified

"German for foreign workers" classes, many individual officers refused to accept these certificates and imposed their own arbitrary tests.[49] Married teenagers also ran into problems. Many young women who fulfilled all of the supposed preconditions for integration found that they were denied permits because their husbands did not fulfill the same requirements. Women who spoke German fluently and had lived in Germany for nearly their entire lives were denied permits because their husbands had resided there for only three years.[50]

Officials were also very reluctant to grant long-term residence permits to foreign youth. Many who were still in secondary school received residence permits that were in effect only until the end of the school term; one group of teenagers taking a German language course that ended in January 1982 were granted extensions that ranged from just one to three months when they applied in December 1981.[51] Already in 1979, 150 foreign youth in West Berlin had signed a letter protesting the fact that the Foreigners' Offices often refused to issue them long-term residence permits once they reached the age of sixteen. One Turkish teenager who signed the letter had lived in Germany since he was three but had received only a six-month permit when he turned sixteen, and a Greek teenager reported that he could receive a permit for only a month at a time.[52] These short-term residence permits increased insecurity among foreign youth, particularly because they made it very difficult for them to get the jobs that they needed to qualify for another residence permit. No employer wanted to hire somebody who might be gone in a month.

Teenagers mobilized on their own behalf against the new administrative regulations. Only ten days after the decree was announced, *Milliyet* published an article encouraging Turks to take the new decree to court in Germany as a violation of Article 6 of the West German Basic Law.[53] Protest ultimately preempted the need for legal action. Several civil society organizations staged the mass November 1981 protest, and teenagers also organized school boycotts and strikes at schools across the city. The Senator of the Interior issued a second decree on December 12, 1981, exactly one month after the first decree. The second clarified that youth who had come to Germany before November 20, 1981 would not be subject to the new requirement of five years of residence to receive a residence permit on turning eighteen. That particular part of the decree was intended only to change behavior in the future and would not be applied to teenagers who were already in West Berlin. The city weakened the requirement of five years of residence again in July 1982.[54]

Even though the federal state had already been discussing similar measures for nearly a year, when the national Interior Ministry introduced a package of administrative "emergency measures" on December 2, 1981, it claimed that its hand had been forced by the administrative decree in West Berlin and a similar proposal in Baden-Württemberg.[55] The federal December 1981 "emergency

measures" did not include West Berlin's controversial "integration test" for children turning eighteen, but it did include the restriction on migration to single
parents and the age limit of sixteen. The federal "emergency measures" were
no more popular than the West Berlin measures. At the Foreigners' Council
in Gelsenkirchen, every single national representative was appalled by the
new restrictions.[56] Diplomats from both Turkey and Yugoslavia lodged official
complaints. Turkish journalists lamented that the single parent restriction would
likely accelerate the migration of spouses, while Yugoslavian journalists echoed
their earlier criticism of the child allowance reform when it argued that the age
limit of sixteen was just another "Germanization" policy aimed at taking children away.[57]

In response to criticism of the "emergency measures," the federal government reiterated its claim that the German population was demanding the
implementation of new restrictions on migration. The Labor Ministry prepared a speech defending the measures that originally included the statement
discussed in the introduction to this book: "our history means that we cannot
afford a domestic political situation that is marked by open xenophobia and related unrest."[58] Although the term "our history," with the implicit reference to
National Socialism, was omitted from the final draft, it retained a very similar
logic, explaining that restriction was necessary because "it will be easier to defend restrictions on family reunion, than to defend the conditions that would
inevitably arise when the foreign population grows further. Our country cannot
defend internationally a domestic situation that is defined by open xenophobia
and the associated disorder. It is better to act on the motto 'as far as possible, no
more foreigners' than to be forced to act later on the motto 'foreigners out.'"[59]

West German officials feared that their international reputation would suffer
more from popular outbreaks of racist violence than from harsh state migration policies. Civil society groups and liberal academics have tended to invoke
the Nazi past in favor of liberalizing migration policy, but the West German
state has consistently invoked the same past as a reason to restrict migration to
avoid racist violence and to limit access to citizenship to avoid accusations of
Germanization. In the 1950s and 1960s, the FRG's migration regime had been
significantly de-regulated compared to its neighbors, even lacking control over
child migrants. However, as the FRG introduced new restrictions in the 1970s,
its migration regime came to more closely resemble post-colonial migration
regimes in France, which had briefly excluded all family migration, and the UK,
which was in the process of redefining its citizenship law to more effectively exclude non-white Britons. Open xenophobia might indeed provoke embarrassing
comparisons to the Nazi past, but paternalist migration regimes that claimed to
protect people by preventing their movement emerged from a proud "Western
European" liberal tradition.[60]

Although parts of the West Berlin administrative decree were softened in re-sponse to mass protest, the "integration" aspect of the measure, whereby chil-dren turning eighteen had to be in school or have a job as well as be able to speak German, was arguably the first example of a coming trend. After 2000, several European Union states began to impose "integration tests" for permanent resi-dency, with a test introduced by the Netherlands in 2003 frequently considered the first such "integration test."[61] The 1981 West Berlin decree features many of the same provisions directed at teenagers on reaching the age of majority—and not for permanent residency, as in the Dutch test, but for a temporary residence permit. Migrants who had been shielded from state power as children were sub-ject to scrutiny immediately on reaching the age of majority. Even children who had grown up in the FRG and who had no relatives elsewhere had to prove their "integration" through finding a job and proving their language skills to a poten-tially hostile bureaucrat. Models of neoliberal citizenship that exhort individuals to make themselves more responsible were tested on foreign residents decades before those models would be adopted more broadly in welfare reform.

"Second Generation" Research and the Doomed Foreign Child

Politicians who claimed that foreign youth who came to Germany were doomed drew on an expanding body of social scientific literature to support their claims. Social scientific knowledge had become much more important for family policy under the SPD-FDP coalition than it had been under previous CDU governments. Unable to draw on a religious belief that the family was a sacred institution, SPD politicians promoted a "rational family policy" that relied on social scientific data about the family as an institution that socialized the next generation.[62] This turn to "rational family policy" coincided with a broader cul-tural shift whereby an increasing number of West Germans believed that the future of democracy depended on reforming the family as an institution.[63] As West Germans scrutinized their own families for the key to democracy, they also tried to understand the migrant families who lived alongside them. By the end of the decade the state was funding three times as many projects on the "second generation" of migrant workers and their prospects for success in Germany as on either "xenophobia" or "state policy on foreigners."[64] The framing of many of these projects on the "second generation" assumed that the foreign family's failures had to be due to problems rooted within the family. While these research designs reflected a much broader cultural concern with the role of the family, it also led to a blinkered focus on the cultural difference of the foreign family, one that arguably obscured the role of state policy and everyday racism in shaping migrants' experiences.

The 1976 study *The Second Generation: Socialization and Acculturation of Foreign Children in the Federal Republic* became one of the most influential texts in this burgeoning field. The study emerged from the research of three sociologists funded by the Ministry for Science and Research in North Rhine-Westphalia to work in schools in and around Duisburg beginning in 1971. The sociologists used the idea of "stigma management" developed by American sociologist Erving Goffman to theorize that successful adaptation would primarily depend on the individual child's ability to successfully manage his stigma around West Germans. This methodological individualism produced a troubling account of how discrimination worked in the FRG. Defining "stigma" as "biological and cultural inheritance," the authors wrote that for children who came after the age six, their "stigma is manifest," and so their attempts to manage it were destined to fail, forcing them to adopt a social identity as a permanent outsider.[65] For children who came between the ages of one and five, their ability to become German would depend on how well they could manage their inherited stigma. Their "adaptation and deception can go so far that inherited biological characteristics like hair and skin color are retouched (as we know from many Negroes in the United States) and the previously acquired ethnic characteristics (language, attitudes, values, etc.) are denied or kept latent."[66] Foreign children born in Germany might "adapt so far in language and in appearance . . . that their stigma will hardly be recognized. . . . That means however, that situations in which one can still recognize their otherness (i.e. through their name, contact with their family, etc.) will be avoided."[67] Children's prospects for success in managing their stigma could be determined by their age of arrival, followed by their willingness to hide their families from Germans.

The *Second Generation* authors began from the premise that there was no biological racial difference between Germans and foreigners and that foreign children could "become German." At the same time, the authors intuitively understood how racialization worked. They knew that to integrate into German society, foreign children would have to "pass" by changing their names, lightening their skin, hiding their families, and changing the way they were perceived in the world.[68] Children who came before six or who were born in West Germany could become German if they were able to manage their life such that people did not know their names, did not see their foreign families, and thought they were tanned, not dark—perhaps by using skin lightening creams like "many Negroes in the United States." Later in the study, the authors acknowledged that making their origins invisible would be difficult, and many children would struggle to manage their stigma, becoming "children who feel themselves to be German but who are not perceived as German." These children might react in ways "that are not dissimilar to those of the Puerto Ricans and Negroes in Manhattan."[69] Once again, the deliberate choice of analogy was telling because it was not an analogy to an immigrant group defined by citizenship status but to a group of citizens defined by their racialization. Without ever using the word "racism," the authors described race through analogy.

Although the authors did not believe in race, their failure to use "racism" or even "xenophobia" as an analytic category distorted their understanding of the situation. Filtering the social phenomenon of racial discrimination through the theory of "stigma management" led the authors to propose an individual solution to the social problem of race. By the end of *The Second Generation*, the success of integration appeared to depend entirely on the foreign child's ability to "pass" as German. The schema offered by the study located the root of the "problem" in children who came to Germany "too late," and the book's theory that children who came after the age of six would be doomed to life as social outsiders became the social scientific justification for new restrictions on child migration.[70] One of the authors of the original study, Hartmut Griese, would publicly apologize for his role in the study only eight years after its publication. He regretted his previous fifteen years of work, explaining that he had come to understand that the more social scientists used their methodologies to study foreigners, "the more people come to believe that foreigners are the source of their own problems."[71]

Griese was upset that a great deal of "second generation" research continued to locate "the source of their own problems" in the structure of the foreign family while failing to even consider the possible impacts of state policy or of German society. Educational researchers were especially concerned about what they took to be the deficient parenting practices of foreign parents. One study funded by the German Youth Institute explained that foreign parents thought that "good parenting" consisted of "good nourishment and physical care. They do not think about personality development" and did not understand the importance of playing with children.[72] Another German Youth Institute study complained that Turkish parents did not buy enough toys for their children and described the Federal Republic as a place "where a toy industry not only flourishes, but children's play is recognized as promoting children's creativity."[73]

Child psychologist Anneliese Ude-Pestel wrote an entire book describing how she had helped a Turkish child overcome his challenges through play therapy. Ude-Pestel had previously written a classic case study of play therapy about "Betty," and her book about "Ahmet" described similar techniques. Ahmet's parents brought him to West Germany at the age of seven, and his parents initially sought help because their twelve-year-old son was still wetting the bed. Usually Ude-Pestel preferred to work with the entire family, but, in this case, the language barrier made that impossible. In the book, Ahmet's mother is described as a depressed woman who has hurt the entire family through her

selfish decision to leave for the FRG alone and only bring her husband and children later. The therapist blames Ahmet's mother for responding appropriately to
German employers' strong preference for employing women.[74]

The zeal of the educational researchers was the zeal of the recently converted,
as West Germans had only begun to embrace play as a pedagogical technique
during the previous decade.[75] The parents in these studies are often recogniz-
able as stressed working-class parents, and it is likely that many working-class
German parents also struggled to find the time and emotional resources to engage in imaginative play with their children. Foreign families did not reject the
idea of play because of their cultural background. Some had even participated in
protests criticizing the state for failing to create safe spaces for their children to
play and demanding the construction of playgrounds. By insisting that "play" is
a particular German quality, the pedagogical manuals criticize foreign parents by
comparing them to an idealized image of the middle-class German family.

Another way to shift the focus to what was distinctive about foreign families
was to stress the role of Islam, which did not become a prominent part of the
West German understanding of Turkish culture until the 1980s. The same year
as the Iranian Revolution, West Berlin commissioned Christoph Elsas to write
the first state-funded report on the role of Islam in the migration process.[76] In
his report, Elsas singled out gender roles as a particular difference: "It is precisely the expectations of marriage and attitudes about the role of women that
are particularly attached to religious traditions and felt traditions. Adoption of
these norms must be understood as the highest level of assimilation to German
culture."[77] Elsas argued that the family reproduced gender norms, particularly in
Turkish girls, who tended to adopt the values of their parents without criticizing
those values. To prevent this value transmission "it is necessary . . . to watch the
parental household more closely than has previously been anticipated."[78] Any of
these sentences could have fit just as well in texts about "Mediterranean" families
published two years earlier.

One year later, educational researcher Petra Zemlin's German Youth Institute
study on *Upbringing in Turkish Families* underlined Elsas's concern about the
"parental household," arguing that Islam was characterized by "subordina-
tion, obedience, acceptance of authority and the blind devotion, the desire to
integrate into existing structures."[79] Although Zemlin was clear that she was
speaking about working-class and middle-class Turkish families rather than elite
Turkish families, she did not make a distinction between secular and religious
families when she explained that, for Turkish parents, their goals for their children "are oriented closely to the behavior norms prescribed in the Koran," with
the primary goal of "educating the children to obey authority."[80] She concluded
that Turkish parents did not try to "change children's behavior through cogni-
tive processes of understanding . . . which could be regarded as the basis for the

children's ability to control their behavior internally."[81] The behavior of Turkish children was motivated exclusively by their desire to avoid external punishment, which meant that "children are deprived of possibilities to develop independence that are not oriented to the norms of their parents: the possibility of criticizing parental ways of thinking and behaving is shut out from the beginning."[82] Zemlin was not alone. Sociologist Hanns Thomä-Venske's 1981 book about Islam and integration warned that behavioral expectations like keeping Friday as a holy day, praying five times a day, and fasting for Ramadan were incompatible with industrial society.[83] Thomä-Venske quoted an unnamed expert as saying, "These parents want their children to be like sheep, without resistance. They also use Islam to apply pressure, as a regulative factor."[84] Zemlin and Thomä-Venske worried that Islamic education created children ruled by bodily discipline rather than internal motivation, automatons who could not function in industrial society. They both drew on a much older European discourse that stigmatized Islamic religious practices for being rooted in the body rather than the mind.[85]

In the eyes of these authors, foreign parents created obstacles for their children in becoming independent thinkers and democratic citizens. As another 1980 report explained, "The hierarchical and patriarchal structure of authority in many guest worker families makes it difficult for the youth—especially the girls, who are more strongly tied to the family—to develop fundamental political skills of critical and rational self-determination."[86] The research became only more pessimistic over time. The 1976 study on the *Second Generation* had only worried about children who came to Germany after the age of six, but the pedagogical manuals of the early 1980s painted a dismal picture even for foreign children born in Germany.

West German educational researchers also worried that foreign children were in danger of failing to develop a national identity and becoming "artists of adaptation, who feel at home neither in the culture of the homeland nor of the foreign culture."[87] Should children be made to feel German? Even self-consciously anti-racist West Germans sometimes struggled with the idea of liberalizing access to citizenship for children in the context of the Nazi past.[88] The Third Reich interfered with families when it searched for children and populations that could be "made German" during its occupation of Eastern European territory, a policy of forced Germanization that was "widely remembered as one of the Nazi regime's greatest offenses against humanity."[89] Fearful of the "Germanization" accusation, many progressive researchers were overjoyed when children had positive feelings about being Turkish. Ude-Pestel, the play therapist, tells Ahmet that he will solve his problems "as a Turk" early in the treatment.[90] Close to the end of the book, she feels that her project has succeeded when Ahmet draws a Turkish flag and a Turkish man wearing a fez, writing "This picture made me happy. Now

Ahmet could recognize his Turkishness with pride. Did he know now where he belonged?"[91]

Pedagogues were primarily worried about the national identities of Turkish and, to a lesser extent, Yugoslavian children. Parents with EEC passports could send their children back and forth as it suited them, and many did just that. Sociologist Barbara von Breitenbach found in 1982 that Italians felt more capable of leaving bad work situations because they did not fear losing their German work permits if they became unemployed. Italians also exhibited an extremely high rate of circular migration, knowing that they could return to relatives in the FRG if opportunities opened up in the future.[92] When Breitenbach spoke to Italian parents about what they wanted for their children, they did not talk about national identity. They said that the most important thing was identification with the family, because whether they chose to make their lives in Italy, Germany, or both, they would still be able to fall back on the family. She found that Italian parents also put a high value on bilingual education, seeing their children as the "generation of the first Europeans," and often sent their children between Germany and Italy repeatedly to help them acquire both languages.[93] The parents' attitudes were also reflected in the official policy of the Italian state, which embraced a philosophy of multiculturalism and stressed the importance of Italian children abroad seeking to become bilingual.[94] Italian parents recognized that children who could move easily between communities would have the best opportunities to meet future challenges.[95]

Politicians could not stop Italians and other newly "European" parents from shuttling their children between states. However, when parents from outside Europe articulated a similar interest in allowing their children to move back and forth, their own investments in hybrid identities and bilingual education were treated as a problem to be solved. For officials in the FRG, Turkish children could be productive members of society only if they were secure in a single identity— German *or* Turkish, not German *and* Turkish. West German politicians came to understand age limits as helpful tools for forcing non-European parents to make irreversible decisions about their children's future earlier rather than later.

The social scientific works in this period confirm that the way research questions are framed matters profoundly. Research projects that focused on the "second generation" as the problem to be explained located solutions in that population or just as often proposed no solutions at all. Because the state was not funding nearly as much work on "xenophobia" or "state policy" as on the "second generation," the resulting body of social scientific knowledge largely failed to ask questions about how West Germany might change to ensure better outcomes for foreign children. Social science from this period is also remarkably consistent in the way it "write[s] off the first generation as unsalvageable."[96] Social scientists sometimes recognized that their research neglected the parents' generation entirely.[97] Their continued focus on children to the exclusion of parents arguably produced an image of children victimized by shortsighted parents.

Political messages about foreign families, such as *Aktion Gemeinsinn's* 1978 "Foreign Children" campaign, reflected this social scientific knowledge. *Aktion Gemeinsinn* was an organization that developed socially conscious advertising campaigns and then arranged for media outlets to donate ad space to these campaign.[98] When the group first decided to create an advertising campaign about xenophobia in 1977, its members immediately resolved that the campaign should not be overly optimistic: "It should not seem as if a complete solution for the problems can be found. . . . Education in two cultures and languages can never succeed completely satisfactorily."[99] They hoped to provoke sympathy in West Germans but not to ask them to reevaluate multilingualism.

The slogan of the campaign "Foreign Children—Strangers or Friends? It depends on us. Let us approach them" already excludes the parents. The visual material produced to accompany this slogan also excluded the parents. In thirty-nine pages of material, there are no photographs of mothers and children, fathers and children, or adults and children in any configuration. There are only foreign children, standing alone in the world. The written material invariably portrayed children as victims of parents who had initially come to the FRG seeking a better future for their children, as today "ripped from their home soil, not rooted here, their children waste away on the social margins, strangers in the home of their families, strangers here."[100] The campaign included short narratives about children who had been brought to the FRG for short-sighted reasons. In the story of a young girl from Sicily, "the father, who speaks quite intelligible German, tells us at length that other reasons also made it necessary to bring his offspring here—'she was a great burden to my parents'—'there is little opportunity to learn in the village.' It is possible that he still believed in learning in German schools then. The primary reason was definitely the money—and that is quite understandable."[101] The campaign disregarded the father's own reasoning in order to portray him as having made a selfish monetary decision.

In another narrative, Nilgün, a teenage girl from Turkey, wanted to be a hairdresser, "a career aspiration that her father especially approved of, because his daughter would have hardly anything to do with men." Although she was able to pass her practical exam as a hairdresser, she failed her oral exam because of her difficulties with speaking German. She wanted to return home to Istanbul to apprentice with a hairdresser, but her father would not allow her to. The text explained that she had no prospects on the labor market and an equally grim future on the marriage market: "Compared with most of the 350,000 Turkish children who live here, Nilgün's fate is certainly not catastrophic. But the happy girl no longer exists. Her hopes were too great and the disappointment has destroyed her self-esteem. Nilgün would like to get married one day. In Turkey women are

Figure 5.3 Cover of the pamphlet made to accompany the "Foreigners or Friends?" Aktion Gemeinsinn campaign. Pamphlet in author's personal collection.

a year younger when they get married than she will be when she returns there. Her parents work, like almost all parents in Germany, for a better future. But for their children's future?"[102]

The advertising campaign may have provoked sympathy for foreign children, but it did not offer solutions. The poll the organization commissioned from the Allensbach Institute to measure the impact of the campaign showed that between 1978 and 1980, there had been an increase in the number of West German adults who believed that foreign children had serious problems in German schools. But when these same adults were asked if they were willing to help foreign children with their homework for a few hours a week, there was no change.[103] Perhaps the situation of foreign children seemed too hopeless for individual actions to matter.

Social scientists were increasingly coming to a consensus that children were only "capable of integration" if they were young enough when they came to West Germany. Politicians and officials who wanted to restrict migration used

the models of assimilation offered by books like *The Second Generation* to justify their policies. At seven it was simply too late to ever become German, and
children forced to live there despite their status as outsiders would never find a
place in society. Foreign parents who brought their older children to the FRG
despite these dismal prospects were irresponsible. Their choices skirted close to
child abuse.

Restricting Child Migration as Child Protection

After issuing the federal "emergency measures" in December 1981, the Interior
and Labor Ministries continued their discussions about the appropriate next
step. The reduction of the age limit to sixteen, the exclusion on migration to
single parents, and even the new integration test in West Berlin had all been justified with reference to the presumably "economic" motives of teenage migrants,
and all were intensifications of previous policies that had turned labor market
access into a reward for good behavior. These "emergency measures" were also
only administrative decrees rather than laws, which meant that they remained
potentially vulnerable to challenges in court. The Interior Ministry pointed
out that "in the past the courts have more often used Article 6 in a 'foreigner-
friendly' manner. A continuation of this practice cannot be reliably shut out,
as long as family reunification is only restricted through administrative measures."[104] To protect new restrictions on child migration from court meddling, the
state would need to pass a law, but to actually enforce a new age limit, it would
first need to revise the Law on Foreigners to require children under sixteen to
have residence permits.

The SPD-FDP coalition seriously considered revising the law on foreigners
to impose a new age limit. In the first half of 1982, the Interior Ministry drew
up a plan to extend the requirement for residence permits to children.[105] This
proposal was controversial within the coalition. Herta Däubler-Gmelin, an SPD
representative from Tübingen, called the Interior Ministry to express her dis-
like of the idea of extending the residence permit requirement to children "who
cannot be made responsible for the failed decisions of their parents." She preferred a solution that "placed sanctions exclusively on foreign parents, for example by reducing or refusing child allowance payments abroad."[106] In August
1982, Chancellor Helmut Schmidt even wondered whether he could ban family
reunion entirely. He argued that such a measure "would make it clear, that this is
not a question about the family, but about the question of whether a man [*sic*]
wants to stay with his family or live and work in the Federal Republic of Germany
without them."[107] Over two decades after the beginning of foreign recruitment,
Schmidt wanted to turn foreigners back into labor power.

Chancellor Schmidt did not have much longer to ponder what his government would do as in October 1982 he was ousted after a vote of no confidence. Helmut Kohl of the CDU came to power as the head of a new CDU/CSU-FDP coalition cabinet, with Friedrich Zimmermann of the CSU as the new interior minister. Zimmermann assumed the leadership of a ministry that had been under the control of the FDP since 1969. The SPD-FDP coalition under Schmidt had already developed an entire arsenal of liberal arguments for restricting family migration. They had also consistently sought to shield those arguments from public scrutiny, fearing the discussion that would ensue. The CDU/CSU-FDP coalition under Kohl believed that those same arguments would appeal to their voters.[108]

In Kohl's first speech as chancellor, he stated that foreigner policy was the third element of his "emergency program." Kohl explained that his government would focus on "integration," but for the CDU, "integration does not mean loss of identity, but a coexistence of foreigners and Germans that is as tension-free as possible. Integration is only possible, when the number of foreigners living with us does not increase." Kohl argued that one way to accomplish this goal of restricting the number of foreigners would be to "restrict family reunion, especially also in the interest of children, who have a right to their own family."[109] When he cited the specific "interest of children," Kohl was drawing on arguments that had been elaborated by liberal law professors and left-liberal members of the FDP.

To revise foreigner policy, Kohl created a new Federal-State-Municipality commission that began to meet in November 1982. Within the commission, one sub-commission was specifically tasked with devising the best way to restrict family reunion. Over three months of meetings, this sub-commission was unable to come to any consensus about how to best restrict child migration.[110] The final vote on the question of the age limit revealed a wide divergence of views. Bremen voted to reverse the "emergency measures" of the previous year and to restore the age limit for child migration to eighteen years. The Foreign Ministry, Hessen, and Liselotte Funcke—still the Federal Commissioner for the Promotion of Integration among Foreign Workers and Their Family Members—all wanted to keep the status quo of sixteen years old. On the more restrictive side, the Family and Youth Ministry voted to move the age limit to eight years, while the Interior Ministry, the Finance Ministry, Baden-Württemberg, Berlin, and the German Council on Municipalities all voted to move the age limit to six years. The Labor Ministry voted for lowering it to six years with an exception if an older child could prove that he or she knew German. Bavaria and Lower Saxony both abstained, with Bavaria insisting that it needed more data to decide.[111]

Blocked from implementing an age limit, the Kohl government decided to pass the November 1983 "Promotion of Voluntary Return" Law, which offered migrants from outside the EEC a cash bonus if they took their entire family with them and left Germany for good. The remigration law was based on a proposal made by Baden-Württemberg in 1975 and a similar program implemented in France in 1977. According to the return promotion program, migrants who left by September 30, 1984, could receive 10,500 DM for themselves as well as 1,500 DM for each child they took with them on the condition that the entire family would leave together—it was not possible to take the youngest children back to Turkey but leave the older children in Germany. After the first two months of the law failed to produce the desired effect, the state also added an opportunity to receive social security contributions after leaving Germany.[112] Eventually 250,000 individuals left as a result of the Return Promotion Law.

While developing the Return Promotion Law, the Kohl government also continued to use the Labor and Interior Ministries, both under the control of the CDU/CSU, to advocate for a limit of no more than six years of age for a child to enter the FRG. Politicians who advocated an age limit argued that they were protecting children from their parents. In March 1983, Interior Minister Zimmermann complained to Liselotte Funcke that people who opposed the age limit, such as herself, "limit themselves to general remarks about the protection of the family and parental rights without seriously engaging with the counterarguments that must be advanced in the interest of child welfare."[113] He would also argue in a 1983 radio interview that "protection of the family means that the children should come to their parents [in Germany] at the right age, not for the first time when the parents think that they can earn money with their children, which is not even the case. The falsely understood and here falsely applied Basic Law and parental rights lead to criminality and to the opposite of what is humane."[114] The parliamentary secretary of the Interior Ministry, CSU politician Carl-Dieter Spranger, employed similar rhetoric when he insisted that "when parents do not live up to their responsibility for their children, the state must resort to the necessary measures."[115] The CDU Minister for Youth, Family and Health Heiner Geißler explained that for the CDU "it is not just husband and wife, that is, the parents, who belong to the partnership, but also the children. . . . The current family practices of many foreign parents undoubtedly violate the rights of the children. Of course, parents have the right to determine the child's best interests. But we also have certain ideas about what opportunities a child should have and must have. . . . They should not misuse their parental right, by destroying important opportunities for the child and in so doing destroying the child's life."[116] State paternalism was elevated into policy, with CDU/CSU politicians insisting that the state understood the interests of foreign children better than their own parents did.

Each side claimed that it knew what was in the child's best interests. Der Spiegel (a weekly news magazine) published a comic that played up this dimension of the political debate. A woman wearing a headscarf holds up Article 6, Paragraph 1, asserting her constitutional rights, while Friedrich Zimmermann tugs at her child's leg.[117] The title, "Zimmermann's chalk circle," refers to the Bertolt Brecht play *The Caucasian Chalk Circle*. In a pivotal scene, two women are fighting about which one of them is the mother of the child, and a judge decides to place the child in question in the center of a chalk circle. The true mother will be able to pull the child from the circle, but if they both pull, they will tear the child in half and each get half. One of the women refuses to pull because she cannot bear to hurt the child, and the judge declares that she must be the true mother, as she loves the child too much to hurt him. The comic shows the mother refusing to pull her child while Zimmermann pulls the child from her, insisting that he knows the best interest is to be as far away from Germany as possible.

Legal scholars disagreed about whether it was legitimate to interpret Article 6 as requiring an age limit for child migration. The Interior Ministry commissioned three expert opinions on the question in 1983. Josef Isensee, Fritz Ossenbühl, and Helmut Quaritsch all supported the age limit, and all three also believed that it would be legal to impose the age limit without any transition period.[118] Quaritsch, a professor of law at the University of Administrative Sciences in Speyer, wrote a particularly impassioned argument for the age limit, in keeping with his broader legal philosophy in favor of strong state sovereignty, particularly in matters of migration law.[119] His expert opinion on the age limit argued that the state had the right to encroach on "parental rights" when it was manifestly clear that the parents' decisions hurt both their own children and the public interest.[120] He further developed these opinions in a 1984 article in which he made a distinction between affective and economic migration and insisted that most so-called family migration into the FRG was the latter, writing that it was "motivated not by the pain of separation, but by economics.... It is a consciously chosen strategy to prevent 'integration' into the Federal Republic, which the parents fear will lead to 'alienation' of the children."[121] The foreign children who had continued to enter West Germany would "as a general rule become an un-employed subproletariat, susceptible to criminality and revolution." Each new foreign child hurt not just other foreign children, but all children who lived in Germany: "If the potential for achievement of part of the population sinks, the potential for achievement of the entire commonwealth is affected.... Late migration pre-programs the foreign child for a tragic life and burdens the welfare state in an unacceptable fashion."[122] He also argued that the Turkish state opposed an age limit for selfish reasons, betting that children who went to school in Turkey before coming to Germany at the age of ten or fifteen would grow up to be "potential importers of foreign currency" while children who left Turkey before the age of six were less likely to remain emotionally committed to Turkey and therefore less likely to send remittances home.[123] For Quaritsch, the age limit was not just constitutional; it was a moral and humanitarian imperative that would prevent foreigners from ruining their own lives.

While the Interior Ministry chose to solicit expert reports only from legal scholars who agreed with its position, other scholars saw the proposal to create a new age limit for children as an obvious violation of Article 6. Fritz Franz, the judge in West Berlin who had also opposed the settlement ban, described the proposal as "grotesque."[124] Berthold Huber, at the time a legal scholar in Frankfurt, had already criticized the decision to ban sixteen- and seventeen-year-olds as an obviously unconstitutional measure that provoked an unprecedented "level of fear and insecurity" in the foreign population. He suggested that perhaps foreign families who wanted to achieve family reunification in the FRG would do well to adopt a tactic of Soviet dissidents and go on hunger strikes.[125] The Catholic Church split over the age limit in a controversy that the press dubbed the "Catholic Struggle." The Council of German Bishops argued that it was an unacceptable incursion into familial autonomy, while the lay organization—the Central Committee of German Catholics—supported new restrictions on family migration.[126] The Bishop of Cologne was apparently not amused when Interior Minister Zimmerman asked him whether he could still receive communion despite his position on family migration.[127]

Even critics of the age limit tended to agree with the underlying assumption that it would be hard for foreign children to "integrate" into German society. A group of educational researchers based in Neuss and Essen argued that the age limit was unnecessary because it did not offer a "guarantee of integration," since there was a high rate of unemployment even for children who had arrived before the supposedly decisive age of six.[128] Similarly, the German Trade Union Confederation opposed the age limit because "the claim that the children will only have a chance if they are integrated into the educational system here from the beginning is already built on sand, because many children of foreign workers currently have no apprenticeship and no job despite having a German diploma."[129] These critics opposed an inhumane policy while accepting the basic premise that "second generation" children had a gloomy future in Germany.

Debates about the age limit were also debates about the role of national identity in child development. Education is regulated by the federal states in Germany, so foreign governments had to negotiate a separate policy for their own citizens with each one. Throughout the 1960s, the Italian government repeatedly insisted that Italian children be included in compulsory schooling laws to prevent German principals from denying admission to foreign children and Italian parents from keeping their children at home to provide childcare. The state of North Rhine-Westphalia, among others, continued to defend its policy of voluntary attendance, arguing that "to require non-citizens to attend was to deny their right to their ethnonational identity. . . . Requiring non-German students to attend German schools would force them to imbibe 'Germanness' instead of the cultural heritage appropriate to their country of citizenship."[130] When federal states did begin to include foreign children in compulsory schooling laws in the mid- to late-1960s, most foreign children were required to spend additional time in "cultural classes" taught by teachers from the country of their citizenship. This policy supposedly gave foreign children access to their own national identity, but it also offered politicians opposed to migration proof for the idea that foreign children refused to "integrate."[131]

This argument about a child's right to a national identity returned during the age limit debates. One group of educational researchers from Münster wrote to Chancellor Kohl explaining that they opposed the age limit because children who came to the FRG shortly before turning six would experience a disruption to their socialization process that would leave them incapable of developing a stable identity later in life. Children who came later, perhaps after the age of twelve, might well have more problems picking up German, "but their personality is more developed and they feel that they belong to a culture. They will live for some time as foreigners in the Federal Republic and consciously define their role in our society; they will not allow themselves to be Germanized. The entire argument for a reduction in the age limit proceeds from a concept of integration that can only be translated with 'Germanization.'"[132] These pedagogues explicitly invoked the precedent of Nazi policies in Eastern Europe to argue against a policy of enforced "assimilation." They did not embrace a hybrid concept of identity. Instead, they argued that Germany had a historic responsibility to allow parents to raise children in their own national identity, which included encouraging children to complete primary education elsewhere.

Public opinion polling shows that the age limit debate was polarizing. In June 1983, a survey about age limits found that 78 percent of respondents were familiar with the debate. Respondents were subsequently given a sheet with a dialogue about the problem and asked which of the listed positions they identified with, in a tactic that reflected the essentially pedagogical function of opinion polling in the FRG.[133] Of the respondents, 44 percent indicated that they agreed with the age limit because "parents who really want to care for their children should bring them as soon as possible. When the children are over six, they often cannot follow along in school and later they will not find work." Only 35 percent stated that they opposed an age limit and agreed with the statement that "older children also need their parents, and so the family should be able to reunite. When children grow up without parents, big problems will develop." Voters from all political parties except the Greens were slightly in favor of the age limit, and voters for the CDU/CSU and FDP were particularly favorable toward the policy. The author of the report on this poll wrote that while "the position of rejection has always tried to present itself . . . as the more liberal, progressive, and

above all child-friendly position," the results of this opinion poll suggested that
the age limit was in fact better for children.[134] Germans' opinions were taken as a
reasonable guide for the difficult decisions faced by foreign families.

Green Party voters who opposed the age limit aligned with the position that
their party defended at both the local and the national level. After an electoral
breakthrough in Hessen in 1983, the Greens agreed to tolerate a minority SPD
government under Minister President Holger Börner in exchange for a number
of concessions, including the issuing of an administrative circular by the Interior
Ministry that would raise the age limit for family reunion back to eighteen, allow
teenagers to migrate to a single parent, and relax requirements for marriage migration. While foreign families, churches, social work organizations, and some of
the unions reacted positively toward the circular, officials also received dozens of
letters from concerned citizens who claimed that it meant that the "the next president of Hesse will be named Mustafa" or that the SPD wanted "to replace the
German people with a hodgepodge of peoples."[135] Börner himself had previously
argued that an age limit of six was the most "humane" solution. His critics from
the CDU/CSU repeatedly pointed out his own inconsistency on this matter,
seeing his willingness to relinquish his earlier position as a telling example of
the "red-green chaos" in Hesse.[136] The CDU mayors of Wiesbaden, Darmstadt-
Dieburg, and Frankfurt all refused to implement the new circular.[137] Within
the first six months after the circular was issued, a total of ninety-one teenagers
made use of the relaxed requirements, thirty-six of whom were older than sixteen.[138] Despite these relatively small numbers, the federal Interior Ministry sent
a harsh letter asking Hesse to withdraw the circular, arguing the change was unacceptable because "it could lead to migration into other federal states, which
have already shut it out for good reasons. . . . Your circular has struck a path that
cannot be reconciled with the interests of the FRG."[139] The circular remained in
effect until 1987, when the CDU won the Hesse state elections outright and was
able to oust the Greens from power—at which point the CDU quickly returned
Hesse to an age limit of sixteen and to a ban on migration to single parents.[140]

The Age Limit of Six

The Kohl cabinet was ultimately forced to abandon the age limit of six because of considerations of foreign policy rather than because it was considered
unconstitutional or incompatible with German liberalism. Foreign Minister
Hans-Dietrich Genscher of the FDP was specifically concerned about the 1970
Association Agreement with Turkey. He worried that on December 1, 1986,
Turkish citizens might come to West Germany, be denied entry, and then appeal
to the European Court of Justice (ECJ) to uphold the promise of free movement.

If the ECJ chose to uphold the free movement provisions of the Association Agreement, the FRG would lose any possibility of enforcing effective control over the movement of Turkish citizens.

The Foreign Ministry believed that Turkey could be negotiated out of freedom of movement but worried that introducing restrictions on child migration would make those negotiations more difficult. As Genscher explained, "Foreign policy considerations force us to keep the migration regulations for Turks as liberal as it can be justified domestically. . . . We should only give in to domestic pressure when the foreign policy risk of worsening our relationship with Turkey is really worth it."[141] İlter Türkmen, the Turkish foreign minister, had informed the FRG that the imposition of an age limit would be a "bombshell" interpreted as an attempt to separate families.[142] Turkish diplomats would only give up on full freedom of movement in exchange for serious concessions. During one meeting in May 1984, they proposed a set of compensatory measures that included lowering the retirement age for Turkish citizens who worked in Europe to fifty-five to match that in Turkey, getting rid of the visa requirements that had been introduced to curb asylum seekers in June 1980, paying equal child allowances to children who lived in Turkey, repealing the waiting period granting immediate access to the labor market for family members, and expanding the group of people who were eligible for family reunification to include children up to the age of twenty-one and dependent parents of foreign workers.[143]

Within this context, the Foreign Ministry argued that the state should give up on the idea of restricting child migration and move toward restricting marriage migration instead, but the Interior Ministry continued to push for an age limit of six.[144] Genscher raised the stakes in October 1984 by threatening to resign as foreign minister if this age limit was implemented.[145] His threat convinced Kohl to drop the idea. Although Kohl continued to support the age limit in principle, it would not be floated as a possibility again until after EEC institutions defused the threat of free movement.

The dramatic but ultimately fruitless confrontation over the age limit damaged the ability of the FDP-CDU/CSU coalition to compromise or even to discuss migration policy. Liselotte Funcke, federal commissioner for the Promotion of Integration of Foreign Workers and Their Family Members, appears to have lost her ability to intervene in policymaking after her public opposition to the age limit. The Labor Ministry argued that she was overstepping the bounds of her role, that her position against the age limit was not based on reason, and that she was overly "emotional" about the topic when she spoke to the press.[146] She had chosen to display sympathy toward fearful foreign families rather than to adopt the "rational" stance against child migration. After 1984 she was never again invited to a cabinet meeting. By the time she resigned via letter in 1991, she had sent dozens of unanswered letters to Chancellor Kohl, who had repeatedly failed to warn her in advance about any of the policies she was expected to defend to the media and to the public.[147]

Funcke was one of very few women in the Schmidt and then the Kohl cabinet, in which men occupied the overwhelming majority of the top jobs. Her colleagues routinely criticized her for being "emotional," and the hate mail directed toward her office regularly engaged in specifically sexualized and gendered abuse, such as the anonymous letter that threatened to hurt a "whore" who was "syphilitic and horny for Turkish cock."[148] Her colleagues also ridiculed her claims to expertise even though she was the only person in the government who routinely spoke to foreigners.[149] In 1987 she tried to hold a hearing about the Law on Foreigners, but an official from the Interior Ministry warned her that such a hearing would be "provocative" and intimated that his ministry might prevent it from occurring. In response, she limited the topic of the hearing to "Foreign Women and Girls," reasoning that the Interior Ministry had previously accepted her special competence for women's issues.[150] The Interior Ministry responded by advising her to remove any topic that touched on "the legal situation of women." The Labor Ministry went even further, advising her to refrain from discussing both law as it pertained to women and the welfare state as it pertained to women.[151] Once law and the welfare state were removed from the agenda, what would be left to discuss but the women's purportedly deviant culture? The responsible ministries once again sought to erase their own role in exacerbating the problems of foreign women and to obscure their own ability to provide solutions. Although Funcke did hold her hearing about the "Situation of Foreign Women and Girls," she had to substantially limit the agenda to placate the ministries. She knew privately that she primarily fulfilled an "alibi function" for the state.[152] The next significant migration reform of the Kohl cabinet—the 1990 revision of the 1965 Law on Foreigners—would be drafted entirely without her input.

* * *

In Hüseyin Yiğit's 1982 play *What Will Become of Us?*, the Turkish characters are utterly nonplused by the change in political leadership from Helmut Schmidt of the SPD to Helmut Kohl of the CDU/CSU. Asked his opinion of Kohl, one character explains that Kohl certainly doesn't seem to like the Turks very much, but "we've already seen and tested Schmidt. . . . He invented the six-year age limit. He didn't want newly married Turks to bring their wives here."[153] The character was right. The argument that an age limit would allow the German state to protect vulnerable children from uncaring parents was developed by the SPD and the FDP well over a year before Kohl came to power. Many SPD politicians publicly supported the age limit of six before finding themselves in opposition, and the age limit was also a key plank in the 1982 SPD/FDP draft of the Law on Foreigners. It was not the single diabolical plan of Interior Minister and CSU hardliner Friedrich Zimmermann.

Chancellor Kohl ultimately dropped the age limit for tactical reasons of foreign policy rather than as a matter of principle, which means that the logic behind the proposal did not disappear after its initial rejection in 1984. The first draft of the 1990 Law on Foreigners proposed an age limit of six that did not make it into the final draft. The 2002 migration law proposed an age limit of twelve for children of low-skill migrants, and eighteen for children of high-skill migrants. This proposal reflects the long-standing assumption that some children are destined to be cosmopolitan border-crossers while others are destined to be burdens on the welfare state.[154] It was a compromise proposal, as the CDU continued to push for an age limit of six in 2002. The European Union intervened in 2003 when it passed a Directive on Family Reunification, which set a maximum age limit of twelve precisely to prevent the FRG from imposing the lower age limit.[155] Denmark's 2004 response to the EU Directive was to lower its own age limit from eighteen to fifteen. It became the second European state with an age limit for the migration of child dependents that was below the age of majority, joining the FRG on the trail it had blazed in 1981.[156]

The age limit has recurred in policy discussions because it is supported by a powerful set of political emotions. Child migrants produce both fear and the impulse to protect the vulnerable. Age limits respond to both emotions by protecting the German state from children while claiming that it is actually protecting children from their parents. Officials across the political spectrum argued that when the German state allowed family migration for humanitarian reasons, some parents perverted the state's intentions, abusing its generosity not to recreate their family life but to pursue their own economic self-interest. Parents brought children to make money with them rather than to love and care for them. The age limit would force migrants to be better parents, parents who brought children because they intended to give up on their links to the home country and assimilate fully into German life, not because they wanted to maintain a transnational family that exploited opportunities across borders.

Politicians who advocated restrictive policies on child migration also claimed that a respect for the development of children, including the proper development of a national identity, was a particularly German value. When they looked to the Nazi past, they drew the lesson that German identity should not be imposed on others through a policy of forced assimilation. This led to a policy whereby European integration forced the state into a limited acceptance of hybrid identities for some while denying the possibility of German identity to others. The same politicians and officials who advocated restrictions on child

migration also advocated restrictions on marriage migration. Having embraced
state paternalism toward children, they were able to embrace paternalism toward
adult women while claiming that gender equality was a timeless German value,
arguing that new restrictions on marriage migration were in place only to save
women, both German and foreign, from foreign men.

Marriage, Deportation, and the Politics of Vulnerability

In January 1982, a group of social workers from Workers' Welfare (AWO) in North Rhine-Westphalia met to discuss their observation that Turkish women in their region were getting more abortions than had been the norm in the past. Although the written record of the discussion does not establish a baseline, the social workers reported that in the past year 25 percent of the women seeking abortions in Düsseldorf and 16.7 percent of those in Gelsenkirchen had been Turkish citizens. The social workers considered and rejected the idea that women were getting abortions to avoid losing their homes. They did not believe that landlords were systematically evicting large families.[1] The social workers hypothesized that the increasing number of abortions showed that Turkish women were undergoing an "adjustment to the different sociocultural conditions of the Federal Republic."[2] Said "adjustment" was apparently an exclusively female affair, as the social workers also assumed that Turkish men did not allow their wives to use contraception, forcing women who wanted smaller families to seek abortions.[3]

This conversation happened during the same month that a group of university students in Bonn found a disturbing flyer in a phone booth and brought it to their student government. The "Heidelberg Manifesto," as it would come to be known, was signed by over a dozen right-wing professors and retired government officials, including Theodor Oberländer, a former National Socialist turned CDU member who had previously served as Minister for Displaced Persons, Refugees, and War Victims under Adenauer. After the student government of the University of Bonn condemned the text, the *Frankfurter Rundschau* published it for a broader audience in March 1982.[4] The "Manifesto" begins, "We are observing a development with great concern. . . . [I]n 1989 alone, the number of registered foreigners rose by 309,000; 194,000 of those were Turks. The situation has been exacerbated by the fact that little more than half of the

Fear of the Family. Lauren Stokes, Oxford University Press. © Oxford University Press 2022.
DOI: 10.1093/oso/9780197558416.003.0007

necessary amount of children are being born in order to maintain zero growth of the German population in West Germany. A renewal of the procreative function of the German family is urgently needed." Because "only active and viable German families can preserve our people for the future," the authors of the "Manifesto" suggest "reuniting guest workers with their families in the ancestral homeland."[5] Fertile foreigners, in their view, needed to be removed in order for Germans to reproduce the "people."

The social workers and the professors had dramatically different politics and undeniably different goals, but both understood foreign fertility rates as a matter of broad social concern. For the social workers, a rise in the abortion rate meant that Turkish women were beginning to show evidence of "integration." For the xenophobic professors, the fact that Turkish women were continuing to have children demanded intervention in the form of mass deportation. The Interior Ministry drew from the same biopolitical assumptions when it insisted one year later, in 1983, that "the solution of the marriage problem is even more important for the future than child migration, because through marriage the family reunification problem continually renews itself."[6] While the bureaucrats rarely spoke as bluntly as either the social workers or the racist professors, all of the actors shared the assumption that the reproductive potential of the Turkish family demanded a kind of regulation.

This chapter examines how the state decided on restrictions on marriage migration before showing how individual married couples navigated these restrictions, particularly the threat of deportation. The net effect of both the policies themselves and the response to them was to accentuate the perceived difference of the foreign family through a paternalistic gender politics of protection. Policies on spousal migration encouraged activists to use a language of vulnerability as they claimed state protection from harm. Families frequently invoked the existence of gender violence within the foreign family to make claims on the state, so that struggles over deportation significantly drove the "turn to gender" as a marker of irreconcilable cultural difference.[7] Activists found themselves arguing that the state could not deport women to Turkey because they would be abused there. Politicians who wanted to restrict migration and deport migrants were attracted to these images of gendered oppression and to the idea that the foreign family was necessarily an oppressive institution. Why should migration policy bring these patriarchal families together? Wouldn't it be better to exclude the foreign family entirely?[8] The state's embrace of a gendered language of protection accentuated the difference of the foreign family and made its expulsion more thinkable.

This paternalistic gender politics encountered a challenge from binational couples, who had a different set of challenges from those confronting foreign couples. Either member of a foreign couple could be deported—for example, if they were to violate the provision of the Law on Foreigners that prohibited political activity by foreigners. Binational couples were safer because at least one member could not be deported. Women married to foreign men organized in favor of their rights in the Association of Women Married to Foreigners (IAF), a political organization founded in 1972 in response to the attempted deportation of several dozen Palestinian and Middle Eastern men married to German women. The group's founding document stated clearly that "Germany is an immigration country" and developed an explicitly anti-racist and feminist critique of migration policy.

The state received this critique in a one-sided fashion. While state officials were willing to listen to the IAF's arguments about how migration law could better protect German women, they were willing to listen only to arguments that did not challenge the Federal Republic's even more fundamental self-conception as an ethnically and racially homogeneous country. The IAF won several important victories for binational couples, but their consistently one-sided reception by state actors meant that, by the end of the 1980s, officials who called for a reform of migration law described reform not as a way to strengthen the legal rights of migrants but as a way to save women—both foreign and German—from the threat of foreign men.

Marriage Migration and the Problem of "Continual Renewal"

State officials who had argued that age limit policies could protect foreign children from their parents also advocated limits on spousal migration to protect the existing foreign population from its own increase. The SPD-controlled Labor Ministry had proposed in 1981 that the children of the initial generation of foreign migrants, the so-called second generation, should not be able to bring foreign spouses into the Federal Republic. According to the Labor Ministry, family migration was a privilege linked to the labor recruitment contract. Subsequent generations had no such contract, and therefore no independent claims to reproductive space in the FRG. Banning marriage migration "would limit family reunion for once and all and put the end of the integration problems resulting from migration in sight. The obligations that the FRG assumed in the course of the recruitment of foreign workers cannot apply to children and their children's children. Inheritance of claims is ruled out."[9] The Labor Ministry continued to understand labor recruitment as a mistake that could be undone.

The Foreign Ministry, headed by Hans-Dietrich Genscher of the FDP, and the Justice Ministry, headed by Jürgen Schmude of the SPD, both objected to the Labor Ministry's proposal for a complete ban on spousal migration for the second generation. The Foreign Ministry warned that it was almost certain to violate the Helsinki Accords that promised that the FRG would facilitate family reunification, while the Justice Ministry expected the ban to be struck down in the Federal Constitutional Court as a violation of Article 6. The Interior Ministry, headed by Gerhart Baum of the FDP, suggested a compromise whereby "second generation" foreigners from outside of Europe would have to have lived in the FRG for eight years and been married for a full three years in order to sponsor spouses. The Labor Ministry agreed, reasoning that foreigners who had already lived in the FRG for eight years would already be less likely to marry people from their country of origin. Furthermore, because foreign spouses had to be married for three years before coming to the FRG, and then wait another four years to take up work, there would be seven years between marriage and possible employment in West Germany. The Labor Ministry believed that this gap would prevent migrants from using marriage as a way to enter the labor market.[10] This compromise created an ironic congruence between foreigner law and domestic marriage law. For West Germans, a marriage was considered irrevocably broken after the partners lived separately for three years, but for foreigners, a three-year enforced separation was proposed as a prerequisite before the spouse outside the FRG could join the husband or wife in Germany.[11]

West Berlin's November 1981 "emergency measures" short-circuited this ongoing discussion about marriage migration. The "emergency" circular ruled that a foreigner who wanted to sponsor a spouse for migration had to have lived in Germany for eight years and be married for one full year. Just as with child migration, the federal government followed West Berlin's lead, issuing identical restrictions on spousal migration a few weeks after the "emergency measures." Bavaria and Baden-Württemberg were both displeased by the federal government's decision to follow West Berlin's lead, and both issued additional circulars that required not only eight years of residence in Germany but also three full years of marriage, in line with what the Labor Ministry and Interior Ministry had already found themselves agreeing on before copying the West Berlin position in December. If West Berlin had not set a lower requirement, it is likely that the three-year marriage requirement would have been national and not merely a requirement of the conservative southern states.

The Federal-State-Municipality commission on foreigner policy that had failed to come to consensus about the best way to restrict child migration in 1982 was also charged with creating a plan to restrict marriage migration, which proved even more divisive. In the final report, issued in February 1983, eleven commission members had been unable to come to consensus and had remained split between six solutions. Most representatives were able to agree that Article 6 of the Basic Law did not apply to marriage migration, as "purely foreign marriages" could always achieve family unity elsewhere.[12] They reached no consensus about when foreigners should first be able to sponsor spouses for migration. The Foreign Ministry, Bremen, and Hesse voted to keep the status quo of one year of marriage, while West Berlin wanted to liberalize citizenship law and then stipulate that only citizens could sponsor spouses for migration.[13]

The Interior Ministry and the Associations of Local Authorities both voted to impose a yearly quota of spousal migration following a model borrowed from the United States. The United States allowed family reunification for foreigners, but had specific per-country limits each year, leading to long backlogs for countries with high demand such as Mexico and the Philippines.[14] According to the German Embassy in Washington, DC, the US quota system ensured "that the ethnic composition of the entire population does not change too much through disproportionately large migration of specific ethnic groups."[15] The Association of Local Authorities also praised the quota system for creating a predictable burden on the welfare state. However, the Foreign Ministry was concerned that a quota system would lead to bad publicity abroad, while several participants were concerned about the bureaucracy needed to administer such a system.[16]

Two members of the commission wanted to require spouses to learn German in order to come to Germany. Bavaria voted for three years of marriage and proven skills in the German language. Liselotte Funcke voted for a minimum of nineteen years of age and proven skills in the German language. She suggested a model whereby spouses would have to reach a certain level of language proficiency before coming to Germany and then another level when they applied for the first extension of their residence permit. She acknowledged that her proposal might create problems if women failed to learn the language but then became pregnant, as it would be awkward to deport pregnant women. Nobody else supported this policy proposal at the time, possibly seeing it as a drain of administrative resources, but Funcke's proposal proved to be prescient. The FRG introduced language requirements for spousal migrants in 2007, arguing that requirements ensured better integration and helped to prevent forced marriages.[17]

Finally, Baden-Württemberg joined the Family Ministry, the Finance Ministry, and the Labor Ministry in voting for a complete ban on spousal migration.[18] These representatives argued that any spousal migration hurt the cause of integration and that they were protecting the interests of foreigners by banning them from entering the FRG. They drew a direct correlation between the number of foreigners and the number of social problems. The Interior Ministry of Baden-Württemberg had calculated that 900,000 foreign children would reach a marriageable age over the next sixteen years. If only one-third of them chose foreign spouses, 300,000 new foreign spouses would migrate to Germany, which would create "a problem of integration that would hardly be solvable, because the spouses would usually come to the Federal Republic at an age at which they could hardly still be integrated here."[19] The Labor Ministry further warned that these couples would also have a new generation of foreign children, and that "the German population's consent . . . would be completely lost in these conditions. The social peace in the FRG would no longer be sustainable."[20] The Labor Ministry feared both the reproduction of the foreign family and the domestic reaction to said reproduction.

Officials who favored restrictions on spousal migration frequently argued that restriction would specifically protect vulnerable women. The representative from the Interior Ministry of Baden-Württemberg argued that if spousal migration continued to be allowed after three years of marriage, as was currently the case in Baden-Württemberg, the home country might respond by marrying women off at fourteen so that they could join their husbands when they were seventeen. Only a complete ban on spousal migration could protect "very young Turkish girls."[21] The federal Interior Ministry worried that any new restrictive measure would need a transitional period before it could go into effect. Because there were currently more Turkish men than women living in West Germany, it anticipated that the Turkish community might take advantage of a transitional period for "bringing in underage women in view of their demographic constraints on marriage possibilities."[22] The Interior Ministry also approved of a solution whereby only German citizens could sponsor spouses for migration, reasoning that it would "limit or exclude the possibility of misuse of marriage migration, where girls who grew up in Germany are 'sold' by their parents to a young foreigner, who will access the German labor market through marriage."[23] Arguments for restriction suggested that allowing spousal migration opened the door to sex trafficking.

The Federal-State-Municipality Commission never discussed the possibility of setting different legal standards for the spousal migration of men and women. This stands in stark distinction to the United Kingdom, which initially only imposed new restrictions on spousal migration for foreign women who were trying to sponsor husbands, while not restricting foreign men who were trying to sponsor wives. The UK justified this policy by arguing that men would have a greater impact on the domestic labor market and thus that their admission was a more serious matter. Male migrants were defined by their resource effects in the public sphere, while female migrants were expected to remain in the private sphere of the family. In May 1985, the European Court of Human Rights ruled that this practice violated principles of gender equality. The British government's response was not to liberalize practice for foreign husbands but to extend the existing restrictions on husbands to foreign wives, such that "by the end of the 1980s, Britain had probably the most restrictive immigration control system in Western Europe."[24] West German officials never took a gendered approach to spousal migration for foreign couples, perhaps because the German domestic courts had already ruled against explicit gender discrimination in other forms of legislation and administrative circulars. By ruling against explicit gender discrimination in granting work permits, domestic courts may have made federal officials wary of introducing explicit gender discrimination elsewhere within the law.

The Federal-State-Municipality Commission presented its final report in February 1983, but the lack of consensus on a new regulation for spousal migration left the December 1981 "emergency measures" in force. Foreigners who wanted to sponsor a foreign spouse for migration were required to be eighteen, to have lived in the FRG for eight years, and to have been married for at least one year before being able to sponsor their spouse. Bavaria and Baden-Württemberg had both already issued additional circulars specifying three years of marriage, and their circulars remained in force after the commission's report. State officials hoped that putting obstacles in the path of spousal migrants would have a disciplinary function as it would inspire young couples to first consider whether they really wanted to spend their married life in Germany.

Spousal Migration, Deportation, and the Politics of Vulnerability

Foreign spouses were actively finding ways to achieve their migration plans rather than waiting for decrees from the federal government. Their success depended on their ability to deploy the state's discourse of paternalism on their own behalf. Many foreign spouses came to visit their partners on tourist visas and then applied for a residence permit after arriving. In one case in Baden-Württemberg, a Turkish citizen man who had lived in the FRG for ten years and who owned his own guesthouse married a Turkish citizen woman in October 1981. His new wife received a tourist visa valid for three days. Upon arrival she announced her intention not to leave and called on Article 6 of the Basic Law. The Foreigners' Office responded that she had entered the country with fraudulent intent and attempted to deport her. The courts agreed with the Foreigners' Office and upheld the deportation order.[25]

State attempts to deport pregnant women reliably drew public attention. In Hanover, a Turkish citizen man married a Turkish citizen woman in 1983. The man had lived in Germany for only three years instead of the required eight. The local Foreigners' Office rejected his wife's application for a residence permit but agreed to postpone her deportation because she was pregnant when she arrived on a tourist visa. They resumed deportation proceedings two weeks after the child's birth. The churches, the women's organization of the SPD, and the Green Party all protested the decision, but a spokesman from the Interior Ministry of Lower Saxony held firm. He reprimanded his critics for seeking "to criticize foreigner policy by tugging on the heart strings." He argued that if his office allowed any exceptions at all, they would incentivize Turkish women to become pregnant as a way to stay in the country.[26]

Loose coalitions of civil society actors frequently mobilized around deportation cases. The Foreigners' Committee of West Berlin first emerged out of a campaign to stop the deportation of a wife. The Nürnberg Foreigners' Council called a meeting in response to the city's attempt to deport the wife of a Turkish man who had lived in the city for fourteen years and who had "mastered the Nürnberg dialect better than some of the Germans who move here." Over thirty families came to the meeting to create the "Bavarian Working Group Against Family Separation," which organized a three-day protest in September 1985, followed by a hunger strike in December.[27] In January 1986, the group successfully prevented the deportation of a pregnant Turkish woman by storming the runway of the Nürnberg airport.[28] The organization Terre des Femmes (Women's Earth) also frequently paid legal costs for appeals in cases involving pregnant women and young mothers, such as a twenty-one-year-old scheduled to be deported only two weeks after giving birth to her daughter.[29] Women subject to deportation could also argue from their roles as caretakers for adults. In one case that was given much media coverage, the Turkish wife of a double amputee was threatened with deportation because she had come to North Rhine-Westphalia before the couple had been married for a full year. Several of the stories about the case printed a full-body photograph of the disabled husband, underscoring the degree to which activists felt that they had to make their arguments from vulnerability.[30]

Women could also sponsor men for spousal migration, making the foreign husband the dependent "family member" with insecure residency status. In these cases, the Bavarian Working Group Against Family Separation explicitly advised women to invoke their own vulnerability to prevent the deportation of their husbands. They suggested that if a pregnant woman had a secure residency status and her husband was threatened with deportation, she should get a doctor to swear that she was in danger of losing her child if her husband had to leave her while she was expecting. In their experience, local Foreigners' Offices would often allow the husband to stay at least through the birth of the child, although they would routinely resume deportation proceedings shortly after the child was born.[31]

The "pregnancy exception" did not function because pregnant women were seen as subjects with independent rights but because their temporary status impelled state protection. When women lost their vulnerability, they also lost their protection from deportation. In one particularly horrifying case, authorities in North Rhine-Westphalia decided to tolerate the residence of a pregnant woman who had come to visit her husband before they had been married for a full year. Tragically, the couple's child died one day after being born. Even though at this point the marriage had in fact existed for a full year, and the woman's husband had already lived in Germany for fifteen years, the local Foreigners' Office resumed deportation proceedings on the grounds that the woman had overstayed her original visa. Once she was no longer pregnant and no longer had an infant to care for, there were no vulnerable family members to justify the exception to the deportation order.[32] A couple's grief at losing a child was evidently deemed insufficient.

Bureaucrats preferred to use the "pregnancy exception" informally and many opposed attempts to formalize such an exception within the law. This attitude reinforced state paternalism because, so long as the exception remained informal, a Foreigners' Office that decided to make an exception to a deportation order could boast about its own benevolence and generosity. Barbara John, the West Berlin Commissioner for Foreigners, met opposition when she tried to create a formal pregnancy exception in her city after a string of high-profile deportations of pregnant women.[33] Senator of the Interior Heinrich Lummer countered with the suggestion not to issue any visas to foreign couples in the first year after marriage, because "the foreign wife almost always becomes pregnant during the visit."[34] John and Lummer came to an agreement in August 1985 whereby men and women would both be able to stay when a woman was "late" in her pregnancy. Deportation proceedings would resume immediately after the birth of a child for deportable husbands and fathers, and two months after the birth of a child for deportable wives and mothers.[35] The definition of "late" was further contested, with John arguing that the city should not deport women past the fifth month of pregnancy, and Lummer arguing that the city should be able to deport women through the seventh month of pregnancy.[36] Women continued to have difficulties using even this narrow exception. Turkish women applying for visas to visit their spouses found that the German consulates in Turkey frequently demanded either monetary "deposits" to be left in Turkey or a doctor's note stating that they were not and could not become pregnant.[37] The West Berlin Foreigners' Office sometimes demanded that women bring a "deposit" of 2,000 to 5,000 DM that could be recovered only after the woman left Germany.[38]

Other authorities objected to West Berlin's decision to formalize the "pregnancy exception." The German Consul in Istanbul complained that "the Berlin hardship regulation proceeds from the false assumption that every Turk of the 'second generation' will stay in Germany . . . and sooner or later bring his spouse into the Federal Republic."[39] The federal Interior Ministry argued that creating an exception for pregnant women was unreasonable because it was in fact not an exceptional situation for a young marriage to produce a child; in fact, most young marriages produced children. Creating an exception for an everyday occurrence "would mean giving up the regulations on marriage migration upon which the federal government and the federal states agreed in 1981 and 1982."[40] The federal Interior Ministry wrote to the Interior Ministries of the federal states looking for support for its opposition to West Berlin's new policy. It turned out that most of the federal states had an unwritten policy of either not deporting pregnant women or of not deporting pregnant women who had a doctor's note stating that the woman could not travel. West Berlin was different only in having formalized the exception and thus had given up some of its own sovereign power by letting migrants know how they would be treated in advance.[41] Despite the unanimous agreement that the state should not make a habit of deporting pregnant women, the interior minister insisted that adopting a formal "pregnancy exception" on the national level was "out of the question."[42] Formal pregnancy exceptions allowed migrants to make plans. They took sovereign power away from the state. The Interior Ministry wrote to the Foreign Ministry asking that consulates abroad not ask local authorities for guidance but rather seek assistance from the federal Interior Ministry. He was furious to find out that so many of his colleagues were willing to place control over family migration "in the scheduling of foreigners."[43] By seeking to retain the informal exception, he sought to retain a state paternalism, with the state as the ultimate arbiter of family unity.

By the end of the decade, Berlin, Hesse, and North Rhine-Westphalia had all formalized the "pregnancy exception" despite continued opposition from the federal Interior Ministry. Barbara John, the West Berlin Commissioner for Foreigners who had first proposed a formal "pregnancy exception," was frustrated with the results. She had wanted the exception to be a "way out of the administrative anti-integration farce," but recognized that it had created another kind of farce: a "population policy . . . [that] functions according to the motto: residence permit for birth certificate."[44] By allowing young couples to stay together only if there was a child on the way, the "pregnancy exception" forced couples to reproduce the stereotypically fertile foreign family. The "pregnancy exception" did not mean that the state valued foreign families. In West Berlin, a young mother became deportable once again when her child turned two months old. Officials allowed for the informal exception because it enabled the state to appear to generously extend its compassion to pregnant women who "tugged on the heart strings" while denying families predictability and autonomy.

The Constitutional Court Weighs In

Migrants once again brought cases to court, and in 1987 the Federal Constitutional Court ruled on a group of three cases that challenged the eight-year residence requirements for spousal migration, one from Schleswig-Holstein and two from Baden-Württemberg. The two latter cases also challenged the additional three-year marriage requirement that had been in effect in Baden-Württemberg and Bavaria since 1981. During its deliberation period, the Court wrote to the federal Interior Ministry to ask for more detail about the reasoning behind the marriage restrictions. The Interior Ministry replied that the restrictions were intended to "win back some influence on the development of family migration, in order not to be relegated to leaving it up to the individual life decisions of the foreigners."[45] The Interior Ministry expressed its paternalism wherein it wanted to deny foreigners the ability to make their own decisions.

The Federal Constitutional Court ultimately ruled that Article 6 did not establish "a fundamental right" for spousal migration, but that it did require officials to "pay regard to the existing marital and familial ties . . . in a manner corresponding to the great weight that the Basic Law unequivocally assigns to the protection of marriage and the family." The court went on to explain that in its judgment, the eight-year residence period was reasonable, but the three-year marriage period was not.[46] According to the court, the longer residence period worked to ensure that the person who was bringing a spouse had a minimum level of integration into German society, which was good for everyone involved, including any children they had. However, the three-year period of marriage was primarily intended to prevent "visa marriages" and was excessive for this purpose, as the existing four-year ban on work permits for spouses should already have been sufficient to prevent such "visa marriages." The court explained that the three-year requirement was particularly troubling because it posed "a threat to a young marriage in that young married couples are often not in a position to assess the consequences of a lengthy separation" and because "it can occasion young couples to marry too early to avoid a separation of more than three years."[47] The court's decision showed that the language of family protection was somewhat effective but still not as expansive as many activists had hoped for.[48] The court upheld the fundamental logic of state paternalism when it decided to protect young couples from marrying "too early" so as to meet the three-year requirement but did not trust them to make decisions before spending eight years in the FRG.

The Enforced Vulnerability of the Dependent

Even after waiting for a year to be able to join their spouses in the FRG, spousal migrants faced additional obstacles to establishing themselves in the new country. Spousal migrants did not become eligible for their own independent residence permits until they had been in the FRG for five years. Until then, their residence would be linked to their spousal sponsor, which meant that if their sponsor's residence permit were revoked their residence permit would be too. If the sponsor committed a deportable crime, the dependent spouse would also be subject to deportation, and if the sponsor passed away, the dependent spouse would have to leave the FRG. The fact that spousal migrants could not work for the first four years further reinforced their dependency on their sponsor, not just for residency but also for a legal income.

This situation created difficult choices for dependent spouses in abusive relationships, because leaving would place their own residence and that of their children in jeopardy. The first autonomous women's shelter in West Germany was founded in West Berlin in November 1976. Five years later, the workers at the shelter reported that 18 percent of the women living at the shelter were not German citizens.[49] The second women's shelter in West Berlin opened in 1979, and in 1984 workers at that shelter reported that roughly one-third of the women in the shelter were Turkish citizens. In the previous year alone, six women at the shelter had found their right to reside in the FRG threatened because they had left their husbands.[50] Sometimes the wife was sponsoring the residence of an abusive husband. "Fatima" had been the first member of her family in the FRG. After she was able to sponsor her husband, he abused her during the period when he was fully dependent on her income and her residence permit. Once he found work, his abuse only increased.[51] He had manipulated her into tolerating abuse in part by making her feel that she would be at fault if she left the family and jeopardized his residency status. She was not the only woman in such a situation.[52]

Women who left abusive spouses without having a residence permit of their own found themselves forced to appeal to the state to be able to remain in Germany. One such woman, "Yaprak," had worked at Siemens in West Berlin from 1971 to 1974 before deciding to leave her job after the birth of her fourth child.[53] When the family returned to Turkey in 1977 on vacation, Yaprak's husband confiscated her passport and the children's passports so that they would be unable to travel. He returned to West Berlin alone and then sent for the family in 1981, at which time he also began to beat their daughters. One of the daughters was beaten so badly that she was unable to go to school, and the two younger children both began bedwetting. Yaprak's husband had also returned to Turkey to pay a woman to pretend to be his wife so that he could file for divorce without Yaprak's knowledge. In 1982, the Foreigners' Office of West Berlin informed Yaprak that she had to leave Germany because she was no longer married and her and her children's residence had been based on the marriage. Although Yaprak and the children had previously lived in Germany from 1971 to 1977, their absence for the next four years meant that they lost any legal claim to an independent right of residence.

Yaprak wrote a letter to the authorities in which she argued both that she had a right to live in the FRG because of her previous work history and that her continued residence in the FRG would protect her children and herself from violence. She stressed her initial period of work at Siemens and her children's previous period of residence and education, explaining that her children had first begun schooling in West Berlin and that it had been "hard for them to adapt to Turkey. They had hardly adapted when they were brought back to Berlin.... Who has the right to destroy the small world of these small children? Why do the German officials help an irresponsible father, because not he, but we must be deported?" She further emphasized that Turkey would be dangerous for her "because in Turkey a divorced woman is seen as an easy woman. In many places attempts are made to take advantage of the woman." She pleaded that "it would be irresponsible of me, to bring my children to Turkey, where they would be branded as children of a divorced mother. But without my children I cannot and I do not want to keep living. Please help me!"[54] In this first petition Yaprak pointed to her previous work and residence in the FRG as well as her children's preference for German schools, but both of these arguments would gradually disappear from later correspondence about her case.

As Yaprak and her allies continued to press her case, they focused almost exclusively on the argument that she was vulnerable and that a grim future awaited her and her children in Turkey. The Alternative List, a left-wing party unique to West Berlin, advocated for Yaprak along with two other women who had left their husbands. In one of these cases, "Pelin," a Kurdish woman, had discovered on arrival that her husband had had a child with his German girlfriend while she was still living in Turkey. The husband and German girlfriend initially tried to force Pelin to be their live-in maid. When she resisted, they threatened to send her back to Turkey. At this point she fled to a women's shelter. Rita Kantemir of the Alternative List argued that for all three women "return to the home country would lead to ostracism.... Because of the difficulties that they have caused their husbands and the 'shame' that they have inflicted by not following their husband's orders to return, they now find themselves in a life-threatening situation, because the male relatives of their husbands have the duty to restore the man's 'honor.'"[55] Deportation would expose the women to social marginalization and even violence in Turkey.

West Berlin Senator of the Interior Heinrich Lummer responded that the social status of a divorced woman was irrelevant to his decision-making process because "it seems problematic to make the return of foreigners to their home countries dependent on the evaluation of the cultural and social conditions of their home country in comparison to German standards. In the interest of restricting the migration of foreigners, foreigners without a secure residence status can and must be expected to continue living according to the living conditions of their home country."[56] Women who came from a land of gender oppression should be expected to live with it.

Civil society groups kept up the pressure on the Berlin Senate, and Lummer finally relented in November 1983. He decided that Yaprak could stay based on her residence from 1971 to 1977, noting that her unique history "lessens the danger of a precedent." Pelin, whose husband had tried to use her as a live-in maid, did not receive the same reprieve.[57] Kantemir continued to press the point about Pelin's possible victimization, writing a petition on her behalf to Richard Weizsäcker, mayor of Berlin. Kantemir argued that Pelin's male relatives in Turkey might assault her if she returned and that "she will receive no help from the neighbors, because there people believe, that a woman is at fault when she is raped (similar beliefs are said to still exist here as well). She has once again stained the honor of the family and must be punished for it. . . . This is depicted very vividly in the film *Yol*."[58] Kantemir's use of a film to make her point underscores the way that semi-fictionalized tropes of the oppressed Turkish woman were mobilized in political debate. It does not appear that this particular argument persuaded the West Berlin mayor. Unfortunately, it is unclear from the available evidence what happened to Pelin after her deportation.

In late 1983, the Greens in Lower Saxony put forward a resolution that would allow foreign women who fled to women's shelters to stay in the FRG. The local SPD also supported this resolution.[59] The Interior Minister of Lower Saxony, a CDU member, rejected the proposal. He argued that perhaps "precisely the foreign woman's residence in a shelter shows that she has largely emancipated herself from religious ties, perhaps because she grew up in a similarly emancipated family and environment. Then her situation after return to the home country would presumably be very different from what is generally depicted in the petition."[60] His reasoning might have been cynical, but it also exposed one of the potential weaknesses of arguments that dwelled on women as victims. If one accepted the idea that Turkish women were inherently oppressed, any act of individual agency became a sign of exceptional empowerment, and a woman who went to a women's shelter to escape an abusive partner must already be free.

Arguments that relied on images of women as victims also had another potential weakness. If women were inherently unsafe around Turkish men, what was the positive argument for allowing Turkish men into Germany in the first place? The bureaucrats who staffed Foreigners' Offices in the 1980s admittedly did not make this argument. At the time it was easy enough for them to justify deportations and restrictions by reiterating the common sense that an individual foreigner's interest in living in the FRG could not outweigh "the public interest in limiting the migration of foreigners."[61] However, the idea that foreign men oppress foreign women has become a potent weapon for politicians who have wanted to restrict migration since the 1990s. Politicians from across the political spectrum have argued that Muslim populations cannot integrate because they are inherently homophobic and misogynistic.[62]

Turkish and other foreign women were already sounding the alarm about the possible misuse of such arguments at the time. At the 1984 Conference of Foreign and German Women, several of the foreign women in attendance wanted to discuss whether blanket statements criticizing the way that "Islamic culture" treated women could be understood as "a hidden form of racism." However, many of the West Germans in attendance rejected this characterization and only wanted to discuss religion as a problem, "a divisive moment, one that made communication more difficult."[63] At the same conference, a working group on the legal situation of foreign women produced a report about dependent residency laws with another concern: even if the state granted independent residence permits to dependents earlier—for example, after one year instead of five—foreign men would continue to exploit the situation by sending their wives home immediately before the new deadline.[64] The logic of this ostensibly feminist report bears a certain resemblance to the way that officials in the Federal-State-Municipality Commission had discussed restrictions on marriage migration. It assumes that foreign men will find a way to oppress foreign women no matter what the law is. This assumption could be the basis for an argument in favor of immediately granting independent residence permits for spouses, but it could also be the basis for an argument not to grant any residence permits to men.

West German feminists who insisted on depicting men rather than migration law as the enemy also adopted a kind of paternalist attitude toward the foreign family as they spoke past the concerns of the foreign women they claimed to represent. As Turkish social worker and researcher Neval Gültekin wrote in a social work periodical, "If a foreign woman complains about certain troubles or even repression in the family, the European woman in most cases wish that she would make herself independent. This kind of self-sufficiency, however, often means flight from the family. . . . For the majority of women emigrants, the family plays the biggest role in the foreign community."[65] The family undeniably was a dangerous place for many foreign women, but their unique problem—a problem they did not share with German women—was that in many cases their family was the entire basis of their legal relationship to West Germany.

Equating the "spousal migrant" with the "oppressed woman" risks overlooking the serious problems that the "spousal migrant" category created for otherwise happy marriages. "Nermin" was twenty-one years old and a second-generation migrant when she was interviewed by a West German social worker in 1983. She explained that she liked her life in Germany and wanted her Turkish fiancé to join her, but that this was impossible because "we would have to be married for three years, and then he couldn't work for four years. He wouldn't be able to stand it." She was planning on returning to Turkey to marry him, but was not

excited about it, telling the interviewer "I will miss Germany. In Turkey everything will be different. Here I can go into the city alone. There I can't go out
alone. Here I can buy a lot of things, because I work and make good money. In
Turkey everything is different."[66] In another series of interviews conducted with
Turkish women working in West Berlin in 1983 and 1984, one woman told the
interviewer: "I think it is terrible that the spouse has to wait five years in order
to receive a work permit. I want to marry somebody from Turkey, but I can't for
that reason." At the time of the interview, she planned to work in Germany for
three additional years so that she could qualify for a pension when she returned
to Turkey to finally marry her fiancé. Because she did not want to get married
before she could live with her husband, migration law was forcing her to delay
her marriage.[67] "Pinar," interviewed by a researcher in 1989, said that she and
her Turkish husband were not considering life in Germany because "it would be
really hard for me to have to work alone for five years for both of us."[68] Foreign
women also frequently felt pressure to rush through their engagement and to
marry early so that their husbands could start the waiting period for migration and for a legal work permit as soon as possible.[69] Migration policy makers
produced the male leverage over women that they claimed to deplore.

All of these women experienced West German migration policy, not Turkish
culture, as an obstacle to their self-fulfillment. Many of them chose to leave
Germany and to return to Turkey because they did not want to start their married life with one to three years of separation only to have to scrape by on one income while condemning their husbands to four years of enforced idleness. The
spousal migrants who were most likely to come to Germany were those who
could put up with four years of idleness, while those who saw those four years as
impossible—most trailing husbands as well as those trailing wives who wanted
to work outside of the home—were more likely to give up on their migration
plans. By actively encouraging female breadwinners and working women to return to Turkey, the policy only reinforced pre-existing ideas that Turkish women
were confined to the household.

State Paternalism Toward German Women
Married to Foreigners

When the FRG was founded in 1949, women's citizenship status continued to
depend on the citizenship status of their closest male relative, as it had since before 1871. This gendered dimension of German national identity also mattered
for ethnic Germans applying to enter the FRG as co-ethnic migrants. Historian
Jannis Panagiotidis found that several German women married to foreign

men were deemed to have lost their "German" identity through marriage and were thus denied the ability to migrate, while no German men married to foreign women were denied such recognition.[70] The 1957 UN Convention on the Nationality of Married Women built on over half a century of activism when it established the principle that a woman should not automatically lose her citizenship on marrying a foreign man, as well as that a change in a husband's citizenship status should not automatically affect the citizenship of the wife.[71]

The FRG changed its citizenship law in 1957 according to both the new guarantee of gender equality in the Basic Law and this new principle of international law.[72] Although German women who married foreign men no longer automatically lost their German citizenship, in practice they were still less "German" than their male counterparts. German men who married foreign women were able to guarantee that their new wives could also become German citizens, while German women who married foreign men were not able to facilitate citizenship or even permanent residence for their foreign husbands.[73] Men were presumed to be the family members with a link to the state. The bureaucracy continued to assume that a man's citizenship ought to determine the location where the entire family would live, and thus that German women who married foreign men would leave the country to follow their foreign husband abroad.

Women challenged this assumption and eventually forced the FRG to reconsider its policy on binational marriages between a German woman and a foreign man. In 1965, the Interior Minister of Schleswig-Holstein wrote to his colleagues about the women in his state who tried to secure residence permits for their foreign husbands. His office generally expected German women to follow foreign husbands abroad but sometimes made exceptions "when the living conditions that the wife would discover in the foreign state according to general experience are glaringly different from those here." However, in reflecting further on Article 6 of the Basic Law and Article 16 of the UN Convention on Human Rights, both of which guaranteed state protection for marriage and the family, he was beginning to consider that perhaps he should grant even more residence permits for foreign husbands.[74] He wanted to know how the other federal states saw this problem.

The Bavarian Interior Minister rejected Schleswig-Holstein's proposal because "it must be expected of an adult woman that she will inform herself about the living conditions in the home country of her future husband when she enters into a marriage with a foreigner." He believed that any relaxation of this principle would produce undesirable effects. If women were not expected to leave with their husbands, "the number of these marriages would increase, since the woman could count on her husband no longer being deported." He added that "many of these marriages of Germans with foreigners from Asian and African countries are not very stable, and after a divorce the foreigner would have to be retained in the country without any reason."[75] Rhineland-Palatinate and West Berlin both wrote in to support the Bavarian position that there was no good reason to relax the requirements for foreign husbands.[76]

In 1970, two women, one from Bavaria and one from Schleswig-Holstein, brought their cases to court and forced the topic back onto the national agenda. The woman from Bavaria was married to an Iraqi citizen, and the court ruled that her husband had to be granted a residence permit because German women should not have fewer rights than citizens of the European Economic Community. At the time citizens of the EEC living in the FRG were able to get residence permits for their spouses regardless of the spouse's country of origin, while German citizens could not.[77] The Bavarian Interior Minister believed that the court's ruling contradicted the gender order. The entire idea of family migration only applied to family members who were "supported by the working breadwinner," and "in appraising whether the denial of a residence permit should be seen as a hardship or injustice, it must be assumed that the male head of the family is the breadwinner."[78] The woman from Schleswig-Holstein was married to an Iranian citizen, and the Foreigners' Office in Kiel had refused to renew his residence permit, arguing that granting residence permits to men from developing countries would create a "brain drain" from the Third World and contradict German "development policy." Countries like Iran and Afghanistan would stop sending men to study in the FRG if those men could easily obtain residence through marriage to German women. Bavaria also picked up on Schleswig-Holstein's argument in its appeal, explaining that allowing men from developing countries to obtain residency through marriage to West German women would lead to "the complete bankruptcy of German development aid."[79]

The case of the Iranian-German couple in Kiel ultimately reached the petition section of the Bundestag and became the subject of an extended debate between the Interior Ministries of the federal states. Responding to the development aid argument, the couple's lawyer had used a touch of strategic self-ethnicization when he insisted that Iran would not be hurt if his client stayed, because his client was a "rug dealer, and it is certain that Persia is not lacking for these." The heart of the couple's argument was that the refusal to renew the man's residence permit was a violation of Article 6 of the Basic Law—"Marriage and the family shall enjoy the special protection of the state."[80] The ensuing debate about the case hinged on what precisely it meant to "protect" marriages between German women and foreign men. Officials did not debate whether or not they were obliged to protect a German woman's right to choose both her husband and her place of residence. They chose to frame the debate as a question of whether or not they were obliged to protect German women and children from living in "less developed" countries.

Interior ministers who favored granting residence permits to husbands argued that German women were vulnerable and needed state protection. The Interior Minister of Lower Saxony explained that an Egyptian man had tried to move to Egypt with his West German wife and their daughter, but they had developed a skin disease "because his wife and his daughter were not up to the climatic conditions in Egypt." The man had also dropped out of his medical studies to become a photographer, so Lower Saxony decided to give the man a residence permit after all.[81] The Interior Minister in Hesse distinguished between physical vulnerability and economic vulnerability. While he occasionally approved residence permits for husbands when wives suffered from health problems, he rarely granted residence permits to the husbands of women whose reasons for wanting to remain in Germany were merely "economic reasons," since he saw it as the woman's responsibility to educate herself about the economic conditions of her would-be husband's home country before entering into marriage.[82]

Petitions from this period show that many women were aware that the language of vulnerability could be useful for contesting a negative residency decision for a foreign husband. One woman married to a man from Egypt wrote to Chancellor Willy Brandt in the voice of her child, attaching a snapshot of her two-year-old son and beginning the letter as follows: "Why am I writing to you?—Well, although I am so young, I already have great worries. . . . My entire baby existence no longer brings me any joy, when I wake up in the morning and already have to think about how my father and perhaps the entire family will have to leave the country in which I would so like to grow up."[83] The "baby" also explained that his mother cared for his sick grandfather, who would likely die if his granddaughter were to leave the FRG for Egypt.

Another woman explicitly used her pregnancy in a petition on behalf of her Syrian husband. Her pregnancy was particularly vulnerable, she wrote, because she had already suffered two miscarriages. The first had occurred because she heard so many cruel comments about her foreign husband, and "it hurt me so much that I had a miscarriage." A stressful fight to renew her husband's work permit had caused a second miscarriage. Pregnant a third time, she prayed to carry the child to term, which she feared was unlikely if she had to move to Syria. She concluded the letter: "Minister Genscher you are my last hope. Please do not think that I am using the pregnancies as blackmail, oh no. It is the wish of every young couple to have children."[84] This woman's case was particularly difficult because her Syrian husband was trained as a medical doctor, and the state believed that her husband's skilled labor belonged in Syria, not in the FRG.

In the course of the debate on binational marriages, many interior ministers invoked the argument from development policy when they argued against giving residence permits to foreign husbands. If men who came to the FRG to study could remain simply by marrying a German woman, the state's policy of helping developing countries would be worse than useless. The Interior Minister of Schleswig-Holstein wrote a twenty-page letter in which he explained that anybody who was in favor of granting residence permits to foreign husbands of German women was in fact a nationalist who did not care about the rest of the world, since "the suffering of the German wife is usually a consequence of the great differences that exist . . . between the civilizational conditions in Central Europe and in the underdeveloped parts of the world." Although "it seems inhumane to the superficial observer," women needed to leave with their husbands because "the existing need of the people in developing countries is in most cases greater than the prospective suffering of the German wives."[85] For the same reason, he demanded that men from developing countries be ineligible for German citizenship.

The federal Interior Minister suggested that perhaps the solution to the development problem was that scholarships for study in the FRG should be given only to men who were already married, so as to make it less likely that they would marry German women.[86] In at least one case, the officials got their wish to reduce the number of German women married to foreign men in a purely formal sense. A woman who had been living with the Afghan father of her child for six years wrote a petition on behalf of her partner explaining that she had chosen not to marry him because she did not think it was right "to enter a marriage that would be overshadowed from the beginning by the fear that the decision of a bureaucracy might mean that the husband and father would have to leave the family." She had also wanted her child to retain West German citizenship, something that had only been possible if the child were born out of wedlock.[87] She now had a German citizen child whose father was at risk of being deported and no obvious way to appeal his deportation, since he was neither her legal husband nor her child's legal father. This case highlights the ways in which migration and citizenship law weighed heavily on women in relationships with foreign men.

Other interior ministers who weighed in on the debate on binational marriages argued that there was no legitimate reason to grant a foreign husband a residence permit. In West Berlin, a woman married to a Nigerian man had argued both that she could not stand the climate in Nigeria and that her husband's family were against his marriage to a white woman, which would make life in Nigeria for her both physically and psychologically miserable. West Berlin refused to give him a residence permit, a decision upheld by local courts.[88] Bavaria argued that any relaxation at all would "pose the danger . . . of giving up the basic principle that the Federal Republic is not an immigration country." Bavaria did not want to have to "put up with foreigners without integrity, just because they have married a German citizen. The possibility of misuse, particularly through false marriage, is close and impossible to miss."[89] Officials rarely worried that foreign women who married German men were "without integrity," but they constantly worried that foreign men were trying to trick the state. The suspicion of misuse was gendered, linked to both the bureaucracy's unwillingness to question the decisions and motives of German men, and to the assumption that foreign men posed more of a potential threat to public order than foreign women.

Throughout the debate about the couple from Kiel, none of the interior ministries used language about gender equality—for example, by arguing that German women deserved the same right as German men to choose their spouse and to choose their place of residence. Such language was at least theoretically available, not only because gender equality was guaranteed in Article 3 of the West German Basic Law but also because it showed up in the petitions that women with foreign husbands made in their own behalf. One German woman who had been married to a Turkish man for three years wrote to her elected representative to explain that she had a child with her husband, but that local authorities were refusing to extend his residence permit. In response, he had applied for citizenship, but the Foreigners' Office had not only denied his citizenship application, explaining that it did not give citizenship to students from developing countries, but also informed him that he had to leave the country immediately. She asked, "Is it compatible with our Basic Law, which states that all people have the same rights, whether they are men or women . . . that foreign women who marry German men receive German citizenship, but foreign men do not? Must I as a German woman completely change my life, but not a German man? Where is the equality there? In my opinion this is completely against the Basic Law!"[90] Another woman wrote to explain that she wanted to marry a foreign man but was worried because she had heard about other foreign husbands being deported: "I've never heard about the deportation of the foreign wife of a German man. The idea imposes itself that the man is more important than the woman in a German family, since the German wife of a foreigner stands alone if he is deported or sees herself forced to go with him." She also wanted to be able to pass her German citizenship on to any children she had with this man: "The child receives the citizenship of the father and the mother can do nothing about it in this period of women's equality! I find that very sad for the FRG and its women!"[91] Despite these women's arguments, officials almost never cited Article 3 in their debates about the meaning of Article 6. Officials implicitly assumed that protecting marriage and the family meant protecting the ideal of the male breadwinner.

The federal Interior Ministry ultimately issued a decree in May 1972 to the effect that the "protection of marriage and the family" guaranteed in Article 6 should be given more consideration—but still not be the sole consideration—in decisions on residence permits. The decree also extended a limited protection from deportation to men who were married to German women. It did not mention Article 3 and the principle of gender equality.[92] The exact language of the decree continued to give local authorities extremely wide latitude for making decisions about whether to grant residence permits to foreign husbands. The state expanded the rights of men married to German women in May 1972 because it decided that it had a duty to protect its own women from having to go abroad to "intolerable" conditions—not because it had concluded that women were equal citizens with the right to choose where to conduct their marital life.

The Association of Women Married to Foreigners

The limited nature of this new protection from deportation became brutally clear after the terrorist attacks at the 1972 Munich Olympics, when the police moved to deport nearly 200 men who were members of the General Union of Palestinian Students. Many of these men were married to German women, including one man who was spared from deportation only because he had been tipped off by a friend and had gone into hiding before the police arrived. One of these women, Rosi Wolf-Almanasreh, drew on the experience to found what would become the Association of Women Married to Foreigners (IAF). Founded in a moment of crisis, the IAF worked collectively to replace the language of protection with a language of human rights. They hoped that making claims in the language of human rights and gender equality would better protect binational families without limitation.[93]

The IAF was arguably one of the first West German organizations to take anti-racism within the FRG as a central goal of its organizing efforts. Its activism developed from the perspective of white German women who saw their privileges as Germans eroded by their choice of husbands. Foreigners were essentially banned from organizing on their own behalf because the 1965 Law on Foreigners prohibited political activity by foreigners that "hurt the interests of the Federal Republic." In the 1960s and early 1970s, this ban on political activity was used primarily against foreign groups who were protesting their home regimes and hurting German interests abroad, groups like the General Union of Palestinian Students.[94] However, because "the interests of the Federal Republic" were also understood as "not being an immigration country," foreigners were reluctant to explicitly criticize the state's migration policy. German women married to foreign men were safe from deportation, and that space of safety enabled some of them to develop a radical critique of the state's migration policy not just on grounds of gender equality but also on the claim that the state was racist. Because the group's catalyzing event was the deportation of Palestinian activists, the IAF's founding document included the demand that foreigners be able to organize politically in the FRG.[95]

One of the group's first actions was a letter-writing campaign in which they made a series of demands to the interior ministries of the federal states. The federal Interior Ministry produced an internal report about the IAF in September 1973 stating that many of these demands were not only "unworthy of discussion" but also that they were "outside of the group's sphere of interest." These purportedly irrelevant demands were as follows: first, the idea that Germany was an immigration country; second, the demand that the protection for foreign families be explicitly written into the Law on Foreigners rather than dependent on administrative decrees; third, that foreigners married to Germans should receive long-term residence permits; and finally, that requirements for German citizenship should be relaxed for the husbands of German women.[96] All of the demands that the Interior Ministry deemed "irrelevant" and "unworthy" dealt with the treatment of foreigners and the goals of migration policy.

One "irrelevant" demand was that foreign men married to German women should receive permanent residence permits that would allow them to remain in Germany even if the marriage dissolved, which amounted to a demand for the extension of a privilege that had been granted to foreign women married to German men since 1957. This demand was not shared by all of the women who chose to marry foreign men. Some felt that if they divorced they would no longer want their former spouse in Germany.[97] However, other women believed that they would want a former husband to remain even after divorce. For instance, if they had a child before the end of the marriage, the man's subsequent removal from Germany would make it not only impossible for him to continue a relationship with the child but also almost impossible for him to pay child support. As one woman pointed out, a man who earned even a relatively high salary in Afghanistan would never be able to earn enough to pay substantial child support to a woman still living in Munich.[98]

Another "unworthy" demand was that the requirements for German citizenship be relaxed for their husbands. Rosi Wolf-Almanasreh's husband, in Germany since 1962 and married since 1968, had applied to become a citizen in 1971 and was still in limbo three years later. Turkish men who pursued German citizenship were often suspected of wanting to become citizens to avoid military duty in Turkey. One woman who wrote to the Interior Ministry pleading for citizenship for her Turkish husband introduced herself as a member of the IAF and explained that her husband "has no relationship to Turkey . . . and can hardly speak Turkish anymore!" Her husband also feared being called into military service. His asylum application had been rejected and the couple were hoping for German citizenship. Her letter undermined her own case. The Interior Ministry replied that since Turkey was a NATO member, her husband's service should be seen as in the German interest and thus presumably in her own interest.[99]

In December 1974, parliament passed a citizenship law reform that allowed children of German wives and foreign husbands to become German citizens. Women within the political parties as well as the courts had criticized the gendered nature of German citizenship law for years. The reform pre-empted a pending decision from the Federal Constitutional Court about whether patrilineal citizenship violated Article 3 of the Basic Law, the guarantee of gender equality.[100] One of the decisive arguments in favor of the reform was the possibility that a foreign father might take his foreign child abroad with him, leaving the child's German mother with no recourse to claim the child.[101]

While the IAF was pleased by this citizenship law reform, it continued to argue for a more egalitarian practice at the civil registrar and the Foreigners' Office. At the second national meeting of the IAF in 1976, the group staged a "Tribunal of German International Family Law" at which women argued that by interfering in their marriages, the state was interfering with their right to freely choose a spouse as guaranteed by the European Convention on Human Rights. The Tribunal made a special point of criticizing what IAF members saw as a paternalistic discourse of protection. In a typical exchange, a character representing the state announces that "This law is only to protect the woman," and the IAF character replies "Cut it out with the incapacitation of women. Stop the discrimination against our group."[102] This critique crystallized in a section of the Tribunal that examined the common practice of requiring foreign men who wanted to marry German women to produce a doctor's report that they were free of diseases. For men from countries with Islamic legal codes, this included "proof of potency" so that the marriage would be valid in their home country. At this juncture in the script, the character representing the "state" explains that the examination is necessary because "a state must protect itself from diseases which do not exist among us. . . . This is only in service of protection of the woman—and protecting society from foreign influences." The IAF character then reads part of the 1935 Law on the Protection of the Hereditary Health of the German People, which prohibited marriages between people with certain hereditary diseases, in order to link state paternalism with the legacy of National Socialist population policy.[103]

State officials responded to the IAF's demands for more rights for their husbands with further paternalism as they argued that the state needed to protect women from unscrupulous foreign men. The West Berlin Senate issued a press release about the "visa marriage" in September 1977 that inflamed a decade-long panic about binational marriages in a context where family migration was the only legal route into the country. The press release was titled "What does a German woman cost? Or, how a foreigner can use a visa marriage to live and work in Germany in perpetuity." It recounted the story of a woman "with a low IQ" who agreed to marry a brother of her Yugoslavian co-worker for 2,000

DM. In fact, she only received 300 DM, and the man actually moved in with his ex-wife, who already lived in Berlin. Having left her job at a cleaning firm in anticipation of the marriage, she was threatened by imminent homelessness. The authors claimed that such tragic stories were on the increase and that Article 6 of the Basic Law obliged the state to do something, explaining that "if protection of marriage is to have positive content, the state must protect marriage from those who would abuse it."[104] This initial story inspired several articles in the national press and even a television special.[105] Although the original press release featured a Yugoslavian guest worker as the villain, in subsequent permutations the villain was frequently a false asylum seeker from a "Third World" country, lying about both his political persecution and his affective relationships.

The "visa marriage" panic was closely linked to the asylum panic of the late 1970s and early 1980s. Klaus-Peter Wolf used a "visa marriage" to explore the FRG's treatment of asylum seekers in his 1984 young adult novel *The Deportation, or Who Killed Mahmut Perver?*, which won the Anne Frank Prize for Literature and was turned into a television movie by ZDF.[106] Eighteen-year-old Elke marries Mahmut, a Kurdish asylum seeker she meets on the street, in order to save him from deportation. Her heart is in the right place, but the couple has given no thought to their scheme. Elke is surprised by the suggestion that she and Mahmut will have to live together to make his claim to marriage plausible. She has also not considered that as a married woman she will no longer qualify for scholarship assistance from the university. Her father is upset that he will lose child allowances for his daughter. When the German boy she is interested in finds out about her marriage, Elke decides to divorce Mahmut in exchange for a promise from the Foreigners' Office that he will be given a residence permit. The Foreigners' Office gives him a residence permit for two weeks and then deports him as soon as it expires. He is murdered shortly after his arrival in Turkey. Elke and her parents are incredibly naïve at the beginning of the marriage. They are repeatedly shocked by what they see at the Foreigners' Office, such as the absence of translators. They become politicized after they learn about Mahmut's death in Turkey, as they realize that their own blind faith in bureaucracy led directly to the death of this young man.

Real-life German bureaucrats would probably not have allowed Elke and Mahmut to get married in the first place, as they were on high alert for couples who seemed to be marrying for suspicious reasons. During the 1960s, some civil registrars had refused to marry women to Spanish men to protect the women from Spanish law, but the Federal Constitutional Court had declared this practice unconstitutional in 1971 when it ruled that the state could not protect Germans from "foreign ideas of marriage." Only one decade later, state officials argued that there was a new threat at the marriage altar—no longer Spaniards who might take advantage of the law to skip town on divorced German women, but failed asylum seekers marrying German women so they could remain in the country. The Bavarian Interior Minister was one of many officials to favor new obstacles to marriage, as "when marriage to a German partner can be achieved without great effort, when the German partner from this marriage can also get out of it without great difficulty, and when residency rights follow automatically from every marriage to a German, the legal institution of marriage will be misused even more than it is right now."[107] Other officials worried that criminal gangs were drugging and threatening women to force them into marriages.[108]

Civil registrars determined to protect marriage from abuse developed lists of "grounds for suspicion" that could help registrars identify possible false marriages and refuse to conduct them. "Grounds for suspicion" ranged from the "questionable mental state of the German fiancée," including evidence of recent self-harm or drug use, to frequent changes of address, "multiple divorces of the German fiancée," or a registration address on a street where sex workers were known to live. They could also start at the passport. A civil registrar could refuse to marry a couple on the grounds that the prospective groom was from Turkey, Pakistan, India, or Afghanistan—all countries from which asylum claims were regularly denied.[109]

Even once they had successfully cleared the hurdle of the civil registrar, couples from these countries continued to have to prove that their marriages were real. Foreigners Offices' were told that if they suspected a visa marriage, they should initially grant the residence permit for only one year instead of the usual three to test whether the marriage still existed in one year. In practice, IAF members found that their husbands were sometimes given permits for as little as three months at a time. The short-term residence permits made it difficult for the men in question to find jobs.[110] Many Foreigners' Offices also monitored binational couples to make sure that they continued to live at the same address.[111] In West Berlin in March 1981, the "Targeted Foreigner Surveillance" division of the police began to investigate every binational marriage in which either the foreign man would not qualify for a residence permit without marriage or the marriage had already been concluded but "grounds for suspicion" arose after the fact. In one case, when the husband lost his job, the couple could no longer afford their shared apartment. Each moved in with friends while they tried to look for new jobs, but their different addresses triggered an investigation and the man's residence permit was shortened, which in turn made it harder for him to find a new job.[112] According to experiences collected by women in the IAF, it seems that in practice "grounds for suspicion" also frequently included tips from neighbors—raising the question of how many were simply acting out of a desire not to have a foreign neighbor.[113]

The West Berlin Senate invited the women of the IAF to discuss their experiences with marriage investigations in February 1982. The women began their testimony by stating decisively that the climate had worsened since new federal restrictions—the age limit of sixteen, the integration test, and the new requirements for marriage migration—had been announced in December 1981. Racist comments on the street, death threats, and hate mail had all increased.[114] Two women's cars had even been destroyed while they were parked on the street. In response to this opening statement, a senator from the FDP told the women to stick to the topic at hand and not stray off topic. A CDU senator agreed and further reminded the women that migration policy was "not covered by their sphere of interest"—a rebuke that echoed the Interior Ministry's earlier judgment that migration policy demands were "unworthy of discussion" and "irrelevant." During the hearing, senators agreed that it must have been embarrassing for the women to be forced to answer questions such as "which marriage broker introduced you to your husband?" and "what conditions did he place on your pre-arranged divorce?," but the senators refused to engage when the women talked about racist threats and how authorities treated their husbands.[115]

After the hearing, the West Berlin Senate asked the police to estimate the true size of the "visa marriage" threat.[116] The two-page report presented by the police offered virtually no detail about how marriages were ultimately judged to be false but provided a jaw-dropping headline in a press release titled "90 percent only marry for appearances."[117] The city of Mannheim came up with similar numbers in its 1985 investigation, claiming that 90 percent of marriages conducted between German women and foreign men were false. When the local chapter of the FDP filed a request for information, the Mannheim police clarified further that they investigated thirty to forty cases a year, 90 percent of which turned out to be genuine cases of false marriages. In both West Berlin and Mannheim, police publicized the 90 percent figure without mentioning that it applied only to cases that had already come under suspicion and been investigated, not to 90 percent of all binational marriages.[118] In a 1983 survey of civil registrars, most of the registrars believed that roughly 1 percent of all marriages conducted in Germany—in other words, all marriages, including those between two Germans—were false. Two of the registrars asserted that "well over 1 percent" of marriages had been false at the height of the asylum panic between 1979 and 1983.[119]

In their own publications, the women of the IAF developed an argument that redirected attention away from foreigners and toward West German migration policies. They argued that the "primary cause of the 'visa marriage' problem is the employment policies for foreigners of the Berlin Senate and of the German state." They also pointed out that the hysteria around "visa marriages" drew a false distinction between marriage for "love" and marriage for money that ignored the fact that historically "marriage has been nothing but an economic institution."[120] For the IAF, the real "forced marriages" were those marriages forced on foreigners for whom marriage was their only way to stay in Germany. Because it was so difficult for foreign men to obtain a residence permit outside of marriage, binational couples often rushed into marriage to maintain the foreigner's ability to reside in Germany. The stress did not end when the marriage was concluded. Because their husbands had to continually prove their commitment to renew their residence permits, binational couples felt pressure to live in the same residence at all times and worried about what might happen if they chose to live apart because of temporary marital difficulties or for career or education-related reasons. Sometimes they even decided to have children earlier than they wanted to. A German woman married to a Greek man who had not yet completed his military service in Greece tried to get his residence permit extended, and the Foreigners' Office told her that they would tolerate her husband's continued residence only "when completing his military service would lead to an unacceptable separation and when there has been a child in the marriage."[121] The "population policy" of "residence permit for child" had its intended effect. The couple decided to have a child so the husband could stay.

The radical edge of the IAF's feminist and anti-racist critique was alienating to some of its members and to women who might have been potential members. In January 1989, the IAF tried to draft a new "basic program" of its principles, a process that revealed gaps between the leadership and the membership. When the national leadership sent out a draft program, local chapters complained that it was too long and that it made programmatic statements about far too many issues, including the AIDS crisis, abortion reform, and drug reform.[122] Chapters in the cities of Bochum and Duisburg complained that the draft was too "intellectual," with the women in Duisburg explaining that some of their potential members already "don't feel themselves to be intellectual enough" to join the group and that the basic program made the IAF seem like a place where only "left-intellectual" women were welcome.[123] One woman in Duisburg explained that in her opinion, "Women who come to us . . . are looking for solidarity and might want to learn something. They don't (yet?) feel themselves to be trailblazers for a multicultural society, but as people with a very individual view of life, who can find like-minded people in the group."[124]

Such internal debates naturally led to the question of what women expected from the IAF when they joined. For many women, the IAF's most important function was as a self-help group where they could feel safe discussing problems that arose in their relationships. Women expected to find an understanding audience rather than a chorus of people telling them "What did you expect when you married *him*?"[125] Some women experienced the IAF as a consciousness-raising group. They came to discuss problems in their relationship, but through coming to meetings, they started to understand many of those problems as collective rather than individual, and thus demanding a political rather than a psychological solution. Inge El-Himoud, a founding member of the IAF, drew a comic expressing this process in 1979. Her husband, Ismail El-Himoud, was a medical student from Jordan. When the state tried to deport him in 1972, he appealed the case all the way to the Federal Constitutional Court, where he won.[126] In the comic, titled "Marriage Counseling," El-Himoud's counselor tells her that the problems in her marriage have "nothing to do with the fact that your husband is a foreigner" and that she must have deeper psychological reservations about her husband. But the more she thinks about it, the more she realizes that most of her problems do have something to do with the way people treat her husband. They cannot rent a larger apartment because landlords refuse to rent to foreigners. When she looks for a job, the man at the employment agency notes that her husband is a foreigner. "What does my job search have to do with the fact that my husband is a foreigner?" she asks. The employment counselor replies: "Well, when your husband leaves the Federal Republic, then you'll go with him, won't you?" The comic subverts the expectation that cultural difference causes problems in binational relationships by redirecting attention at the surrounding social context. El-Himoud praises the IAF for giving her the perspective to push back on her therapist's assumption that her problems are caused by her own reservations about her husband. She now realizes that her problems are caused by the fact that West German society treats him as a temporary presence.[127]

The women of the IAF consistently criticized the sexism and racism of West German migration policy. Their state interlocutors occasionally engaged with their criticism about gender equality, an ideal that was enshrined in the Basic Law and enforced by German courts, but those same interlocutors were unreceptive, even hostile, to their argument about German racism. Over the years the founding members of the IAF have achieved many of their original goals. The group still exists, having dropped "German" from its name in 1984, created a group for binational same-sex couples in 1996, and changed its name to the "Association of Binational Families and Partnerships" in 1997. The state consistently responded to their activism in ways that produced greater equality between German men and women while reinforcing the inequality between Germans and the foreigners they marry.[128] German men and women today have the same rights to bring people into the community, so German women can also, to quote anthropologist Damani Partridge, "exercise state power through their intimate engagements."[129] German men and women continue to exercise power because one original IAF demand remains unfulfilled. There has been no movement toward independent residence rights for foreign spouses.

* * *

In January 1982, an official at the Foreign Ministry inspected a draft memorandum recommending that the number of foreigners "be brought to a standstill." He penciled in a suggested revision: write that the number of foreigners "be limited," because the current wording "could raise the question of not just birth control, but in the extreme case also the question of forced abortion and even the murder of newborns (Herod!)."[130] This "joke" reveals both the bureaucratic fantasy and its limits. While many state officials were explicit about their hope that the number of foreigners would stop increasing, absolute control over population would have necessitated absolute control over women's bodies. Unable to contemplate "forced abortion and even the murder of newborns" except in jest, officials instead chose to regulate spousal migration. They feared the pregnant woman, who became central to the practice of regulation. She threatened the project of restriction not just because she could reproduce but because the spectacle of a pregnant deportee could briefly "tug on the heart strings" of officialdom.

The state maintained its own prerogatives to make decisions, sometimes even generous decisions, while continuing to deny migrants the status of autonomous rights-bearing subjects. As a result, the policy debate about spousal migration repeatedly collapsed into debates about the future of individual pregnant or abused women. Women who succeeded in contesting their own deportation or their husbands' deportations did so because they were able to work within state paternalism and to depict themselves as victims in need of state protection. Meanwhile, women who tried to use a language of equal rights—initially a language of women's rights, but also the language of migrant and human rights— found their claims rebuffed. The strategy of making a public appeal grounded in vulnerability could and did save individual women from being deported, but this strategy was not as effective for protecting members of the family who were not traditionally understood as vulnerable, especially foreign men. The forced repetition of the story of the vulnerable woman reduced all women to their vulnerability and need for protection, ignoring other rights they might have as members of the community.

The women of the IAF developed an incisive critique of migration law that recognized the limitations of this form of state paternalism. They understood that the obstacles erected to their relationships were not intended to "protect" them but to maintain an idealized fantasy of a homogeneous German community. Their critique remains absolutely essential considering the frequent acceptance of scholars that intermarriage can be taken as an uncomplicated indicator of a given ethnic group's "level of integration" into their host society.[131] By the early 2000s, migrants to Germany who attended integration classes were told as much in their courses, and their acceptance of the idea of intermarriage was seen as a positive indicator of their willingness to integrate.[132] But the question of whether foreigners are willing to allow their children to marry Germans cannot be asked without also considering "will Germans allow their children to marry foreigners?" and "will the state allow its citizens to marry foreigners?" A German woman who married a foreign man in the 1960s would be expected to leave the country with him, while a German woman who married a foreign man in the 1980s would find her marriage subject to investigation by the "Targeted Foreigner Surveillance" division of the West Berlin police—if she was even allowed to marry her husband. Any historical discussion of changing rates of intermarriage that equates intermarriage with "integration" must contend with these facts.

The IAF clearly stated in 1972 that "Germany is an immigration country," but the Interior Ministry filed the group's petition away with a memorandum that called the demand for a recognition of this reality both "unworthy" and "irrelevant." Through the 1970s and the 1980s, the federal state remained profoundly committed to the idea that Germany was not an immigration country and that "the interests of the Federal Republic" should continue to be the primary determinant of foreigners' rights. Because the state was unwilling to hear anti-racist critiques of migration policy, women and men in desperate situations were forced to trade on their own vulnerability. In so doing, they were forced to engage in politics "from the perspective of the injured," a kind of politics that "powerfully legitimizes law and the state as appropriate protectors against injury and casts injured individuals as needing such protection by such protectors."[133] The politics of vulnerability were effective within a legal framework of paternalism within which foreigners' presence in the FRG was dependent on state mercy, but they could not change this framework. This form of inclusion reproduced existing social hierarchies and preserved the state as the final arbiter of what was legitimate and acceptable. In choosing to grant some hardship exceptions while denying others, the state ultimately reinforced its authority as the sovereign with the power to decide who was deserving of state protection.

Between Two Fathers?

The Foreign Child in Citizenship Reform

In 1986 Tahsin Baki arrived in the FRG on a tourist visa and applied for a residence permit. Baki had been born in the Ruhr and had lived there until he was sixteen and his parents decided to return to Turkey. On turning eighteen, he decided to return to Germany on his own. Although the Foreigners' Office denied his application for a residence permit, a local initiative for "social minorities" took an interest in his case, getting him in touch with journalists who wrote stories marveling at his mastery of the local *Ruhrpott* dialect and wondering whether he was a "German Turk (or a Turkish German?)."[1] Those stories brought the case to the attention of Herbert Schnoor, an SPD politician and the Interior Minister of North Rhine-Westphalia. Schnoor agreed to make a temporary exception for Baki to work in Germany on the condition that he first returned to Turkey to apply for a visa and to leave a deposit of 1,200 DM at the consulate that would secure his eventual return "home." Baki's apprenticeship at the Cologne Zoo offered journalists excellent photo opportunities, and they continued to cover his case, putting pressure on the state to find a more permanent solution. Having left West Germany with their parents as minors, Baki and thousands of other young adults in Turkey and Yugoslavia found themselves unhappy at "home" and wanted desperately to return.[2]

A decade later, unified Germany passed a citizenship reform that opened up German citizenship to children like Baki. The 1999 reform introduced automatic German citizenship for a subset of children born in Germany to parents with legal residence statuses while failing to significantly open access to naturalization for those who had been born elsewhere. Reflecting the fact that the state had consistently drawn a distinction between foreign parents and foreign children, the reform changed the conditions under which people could be born into German citizenship but failed to significantly open German citizenship to those who wished to choose it as adults.[3] The specific compromise reached around

Fear of the Family. Lauren Stokes, Oxford University Press. © Oxford University Press 2022.
DOI: 10.1093/oso/9780197558416.003.0008

dual citizenship reflected this division within the foreign family. According to the compromise, foreign children were able to have dual citizenship until they turned twenty-three, at which point they would be forced to choose one of their two citizenships for the future. Lawmakers imagined that young adults, in choosing German citizenship, would choose the state over the family, as their parents became a denied link to a distant homeland.

Until 1990, foreign children under sixteen were not required to have residence permits or visas, making them uncontrollable and uncountable innocents who could not be deported. Precisely their status as children had posed a threat to decades of politicians who wanted to end migration. To reconcile the tension in the German public between seeing a foreign child as a threat and as an innocent, these politicians had repeatedly invoked the idea that parents exploited their foreign children. Politicians and bureaucrats argued that foreign mothers were irresponsible because they left their children at home, that foreign fathers were oppressive because they did not let their daughters go to school, and that foreign parents reproduced in order to access welfare and avoid deportation. These narratives all simplify reality, but in all of them, the child retains its innocence and the threat is placed on the parents' shoulders. A popular narrative that described foreign children as victims of their neglectful parents also opened the possibility that children could be redeemed through state action. The state required foreign children to hold residence permits in two steps, extending it to some children in 1990 and to all children in 1997. This reform made children part of the documentary migration regime, a reform that made the child deportable for the first time, but also potentially available for rehabilitation by the state. When the FRG enacted citizenship reform for these children in 1999, the paternalistic state was finally claiming paternity.

This chapter focuses on the figure of the foreign child from the late 1980s to the 1999 citizenship reform. It explains how the Turkish Association Agreement ceased to be a matter of concern for the FRG in 1987, opening a new possibility for migration reform. It also examines the discussion about opening a "return option" for foreign children whose parents had taken them away from Germany and the 1990/1997 decision to require residence permits for children under sixteen. It looks closely at the figure of the child in the 1990 reform to the Law on Foreigners and the 1999 citizenship reform, even though the thirty-year limit in place in German archives means documents recording interministerial discussions about these reforms were not yet public when I conducted the research. The SPD-Green coalition came to power in 1998 determined to change citizenship law.[4] Their scope for action was overdetermined by the debates of the previous three decades and heavily influenced by a tradition of state paternalism. Just as with earlier discussions about spousal migrants, state actors were more likely to engage with the narrative that cast the state as the protector of vulnerable foreign children and much less willing to engage with explicitly anti-racist arguments.

The historic events of 1989/1990—the fall of the Berlin Wall, the end of the German Democratic Republic, and the unification of East and West Germany—tended to confirm pre-existing trends in attitudes toward foreigners. German unification led to an upsurge of nationalism and racist violence against migrant families.[5] People in the East German towns of Hoyerswerda and Lichtenhagen rioted at dormitories housing asylum seekers, while far-right skinheads in the West German towns of Solingen and Mölln set homes of Turkish families on fire, killing eight and injuring fourteen. Politicians from both the CDU/CSU and the SPD saw these violent attacks as evidence that justified the decision to hollow out the constitutional right to asylum at the end of 1992.[6] The violence also impacted the course of ongoing discussions about residence and citizenship law.

Defusing the Threat of Turkish Association

The 1963 Association Agreement between the EEC and Turkey and the 1970 Additional Protocol had appeared to promise freedom of movement for Turkish citizens beginning no later than December 1, 1986. These pre-existing agreements meant that the FRG might have already lost its sovereignty over Turkish movement, depending on whether and how the EEC would decide to enforce them. German diplomats began to raise the issue with their EEC colleagues as early as 1974 but repeatedly discovered that no other state felt quite as anxious about the prospect.[7] By 1979 the FRG recognized that "we will only achieve agreement from Turkey, when we are ready for financial sacrifice."[8] The Foreign Ministry worked with Turkish diplomats behind the scenes to reach an informal agreement that Turkey would not force the question as long as Germany continued to maintain its existing policies and did not introduce new restrictions on Turkish migration.[9] In 1982, the Schmidt cabinet briefly considered implementing an age limit of six for the migration of foreign children precisely to create a "bargaining chip" for the negotiations with Turkey.[10] When the Kohl cabinet tried to push the age limit through, Foreign Minister Genscher countered that such a policy reversal would be a "bombshell" that would destroy the fragile agreement that Turkey would not further press its position, and his threat to resign temporarily took the age limit off the table.

As the deadline of December 1, 1986, approached, the EEC states remained divided about which concessions were acceptable. Other states wanted to maintain strict restrictions on Turkish mobility within the EEC because they feared migration from the FRG. Other states also placed pressure on the FRG to loosen its restrictions on family reunification, pressure that it resisted as it proposed a

ban on family migration for all but "first-generation" foreigners.[11] The offer finally made to Turkey on November 27, 1986, represented the lowest common
denominator that the member states had been able to agree on. It was a very low
denominator. The EEC's offer stated that the Association Agreement was not
legally binding and that Turkey had failed to hold up its own end of the deal. It
made no promises about family migration and limited itself to promising that
perhaps in the future Turks would be recruited for work again.[12] Chancellor
Kohl's office had judged "that Turkey will not accept the position as a basis for
negotiations" and anticipated a "panic reaction" from Turkey, perhaps even
an application for membership in the EEC. FRG diplomats also hoped to use
the EEC as a way to conceal their own primary responsibility for the lowball
offer.[13] The chancellor's office criticized two newspapers—the conservative *Die
Welt* and the center-right *Frankfurter Allgemeine Zeitung*—for publishing stories
mentioning "German" diplomats, since that adjective would give Turkey a pretext to demand answers when the FRG would prefer to direct all questions to
the EEC.[14]

Turkey responded that the EEC's offer was a "failure to fulfill its commitment"
that would produce "serious adverse effects on our association relations," leaving
it with no option to pursue its rights but to apply for full membership.[15] After
Turkey submitted its application for membership in April 1987, the European
Commission (EC) took over two years to respond to it. By December 1989,
transformations in Eastern Europe had pushed Turkish membership down the
priority agenda. The EC pointed to ongoing human rights abuses and the dispute over Cyprus as proof that it was not the right time to begin the accession
process.[16]

Individuals could also call on the Association Agreement themselves.
Meryem Demirel did so in 1985 in Schwäbisch Gmünd, a town of 56,000 people
in Baden-Württemberg. Demirel had entered the FRG on a tourist visa to visit
her husband in March 1983 but failed to leave after her visa expired in June 1984.
Her husband had lived in the country only since 1979, leaving him four years
short of being able to sponsor a spouse for migration. When the city tried to
deport Demirel, she and her lawyer appealed the decision on the basis of the
Association Agreement. The court in Stuttgart referred the case to the European
Court of Justice in December 1985, asking it to rule on the question of whether
the Association Agreement between Turkey and the European Economic
Community was in fact legally binding on member states.[17]

The court issued a ruling in September 1987 that defused the threat of the
Association Agreement by fully supporting the German position. According to
the European Court of Justice, the Association Agreement and related Protocol
did not "constitute rules of Community law which are directly applicable in the
internal legal order of the Member States." Because the Association Agreement

was insufficiently precise, "there is at present no provision of Community law defining the conditions in which Member States must permit the family reunification of Turkish workers lawfully settled in the Community."[18] The *Demirel* ruling meant that the regulation of migration between Turkey and individual EEC states remained a matter of national sovereignty.[19] It essentially meant that German officials could introduce new restrictions without worrying that they would be struck down by European courts, thus opening the door to the reform of the 1965 Foreigner Law.

Returned Children and the "Return Option"

While waiting for the resolution of the Association Agreement, the Kohl cabinet had pursued a number of other avenues in order to put migration in the past. These included the November 1983 Promotion of Voluntary Return Law, which sought to incentivize foreign families to return home by offering them a lump sum payment if they left together. Some observers had worried that the requirement for family unity would lead to coerced migration within families. Rudolf Dressler, an SPD representative from Wuppertal, brought up this point in the Bundestag debate, arguing that the law would create tragic scenes where children were "ripped out of their school, ripped out of their vocational training, when their unemployed father, seduced by the offer of payment, purchases a return ticket in a panic reaction."[20] Dressler inverted the earlier narrative of the child allowance panic: the father, excited by welfare, had put his children on an airplane to Germany, and now the father, seduced by the prospect of a large pile of cash, was going to force his children to board an airplane heading the other direction.

The Institute for Labor Market Research of the Federal Labor Office conducted a 1984 study of the 250,000 individuals who had left as a result of the Return Promotion Law that confirmed this concern. Researchers interviewed children who had returned to Turkey with their families and found that only one-third had actively wanted to leave Germany. Of the children they asked, 39 percent explained that they "did not contradict" the family's desire to return; 30 percent agreed that they "had to return with their family"; and 2 percent described themselves as having been "forced" to return.[21] Roughly half of the children also described their lives in Germany as better, and half said that if they had the option they would "absolutely" or "very likely" return to Germany.[22] The study also found that the young women who had returned to Turkey felt that the move had also forced them to "return" to the household and the family.[23]

Many of the experiences of Turkish children who returned to Turkey in the 1980s suggested that they had in fact been more "integrated" in Germany than had been suggested by the dominant media discourse about the "second genera-tion." Students struggled to fit in to Turkish classrooms that placed a strong em-phasis on obedience, and they missed the critical inquiry and independence that they had learned in German schools. Media narratives about returned children also focused on young Turkish women, who no longer had the freedom they had felt in Germany and who found that Turkish stereotypes about the sexual availability of "German girls" led to sexualized harassment in Turkey. These chil-dren and their specific difficulties were the subject of extensive concern and re-mediation in Turkey, which created specific "re-integration" classes to help the so-called Germans adjust to life in Turkey.[24] West German politicians and social workers could look at the experiences of these children in two different cultures and use them as proof that West Germany was in fact more democratic, more independent, and above all better for women.

Children like Tahsin Baki also forced the issue as they returned to Germany on tourist visas and sought to secure their own return. In 1985, Bremen and Saarland both issued administrative circulars allowing children to return on a case-by-case basis if they were "largely integrated," could cover their own living expenses, and had a specific reason to be in Germany, usually a vocational training program or job. North Rhine-Westphalia issued a similar circular in 1986, West Berlin in 1987, and Hamburg in 1988. The German Trade Union Confederation endorsed these circulars at its party congress in 1986, and in 1988 the SPD authored a draft law to introduce the "return option" on the national level.[25] The law would have offered foreign youth who had left the FRG with their parents the ability to choose to return between the ages of eighteen and twenty-one. This possibility would be open to youth who had either finished school in the FRG or had lived there for the majority of the period when they had been ten to eighteen.[26] Elmar Hönnekopp, the researcher who had conducted the 1984 study on the youth who had returned to Turkey, believed that perhaps 4,000 children in total could be expected to make use of this option.[27] Some segments of the CDU also came to support a modified version of the proposal over the course of the next year.[28] The Green Party insisted that the "right to return" ought to extend to all members of the family, not just children, but it was an outlier. Every other political party and civil society organization wanted to limit the option to youth. In December 1988, the federal Interior Ministry responded to these initiatives by issuing a national circular that allowed foreign children to return to Germany within five years of their original departure on the condition that they possess several important markers of "integration," most prominently, a high school degree and proof that they could participate in further vocational training.

The return policy for foreign youth rested on the figure of the traumatized child who could not stand life in Turkey. At a press conference that Liselotte Funcke organized in favor of the measure in 1987, she paraphrased a letter by a young man who had returned from Schleswig-Holstein to Istanbul with his parents in 1984. He described the intervening three years as "torture" during which he had had "suicidal thoughts."[29] At a hearing on the draft law, Gerd Wartenberg, an SPD representative from Kreuzberg in Berlin, made the case for the return option by reading from a letter by a Turkish teenager who had been born in Germany before leaving with his parents in 1983. He could not speak Turkish well and was deeply uncomfortable living in Turkey: "When I speak, everyone laughs. All of my friends, who I love, are in Germany. Everything happened because of my parents. If they had not returned, none of this would have happened! Is that my fault? If I were an adult, I would have stayed in Germany, and would have applied for German citizenship. . . . I am in my fatherland, but where is my homeland? For me it is Germany!"[30] The letter specifically blamed his parents as the source of his misery. While most experts anticipated that more men than women would choose to return within the three-year window, the specific assumption that teenage women were vulnerable was also invoked as a reason to implement the "return option." Even CDU/CSU representatives could agree that it was "barbaric" to send an "enlightened Turkish girl, who earned a high school diploma here, back to an Anatolian village."[31] The statement reflected the popular assumption that Turkish society was significantly worse for women than German society.

Authorities who implemented the circular often proceeded from the assumption that foreign children could be at home either in Turkey or Germany but not in both. According to this logic, children who wanted to return had to prove that they were completely unable to adapt to Turkey and had no prospects anywhere but Germany. The embassy in Ankara frequently rejected applications from children who were doing well in a Turkish school because the "return option" was understood a way "to aid children who cannot integrate in Turkey . . . who were integrated in Germany and who were ripped away from integration by their parents."[32] The embassy's language imputes violence to the parents who "rip" their children away from integration, rather than considering the very real possibility that a child might have strong attachments to both Germany and to their foreign parents. The embassy refused to consider applications from youth who could be happy in either place but who would prefer Germany. One Turkish girl remembered that when her parents announced that they were returning to Turkey when she was sixteen, she went to the local youth office, and the advisor there told her to play the part of the traumatized child: "If you say that you will kill yourself if you return, then you won't have to go back." Because her parents wept at the thought of being separated from their daughter, she decided to return with them. Two years later, she still considered the possibility of making use of the "return option," but she had integrated well in Turkish school and still loved her parents, and thus felt uncomfortable displaying the kind of desperation that the "return option" required.[33] Other young women married upon returning to Turkey, which made the "return option" almost impossible. One woman tried to make it work anyway, returning to Germany to visit her old friends with her new husband and scheduling an appointment with the Foreigners' Office so that the couple could beg for residence permits. The official told her "that it wouldn't work. Either marry someone from Germany or go back to Turkey."[34] As social scientist Gaby Straßburger put it in one of the only studies ever conducted on this measure, the law was not really designed for foreign children "but for children of German society, who have a right to return to the 'Federal Republican parental home.'"[35] The "return option" allowed for the fact that some children might feel more at home in Germany than in Turkey, but it was still predicated on the assumption that children could only belong in one place. Authorities who implemented the circular did not understand it as giving children a choice, but as saving children for whom Germany had taken the place of their parents.

The Reform of the Law on Foreigners

Helmut Kohl had promised that a reform of the Foreigner Law would be one of the signature achievements of his chancellorship. The unresolved nature of the Association Agreement prevented his cabinet from issuing any concrete proposals until after 1987, but a September 1983 draft memorandum began with the statement, "The basic principle remains restriction of immigration." It specifically proposed introducing residence permits and visa requirements for children under sixteen. It also sought to move power from local Foreigners' Offices to the national level. In a practical sense, this meant giving the federal Interior Ministry the ability to issue emergency administrative orders to ban local authorities from issuing residence permits for specific groups of foreigners or for all foreigners so that the federal office could react more quickly to "combat potential undesirable developments."[36]

The Interior Ministry's 1983 memorandum uniformly described migration as an event that had happened in the past rather than as an ongoing reality that would continue to need regulation in the future. The author of the memorandum insisted that any new Law on Foreigners would have to make "a legally and socially important distinction" between the "first generation" and the "second generation" on the "basis of the contract." This distinction needed to be preserved in both the migrant's ability to bring family members to Germany and in his or her access to citizenship. The "first generation" should have more ability to bring family members into the country, but no increased access to naturalization because the "'basis of the contract' of recruitment offers no such expectation or reason." The second generation should have increased access to naturalization for reasons of the "public interest," but no ability to sponsor family members for migration. Specifically, "second generation" foreigners would be able to marry a foreigner and bring that foreigner to the FRG only if they had previously tried to naturalize as a German and failed through no fault of their own—typically because the other state had refused to cancel their previous citizenship status.[37] The parents would still have claims on German society based on their labor contract, but the children would have to naturalize in order to have claims of their own. There would be no new sources of migration and no new transnational families.

After the threat of the Association Agreement was defused in 1987, the Kohl government determined that it was time to revisit this memorandum. In January 1988, the Interior Ministry under Friedrich Zimmermann authored a sweeping proposal for reform that closely followed the logic of the 1983 memorandum by splitting the Law on Foreigners into two separate laws based on generations. The "first generation" and their immediate family members already living in the FRG would be regulated by the Law on the Integration of Foreigners (AIG), while all other foreigners, including current students, current asylum seekers, and any foreigners who came to Germany in the future, would be regulated by the Law on the Residence of Foreigners (AAG). In the eyes of the Interior Ministry, the guest worker program had been a mistake, and the "integration" law was a one-time-only offer to resolve that mistake. The offer of "integration" would be withdrawn for future foreigners, who would never be offered anything but residence.

The AIG for the first generation of "guest workers" allowed them to apply for a secure residency status after five years and to sponsor spouses and children under sixteen to migrate to West Germany as long as both parents lived there. These immediate family members would be eligible for a newly created status, the "Family Residence Permit." The "Family Residence Permit" was an entirely new residence category that did not entitle the holder to sponsor further family members and which could be converted into an independent right to residence only after five years. This meant that the "second generation" would have to become German citizens to be able to sponsor their own spouses for migration.

The AAG for students, asylum seekers, and future migrants would have made secure residence status the exception rather than the rule. It proceeded from the assumption that there was a "primacy of public interest before the interest of the foreigner" because "every state has the right and the duty, first to care for the welfare of its own people." This meant that "foreigner law is not immigration law. Foreigners should from now on only be granted limited residence." All residence permits would be linked to a specific purpose and no residence permits could be issued for longer than eight years. Future workers would be able to bring their spouses, but students would be allowed to bring spouses only on a case-by-case basis, and asylum seekers would be able to bring spouses only if they were already married when they entered the FRG and were unable to safely leave the FRG. Children would have the right to move with their parents only if they were under the age of six. Children who were between the ages of six and fifteen would be allowed to come on a case-by-case basis and only if both parents already lived in Germany. Parents also had to bring children quickly, as children became ineligible for migration after one parent had been in possession of an unlimited residence permit for more than a year. Children could achieve secure residency status once they turned eighteen, had lived in Germany for at least eight years, had a parent with a secure residency status, and were economically self-supporting.[38]

What would navigating such a law have looked like for an individual trying to achieve a secure residence status? A foreigner who had come to the FRG to work could first apply for an "unlimited residence permit" after five years of residence, at which point officials would have the discretion to decide if there was in fact a "public interest" in her continued residence. If this was granted, she could continue to live in the Federal Republic. After ten years of residence she could apply for a long-term residence authorization providing enhanced protection from deportation. If she had worked for the entire decade, she would have a right to such a document, but if she had been unemployed for any part of that period, officials would again have full discretion over whether to grant the more secure residence status. Although her spouse would be allowed to join her, he would receive a Family Residence Permit, a status that gave him no right to an independent residence status in the case of divorce, death, or deportation in the first five years. The couple's children could come once both parents lived in Germany, but if they were over six, officials would once again have discretion over whether to allow the children to come to Germany to live with their parents. The children would again be subject to administrative discretion about their future status on turning eighteen, at which point they would have the right to a secure residence status only if they could prove that they could support themselves financially on their eighteenth birthday. The children would have to become German citizens if they wanted to marry a foreign spouse and sponsor that spouse for marriage. The law was intended to make it impossible for foreigners to make long-term plans about life in the FRG. The Interior Ministry claimed that it was defending the FRG against "advance troops of minors" and insisted "the personal plan that is demanded from these foreigners is their return."[39]

The AIG/AAG draft leaked first to the social work associations and then to the press. *Der Spiegel* reported on the draft on April 4 and April 18, 1988. This series of events echoed the 1977 leak of the Schmidt cabinet's "17 theses," which had revealed to the public the divergence between the hardline Labor Ministry and the other ministries. In this case, the AIG/AAG draft "proved to be political dynamite," and the hardline Interior Ministry met with nearly universal disapproval.[40] Wolfgang Pahle of the German Confederation of Unions criticized the bifurcation of the law, writing that while the AIG appeared to respond to criticism, the AAG "only treats foreigners as burdensome objects and is shaped by the spirit of nationalist ideas."[41] Liselotte Funcke made a similar critique when she told a reporter, "We have a crack straight through the families—I am allowed to care about some of them and not about others."[42] She wrote a letter to Chancellor Kohl in which she called it "incomprehensible and unjustifiable from a standpoint of family policy," in part because it would "unleash a hurried practice of marriage and family migration." She did not understand why the proposed law had done nothing to improve the status of dependent family members: "women will be prevented from finding shelter from abuse in women's shelters, and men will be able to rid themselves of their families more easily, by no longer paying support."[43] These letters to Kohl, like every letter for the last seven years of her tenure, went unanswered.

The proposal proved such a political disaster that Zimmermann was demoted to transport minister in April 1989 and replaced by Wolfgang Schäuble as interior minister.[44] Schäuble was a CDU member who had first been elected to the Bundestag in 1972 and who had become one of Chancellor Kohl's closest advisors, appointed a federal Minister for Special Affairs in 1984. The role in the Interior Ministry was his first national role with a portfolio, and it would become the launchpad for an exceptional career that would include Finance Minister and President of the Bundestag. In 1989, however, he was new on the national stage. By the time he was appointed, the CDU/CSU had lost its majority in the Bundesrat, so passing a Foreigners' Law would require more compromise, and the proposal he presented in October 1989 reflected an accommodation of this fact.

The Schäuble proposal represented a liberalization of the AIG/AAG draft in several ways. First, it codified existing practice on family reunion into national law for the first time, giving foreigners far more predictability than they had had in the decades of circulars subject to local administrative discretion. Foreigners who had lived in the country for eight years would have the right to bring a spouse, while children who were over the age of sixteen could not move to Germany to be with their parents. Second, it turned the "return option" administrative circular issued in December 1988 into national law. Youth who had left with their parents would be able to return between the ages of fifteen and twenty-one if they had lived in the FRG for at least eight years, gone to school in the FRG for at least six years, and could provide for themselves financially.[45] These improvements would be possible because the law also proposed that children under sixteen would require residence permits and visas starting from the age of six months. Children's incorporation into the state would depend on the state's ability to see them.

The proposal also included significant improvements in citizenship entitlement for adults and independent residency rights for spouses. First, it stated that citizenship should "as a general rule" be granted for first-generation immigrants who had lived in Germany for at least fifteen years and for second- and third-generation immigrants who applied for citizenship between the ages of sixteen and twenty-four, having previously lived in the FRG for at least eight years, attended school in the FRG for at least six years, and given up any other citizenships.[46] This was a significant change that still stopped short of providing a full entitlement to citizenship. Second, it reduced the period of forced dependent residency for spousal migrants from five years to four years, or three years in "hardship cases," which included cases in which the sponsor had passed away.

Many of the jurists and legal scholars who had criticized the Law on Foreigners since 1965 saw the proposal as one more artifact of a quarter century of failed policy on foreigners. West Berlin judge Fritz Franz argued that the new proposal contradicted the Basic Law.[47] Helmut Rittsteig, the specialist in international law who had first elaborated the legal justification for an age limit of six, was particularly critical of the new law's effects on young families, including the new visa requirement for children and the fact that children born in the Federal Republic would require a residence permit within six months of birth, especially because this baby's residence permit would require "sufficient housing." He warned that this turned "the housing shortage into an instrument of the exclusion of people who are born here without German citizenship. . . . It can make abortion into an unavoidable necessity."[48] He also criticized the proposal for clinging to the idea of separate regulation of residence permits and work permits, which would continue to create populations of legal residents who could not work legally and thus force people onto the illegal labor market.

The discussion over the Schäuble proposal was cut short by other events, as the Berlin Wall fell less than a month after the proposal's first public hearing. Turks in Berlin would feel that "the wall fell on our heads" as the process of German unification was accompanied by an intensification of racist violence.[49] Within the Kohl cabinet, unification legitimized previously held positions about migration and citizenship. When Schäuble introduced his second draft of the Law on Foreigners to the Bundesrat in February 1990, he explained that unification had only been possible because the Federal Republic had never changed its citizenship laws, explaining that "precisely the most recent developments in Europe and in Germany show that national identity is a necessary element that stabilizes and secures freedom."[50] People who suffered the intensification of everyday racism and racist violence in this period would likely not have agreed, but their perspectives had not been sought by those preparing the new proposal.

The new proposal presented in the early months of 1990 continued to maintain that migration and integration could be put in the past tense, insisting that the FRG would be able to integrate guest workers successfully only if it could guarantee that migration was "a finite process."[51] In the parliamentary debate on the proposal, several members of the Green Party and the SPD argued that migration was an ongoing reality rather than a single aberration. Cornelie Sonntag-Wolgast, an SPD representative from Nürnberg, argued that "migration cannot be shut off with the press of a button. As long as there is still unfreedom and economic need, it is certainly not a process with a foreseeable end. In this area . . . we still have infinitely more to experience."[52] German Meneses Vogl of the Green Party, who represented Berlin and had been born in Peru, insisted that "in a few years—you will see—laws will no longer suffice. We will have to put up walls and borders with barbed wire, because the poverty and the misery in the world grow, and people will continue to flee. Then as democrats we will probably have to become murderers."[53] These speakers called for a law that responded to the ongoing reality of migration rather than the fantasy of a reconstituted and purified German nation.

The second hearing on the Schäuble proposal in April 1990 was "ill-tempered" and "marred by personal insults."[54] The Interior Ministry had responded to criticism of the proposal with a few minor changes—for example, to the provision requiring residence permits for six-month old children. This requirement was opposed by groups from across the political spectrum, from conservative Catholics, who saw it as a provision that would force foreign women to have abortions, to radical feminists, who saw it as a racist provision intended to force foreign women to have abortions.[55] The new proposal only required that children have "sufficient housing" for their residence permit upon turning two years old, giving parents time to find a larger apartment before the child learned to walk. Catholics and feminists were both disappointed.

Green Party representatives uniformly opposed the new law. During the April hearings, Meneses Vogl repeated his prediction that closed borders would lead to dead bodies and called for a minute of silence for "the future victims of this law," warning, "The new Law on Foreigners remains a wall."[56] Erika Trenz of the Green Party had previously described the AIG/AAG proposal as "racist" in 1988, when she had been rebuked by Richard Stücklen, CSU member and Vice-President of the Bundestag, who told her that "comparisons with the Third Reich, with National Socialism," were not allowed in the Bundestag.[57] In April 1990, Trenz repeated her charge that the Schäuble proposal represented "institutionalized racism." This time Hildegard Hamm-Brücher of the FDP criticized Trenz's choice of words. Hamm-Brücher had been born in 1921 and forced to leave her school during the Nazi period because her grandmother was Jewish. She told Trenz that "since the older members of this body had to live twelve

years under institutionalized racism, ladies and gentlemen, I ask you, especially the younger colleagues, to have respect for these horrible experiences and
not to introduce such terms into everyday political business."[58] Because "race"
remained taboo within political speech, explicitly anti-racist critiques were difficult to articulate in parliament.

The 1990 Law on Foreigners passed both houses of parliament on May 11,
1990. The vote was deliberately scheduled only two days before a regional election in Lower Saxony that would lead to the CDU/CSU losing its majority in
the Bundesrat. Contemporaries criticized the CDU for taking an "unashamedly
majoritarian" approach to pushing through the law. The 1990 revision to the
Law on Foreigners created significant new rights for dependent children, most
prominently the "return option," but it did little to improve rights for spouses.
Following years of debate on the true motives of family migrants, the "return option" for youth functioned as a kind of family romance for the Federal Republic.
Foreign children would have the opportunity to choose Germany over their
own bad parents, who remained on the outside looking in.

The Introduction of Residence Permits for Minors

This new inclusion of children was predicated on their documentation, which
for the first time was required for children under sixteen. The Interior Ministry
had wanted to introduce these required residence permits and visas to increase
the state's knowledge of its population and, with it, its capacity for action for
over a decade. In 1982, the state interior ministries debated the appropriate
response to adult women who arrived with children and without appropriate
entry documents. The Bavarian Interior Ministry felt strongly that if it could
turn away the woman, it should also be able to turn away children without adult
supervision. The federal Interior Ministry explained that such a practice would
be illegal, because as long as children did not require entry documents, there
was no legal basis to exclude them. The absurd situation underscored the need
for the law to state that residence permits and visas were required for minors.[59]

Six years later, the federal Interior Ministry saw that unaccompanied minors
were arriving at the Frankfurt airport and applying for asylum, seizing this as
an opportunity to put the issue on the national agenda.[60] The Interior Ministry
argued that the introduction of residence permits and visas for children under
sixteen should not have been controversial when compared to international
standards, particularly since the FRG, Spain, Andorra, and South Africa were
the only four countries that did not require such documentation.[61] Even though
the FRG was an outlier internationally, the Interior Ministry faced vigorous domestic opposition to its plan to require children to have documents.

Domestic civil society groups opposed what they saw as an attempt to keep minors from seeking asylum in Germany. The Foreigners' Council of Essen passed a measure condemning the requirement as an example of the "hollowing out of Article 16."[62] Pro Asyl and a number of left-leaning Christian groups organized a letter-writing campaign to persuade the government that the measure was un-Christian and that it violated Germany's obligation to atone for Nazi crimes.[63] One group took out a full-page advertisement in the *Frankfurter Allgemeine Zeitung* with the title "Anne Frank Could No Longer Flee."[64] The growing anti-racist movement in the FRG focused on its obligation to keep its borders open to minors fleeing danger.

The more consequential domestic opposition was a response to the Interior Ministry's well-known desire to impose an age limit of six for all child migration. The Labor Minister and Foreign Minister both worried that, if residence permits for children were introduced, the Interior Minister would unilaterally impose the age limit by administrative circular. Both ministries would agree to support residence permits for children only if children from former guest worker countries were exempt from the requirement.[65] The FDP, the Justice Ministry, and the German Embassy in Ankara also took a strong stance against residence permits for minors.[66] As a result, the reform to the Law on Foreigners passed in 1990 included the curious provision that residence permits and visas would thereafter be required for children from every country but Turkey, Yugoslavia, Morocco, and Tunisia.

Interior Minister Manfred Kanther of the CDU proposed to end the exemption in January 1997. He pointed to a dramatic increase in unaccompanied minors from these four countries to justify ending the exemption. In 1994 only 198 unaccompanied minors had arrived in the FRG, but in 1996, that number had swelled to 2,068. Parents or relatives collected 1,300 of the unaccompanied minors at the airport—making them only briefly "unaccompanied"—while 352 of the remaining children applied for asylum. Kanther invoked the image of a child as a victim when he variously described the requirement as an anti-smuggling measure and as an anti-drug-trafficking measure. He claimed that parents "smuggled" children to the FRG hoping that their children would be able to receive residency and sponsor other family members for entry. He also claimed that Kurdish adults sent their children to Germany as drug couriers: "The mini-dealers are especially useful for the scene, because children cannot be charged as criminals." Barbara John, Commissioner for Foreigners in Berlin who had previously fought for a pregnancy exception in the 1980s, also used the language of protective paternalism, explaining that the measure would protect children from being "carried here and there and being misused for purposes that are more than suspicious."[67] Neither considered the possibility that children might in fact be fleeing danger and coming to the FRG for refuge.

The Turkish Community in Germany and the Green Party launched a national protest against the measure. They argued that it would not just make it harder for

Figure 7.1 Child carrying "Does my doll also need a visa?" sign at July 1997 protest in Berlin against new visa requirements for foreign children. Agencja Fotograficzna Caro/ Alamy Stock Photo.

unaccompanied minors to apply for asylum in Germany, but that it would also create problems for approximately 800,000 foreign children who already lived in Germany.[68] The Turkish Community in Germany called for children to boycott school on February 27, 1997. The Greens also used the protest to raise the issue of citizenship, with Özdemir telling *Der Spiegel* that "the paper that would be appropriate for children from the former recruitment countries, is not a residence permit, but a German passport."[69] Despite the protest, Kanther's proposal passed in March 1997, ending an exception within the Schengen Zone that was itself a legacy of the contestation over the age of limit of six years. The requirement that minors have residence permits was a watershed in German migration history, one that made children both knowable and excludable. This possibility of exclusion appears to have been a precondition for inclusion in the form of citizenship.

Citizenship Reform and the Problem of Dual Citizenship

The SPD had promised to support new restrictions on asylum in 1992 in return for comprehensive citizenship reform that would include a form of birthright citizenship for foreign children born in Germany. As the SPD and CDU debated the precise form that this new citizenship would take, dual citizenship emerged as a particular point of conflict. If citizenship were extended to the "second" and "third" generation of guest workers, would those new citizens be able to retain their old citizenship, or would they have to relinquish it? The CDU/CSU maintained a steadfast opposition to the idea of dual citizenship for the "second generation" of guest workers. Edmund Stoiber, CSU chairman and Interior Minister of Bavaria, quipped in 1999 that dual citizenship was "more dangerous than the RAF," the terrorist organization responsible for thirty-four deaths between 1970 and 1998. This hyperbole distracted attention from the hundreds of thousands of German dual citizens who already existed and who as a group were not known for assassinations or kidnappings. German women had been able to pass their citizenship down to children since 1974, which meant that thousands of children had been born with irrevocable dual citizenship every year since then.[70] At the time, co-ethnic German migrants who left communist countries for the FRG could also retain dual citizenship. Former Germans whose citizenship had been stripped by the Nazi regime could also apply to have that citizenship restored without renouncing other citizenships.[71]

As Germany was already home to hundreds of thousands, perhaps even millions, of dual citizens, the CDU/CSU hostility to dual citizenship for "guest workers" and their children arose from the fear of a specific Turkish-German hybridity. Turkey had changed its citizenship law significantly since the 1964 law allowing both men and women to pass Turkish citizenship on to their children. The military government introduced new reforms in 1981 that made it possible for the state to strip citizenship from individuals charged with endangering national security, but that also introduced widespread toleration of dual citizenship.[72] Even though Turkey tolerated dual citizens, Germany did not, which meant that many Turkish citizens in Germany remained reluctant to acquire German citizenship so long as it would require them to renounce their Turkish one. Turkey responded to these concerns in 1995 by introducing a "pink card" that enabled people who had renounced Turkish citizenship to continue to be treated like Turkish citizens in matters such as purchasing property and taxation.

The CDU/CSU opposed dual citizenship. It tried to avoid the problem by proposing a new revocable category of citizenship for children: not Staatsangehörigkeit but rather Staatszugehörigkeit, a change without a self-evident semantic meaning in German. The new category avoided the legal difficulty whereby Article 16 of the Basic Law declared that German citizenship— Staatsangehörigkeit—was irrevocable and could not be stripped of someone without his or her consent. Under the new proposal, foreign children under twelve with two parents who had been resident in Germany for ten years would receive a revocable Staatszugehörigkeit. If children obtained release from their foreign citizenship by the age of nineteen, they would graduate to full German citizenship—*Staatsangehörigkeit*—but if they did not, they would lose the revocable citizenship. Since *Staatszugehörigkeit* was only a quasi-citizenship, the issue of consenting to loss of citizenship no longer mattered.[73]

Citizenship comes with a host of political rights that are not very relevant for minors, so what was the purpose of giving minors revocable citizenship at all? It might be understood as a kind of "training period" for national identity, a way for children to practice thinking of themselves as Germans as they grew up and interacted with German society. To graduate to full German citizenship and shed their provisional and revocable citizenship, children would have to actively reject the foreign citizenship that their parents still held. The proposed category was designed to avoid accusations of Nazi-era "Germanization" by giving children born in the FRG a choice about whether they wanted to become German adults. It did so by creating a revocable citizenship status, which was a particularly odd choice when the Nazi legal system had also been infamous for revoking the citizenship of Jewish Germans.

The CDU/CSU coalition splintered around the proposal. Interior Minister Manfred Kanther and the entire CSU favored the revocable citizenship model of *Staatszugehörigkeit*, but in October 1995, a group of CDU members who found it unwieldly presented a proposal for the more traditional *Staatsangehörigkeit*. This second proposal would have given full German citizenship to all children born in Germany as long as at least one parent was resident—but once again, it would have required these children to choose a single citizenship by the age of twenty-one. This model stood little chance as long as the Interior Ministry opposed it.

When the SPD won the general election and, with it, the chancellorship in 1998, it entered a governing coalition with the Green Party that promised citizenship reform as one of its signature achievements. The "Red-Green coalition" initially had enough votes to pass its own reform without any votes from the CDU/CSU, which opened the possibility for extensive dual citizenship. The Red-Green coalition lost its majority in the Bundesrat after the CDU/CSU won the February 1999 elections in Hesse on a campaign against dual citizenship. After those elections, the Red-Green coalition was forced to compromise on its initial plan in order to get the needed votes. The eventual result of this compromise was the 1999 "option model," whereby a child born in Germany to foreign parents would be granted German citizenship at birth; however, he or she would be forced to choose between German citizenship and the citizenship of the child's parents between the ages of eighteen and twenty-three. This child could become a German citizen only if his or her parents had lived in the FRG for at least eight years and if at least one of them already possessed a permanent residence permit. The reform excluded the possibility that undocumented migrants could have children who would become German citizens.

Only the FDP was truly happy with the compromise. Guido Westerwelle of the FDP supported giving children full citizenship because it would enable them to feel German from an earlier age: "If you allow the children to grow up with a foreign consciousness, in order to have to integrate them later, I have to tell you, that [you] do not solve the problem. It would be better to first integrate the children and give them the feeling that they belong to us."[74] His reasoning echoes the formula for integration from the *Second Generation* study—to successfully achieve a German identity, it is vitally important that children first feel themselves to be German.

The other parties saw the "option model" as a "ticking time bomb" destined to create conflicts within families as children were forced to choose between their identities on reaching the age of majority. Kerstin Müller, head of the Green Party in parliament, explained that "many parents will understand their children's choice in favor of German citizenship as a renunciation of their own connections to their home country, that means as a choice against their parents. I ask you: do you really want that?"[75] CDU representative Wolfgang Bosbach, of Bergisch Gladbach, echoed her reasoning when he explained that the "option model" would "create conflict inside foreign families at the moment when the young adults must choose between two citizenships and the parents insist that they hold on to the ancestral citizenship."[76] The Greens and the CDU/CSU agreed that the proposal would create conflict, but had different ideas about how to resolve these conflicts within families.

The Green Party wanted to significantly open access to citizenship for adults, including the possibility of dual citizenship for adults.[77] Their representatives also repeatedly pointed out that legal citizenship was not enough, because society would also have to recognize these new citizens as Germans. This is the context in which Özdemir, a German citizen since 1984 and one of the first two Turkish-Germans elected to the Bundestag, asked, "How will we deal with the fact that the hair color and the skin color will not change? We will have German citizens with darker skin colors. We will have German citizens, who have taken somewhat more sun than the average in this republic." He argued that Germany would need to pass anti-discrimination laws to protect these citizens.[78] Marieluise Beck, at the time the Federal Commissioner for Migration and Integration, explained that "it is about the question of whether this society can recognize it as normal that black people with a German passport also belong to us. . . . As a majority society we have not learned that people who look different, people who are different have also become an integral part of our society."[79] The Greens deliberately did not use the language of racism or racialization, but their language consistently pointed to the social problem of race.

The CDU/CSU had a different solution for family conflict: to refuse to grant birthright citizenship to foreign children. They argued that such a policy would actually violate the rights of foreign parents. Meinrad Belle of the CDU worried that "because the parents do not have a right of refusal, German citizenship will be forced on foreign children and will perhaps plant the seed of conflict in these families."[80] Erwin Marschewski of the CDU rejected the proposal "because it is wrong to give children dual citizenship at birth—and against the will of their parents."[81] CSU chairman Stoiber, who had previously compared dual citizenship to domestic terrorism, worried that children would "automatically receive German citizenship, without their foreign parents having the right to reject German citizenship."[82] This argument for parents' rights was a kind of ironic reversal. The CDU/CSU had styled itself as the party of children's rights in the 1980s when it argued for an age limit of six to protect children from being brought into Germany by their parents at the wrong time. In the fight against dual citizenship, it styled itself as the party of parents' rights, because parents ought to be able to protect their children from German citizenship. These two arguments clearly did not derive from a coherent position on the role of parental authority within the family but instead from a coherent position that Germany needed to be protected from foreigners at any cost.

CDU/CSU members also worried about foreign teenagers. Günther Beckstein, Interior Minister of Bavaria, was concerned that Turkish parents might take advantage of birthright citizenship by having children in the FRG and then sending them to Turkey for education, bringing them back on German passports only when they were already eighteen or nineteen years old.[83] Other CDU/CSU members worried about the possibility that young foreign mothers might create a kind of sleeper generation of Germans-in-waiting. An eighteen-year-old woman with German citizenship could move to Turkey, where she could have a child who became German by virtue of the principle of descent. The woman could then relinquish her German citizenship in favor of Turkish citizenship upon turning twenty-three, but her child would retain its German citizenship despite never having been there. The child would then have the right to enter Germany whenever it wanted.[84] CDU/CSU politicians were only willing to consider what they called a "citizenship assurance," a promise that foreign children born in Germany to parents who had unlimited residence permits could receive German citizenship upon turning eighteen provided they fulfilled all of the requirements. These requirements included having lived in Germany for the previous ten years, not having committed any deportable offenses, and renouncing any other citizenships. Giving German citizenship to children who had not yet proven themselves represented a threat to social order. Foreign parents would be unwilling to imagine their children as German citizens, who would in turn misuse their citizenship.

Citizenship reform took the shape that it did because politicians had spent decades describing children as "ticking time bombs" in the hands of parents who were already irrevocably lost. Politicians in the 1980s had argued that it was more important to solve the "marriage problem" than the child migration problem, because limiting marriage migration might bring the creation of new foreigners to an end. The same tortured logic applied to the decision to focus on birthright citizenship. In the most cynical account, some politicians who agreed to the citizenship reform imagined that turning children into Germans would end the "infinite renewal" of non-Germans into the future.

The state extended the new entitlement to birthright citizenship retroactively ten years, so that children born after January 1, 1990, could receive German citizenship. Their parents had until the end of 2000 to pay 500 DM to make the application. The high fee, the short open period, and the fact that the cut-off date split up pairs of siblings all proved to be significant obstacles. Parents filed retroactive citizenship applications for only about 10 percent of the children who were eligible.[85] The requirement that one parent of a child already have a permanent residence status continues to be very effective in restricting citizenship access. Even in 2012, roughly half the children born to foreign parents in Germany were ineligible for citizenship because neither of their parents possessed a permanent residence status.[86]

These new citizens also anticipated having to choose between their two citizenships. When sociologist Çetin Çelik studied Turkish teenage boys in Germany in 2011, he found that many were opting for the Turkish passport. Their everyday experiences meant that they had come to believe that "the German passport will not protect them from being discriminated against. . . . From their perspective, if they decide to carry a German passport, they will sacrifice their identity for nothing."[87] Criminologist Sandra Bucerius came to similar conclusions in her fieldwork with young Turkish men in Frankfurt, who had "experienced the exclusionary German rhetoric for so long that they simply did not know what to make of the change."[88] Citizenship reform did not solve the challenges of social recognition for Germans "who have more sun than other Germans," to use Özdemir's tongue-in-cheek phrase. Because German society continued to produce German citizen children who were not socially recognized as Germans, many of these new citizens feel ambivalent about the prospect of retaining German citizenship as adults.

Integration Tests in the Twenty-First Century

Several federal states responded to the new citizenship reform by using administrative circulars to introduce new requirements for citizenship, particularly tests for adult applicants. In 2006, Baden-Württemberg introduced a test that asked applicants from majority-Muslim countries highly leading questions about their attitudes toward gender relations and terrorism. The national government responded to the ensuing controversy with the 2007 law on German citizenship, which ruled out local innovations by creating a single national standard for citizenship. Prospective citizens would have to make a spoken declaration of loyalty to the Federal Republic and its laws, prove that they had German language skills at level B1, and pass a standard naturalization test including questions about German history, culture, and politics. In the "integration courses" that sociologist Jessica Autumn Brown attended, she found that German instructors lecture their foreign students about the deviant gender relationships within Islam and inform migrants that intermarriage is a German value and a positive indicator of their own willingness to integrate.[89] The function of these courses is to present German liberal values as timeless and unchanging. In so doing, they overlook not just the fact that many Germans would still be uneasy about allowing their daughters to date foreign men, but also that the German state has been actively placing obstacles in the paths of binational couples for a long time.[90]

Would-be citizens also had to prove that they would be responsible members of the community, and the 2007 reform raised the requirements for citizenship in two different ways. First, it stated that a possible disqualification for a citizenship application was having been sentenced to a cumulative three months of prison. Before 2007, six months of prison had been the disqualifying threshold. This new requirement poses an insurmountable obstacle for many young men who might otherwise apply for citizenship.[91] Second, young applicants for citizenship between the ages of eighteen and twenty-three also had to be able to prove that they could provide for themselves and their dependents financially. Before 2007, young applicants were eligible for citizenship even if they had previously used social welfare. These two reforms together raised the standard in ways that excluded a larger number of youth.

The reforms introduced in 2007 also created new barriers for would-be family migrants, most notably language tests for dependent spouses—an "integration" measure first suggested by Liselotte Funcke in 1981. Politicians frequently describe these tests as an excellent way of protecting foreign women from forced marriage, although one wonders why a forced marriage could not include a forced German class. Scholars have shown that the measure penalizes low-income and rural migrants as well as those who lack access to German language classes in their home country.[92]

The state's reluctance to accept dual citizenship remained perhaps the most important obstacle to increased naturalization in 2007. The first group of children who had acquired German citizenship based on birth on German soil in 1990 began to turn twenty-three in 2013, which meant that they had to choose between their German and foreign citizenships. These young adults organized into groups like DeuKische Generation to defend their ability to retain the citizenship of their parents as well as German citizenship. The opposition parties in the Bundestag—at the time the Green Party, Die Linke, and the SPD—united to introduce a measure to support this demand. They argued that dual citizenship was becoming more common every year, particularly since 2007, when the German state decided that dual citizenship between Germany and another country within the EU was generally acceptable. In light of this change, the continued refusal to grant dual citizenship beyond the EU appeared to reflect a specific prejudice against Turkish German hybridity.[93]

CDU/CSU politicians responded to this proposal by arguing that the European Union was based on a shared community of values, so dual citizenship with another EU state did not create the same conflicts in values and loyalty as for potential Turkish-German citizens. Reinhard Grindel of the CDU was one of the few politicians to specify possible conflicts when he argued that Turkish families continued to present an obstacle to integration. Children from Turkish families might have German passports so that they could go on class trips, "but the problem is . . . that today they can all go along, yes, but many— precisely Turkish girls—may not go along, because their parents forbid them. As long as we have these parallel structures, that means that children cannot play sports together. . . . We will be cementing parallel societies."[94] Later in the debate he defended the new requirements for marriage migration by explaining that requiring spouses to take language courses before entering Germany was good for women because the courses "give women above all self-confidence and strength, so that they come to Germany better prepared than was previously the case. For this reason I say to you: whoever wants to do away with this instrument, is anti-women and anti-integration."[95] Ingo Wellenreuther, also of the CDU, argued that toleration of dual citizenship was unnecessary because most dual citizens were already opting for German citizenship, noting that "it is specifically young women who have said that they choose German citizenship, because they find the image of women in their home country problematic."[96] With their allusions to Turkish gender roles, Grindel and Wellenreuther subtly supported their party's claim that Turkish-German dual citizenship was fundamentally different from European-German dual citizenship because Turkish values were incompatible with German ones. The unanimous opposition of the governing CDU/CSU meant that the dual citizenship measure failed in June 2013.

Later that year the CDU/CSU and SPD both gained seats in the 2013 federal elections, while support for the FDP collapsed, with the party failing to meet the 5 percent threshold to qualify for seats in the Bundestag. Unable to form a governing coalition with the FDP, the CDU/CSU was forced to make a coalition deal with the SPD, which insisted that the law tolerating dual citizenship for children needed to be part of the deal. The new law went into effect on November 23, 2014. While adults continue to be left out of the reform, the new law allows children who received German citizenship at birth to hold dual citizenship indefinitely as long as they have lived in Germany for eight years and either attended a German school for six years or completed vocational training in Germany.[97] Foreign youth themselves brought about this change through their own activism, and it is a monumental change. In 1981, eighteen-year-olds in West Berlin needed to be able to prove eight years of residence simply to receive a residence permit that allowed them to continue to live in Germany. By 2014, those same eight years of residence allow a new generation of eighteen-year-olds to maintain dual citizenship.

* * *

The foreign children who grew up in Germany in the 1970s and early 1980s had integrated into German society far better than the panicked discourse of national politics had ever predicted. That surprisingly integrated foreign child would come to play a starring role in a story that the German state told itself about its own liberalization. The state could save the child it had liberated from a dismal life outside of Europe, and it did so, first with the 1988 "return option" circular, later with the 1990 Law on Foreigners, and finally with the 1999 citizenship law. The 1988 "return option" was an important step because it recognized that youth could make autonomous decisions apart from their parents and, in so doing, irrevocably split the family within migration policy. Children who used the "return option" were unable to sponsor their parents or siblings for family migration. They had chosen the FRG over the family.

The 1990 Law on Foreigners created the documentary basis for future child-centered legislation because it extended the residence permit requirement to children. The bureaucratic fantasy of the deportable child was whispered in youth service offices in the 1960s, enacted on a de facto basis through forensic age verification at the Frankfurt airport in the 1970s, circulated in draft form by the Interior Ministry in the 1980s, and finally enshrined in the law in 1990. The Interior Ministry had been so vocal about its desire to enact an age limit of six years that children from the former "guest worker" countries were initially excluded from this new requirement. The ministry used another increase in unaccompanied minors seeking asylum in the mid-1990s to argue that it was necessary to extend the residence permit requirement to all children, something that happened in 1997.

The fact that the child was finally excludable likely played a large role in enabling its inclusion in the form of the child-centric 1999 citizenship reform. The reform enables children born in the Federal Republic to acquire German citizenship as long as they were born to two parents with a legal residence status, at least one of whom had already been in the country for eight years. Birthright citizenship for children represents a significant shift in German citizenship policy, but the compromise that was reached reflects much older parts of the German discourse on migration. The compromise rejected the idea of hybridity by excluding dual citizenship, and it emphasized the possibility of being born into German identity over the possibility of actively choosing German identity.

The Green Party repeatedly rejected measures that helped foreign children while leaving their parents on the outside looking in. Green politicians advocated expanding the "return option" to all foreigners and not just youth, opposed the introduction of residence permit requirements for youth, and supported both dual citizenship and significant liberalization in adult access to German citizenship. It grounded all of these arguments in a new language of international human rights rather than calling on the FRG's constitutional imperative to defend the family. Although an alternative vision was presented, the state consistently reached compromises that incorporated children and not adults. This is not a surprise. The image of the oppressed child had been central to the migration discussion ever since the 1974 panic about child allowance migrants seeking higher welfare payments. Supporters of migrant rights successfully used images of unhappy foreign children to secure more rights for those children, but those rights were contingent on the continued exclusion of their adult family members. The state cast itself as the paternalist protector of foreign children, who were recuperated insofar as they had made efforts to integrate themselves into German society against the wishes of their allegedly repressive parents.

The paternalist state passed significant reforms in the 1990s but consistently failed to incorporate the more radical critique advanced by the Green Party and by migrant activists themselves. The reforms of the 1980s and 1990s made a concrete difference for millions of foreigners while leaving in place both the idea that Germany was not an "immigration country" and the paternalism of migration law—the assumption that the state always knows better than the foreign family. The FRG entered the twenty-first century with a new citizenship law as well as a political approach to migration that continued to lurch from crisis to crisis, approaching each new migrant as if she or he were the first one.

Conclusion

Migration Without End

The federal administrative court recognized broad family migration rights in 1973 with the expectation that family migrants would perform the "reproductive labor" of raising children, caring for ill family members, and running a household. Nearly from the moment the court issued this decision, the migration bureaucracy sought to limit its significance in practice by restricting family migration. Officials depicted family migrants as a group of burdensome dependents seeking to defraud the welfare state, and the child allowance panic made this narrative inherently plausible. Officials also attacked the court's argument that family migrants could perform socially valuable labor by describing their care work as a dangerous source of foreign values. This argument continues to surface whenever politicians complain about "Muslim patriarchs" who teach their sons to dominate women and who force their daughters to wear headscarves.

The history of family migration proves that the FRG liberalized and Westernized its political culture, but it also shows that this process entailed adopting the exclusions of gender and race inherent to liberalism. Officials initially expected the migrant family to resemble their limited understanding of the German family: a primary male breadwinner and a woman who perhaps was a secondary wage earner but was always a homemaker first. Families that appeared to violate this ideal were unable to gain admission into Germany. Although the limits of the acceptable "German family" expanded in the 1970s with the reform of marriage law, migration law lagged behind. Officials accused migrants and "foreigners," including the migrants' German-born children and grandchildren, of importing retrograde practices that West Germans had purportedly rejected. As West German women gained the ability to pass down their own citizenship in 1974, they became more a part of the nation and were able to retain their German identity even after marrying foreign men. German women dramatized

Fear of the Family. Lauren Stokes, Oxford University Press. © Oxford University Press 2022.
DOI: 10.1093/oso/9780197558416.003.0009

the progress that had been made by means of comparison to a composite foreign family with the wrong, patriarchal, backward values.

Migration law has also made the migrant community appear more uniformly heterosexual than it actually is. Politicians and scholars who complain about migrant homophobia rarely mention that Germany introduced same-sex civil unions only in 2001, which meant that for decades migrants who wanted to live with same-sex partners were cut off from legal migration through family reunification. When Turkish citizens living in the FRG formed the organization Türk-Gay in 1996, they were flooded with letters from Turkish citizens living in Turkey who were unable to get residence permits based on same-sex partnerships with either Germans or with Turks who lived in Germany.[1] These denied queer migrants might have had a lot to say to the working women who left Germany in the 1980s because they did not want to condemn their "trailing husbands" to idleness. Both experienced firsthand the effect of the migration law that created a particular form of family—a heterosexual couple that depends on the wages of a single breadwinner. Migration law ensures that precisely those migrants who might challenge the dominant family form are the ones most likely to be excluded from Germany.

The federal government has been slow to accept the reality that the FRG has become an "immigration country" and clumsy about dealing with the systematic effects of its own policies. Officials on the national level rarely treat the welfare state as an institution that can integrate foreign families. They have tended to manage their failure to recognize social reality by disavowing their own responsibility for the situation they created and placing the blame at the feet of the foreign family. When SPD member Thilo Sarrazin published *Germany Abolishes Itself* in 2010, mainstream commentators seized on his arguments about Muslims "reducing the quality of the German workforce upon which the nation's fate hangs" as a useful examination of "failed" integration while avoiding an explicit discussion of Sarrazin's racism.[2] Sarrazin's book rehearsed tropes that had long been bureaucratic common sense. Should the state build more affordable housing? No, it should blame migrants for moving into unsuitable housing and create punitive housing ordinances in the name of preventing overcrowding, only to restrict the number of places migrants could live and thereby worsen overcrowding. Should the state admit that its reform to child allowance payments failed to meet its objective of controlling migration flows? No, the state should blame foreign parents as morally reprehensible for responding to economic incentives intended to encourage German reproduction. Should the state try to integrate "family migrants" into the labor market? No, it should use work permits as a tool of labor market discipline and then blame people locked out of the legal labor market for working without papers. Should the state acknowledge the existence of racism in Germany and think seriously about what it means for a society in which migration continues to occur every year? No, it should embrace the idea that only very young children can become German and accuse migrants of fomenting racism through their presence in the country. Should the state change the law to emancipate foreign spouses and make it possible for them to establish a right of independent residence? No, it should make it more difficult for them to get married and to establish an independent economic or legal existence, then blame their resultant dependency on the purported male chauvinism of their home country. While hidebound and unresponsive in other ways, the federal state has never failed to invent new ways of blaming its own shortcomings on foreigners.

The state has tended to operate based on the fear of creating moral hazards for would-be migrants. It consistently fears that if it does too much for foreigners, it will encourage them to risk the journey to the FRG and to assume that the state will take care of them if their migration project fails. The repetitive mantra that "Germany is not an immigration country" has never been an accurate reflection of reality. It is better understood as a warning sign to potential migrants: enter at your own risk, because the state does not intend to take responsibility for any migration that may occur. Migration is a personal rather than a state project, which means that the state can hold foreigners personally responsible for bearing the costs of their decision to migrate to a state indifferent to their well-being. To reduce the risk of moral hazard to itself, the state further makes access to residence permits, work permits, and citizenship contingent on the migrant's passing a series of "integration" tests. Foreigners who wish to gain access must first demonstrate not just their ability to currently take care of themselves without recourse to the welfare state, but also their willingness to adapt to anything the labor market might ask of them in the future.

The 2003 unemployment reforms known as "Hartz IV" extended this logic of moral hazard to native-born Germans, who must no longer believe that the state is there to take care of them if they become unemployed. To receive benefits, the unemployed must consistently prove their "willingness" to work by accepting any job offered to them, including the "one Euro jobs" that pay 1 to 2 Euros per hour. Working-class, native-born white Germans accurately perceived the introduction of Hartz IV as the breaking of a social contract, and the SPD's decision to break this contract drove many working-class German voters away from the party. One of the parties that has benefited in recent years is the Alternative for Germany, an anti-immigration party that promises to repair the broken covenant in part by explicitly racializing the welfare state.

The fear that migration creates a moral hazard is not a uniquely German phenomenon. In 2003 the European Union passed a Family Reunification Directive that created minimum standards for family reunification for non-EU, or "third-country," nationals migrating to the EU. German diplomats succeeded in their goal of ensuring that the directive would preserve a maximum level of national sovereignty, prevailing over a French delegation that wanted to strengthen the EU-wide family reunification rights of migrants no matter what a given national government might legislate.[3] The directive allows states to require sponsors to provide evidence of income sufficient to support their family members as well as proof of sufficient housing. It allows states to raise the age limits for spousal migration to "ensure better integration and to prevent forced marriages" and also allows the use of pre-entry "integration measures" such as language tests.[4] States may require a would-be sponsor to first establish two years of legal residence, and family migrants must be able to acquire an independent resident status, one not yoked to the status of their sponsor, after no more than five years. Finally, EU countries must allow children to migrate to their families up to the age of fifteen; no country can impose an age limit lower than fifteen.

The directive was meant to create minimum norms for the migration of non-EU nationals to the EU, and it does exclude some of the most restrictive ideas that had previously been floated in the FRG, most notably the age limit of six years. However, officials in several European states "presented convergence towards these minimum norms as a desirable form of European harmonization," enabling politicians to justify new restrictive measures in states where a trend toward restriction had not previously been evident.[5] Denmark followed the FRG to become the second country in Europe to implement an age limit for child migration shortly after the directive. Denmark also created an age limit for spouses and an "attachment requirement" whereby a couple must prove a stronger "subjective attachment" to Denmark than to any other country for a Danish resident to be able to sponsor a dependent spouse for migration. Countries including Norway and the UK considered age limits but ultimately turned higher income requirements into the centerpiece of their new restrictions on family migration.[6]

While the widespread use of income requirements is new, these requirements are logical extrapolations from the reasoning that the Federal Administrative Court drew on in 1973 when it permitted the residence of the "Spanish grandmother." Family reunion has never been based on an abstract ideal of a right to family unity but on the concrete idea that unified families can take care of their own costs of social reproduction and in so doing unburden the welfare state. Having taken care of themselves, they are also drafted into caring for others. In her comparative study of France, Italy, and the Netherlands, Sara Farris shows that contemporary family migration regimes tend to direct newly arrived family migrants (gendered as female) into paid care work. This female migrant labor plays an important role in the ongoing restructuring of welfare regimes in Europe by lowering their labor costs as demands for their services rise in the context of aging European populations.[7] This situation has a particular irony in the FRG. In the 1960s, foreign women were recruited to German factories to enable German women to remain at home, but in the present, foreign women are increasingly the maids, home health aides, and nannies who enable German women to pursue careers outside the home.

Given the surprising consistency of German migration policy in the past, did the underlying logic of German migration policy shift in response to more recent migration crises? In the summer of 2015, when asylum seekers fleeing ongoing war in Syria, Afghanistan, and Iraq traveled over sea and over land to enter Europe, many states reacted by shutting their borders and refusing to accept any more asylum seekers. The FRG reacted differently when Chancellor Angela Merkel announced that it would accept every asylum seeker who arrived, a policy that enabled over 1 million people to register for asylum that year. This is the largest number of asylum seekers to have arrived in a single year since the 1992 constitutional amendment that limited access to asylum on German soil.

Over the next year, the reactions to this arrival played themselves out with breathtaking speed. State institutions struggled to process the number of asylum seekers. A grassroots "Welcome Refugees" movement stepped in, providing warm clothing, offering language courses, and placing asylum seekers with German families. Germans opposed to the arrival of the refugees also founded their own civil society organizations, including the "Patriotic Europeans Against the Islamization of Europe," in existence since 2014. The Alternative for Germany (AfD), a political party founded in 2013 as a Euroskeptic and anti-Euro party, opposed the acceptance of refugees, a stance it turned into electoral success in 2017.

Family migration was a significant part of the larger debate. In November 2015, Interior Minister Thomas de Mazière publicly opposed Chancellor Merkel's policy of welcome. He proposed creating a new asylum status whereby asylum seekers would not be eligible to bring their families with them. His proposal was criticized, particularly after New Year's Eve of 2015–2016, when foreign men living in Cologne and other German cities sexually harassed and assaulted German women, provoking a national and international scandal. Echoing a pattern familiar from the beginning of the guest worker recruitment, opponents of the proposal to ban family reunion now advocated family reunion to satisfy the purported sexual urges of young Muslim men. The figure of the dangerous foreign man is invoked to argue that foreign women should be able to domesticate him, but he is also invoked to argue that Germany should simply rid itself of foreigners altogether.

The desire to curb the number of asylum seekers in Europe also led to a dubious deal with Turkey in March 2016, in which the EU traded asylum seekers whose claims were still being considered in Europe for refugees whose claims had already been recognized as legitimate in Turkey. The first recognized refugees from Turkey arrived in Germany and Finland shortly after the agreement was reached.

Press coverage and photographic records of the transfer reiterated a consistent visual message about the nature of the deal that Europe had struck: young men were being sent back to camps in Turkey, while families with young children were being allowed to settle in Europe. Young men were portrayed as sources of sexual and political danger, but young families were depicted as grateful, hard-working, and, crucially, self-contained.

This deal applied only to families who could be recognized as refugees under international refugee law. It did not solve the question of what to do with the vast majority of asylum seekers. The state had granted over 125,000 Syrians "subsid-iary protection," a status short of "refugee" that provided only temporary protec-tion for people deemed to be at risk in a warzone but not specifically persecuted in a way that would qualify them as a refugee. In March 2016, a new measure suspended the right to bring family members for Syrians with "subsidiary pro-tection" for two years, with the state promising to revisit the decision in two years. The 2016 and 2018 debates about family reunification for Syrians with "subsidiary protection" are the longest debates about the topic of migration and foreign families that have ever occurred in the Bundestag. Although the political parties currently sitting in parliament have changed, the underlying logic of their speeches is familiar. As politicians argue for and against family migration, they are debating the nature of gendered division of labor within the family, the ques-tion of whether families help or hinder the "integration" of their members, and the question of whether families are "genuine" or opportunistically exploiting the fact of kinship to grasp material advantage. Some of the politicians call into question whether the foreign family is worth supporting at all.

In the 2016 debates, members of the Christian Democratic Union—the party of Angela Merkel and at the time the largest party in the Bundestag—repeatedly argued that they needed to enact restrictions to protect women, mentioning the events in Cologne to suggest that asylum seekers posed a generalized danger to "the equal rights of men and women."[8] In this familiar rhetorical move, main-stream political culture assumed that the German gender order is equitable in itself and that it consistently falls short of equality only because foreigners keep disturbing it from the outside.

CDU/CSU members argued not just that they were protecting German women but also that they were protecting foreign children. Several claimed that if they allowed family reunion, it would lead to child endangerment, because parents would respond by sending unaccompanied children to Germany in order for the parents to plan to use the family reunion program to rejoin their children later. Banning family reunion would prevent families from callously sending their children away on their own.[9] Martin Patzelt, a CDU representative from Frankfurt an der Oder, pointed out, "We are not the ones who separated the children from their parents. In most cases the parents separated themselves from their children." When Franziska Brantner, a Green Party representative from Heidelberg, challenged Patzelt's argument by pointing out that it was more common for heads of family to risk the dangerous journey alone than to send their children, he responded, "I cannot imagine that I would have left my family and my underage children in such a situation." He continued that the decision to travel to the FRG and to leave children in a refugee camp was "an intentional and planned behavior of the parents," who should live with the consequences. Although he did not name a specific family that had made this particular choice, the lack of factual precision made the problem loom even larger. Parents fleeing Syria were making choices in a situation where there were no good options, but by insisting that their actions were literally incomprehensible, Patzelt insinuated that they were bad parents who did not love their children correctly.[10] For Patzelt and others, instituting an explicit policy to reunify families would create moral hazard by encouraging families to look to the state to help them after they had failed their responsibility to stay together in the first place.

The Green Party and the Left—a successor to the Socialist Unity Party that governed the East German dictatorship, and a party that retains a strong base of support in the former East—both used the 2016 debate to argue in favor of a generous family reunification policy for the Syrian citizens who had been granted subsidiary protection but not full refugee status. Representatives from these parties brought up multiple concrete cases of families being hurt by the requirements of the reunification law, such as a Syrian woman whose two oldest daughters were fifteen and sixteen. If this mother had to wait for two years before she could even apply for family reunification, both of her daughters would have aged out of the possibility.[11] They also insisted that family migration was a precondition for any possibility of integration.[12] Some representatives directly accused the Christian Democrats of a form of cultural racism, such as Katja Dörner, a Green representative from Bonn, who insisted that "the [Christian Democratic] Union always puts marriage and family up so high. But family cannot be so valuable to someone for whom the Muslim family has less value than the Christian family and the Syrian family has less value than the German family."[13] Gökay Akbulut, a representative of the Left party from Mannheim and a Kurdish-German who has lived in the FRG with her parents since 1990, asked her CDU colleagues to "in the future please stop uttering the word 'Christian' and the word 'family.' "[14] Both of these politicians observed the taboo on using the language of race in parliament while accusing the CDU of caring about some families more than others using a language of religious and ethnic difference.

The governing CDU/CSU decided to suspend family reunification for two years beginning in March 2016. In the intervening period, Germany held the first national election since the 2015 refugee crisis. The result of the September 2017 voting was an unprecedentedly fractured parliament with six parties entering the

Bundestag, including the Alternative for Germany (AfD) for the first time. After the two-year suspension ended in March 2018, the Bundestag was once again faced with the question of whether asylum seekers with subsidiary protection should have access to family reunification, but now with six parties discussing this in the chamber rather than four. The governing coalition of the Christian Democrats and the SPD had proposed a compromise solution whereby family migration would be regulated by quotas. Starting in August 2018, 1,000 family members of asylum seekers with subsidiary protection would be able to come per month. Given that at least 60,000 family members were thought to be on the wait list, this proposed solution meant that the vast majority of families would continue to be separated for the foreseeable future.

The discourse on the foreign family did not shift much in response to this unprecedented situation. The CDU continued to depict generous family reunification policies as dangerous, arguing that such policies were an "incentive" that produced a "strong magnetic effect" pulling would-be asylum seekers to the FRG.[15] They depicted restrictions on family reunification as a way to protect families from the temptation of separating themselves in the short term. At times, these arguments were made by figures who had literally been repeating them for decades. Horst Seehofer, a CDU member and the newly appointed minister for the Interior, Construction and the Homeland—the last word recently added in an appeal to the far right—explained that restrictions on family reunification protected children. If Germany was too generous, "minors will be sent by their parents ahead on the dangerous trip, endangering child welfare."[16] Events had not changed Seehofer's basic attitude. Since 1983 he had used his platform in the Bundestag to argue that encouraging foreigners to leave Germany was in their best interests, even if they didn't know it.[17]

The Alternative for Germany criticized the proposed quota policy by insisting that even one refugee was too many. Martin Sichert, an AfD representative from Nürnberg, insisted that "in the asylum seeker hostels, antisemitism, racism, persecution of Christians and the oppression of women and minorities are the order of the day."[18] He described asylum seekers as threats to Germany's liberal order who imported homophobia, sexism, and racism. AfD members heckled other parties when they tried to bring up individual cases. When a Green Party representative presented a case of a husband who was trying to bring his wife to Germany, AfD representative Jürgen Braun shouted "His second wife?"[19] Frauke Petry, who had been a leader of the AfD before resigning from the party to promote her anti-immigration policies as an independent, argued that "families in Europe and families in the Middle East are light years apart from one another. Here we speak of equal rights. . . . There we speak of the oppression of women, of the disadvantage of girls, of domestic violence that the state does not investigate."[20] Bernd Baumann, chief whip of the AfD, warned that foreigners would trick authorities to import entire extended families.[21] Left parties described individual families making wrenchingly difficult choices, while the AfD consistently depicted the foreign family as a threatening monolith. Their party might be new, but the AfD representatives' arguments were rooted in the history of decades of debates about whether the foreign family was worthy of inclusion.

Centrist parties denounced the far right as morally repugnant, but they also made significant concessions to its worldview when they deemed quotas and integration tests to be acceptable limits on the right to family life. The SPD—at this point the junior partner in the "Grand Coalition" between the two largest, most centrist parties—continually insisted that while it would prefer a more generous policy, it saw the decision to set quotas to limit family migration as a necessary form of pragmatism. The FDP had fallen below 5 percent of the national vote and thus out of the Bundestag between 2013 and 2017, before returning to the national stage in the 2017 election. Sensing the tenor of the times, representatives of this liberal party proposed making family reunification contingent on proof of integration, explaining that "we want people who show effort to be able to bring their families."[22] The FDP was rehearsing the argument that it had made in 1979 about the "Waiting Period Law," on that occasion in reference to work permits. The belief that family reunion should be an earned privilege rather than a basic human right proved broadly appealing. Stephan Mayer of the CSU, state secretary of the Interior Ministry under Horst Seehofer, promised that his ministry would privilege people for family reunion who "can express that they are particularly ready and willing to integrate themselves into German society."[23] By the end of the debate about family life for Syrians with subsidiary protection, family life had become a reward for good behavior, an entitlement that must be earned to avoid moral hazard—as well as a strategy for centrists to signal to white voters that they could also be tough on migrants.

While many politicians have insisted that their actions since the summer of 2015 have been reactions to an unprecedented "refugee crisis," *Fear of the Family* has shown that these lawmakers are in fact drawing on a repertoire of arguments that has existed for decades. Some of them are literally the same people—as in the case of Horst Seehofer—while others are simply enacting and reenacting a well-established political culture whereby family reunion is not a human right but an entitlement on the basis of utility and effort. While the 1973 "Spanish grandmother" case was based on patriarchal, functionalist, and utilitarian presumptions, there remains something hopeful and something worth retaining in its recognition of the social value of reproductive labor. The "permanent consensus" produced every day by the process of economic growth in the Federal Republic has already expanded to include those foreigners who engage in production. It must further expand to include those foreigners who engage in reproduction. An emancipatory migration politics would not only recognize care as a valid claim to social belonging. It would also recognize that family is not the only social institution that can provide care. In a just society it surely must not be incumbent on families to prove themselves worthy of the standards set by politicians, but the other way around.

NOTES

Introduction

1. Information about the preparations for Rimski's arrival is in Bundesarchiv [BArch] B 119/ 6780. All translations in this book are mine unless otherwise specified.

2. Armando Rodrigues da Sá is pictured on the cover of Rita Chin, *The Guest Worker Question in Postwar Germany* (Cambridge: Cambridge University Press, 2007), and is the first primary source document included in Deniz Göktürk, David Gramling, and Anton Kaes, eds., *Germany in Transit: Nation and Migration, 1955-2005* (Berkeley: University of California Press, 2007). The moped has been on display in the permanent exhibition at the national history museum in Bonn since 2001. Yasemin Şamdereli's 2011 film *Almanya: Welcome to Germany* features the "one-million-and-first" guest worker as a protagonist, with a scene where the protagonist looks on as the man before him in line is gifted with a motorcycle. The mediatization of the Rodrigues da Sá image is discussed in Christoph Rass and Melanie Ulk, "Armando Rodrigues de Sá revisited. Bildwissenschaftliche und historische Analysen im Dialog," *in Migration ein Bild geben: Visuelle Aushandlungen von Diversität*, ed. Christoph Rass and Melanie Ulk (Wiesbaden: Springer, 2018), 419-446.

3. Historical Archives of the European Union [HA-EU], EN-1148.003, "Call by the president of the EC on the Federal German Chancellor, 27 October 1978." For more on Greece's accession to the European Economic Community, see Erini Karamouzi, *Greece, the EEC and the Cold War 1974-1979: The Second Enlargement* (New York: Palgrave Macmillan, 2014); and Antonio Varsori, "The EEC and Greece's Application to join the Community, 1959-1976," in *Institutions and Dynamics of the European Community, 1973-1983*, ed. Johnny Laursen (Baden-Baden: Nomos, 2015).

4. "Çocuklarımızı Sokağa Mı Atalım?," *Emekçi Kadın*, November 2, 1976, trans. Lizzie Howell and Hazal Özdemir. Similarly, when Esra Akcan conducted fieldwork in Kreuzberg in the 2010s, she writes that one woman "still recalls the day when the police showed up the minute she tried to boil water to make tea at Schinkelplatz, and that memory prompts her to list all her other fears: the fear of being held by the police for having a picnic in a park, the fear of having neighbors call the police because she and her family make too much noise, and the fear of their children being taken by the police for disturbing Germans," a list that suggests the way that encounters with the bureaucracy produced a sense of insecurity and fear that pervaded everyday existence. *Open Architecture: Migration, Citizenship, and the Urban Renewal of Berlin-Kreuzberg by IBA-1984/87* (Basel: Birkhäuser, 2018), 81.

5. In *German Angst* (New York: Oxford University Press, 2020), 366, Frank Biess reminds us that "whose emotions are being heard is ultimately a question of political and cultural power."

6. Eleonore Kofman, "Female 'Birds of Passage' a Decade Later: Gender and Immigration in the European Union," *International Migration Review* 33, no. 2 (Summer 1999): 269-299;

and "Family-Related Migration: A Critical Review of European Studies," *Journal of Ethnic and Migration Studies* 30, no. 2 (March 2004): 243–262.

7. Emmanuel Comte, *The History of the European Migration Regime: Germany's Strategic Hegemony* (New York: Routledge, 2018).

8. Documentation about this case can be found in BArch B 149/47278. All identifying details have been changed.

9. The framework of "autonomy of migration" has been forwarded by critical sociologists in the German context. See Manuela Bojadžijev, *Die windige Internationale: Rassismus und Kämpfe der Migration* (Münster: Westfälisches Dampfboot, 2008); Serhat Karakayali, *Gespenster der Migration. Zur Genealogie illegaler Einwanderung in der Bundesrepublik Deutschland* (Bielefeld: transcript Verlag, 2008); Miltiadis Oulios, *Blackbox Abschiebung. Geschichte, Theorie und Praxis der deutschen Migrationspolitik*, 2nd ed. (Berlin: Suhrkamp Verlag, 2015). The "autonomous migrant" resembles the *eigensinnig* subject whose behavior is characterized by a "misanthropic distancing from all constraints or incentives." Alf Lüdtke, ed., *The History of Everyday Life: Reconstructing Historical Experiences and Ways of Life*, trans. William Templer (Princeton, NJ: Princeton University Press, 1995), 313–314. Both also resemble the figure of the "willful subject" who does not will in the socially acceptable way who is celebrated by critical theorist Sara Ahmed, *Willful Subjects* (Durham, NC: Duke University Press, 2014).

10. Robert G. Moeller, "The Elephant in the Living Room: Or Why the History of Twentieth-Century Germany Should Be a Family Affair," in *Gendering Modern German History: Rewriting Historiography*, ed. Karen Hagemann and Jean H. Quataert (New York: Berghahn, 2007), 237.

11. Alexandria N. Ruble, "Creating Postfascist Families: Reforming Family Law and Gender Roles in Postwar East and West Germany," *Central European History* 53 (2020): 414–431. For Christian ideas of the family, see Maria D. Mitchell, *The Origins of Christian Democracy: Politics and Confession in Modern Germany* (Ann Arbor: University of Michigan Press, 2012). For an account that focuses on the Catholic milieu, see Lukas Rölli-Alkemper, *Familie im Wiederaufbau: Katholizismus und bürgerliches Familienideal in der Bundesrepublik Deutschland 1945–1965* (Paderborn: Schöningh, 2000). For family politics in general, see Robert G. Moeller, *Protecting Motherhood: Women and the Family in the Politics of Postwar West Germany* (Berkeley: University of California Press, 1993); Elizabeth D. Heineman, *What Difference Does a Husband Make? Women and Marital Status in Nazi and Postwar Germany* (Berkeley: University of California Press, 1999); Christiane Kuller, *Familienpolitik im föderativen Sozialstaat: Die Formierung eines Politikfeldes in der Bundesrepublik 1949–1975* (Munich: R. Oldenbourg Verlag, 2004).

12. Wiebke Kolbe, "Gender and Parenthood in West German Family Politics from the 1960s to the 1980s," in *State Policy and Gender System in the Two German States and Sweden 1945–1989*, ed. Rolf Torstendahl (Uppsala: Uppsala University Press, 1999), 133.

13. Christine von Oertzen, *Teilzeitarbeit und die Lust am Zuverdienen. Geschlechterpolitik und gesellschaftlicher Wandel in Westdeutschland 1948–1969* (Göttingen: Vandenhoeck & Ruprecht, 1999); Karen Hagemann, "Between Ideology and Economy: The 'Time Politics' of Child Care and Public Education in the Two Germanys," *Social Politics* 13, no. 2 (2006): 217–260, and Kolbe, "Gender and Parenthood."

14. When I refer to "reproductive labor" or to the "social reproduction" such labor accomplishes, I mean those activities which maintain human beings on an everyday basis, including caring for children, obtaining and preparing food, cleaning clothing, and all of the other tasks that go into running a household and having a family life. Such labor is necessary to reproduce human life, but it is not "productive" inasmuch as it produces no saleable commodity— except, perhaps, for the capacity of the family members to subsequently enter the labor market. I draw on scholarship including Evelyn Nakano Glenn, "From Servitude to Service Work: Historical Continuities in the Racial Division of Paid Reproductive Labor," *Signs* (Autumn 1992): 1–43, Silvia Federici, *Revolution at Point Zero: Housework, Reproduction, and Feminist Struggle* (Oakland, CA: PM Press, 2012); and Tithi Bhattacharya, ed., *Social Reproduction Theory: Remapping Class, Recentering Oppression* (London: Pluto Press, 2017).

15. Monika Mattes, *"Gastarbeiterinnen" in der Bundesrepublik: Anwerbepolitik, Migration und Geschlecht in den 50er bis 70er Jahren* (Frankfurt: Campus Verlag, 2005), 9–10.

16. On Jamaicans: Cindy Hahamovitch, *No Man's Land: Jamaican Guestworkers in America and the Global History of Deportable Labor* (Princeton, NJ: Princeton University Press, 2011). On Puerto Ricans: Eileen J. Suárez Findlay, *We Are Left Without a Father Here: Masculinity, Domesticity, and Migration in Postwar Puerto Rico* (Durham, NC: Duke University Press, 2014). On the "bracero" program: Deborah Cohen, *Braceros: Migrant Citizens and Transnational Subjects in the Postwar United States and Mexico* (Chapel Hill: University of North Carolina Press, 2011); Mireya Loza, *Defiant Braceros: How Migrant Workers Fought for Racial, Sexual, and Political Freedom* (Chapel Hill: University of North Carolina Press, 2016); and Ana Raquel Minian, *Undocumented Lives: The Untold Story of Mexican Migration* (Cambridge, MA: Harvard University Press, 2018).
17. Max Frisch, foreword to *Siamo Italiani/Die Italiener: Gespräche mit italienischen Arbeitern in der Schweiz*, ed. Alexander J. Seiler (Zürich: EVZ-Verlag, 1965), 1.
18. Leslie Adelson is one of the few to quote the entire phrase in *The Turkish Turn in Contemporary German Literature: Toward a New Critical Grammar of Migration* (New York: Palgrave Macmillan, 2005), 124.
19. Maria Alexopoulou develops a similar critique in "Vom Nationalen zum Lokalen und zurück? Zur Geschichtsschreibung in der Einwanderungsgesellschaft Deutschland," *Archiv für Sozialgeschichte* 56 (2016): 463–484; and "'Ausländer'—A Racialized Concept? 'Race' as an Analytical Concept in Contemporary German Immigration History," in *Who Can Speak and Who Is Heard/Hurt? Facing Problems of Race, Racism, and Ethnic Diversity in the Humanities in Germany*, ed. Mahmoud Arghavan, Nicole Hirschfelder, Luvena Kopp, and Katharina Motyl (Bielefeld: transcript, 2019): 45–67.
20. Helma Lutz, *Welten verbinden. Türkische Sozialarbeiterinnen in den Niederlanden und der Bundesrepublik Deutschland* (Frankfurt: Verlag für Interkulturelle Kommunikation, 1991), 74.
21. Rita Chin, Heide Fehrenbach, Geoff Eley, and Atina Grossmann, *After the Nazi Racial State: Difference and Democracy in Germany and Europe* (Ann Arbor: University of Michigan Press, 2009).
22. Tina Campt, *Other Germans: Black Germans and the Politics of Race, Gender, and Memory in the Third Reich* (Ann Arbor: University of Michigan Press, 2004).
23. For "racialization" as applied to the Federal Republic, see above all Maureen Maisha Eggers, Grada Kilomba, Peggy Piesche, and Susan Arndt, eds., *Mythen, Masken und Subjekte: Kritische Weißseinsforschung in Deutschland*, 4th ed. (Münster: UNRAST-Verlag, 2020, [original 2005]); and Fatima El-Tayeb, *Undeutsch: Die Konstruktion des Anderen in der Postmigrantischen Gesellschaft* (Bielefeld: transcript, 2016). For the "racialization" paradigm as applied to the United States, see Michael Omi and Howard Winant, *Racial Formation in the United States. From the 1960s to the 1990s*, 2nd ed. (New York: Routledge, 1994). For a philosophical treatment of "race" as a structure of perception, see particularly Paul C. Taylor, *Race: A Philosophical Introduction* (Cambridge: Polity Press, 2004); and Linda Alcoff, *Visible Identities: Race, Gender, and the Self* (Oxford: Oxford University Press, 2006).
24. Deutscher Bundestag, Plenarprotokoll 14/40, May 7, 1999, 3432.
25. Yvonne Rieker, "Südländer, Ostagente oder Westeuropäer? Die Politik der Bundesregierung und das Bild der italienischen Gastarbeiter 1955–1970," *Archiv für Sozialgeschichte* 40 (2000); *"Ein Stück Heimat findet man ja immer." Die italienische Einwanderung in die Bundesrepublik* (Essen: Klartext Verlag, 2003); Grazia Prontera, *Partire, Tornare, Restare? L'esperienza migratoria dei lavoratori italiani nella Repubblica Federale Tedesca nel secondo dopoguerra* (Milan: Guerini e Associati, 2009); and Oliver Janz and Roberto Sala, eds., *Dolce Vita? Das Bild der italienischen Migranten in Deutschland* (Frankfurt: Campus Verlag, 2011).
26. Christopher A. Molnar, "Imagining Yugoslavs: Migration and the Cold War in Postwar West Germany," *Central European History* 47, no. 1 (2014); and *Memory, Politics, and Yugoslav Migrations to Postwar Germany* (Bloomington: Indiana University Press, 2018). Also see Kaja Shonick, "Émigrés, Guest Workers, and Refugees: Yugoslav Migrants in the Federal Republic of Germany, 1945–1995" (PhD diss., University of Washington, 2008).
27. Karin Hunn, *"Nächstes Jahr kehren wir zurück . . ." Die Geschichte der türkischen "Gastarbeiter" in der Bundesrepublik* (Göttingen: Wallstein Verlag, 2005); Jennifer A. Miller, *Turkish Guest Workers in Germany: Hidden Lives and Contested Borders, 1960s–1980s* (Toronto: University of Toronto Press, 2018): Sarah Thomsen Vierra, *Turkish Germans in the Federal Republic of*

Germany: Immigration, Space, and Belonging, 1961–1990 (Cambridge: Cambridge University Press, 2018); and Michelle Lynn Kahn, "Foreign at Home: Turkish German Migrants and the Boundaries of Europea, 1961–1990" (PhD diss., Stanford University, 2018). Christopher Ewing shows that the Iranian Revolution was also an important event in the gay press. "The Color of Desire: Contradictions of Race, Sex, and Gay Rights in the Federal Republic of Germany" (PhD diss., City University of New York, 2018).

28. Helma Lutz and Christine Huth-Hildebrandt are early analysts of this phenomenon in "Geschlecht im Migrationsdiskurs. Neue Gedanken über ein altes Thema," *Das Argument* 224 (1998), later to be joined by Petra Rostock and Sabine Berghahn, "The Ambivalent Role of Gender in Redefining the German Nation," *Ethnicities* 8, no. 3 (2008); Susan B. Rottmann and Myra Marx Ferree, "Citizenship and Intersectionality: German Feminist Debates About Headscarf and Antidiscrimination Laws," *Social Politics* 15, no. 4 (2008); and Rita Chin, "Turkish Women, West German Feminists, and the Gendered Discourse on Muslim Cultural Difference," *Public Culture* 22, no. 3 (2010).

    Rita Chin makes this argument in more detail in *The Guest Worker Question* and extends it to other European countries in *The Crisis of Multiculturalism in Europe: A History* (Princeton, NJ: Princeton University Press, 2017). Chin argues that the "turn to gender" happened because of family reunion, but her account of causality derives from the fact that there were more women coming to Europe rather than from the internal dynamics of bureaucracy, which I argue endowed that fact with symbolic power.

29. Laura Block makes a similar argument for 2005–2010 in *Policy Frames on Spousal Migration in Germany: Regulating Membership, Regulating the Family* (Wiesbaden: Springer, 2016).

30. The scholarship on "homonationalism" in the German context includes Fatima El-Tayeb, *European Others: Queering Ethnicity in Postnational Europe* (Minneapolis: University of Minnesota Press, 2011); "'Gays Who Cannot Properly Be Gay': Queer Muslims in the Neoliberal European City," *European Journal of Women's Studies* 19, no. 1 (2012); Jin Haritaworn, "Queer Injuries: The Racial Politics of 'Homophobic Hate Crime' in Germany," *Social Justice* 37, no. 1 (2010); *Queer Lovers and Hateful Others: Regenerating Violent Times and Places* (London: Pluto Press, 2015); and Damani Partridge, *Hypersexuality and Headscarves: Race, Sex, and Citizenship in the New Germany* (Bloomington: Indiana University Press, 2012).

31. *Familiennachzug* does not appear in *Duden,* while the *Digitale Wörterbuch der deutschen Sprache* does not show it until 1982. My analysis is based on a Google Ngram of "Familiennachzug" in a German corpus, which first finds the word in 1962/1963 in publications about guest workers in Switzerland. In a 1970 memorandum about a new demographic research institute, the author writes *"Familiennachgang"* before making a handwritten correction, crossing out *"gang"* in favor of *"zug,"* also suggesting the term's apparent novelty. BArch B 106/45157, 9. Dezember 1970 memo by Referat V II 6.

32. Politisches Archiv des Auswärtigen Amtes [PAAA], B 85/1459, B 85/1603, and B 85/1613.

33. For example, the Turkish communist group Federation of Turkish Workers' Associations in West Germany [FIDEF] accused the state of violating its Helsinki Accord obligations to facilitate "family reunion" when it came to Turkish workers. IG Metall-Archiv im Archiv der sozialen Demokratie [IG Metall-Archiv], ZWA013704, October 8, 1977, FIDEF letter to Konferenz über Sicherheit und Zusammenarbeit in Europa.

34. The other languages used in the source base for this study—Spanish [*reagrupación familiar*], Italian [*ricongiungimento familiare*], and Turkish [*aile birleşme*]—do not to my knowledge have a similarly consistent split in the terms used to describe family migration.

35. Ulrich Herbert, *Hitler's Foreign Workers: Enforced Foreign Labor in Germany Under the Third Reich,* trans. William Templer (Cambridge: Cambridge University Press, 1997 [original 1985]).

36. Konrad Jarausch, *After Hitler: Recivilizing Germans, 1945–1995,* trans. Brandon Hunziker (New York: Oxford University Press, 2006), 17.

37. Jennifer Miller, "On Track for West Germany: Turkish 'Guest-Worker' Rail Transportation to West Germany in the Postwar Period," *German History* 30, no. 4 (2012).

38. BArch B 149/59888, November 26, 1981, RD Dr. Fendrich to Herrn Staatssekretär.

39. BArch B 149/59889, November 30, 1981 memorandum.

40. The president's office did begin to keep a series of files under the title "Xenophobia in the German Federal Republic—Petitions from Citizens" in the 1970s, which significantly swells in volume in the 1980s. However, the point here is that racist letters appear in seemingly *every* series that has to do with foreigners, that they overspill the confines of "Xenophobic Petitions" to be filed everywhere. Thank you to Christopher Molnar for alerting me to the existence of this archival series.
41. "Wolfgang Seeger zur Erinnerung," *Mensch und Maß* 22 (2006): 1020–1026. Thank you to Ulli Jentsch at the anti-fascist archive in Berlin for providing me with biographical material about Seeger.
42. Stadtarchiv Nürnberg [StadtAN] E 52, Nr. 37, Wolfgang Seeger, *Ausländer-Integration ist Völkermord. Das Verbrechen an den ausländischen Volksgruppen und am deutschen Volk*, Verlag Hohe Warte, 1980.
43. Author's correspondence with Ulli Jentsch at Apabiz, November 19, 2019.
44. Hessisches Hauptstaatsarchiv Wiesbaden [HHW] Abt. 502, Nr. 7411, 7. Sept. 1984, Eduard Stöcker to Holger Börner, and Abt. 502, Nr. 7414, 21. Mai 1985, Dr. Otto Uhlitz to BMI.
45. Catherine Puzzo, "British and French Immigration Policy in the 1970s: A Comparative Analysis," *Contemporary European History* 12, no. 1 (2003); Helena Wray, "An Ideal Husband? Marriages of Convenience, Moral Gate-keeping and Immigration to the UK," *European Journal of Migration and Law* 8, no. 3 (2006).
46. There is a growing literature on the intellectual foundations of neoliberalism in West Germany. My own approach is influenced by Anthony J. Nicholls, *Freedom with Responsibility: The Social Market Economy in Germany, 1918–1963* (Oxford: Oxford University Press, 1994); Alfred C. Mierzejewski, *Ludwig Erhard: A Biography* (Chapel Hill: University of North Carolina Press, 2004); Ralf Ptak, *Vom Ordoliberalismus zur Sozialen Marktwirtschaft. Stationen des Neoliberalismus in Deutschland* (Wiesbaden: VS. Verlag für Sozialwissenschaften, 2004); James C. Van Hook, *Rebuilding Germany: The Creation of the Social Market Economy, 1945–1957* (Cambridge: Cambridge University Press, 2004); Ralf Ptak, "Neoliberalism in Germany: Revisiting the Ordoliberal Foundations of the Social Market Economy," in *The Road from Mont Pelerin: The Making of the Neoliberal Thought Collective*, ed. Philip Mirowksi and Dieter Plehwe (Cambridge, MA: Harvard University Press, 2009), 98–138; and Quinn Slobodian, *Globalists: The End of Empire and the Birth of Neoliberalism* (Cambridge, MA: Harvard University Press, 2018).
47. Michel Foucault, *The Birth of Biopolitics. Lectures at the Collège de France 1978–1979*, ed. Arnold I. Davidson, trans. Graham Burchell (New York: Picador, 2008), 84.
48. Margaret Haderer, "'Economic Policies Are the Best Social Policies': West German Neoliberalism and the Housing Question After 1945," *American Journal of Economics and Sociology* 77, no. 1 (January 2018): 149–167.
49. Philip Zölls also interprets the bilateral agreement as part of Erhard's "ordoliberal understanding of the economy" in *Regieren der Migration. Von Einwanderungsprozessen und Staatlichen Regulierungspolitikern* (München: Allitera Verlag, 2019), 29–31.
50. Melinda Cooper, *Family Values: Between Neoliberalism and the New Social Conservatism* (New York: Zone Books, 2017), 57.
51. Cooper, *Family Values*, and Laura Briggs, *How All Politics Became Reproductive Politics: From Welfare Reform to Foreclosure to Trump* (Berkeley: University of California Press, 2017).
52. James Chappel, *Catholic Modern: The Challenge of Totalitarianism and the Remaking of the Church* (Cambridge, MA: Harvard University Press, 2018); and Mitchell, *The Origins of Christian Democracy*.
53. Kolbe, "Gender and Parenthood," 144. Christiane Kuller points out that subsidiarity makes unpaid care work within the family "a permanent part of the idea of the welfare state," "Soziale Sicherung von Frauen—ein ungelöstes Strukturproblem im männlichen Wohlfahrtsstaat. Die Bundesrepublik im europäischen Vergleich," *Archiv für Sozialgeschichte* 47 (2007): 218.
54. For an example of cooperation, see Haderer, "West German Neoliberalism and the Housing Question," on the overlapping interests in owner-occupied housing. For an example of conflict, see Mark Jakob, *Familienbilder: Sozialer Wandel, Wissenschaft und Familienpolitik in der BRD 1954–1982* (Wiesbaden: Springer VS, 2019), 225, on the clash between Ludwig Erhard and Catholic politicians on family allowances.

55. Michael N. Barnett, "Introduction," in *Paternalism Beyond Borders* (Cambridge: Cambridge University Press, 2017), 1–43, 13.

Chapter 1

1. Häuserrat Frankfurt, *Wohnungskampf in Frankfurt* (Munich: Trikont-Verlag, 1974), 130.
2. Qtd. in Heike Knortz, *Diplomatische Tauschgeschäfte: 'Gastarbeiter' in der westdeutschen Diplomatie und Beschäftigungspolitik 1953–1973* (Köln: Bohlau, 2008), 87.
3. Mathilde Jamin argues that the initial omission of this provision reflects the suspicion that Turks would be unable to integrate, while Karin Hunn believes that it was simply a function of chronology as the state became more nervous about family migration. Mathilde Jamin, "Fremde Heimat: Zur Geschichte der Arbeitsmigration aus der Türkei," in *50 Jahre Bundesrepublik—50 Jahre Einwanderung: Nachkriegsgeschichte als Migrationsgeschichte*, ed. Jan Motte, Rainer Ohliger, and Anne von Oswald (Frankfurt: Campus Verlag, 1999), 148–149; and Hunn, *"Nächstes Jahr,"* 56.
4. Karen Schönwälder, "'Ist nur Liberalisierung Fortschritt?' Zur Entstehung des ersten Ausländergesetzes der Bundesrepublik," in *50 Jahre Bundesrepublik—50 Jahre Einwanderung: Nachkriegsgeschichte als Migrationsgeschichte*, ed. Jan Motte, Rainer Ohliger, and Anne von Oswald (Frankfurt: Campus Verlag, 1999); and Karen Schönwälder, *Einwanderung und ethnische Pluralität. Politische Entscheidungen und öffentliche Debatten in Großbritannien und der Bundesrepublik von den 1950er bis zu den 1970er Jahren* (Essen: Klartext-Verlag, 2001), 218–245.
5. Schönwälder, *Einwanderung und Pluralität*, 323–329.
6. Qtd. in Schönwälder, *Einwanderung und Pluralität*, 262.
7. Their country had signed an Association Agreement with the European Economic Community in 1963, and the Federal Statistics Office listed Turks as "Europeans" in the annual statistical bulletin of migration through 1973. At this point "Europe" stops being a category, replaced by "recruitment stop countries" and "non-recruitment stop countries."
8. BArch B 106/69872, "Sprechzettel . . . am 12. Oktober 1965."
9. BArch B 106/69872, September 14, 1965, BMWi to BMI.
10. Karakayali, *Gespenster der Migration*, 139–143.
11. Qtd. in Schönwälder, *Einwanderung und Pluralität*, 329. Also see BArch B 149/62775, "Niederschrift . . . 6. Dezember 1965."
12. For more on the strong pull of the male-breadwinner, female-homemaker model in the postwar Federal Republic, see Karin Hausen, "Frauenerwerbstätigkeit und erwerbstätige Frauen. Anmerkung zur historischen Forschung," in *Frauen arbeiten: weibliche Erwerbstätigkeit in Ost- und Westdeutschland nach 1945*, ed. Gunilla-Friederike Budde (Göttingen: Vandenhoeck and Ruprecht, 1997); and Sarah E. Summers, "Reconciling Family and Work: The West German Gendered Division of Labor and Women's Emancipation, 1960s to 1980s" (PhD diss., University of North Carolina, 2012).
13. Christine von Oertzen also makes this point in *Teilzeitarbeit*, 251, 274–275.
14. Mattes, *"Gastarbeiterinnen,"* 34.
15. Mattes, *"Gastarbeiterinnen,"* 63–66, 82–84. The German Embassy in Portugal pushed for liberal family reunification policy for this reason. BArch B 106/69872, November 8, 1965, Botschaft Lisbon to AA. Also see BArch B 106/69872, November 11, 1965, BMA to BMI.
16. Mattes, *"Gastarbeiterinnen,"* 39–44.
17. Knortz, *Diplomatische Tauschgeschäfte*, 140–151.
18. Rieker, *Italienische Einwanderung*, 103.
19. Roberto Sala, *Fremde Worte: Medien für 'Gastarbeiter' in der Bundesrepublik im Spannungsfeld von Aussen- und Sozialpolitik* (Paderborn: Ferdinand Schöningh, 2011), 202–206. "Native expert" Maturi was from *Northern* Italy, and his work reproduced stereotypes that Northern Italians held about Southern Italians and extended them over the larger cultural space of the European "South." For more on the "Southern Italian" stereotype, see Aliza S. Wong, *Race and the Nation in Liberal Italy, 1861–1911: Meridionalism, Empire, and Diaspora* (New York: Palgrave Macmillan, 2006).

20. Giacomo Maturi, "Die Eingliederung der Südländischen Arbeitskräfte und ihre besonderen Anpassungsschwierigkeiten," in *Ausländische Arbeitskräfte in Deutschland*, ed. Hessisches Institut für Betriebswirtschaft (Düsseldorf: Econ-Verlag, 1961), 129, 131. Maturi made similar arguments in a 1961 report for the German Association for Public and Private Welfare. LA-B, DST 4/44-49, Band 1, Giacomo Maturi "Zur Frage der ausländischen Arbeiter."
21. Amelia H. Lyons, *The Civilizing Mission in the Metropole: Algerian Families and the French Welfare State During Decolonization* (Stanford, CA: Stanford University Press, 2013), 13; and Jordanna Bailikin, *The Afterlife of Empire* (Berkeley: University of California Press, 2012), 170.
22. Giacomo Maturi, "Weibliche Arbeitskräfte aus den Mittelmeerländern," in *Ausländische Arbeitskräfte in Deutschland*, ed. Hessisches Institut für Betriebswirtschaft (Düsseldorf: Econ-Verlag, 1961), 183.
23. Maturi, "Weibliche Arbeitskräfte," 185.
24. Maturi, "Weibliche Arbeitskräfte," 186.
25. ADCV, 380.20 + 172 Fasz.01—Sozialdienst des DCV fuer auslaendische Mitbuerger Vermischtes Schriftgut 1960–65, March 10, 1960, "Thema: Regelungen fuer auslaendische Arbeiterinnen aus fremden Laendern."
26. Archiv des Deutschen Caritasverbands [ADCV], 380.20 + 172 Fasz.01—Sozialdienst des DCV fuer auslaendische Mitbuerger Vermischtes Schriftgut 1960–65, April 7, 1960, Wilhelm Wissing (Catholic Office in Bonn) to the President of the Bundesanstalt fuer Arbeitsvermittlung und Arbeitslosenversicherung.
27. Zölls, *Regieren der Migration*, 109.
28. Landesarchiv Berlin, Deutsche Städtetag [LA-B, DST], 4/44–49, February 12, 1963, Georg Albrecht, "Anmerkung zu meiner Denkschrift vom 15.1.1963."
29. Archiv des Diakonischen Werkes der EKD [ADW], HGSt Nr. 2973, Ausländische Arbeitnehmer, 1965–1967, March 1, 1967, "Vermerk"; and BArch B 189/6798, November 12, 1964, Siemens-Schuckertwerke Aktiengesellschaft Sozialpolitische Abteilung to Dr. Zöllner, December 6, 1966, Senator für Inneres Berlin to BMI, and October 6, 1967, BMI to BMJ and BMFa.
30. Vittorio Bifulco, "Die Auswahl Italienischer Arbeitskräfte für Deutschland und ihr Einsatz in deutschen Betrieben," in *Ausländische Arbeitskräfte in Deutschland*, ed. Hessisches Institut für Betriebswirtschaft (Düsseldorf: Econ-Verlag, 1961), 66.
31. Gerassimos B. Papavassiliou, "Die Auswahl griechischer Arbeitskräfte und ihr Einsatz in deutschen Betrieben," in *Ausländische Arbeitskräfte in Deutschland*, ed. Hessisches Institut für Betriebswirtschaft (Düsseldorf: Econ-Verlag, 1961), 87.
32. LA B-W, EA 8/201 Bü 664, Memo from November 23, 1960. See similar arguments in Helmuth Weicken, "Anwerbung und Vermittlung Italienischer, Spanische und Griechischer Arbeitskräfte im Rahmen Bilateraler Anwerbevereinbarungen," in *Ausländische Arbeitskräfte in Deutschland*, ed. Hessisches Institut für Betriebswirtschaft (Düsseldorf: Econ-Verlag, 1961), 37; and LA-B, DST, 4/44-49, Band 1, Dr. Valentin Siebrecht report, "Aufgaben der Fürsorge im Zusammenhang mit der Beschäftigung von Ausländern in Deutschland."
33. Giacomo Maturi, *Hallo Günther! Der Ausländische Arbeiter Spricht zu Seinem Deutschen Kollegen* (Heidelberg: Curt Haefner Verlag, 1966). This booklet was funded by the German Labor Ministry and translated into all of the national recruitment languages for guest workers. The guest worker was referred to as the "Southerner" across all of the languages I have been able to check (German, Spanish, Portuguese, Italian, and Turkish), homogenizing the guest workers into a single "Southern" culture positioned against German culture.
34. Maturi, *Hallo Günther!*
35. For another discussion of this phenomenon, see Grazia Prontera, "The Migration Experience of Italian Workers in the Federal Republic of Germany in the Postwar Years," in *Postwar Mediterranean Migration to Western Europe: Legal and Political Frameworks, Sociability and Memory Cultures*, ed. Clelia Caruso, Jenny Pleinen, and Lutz Raphael (Frankfurt: Peter Lang, 2008).
36. BArch B 119/3038, July 16, 1962, Bundesanstalt to Landesarbeitsämter.
37. Quote from BArch B 119/3038, August 25, 1962, Landesarbeitsamt NRW to Bundesanstalt, also see October 15, 1963, Landesarbeitsamt B-W to Bundesanstalt.
38. BArch B 119/3038, November 2, 1962, Arbeitsamt Köln to German Commission in Rome.

39. BArch B 119/4727, March 20, 1969, Landesarbeitsamt Nordbayern to Bundesanstalt.
40. BArch B 119/3038, August 24, 1962, Landesarbeitsamt B-W to Bundesanstalt.
41. BArch B 119/3038, February 26, 1963, Deutsche Kommission in Türkei to Bundesanstalt.
42. Ahmet Akgündüz, *Labour Migration from Turkey to Western Europe, 1960-1974: A Multidisciplinary Analysis* (Aldershot: Ashgate, 2008), 77.
43. For an extended discussion on the train journey, see Miller, "On Track for West Germany."
44. BArch B 119/3038, January 24, 1964, Präsident Sabel to Oberdirektor Dr. Kästner.
45. BArch B 119/3038, January 30, 1964, Bundesanstalt to Deutsche Kommissionen, February 17, 1964, Deutsche Verbindungsstelle in der Türkei to Bundesanstalt, and July 2, 1964, Bundesanstalt to Deutsche Kommissionen.
46. BArch B 106/60276, December 17, 1970, *Süddeutsche Zeitung* story, "Dunkle Geschäfte mit Türken," by Karl Heinz Eckert, Dokumentationszentrum über die Migration in Deutschland [DOMiD], interview with Anestis Kellidis from June 25, 2004; and Ali Uçar, *Die soziale Lage der türkischen Migrantenfamilien. Mit einer empirischen Untersuchung unter besonderer Berücksichtigung der arbeits- und sozialrechtlichen Fragen*, 2nd ed. (Berlin (West): EXpress Edition, 1982), 30–31.
47. Lea Nocera, *Cercasi Mani Piccole E Abili: La Migrazione Turca in Germania Occidentale in una Prospettiva di Genere 1961-1984* (Istanbul: Edizione Isis, 2012), 102.
48. Nocera, *Cercasi Mani Piccole E Abili*, 102–103.
49. BArch B 119/4735, October 15, 1963, Landesarbeitsamt B-W to Bundesanstalt.
50. BArch B 119/4727, September 16, 1969, Bundesanstalt circular to Dienststellen.
51. BArch B 119/4728, October 27, 1962, Landesarbeitsamt B-W to Bundesanstalt, and September 16, 1962, Landesarbeitsamt B-W to Bundesanstalt.
52. BArch B 119/4728, February 18, 1963, Landesarbeitsamt B-W to Bundesanstalt.
53. BArch B 119/4727, March 20, 1969, Landesarbeitsamt Nordbayern to Bundesanstalt.
54. BArch B 119/4727, May 10, 1969, Deutsche Verbindungsstelle in der Türkei to Bundesanstalt, and September 16, 1969, Bundesanstalt circular to Dienststellen.
55. BArch B 119/4727, November 18, 1969, Botschaft Ankara to AA.
56. BArch B 119/4727, April 24, 1970, BMI to Innenminster der Länder.
57. Many Turkish men used named recruitment to get around informal prohibitions on recruiting men with large families, a practice that is mentioned in BArch B 119/4728, June 4, 1968, memorandum and June 30, 1968, memorandum, and in BArch B 119/4727, May 10, 1969, Deutsche Verbindungsstelle in der Türkei to Bundesanstalt.
58. StadtAN F 21, Nr. 57; and Barbara Wolbert, *Der getötete Paß: Rückkehr in die Türkei: Eine ethnologische Migrationsstudie* (Berlin: Akademie Verlag, 1995), 77.
59. PAAA B 85/1033, July 5, 1972, Innenminister NRW to BMA.
60. PAAA B 85/1033, March 14, 1973, "Ergebnisprotokoll," and April 25, 1973, BMI to BMA. There were also at least two debates about whether minor children with contagious diseases could be deported. Bavaria defended deporting these children in 1968, but Rhineland-Palatinate and Berlin both thought it might be unconstitutional. The Interior Ministry speculated that it might in fact be more workable to deport the *mother* of a sick child. In 1975 Baden-Württemberg raised the question once again, and the Interior Ministry responded by issuing a circular stating that minor children with illnesses should not be deported. Correspondence in LA B-W, EA 2/303, Bü 176.
61. Julia Woesthoff, "Ambiguities of Anti-Racism: Representations of Foreign Laborers and the West German Media, 1955–1990" (PhD diss., Michigan State University, 2004), 49–50.
62. Qtd. in Schönwälder, *Einwanderung und Pluralität*, 189.
63. Karl Bingemeier, Edeltrud Meistermann-Seeger, and Edgar Neubert, *Leben als Gastarbeiter. Geglückte und mißglückte Integration* (Cologne: Westdeutscher Verlag, 1970), 178–188. Bingemeier's hypothesis about guest workers using older women to meet their sexual needs could read as a plot description of Rainer Werner Fassbinder's 1974 film *Ali: Fear Eats the Soul*—it seems possible that Fassbinder read either press coverage or the study itself.
64. Bingemeier, Meistermann-Seeger, and Neubert, *Leben als Gastarbeiter*, 171.
65. Mark E. Spicka, "City Policy and Guest Workers in Stuttgart, 1955–1973," *German History* 31, no. 3 (2013): 345–365.

66. LA-B, DST, 4/44-49, Kommunale Korrespondenz Pressedienst des DST October 8, 1962, Nr. 98. Here he makes a reference to the influence of the Napoleonic Code over legal regimes in Southern Europe.

67. LA-B, DST, 4/44-49, March 4, 1964, "Kurzfassung der Ausführungen von Frau Ministerialrätin Dr. von Loeper."

68. Sybille Buske, "'Fräulein Mutter' vor dem Richterstuhl: Der Wandel der öffentlichen Wahrnehmung und rechtlichen Stellung lediger Mütter in der Bundesrepublik 1948 bis 1970," *WerkstattGeschichte* 27 (2000): 48–67, and *Fräulein Mutter und ihr Bastard: Eine Geschichte der Unehelichkeit in Deutschland, 1900–1970* (Göttingen: Wallstein Verlag, 2004).

69. LA-B, DST 4/44-49, September 18, 1962, letter from Bürgermeisteramt Stuttgart to the DST.

70. LA-B, DST, 4/44-49, June 20, 1962, Deutscher Städtetag Abt. 4 Vermerk and July 21, 1961, "Auszug aus der Niederschrift über die 9. Sitzung des Sozialausschusses."

71. LA-B, DST, 4/44-49, Beiheft: Rundfrage vom 13.1.64, July 16, 1964, Stadt Bielefeld to DST, and March 13, 1964, Behörde für Inneres Hamburg to DST.

72. LA-B, DST, 4/44-49, Beiheft: Rundfrage vom 13.1.64, May 11, 1964, Stadt Reutlingen Bürgermeisteramt to DST.

73. LA-B, DST, 4/44-49, Beiheft: Rundfrage vom 13.1.64, March 10, 1964, Stadt Bayreuth Oberbürgermeister to DST.

74. LA-B, DST, 4/44-49, Beiheft: Rundfrage vom 13.1.64, March 16, 1964, Stadt Duisburg Oberstadtdirektor Einwohnermeldeamt Ausländeraufsicht to DST.

75. W. Steuer and K. Schramm, "Ehen zwischen deutschen und ausländischen Arbeitnehmern," *Das öffentliche Gesundheitwesen* 1, no. 27 (1965).

76. Maria Höhn, *GIs and Fräuleins: The German-American Encounter in 1950s West Germany* (Chapel Hill: University of North Carolina Press, 2002), 235.

77. Heide Fehrenbach, *Race After Hitler: Black Occupation Children in Postwar Germany and America* (Princeton, NJ: Princeton University Press, 2005).

78. Henner Hess and Achim Melcher, *Ghetto ohne Mauern. Ein Bericht aus der Unterschicht* (Frankfurt am Main: Suhrkamp Verlag, 1973), 67.

79. Woesthoff, "Ambiguities of Anti-Racism," 54.

80. Comments to this effect in LA-B, DST, 4/44-49, June 25, 1962, Oberstadtdirektor Oberhausen Dr. Peterssen to DST. In the Netherlands, Sarah van Walsum reports that when the dancing halls in Oldenzall decided to exclude Italian and Spanish foreign workers, riots and strikes broke out. Sarah van Walsum, *The Family and the Nation: Dutch Family Migration Policies in the Context of Changing Family Norms* (Newcastle: Cambridge Scholars, 2009), 121.

81. LA-B, DST 4/44-49, "Bericht des Landesjugendamtes Rheinland . . . vom 28–30 November 1966"; and H. Meid "Bericht über die Betreuung der ausländischen Arbeitnehmer."

82. BArch B 141/36536, July 10, 1965, SZ clipping, Wolfgang Kuballa, "Senor Rodriguez heiratet Fräulein Meier . . . Eheschließungen zwischen Deutschen und Gastarbeitern werfen schwierige rechtliche Probleme auf."

83. Qtd. in Woesthoff, "Ambiguities of Anti-Racism," 103.

84. LA-B, DST, 4-44/49, Nr. 7107, "Protokoll der 19. Konferenz für Ausländerfragen am 2. Juni 1966."

85. Walter Becker, *Ehen mit Ausländern* (Münster: Aktion Jugendschutz, 1966).

86. For more on this topic, including on this pamphlet, see Julia Woesthoff, "'When I Marry a Mohammedan': Migration and the Challenges of Interethnic Marriages in Post-War Germany," *Contemporary European History* 22, no. 2 (2013): 199–231.

87. Becker, *Ehen mit Ausländern*, 30.

88. For more on changing gender relations in Franco's Spain: Aurora G. Morcillo, *True Catholic Womanhood: Gender Ideology in Franco's Spain* (DeKalb: Northern Illinois University Press, 2000); and Antonio Cazorla Sánchez, *Fear and Progress: Ordinary Lives in Franco's Spain, 1939–1975* (Oxford: Wiley-Blackwell, 2010), 144–171.

89. BArch B 141/36539, December 18, 1962, letter from "Herr W" to BMFJ.

90. BArch B 141/36536, May 26, 1965, letter from "Frau S" to BMFa and December 8, 1966, clippings from *Frankfurter Rundschau* and *Frankfurter Allgemeine*, "Weder ehelich noch unehelich. Zwei Kinder von Gastarbeitern ohne Familiennamen."

91. Sozialdemokratischer Pressedienst, "Deutsch-spanische 'Tondern-Ehen,' November 15, 1968, http://library.fes.de/spdpd/1968/681115.pdf; and Christof Böhmer, "Die Gültigkeit der 'Tondern-Ehen' in Deutschland," *Standesamt* 22, no. 4 (1969).

92. BArch B 141/36536, clipping *Stuttgarter Zeitung* July 23, 1966, by Heinz Kohl, "Der König hilft dem Heiratsvogt."

93. BArch B 141/49469, December 12, 1966, Evangelischer Presseverband für Bayern to BMJ.

94. BArch B 141/49475, December 13, 1966, Helmut Aschbacher to BMJ.

95. BArch B 141/36539, December 18, 1966, clipping from *Sonntagsblatt Hamburg*, "Ohne Priester geht es nicht. Heirat zwischen Deutschen und Spaniern: Das spanische Eherecht gilt in Deutschland."

96. Bundesverfassungsgericht [BVerfGE] 31, 58—Spanier-Beschluß, May 4, 1971.

97. BArch B 141/49478, June 25, 1971, "Verlautbarung der Pressestelle des Bundesverfassungsgerichts."

98. Richard Schmid, "Nicht mehr nach Tondern. Das 'Kanonische Hindernis' ist gefallen," *Die Zeit*, July 7, 1971.

99. Thomas T. Kane, *Streams of Change. Fertility, Nuptiality, and Assimilation of Guestworker Populations in the Federal Republic of Germany* (New York: Garland, 1989), 139, 154–155.

100. Ralph Jessen argues that because it disincentivized employers from making changes to accommodate mothers working full-time, migration "worked indirectly as an obstacle to equality and a support for traditional concepts of gender roles." "Bewältigte Vergangenheit— blockierte Zukunft? Ein prospektiver Blick auf die bundesrepublikanische Gesellschaft am Ende der Nachkriegszeit," in *Das Ende der Zuversicht? Die siebziger Jahre als Geschichte*, ed. Konrad Jarausch (Göttingen: Vandenhoeck & Ruprecht, 2008), 189.

101. Karen Hagemann, "A West German 'Sonderweg'? Family, Work, and the Half-Day Time Policy of Childcare and Schooling," in *Children, Families, and States. Time Policies of Childcare, Preschool, and Primary Education in Europe*, ed. Karen Hagemann, Konrad H. Jarausch, and Cristina Allemann-Ghionda (New York: Berghahn Books, 2011).

102. Hermann Schubnell, "Die Erwerbstätigkeit von Frauen und Müttern und die Betreuung ihrer Kinder," *Wirtschaft und Statistik* no. 8 (1964); and Sabine Chelmis, *Die Betreuung ausländischer Kleinkinder in Krippen, Tagespflegestellen und bei Verwandten* (Munich: DJI Verlag, 1982), 4.

103. LA-B, DST, 4/44-49, Beiheft: Rundfrage vom 13.1.64, March 12, 1964, Stadtverwaltung Ludwigshafen am Rhein to DST.

104. LA-B, DST, 4/44-49, Beiheft: Rundfrage vom 13.1.64, March 11, 1964, Landeshauptstadt München Schulreferat to DST.

105. LA-B, DST, 4/44-49, Beiheft: Rundfrage vom 13.1.64, March 9, 1964, Der Magistrat der Stadt Kassel to DST.

106. LA-B, DST, 4/44-49, Beiheft: Rundfrage vom 13.1.64, March 10, 1964, Stadt Wilhelmhaven to DST.

107. LA-B, DST, 4/44-49, Beiheft: Rundfrage vom 13.1.64, March 4, 1964, Der Magistrat der Stadt Hanau a.M. to DST, and March 17, 1964, Stadt Heilbronn Bürgermeisteramt to DST.

108. Stadtarchiv Frankfurt, Fürsorgeamt 4827, January 5, 1967 report from Caritas Frankfurt.

109. LA-B, DST, 4/44-49-7, Band 20, "Ergebnisprotokoll . . . vom 3. Oktober 1968.

110. Hasan Çil, *Anfänge einer EPOCHE. Ehemalige türkische Gastarbeiter erzählen/bir DÖNEMin başlangıçları. Bir zamanların konuk işçileri anlatıyor* (Berlin: Verlag Hans Schiler, 2003), 43.

111. Charity Goodman, "The Decision Makers: Spanish Migrant Women in West Germany" (PhD diss., Rutgers University, 1984).

112. Javier Dominguez, *El hombre como mercancia: españoles en Alemania* (Bilbao: Desclée de Brouwer 1976), 167–169.

113. Summers, "Reconciling Family and Work." For the reception of feminist demands for childcare, see also Kuller, *Familienpolitik*, 311–325.

114. Landesarchiv Baden-Württemberg [LA B-W], EA 2/303, Bü 204, March 2, 1971, Antonios Rodopoulous to IM B-W.

115. LA B-W, EA 2/303, Bü 276, April 26, 1972, Innenministerium B-W to BMI and Innenministerien.

116. LA B-W, EA 2/303, Bü 276, January 22, 1970, Innenminister NRW to Regierungspräsidenten.

117. Mattes's case study of Siemens in West Berlin is excellent on this point. *Gastarbeiterinnen*, 159–182.

118. LA B-W, EA 2/303, Bü 275, April 6, 1970, IM Berlin to BMI and Innenministerien.

119. Landesarchiv Berlin, B Rep 002 Nr. 17348, January 15, 1973, "Niederschrift über die 7. Sitzung . . . am 12. Januar 1973."

120. Deutscher Bundestag, Plenarprotokoll 6/42, April 15, 1970, 2125–2126. Also see LA B-W, EA 2/303, Bü 204, April 29, 1971, BMI to Antonios Rodopoulos of Mannheim.

121. PAAA B 85/1272, August 14, 1970, "Protokoll über das Gespräch des Herrn Bundespräsidenten mit Vertrauensleuten ausländischer Arbeitnehmer."

122. LA B-W, EA 2/303, Bü 276, April 26, 1972, Innenministerium B-W to BMI and Innenministerien.

123. LA B-W, EA 2/303, Bü 277, Verwaltungsgerichtshof B-W decision from April 7, 1972, I 312/71.

124. Miller analyzes a similar dynamic at work in the ways in which observers described guest worker women's participation in strikes in *Turkish Guest Workers in Germany*, 156–158.

125. Bundesverwaltungsgericht [BVerwG] I C 35.72, 2, a, 24.

126. B VerwG I C 35.72, 2, a, 28.

127. B VerwG I C 35.72, 2, c, 39.

128. B VerwG I C 35.72, 2, c, 34.

129. LA B-W EA 2/303, Bü 277, "Ausländerreferentenbesprechung am 12/13 März 1974 in Mainz."

130. B VerwG I B 821.80.

131. B VerwG 1 B 40.83.

132. BArch B 149/121743, BMA IicI—24 200/17, January 27, 1983, "Kommission 'Ausländerpolitik' Bericht des Ausschusses 2 'Familienzusammenführung.'"

133. For more background on the production and reception of this report, see, *Regieren der Migration*, 167–175, 186–190.

134. Underline in copy from PAAA B 85/1033, "Kommunalpolitische Aspekte des wachsenden ausländischen Bevölkerungsanteils in München."

135. LA-B, DST, 4-44/49, June 16, 1971, letter from Dr. Elsholz to Dr. Vogel.

Chapter 2

1. Gaby Franger, *Wir haben es uns anders vorgestellt. Türkische Frauen in der Bundesrepublik* (Frankfurt: Fischer Taschenbuch Verlag, 1984), 50.

2. StadtAN F 21, Nr. 57.

3. StadtAN F 21, Nr. 58.

4. Raika Espahangizi, "Migration and Urban Transformations: Frankfurt in the 1960s and 1970s," *Journal of Contemporary History* 49, no. 1 (2014): 202.

5. Ruth Mandel describes migrants "gerrymandering their ways around the law with false residency registration," *Cosmopolitan Anxieties. Turkish Challenges to Citizenship and Belonging in Germany* (Durham, NC: Duke University Press, 2008), 148. This form of "undocumented" status has also been discussed by Karakayali, *Gespenster*, 158–160.

6. Dormitory housing has been discussed extensively by other scholars, including Barbara Sonnenberger, *Nationale Migrationspolitik und regionale Erfahrung. Die Anfänge der Arbeitsmigration in Südhessen 1955–1967* (Darmstadt: Hessisches Wirtschaftsarchiv, 2003); Miller, *Turkish Guest Workers*, chapter 3; Vierra, *Turkish Germans*, chapter 2; and Anne von Oswald and Barbara Schmidt, "'Nach Schichtende sind sie immer in ihr Lager zurückgekehrt . . .' Leben in 'Gastarbeiter'-Unterkünften in den sechziger und siebziger Jahren," in *50 Jahre Bundesrepublik—50 Jahre Einwanderung: Nachkriegsgeschichte als Migrationsgeschichte*, ed. Jan Motte, Rainer Ohliger, and Anne von Oswald (Frankfurt: Campus Verlag, 1999).

7. BArch B 134/6926, August 5, 1960, DST to BMA. Also see "Deutsches Barack?" *Die Städtetag*, March 1960, 11.

8. Rieker, "Südländer, Ostagente oder Westeuropäer?," 245.

9. BArch B 106/81059, March 10, 1965, Botschaft Rom to AA, attached a February 26, 1965, clipping from "UNITA," and July 26, 1965, Niedersachsische Minister des Innern to BMI.

10. BArch B 134/6926, August 25, 1960, letter from Bundesminister für Wohnungsbau to the Wohnungsministerien der Länder, and "Kein deutsches Barack!" *Die Städtetag,* October 1960, 491–492.

11. Rölli-Alkemper, *Familie im Wiederaufbau,* 434, 446.

12. Sonnenberger, *Arbeitsmigration in Südhessen,* 371. Lücke came from a similar intellectual milieu to Family Minister Franz-Josef Würmeling, whose politics of "familialism" are elucidated by James Chappel, "Nuclear Families in a Nuclear Age: Theorising the Family in 1950s West Germany," *Contemporary European History* 1, no. 26 (2017): 85–109 .

13. BArch B 134/6927, "Eröffnungsrede des Präsidenten des 79. Deutschen Katholikentages in Hannover Paul Lücke," and BArch B 134/6928, September 29, 1964, Abteilung II Vermerk.

14. BArch B 134/6926, September 19, 1960, Deutscher Industrie- und Handelstag to BMWo.

15. BArch B 234/6928, June 1964 draft letter from BMWo to Bundeskanzleramt, and August 5, 1964 Referat IIA1 memorandum.

16. Rölli-Alkemper, *Familie im Wiederaufbau,* 481.

17. BArch B 134/6928, October 20, 1964, Referat IIA1 memorandum.

18. Qtd. in Sonnenberger, *Arbeitsmigration in Südhessen,* 371.

19. BArch B 134/6929, July 6, 1965, Unterabteilung IIB memorandum.

20. Sonnenberger, *Arbeitsmigration in Südhessen,* 373–374.

21. BArch B 106/69872, December 28, 1965, BMWi to BMI.

22. To draw on Foucault's concept of the role of the market in German ordoliberalism, the housing market assumes the role of "verification" as it reveals the "truth" of whether the foreign family can succeed in West Germany. Thomas Biebricher and Frieder Vogelmann, "Introduction," in *The Birth of Austerity: German Ordoliberalism and Contemporary Neoliberalism* (London: Rowman & Littlefield, 2017), 14.

23. Schönwälder, *Einwanderung,* 584–587; and Karl Christian Führer, *Die Stadt, das Geld und der Markt: Immobilienspekulation in der Bundesrepublik 1960–1985* (Berlin: Walter de Gruyter, 2016), 299–314. The Interior Ministry specifically mentions the "daily press" as an impetus in BArch B 106/81065, December 29, 1969, BMI to Innenministerien, and repeats the point about public attention in "Ausländerreferentenbesprechung am 18/19 März 1970 in Bonn."

24. BArch B 106/81065, January 16, 1970, Saarland Minister des Innern to BMI.

25. BArch 106/81065, July 10, 1969, Innenminister Schleswig-Holstein to BMI and IM der Länder, August 27, 1969, Innenminister NRW to IM der Länder, September 17, 1969, BMI to BMWo, and October 31, 1969, BMWo to BMI.

26. BArch 106/81065, August 12, 1972, *FAZ* clipping, "Familien dürfen nur bei Wohnungsnachweis kommen. Neue Regelung für Gastarbeiter in Bayern und Rheinland-Pfalz. Scharfe Kritik seitens katholischer Stellen."

27. LA-B, DST, 4/44-49 Ausländische Arbeitnehmer, Nr. 7118, Band 39, 7/1976, Nr. 15, Information des Deutschen Caritasverbandes, "Familienglück mit Hindernissen."

28. BArch B 106/81065, "Ausländerreferentenbesprechung am 18/19 März 1970," "Ausländerreferentenbesprechung am 25/26 Mai 1971," August 9, 1974, memorandum, "Ausländerreferentenbesprechung am 25/26 September 1974," and December 10, 1974, BMI to BMA.

29. BArch 106/81065, FAZ clipping August 12, 1972, "Familien dürfen nur bei Wohnungsnachweis kommen. Neue Regelung für Gastarbeiter in Bayern und Rheinland-Pfalz. Scharfe Kritik seitens katholischer Stellen," and Cihan Arın, "The Housing Market and Housing Policies for the Migrant Labor Population in West Berlin," in *Urban Housing Segregation of Minorities in Western Europe and the United States,* ed. Elizabeth D. Huttman (Durham, NC: Duke University Press, 1991).

30. BArch 106/81065, July 10, 1969, Innenminister Schleswig-Holstein to BMI and IM der Länder.

31. BArch 106/81065, "Ausländerreferentenbesprechung am 18/19 März 1970 in Bonn."

32. Führer, *Immobilienspekulation in der Bundesrepublik,* 312.

33. Cihan Arın, Sigmar Gude, and Hermann Wurtinger, *Auf der Schattenseite des Wohnungsmarkts: Kinderreiche Immigrantenfamilien. Analyse mit Verbesserungsvorschlägen in*

Wohnungsbelegung, Erneuerung, Selbsthilfe und Eigentum. Studie im Auftrag der Internationalen Bauausstellung Berlin 1987 (Basel: Birkhäuser Verlag, 1985), 29.

34. Ursula Mehrländer, *Situation der ausländischen Arbeitnehmer und ihrer Familienangehörigen in der Bundesrepublik Deutschland. Repräsentativuntersuchung '80* (Bonn: Forschungsbericht im Auftrag des Bundesministers für Arbeit und Sozialforschung, 1981), 469–476.

35. Qtd. in Prontera, *Partire, Tornare, Restare?*, 266.

36. Manfred Budzinski and Mechthild Schirmer, "Wirkungen der Beschränkung des Familiennachzugs für Ausländer," *Evangelischer Pressedienst Dokumentation* 5a (January 24, 1983); and Manfred Budzinski and Mechthild Schirmer, "Wie Ausländerbehörden mit Ausländerfamilien umgehen," *Evangelischer Pressedienst Dokumentation* 43a (October 17, 1983).

37. Budzinski and Schirmer, "Beschränkung des Familiennachzugs," 22.

38. Budzinski and Schirmer, "Beschränkung des Familiennachzugs," 22.

39. Budzinski and Schirmer, "Ausländerbehörden," 17.

40. Franz Hamburger, Lydia Seus, and Otto Wolter, *Zur Delinquenz ausländischer Jugendlicher. Bedingungen der Entstehung und Prozesse der Verfestigung* (Wiesbaden: Bundeskriminalamt, 1981), 75.

41. Budzinski and Schirmer, "Beschränkung des Familiennachzugs," 23–24.

42. Budzinski and Schirmer, "Beschränkung des Familiennachzugs," 20, 23.

43. Budzinski and Schirmer, "Ausländerbehörden," 20–21.

44. Matthew G. Hannah, *Dark Territory in the Information Age. Learning from the West German Census Controversies of the 1980s* (Farnham, UK: Ashgate, 2010), 48.

45. Archiv der Sozialen Bewegungen Freiburg [ASB Freiburg], Sigle 17-a4-264, *Dokumentation des bundesweiten Treffens der Initiativen zum Volkszählungs-Boykott 1983 in Bochum*, 1983, 13–16.

46. "Chronologie—Über die Geschichte der Rechtshilfe," http://www.rechtshilfe-muenchen.de/chronologie/.

47. DOMiD, FL0255—Volkszählung in Berlin, 1987.

48. "Heiße Ohren," *Der Spiegel*, April 11, 1983; "Volkszählung: Laßt 1000 Fragebogen glühen," *Der Spiegel*, March 28, 1983; and Larry Frohman, "'Only Sheep Let Themselves Be Counted': Privacy, Political Culture, and the 1983/87 West German Census Boycotts," *Archiv für Sozialgeschichte* 52 (2012), 345.

49. Deutscher Bundestag, Plenarprotokoll 10/3, March 30, 1983, 40.

50. Feride Erdoğmuş, "'Am Großmarkt wartet schon die Polizei.' Bericht eines 'Illegalen' aus der Türkei," in *Ausländer, die verfemten Gäste*, ed. Christian Habbe (Reinbek bei Hamburg: SPIEGEL-Verlag, 1983), 73.

51. I have been unable to determine whether Vogel ever published this particular essay in a final form. His larger body of writing on urban problems was influenced by his reading of American urbanists including Jane Jacobs. Kay Schiller and Christopher Young, *The 1972 Munich Olympics and the Making of Modern Germany* (Berkeley: University of California Press, 2010), 28.

52. LA-B, DST, 4/44-49, Band 22, June 16, 1971, letter from Dr. Elsholz to Dr. Vogel, undated essay is attached.

53. "Kulis der Nation," *Die Zeit*, October 20, 1972.

54. "Markt der Menschenhändler," *Der Spiegel*, March 26, 1973, 61. This analogy was also sometimes used to borrow solutions from the United States: at one point, FDP politicians suggested borrowing a measure from the United States and "busing" foreign children to other schools. See Kreuzberg Museum, SO 36 Archival Collection, Inv. Nr. 131, Lfd. Nr. 137, May 26, 1981, FR clipping "FDP: 'Bussing' für Ausländer. Kinder von Gastarbeitern sollen Schulen nicht überfremden."

55. LA B-W, EA 2/303 Bü 277, August 25, 1971, Landeskriminalamt Bremen.

56. "Die Türken kommen—rette sich wer kann," *Der Spiegel*, July 30, 1973, 26. Maria Stehle analyzes reporting on foreigners in *Der Spiegel*, including this article, in her "Narrating the Ghetto, Narrating Europe: From Berlin, Kreuzberg to the Banlieues of Paris," *Westminster Papers in Communication and Culture* 3, no. 3 (2006).

57. LA-B, B Rep 002 Nr. 10434 and 10436, and Camillo Noel, *Kommunalpolitische Aspekte des wachsenden ausländischen Bevölkerungsanteils in München. Problemstudie* (Munich: Stadtentwicklungsreferat, 1972). The entanglements of German and American social science have a longer history explored by, among others, Mary Nolan, *Visions of Modernity: American Business and the Modernization of Germany* (New York: Oxford University Press, 1994); and, with particular relevance for the entanglement of racial science, Fatima El-Tayeb, "Dangerous Liaisons. Race, Nation, and German Identity," in *Not so Plain as Black and White. Afro-German Culture and History, 1890–2000,* ed. Patricia Mazón and Reinhild Steingröver (Rochester: University of Rochester Press, 2005); and Andrew Zimmerman, *Alabama in Africa: Booker T. Washington, the German Empire, and the Globalization of the New South* (Princeton, NJ: Princeton University Press, 2012). The 1960s "globalization of the inner city" would be criticized by a later generation of German urbanists. See Arın, "Housing Market," 210–213.

    Ursula Kurz offers a contemporary critique of uncritical usage of American models in "Partielle Anpassung und Kulturkonflikt. Gruppenstruktur und Anpassungsdispositionen in einem italienischen Gastarbeiter-Lager," *Kölner Zeitschrift für Soziologie und Sozialpsychologie* 17 (1965). She argues that researchers who draw on American models implicitly assume the end goal of assimilation and absorption into a "melting pot" rather than the German goal of preservation and return.

58. Noel, *Kommunalpolitische Aspekte*, 179, 104.

59. LA-B, B Rep 002 Nr. 10436, "Abschlußbericht des Planungsteams 'Eingliederung der ausländischen Arbeitnehmer und ihrer Familien'" also singled out for analysis in Ausländerkomitee Berlin (West), *Gleiches Wohnrecht für Alle! Dokumentation zur Zuzugssperre für Ausländische Arbeiter* (Berlin: self-published, 1978), 3.

    Raika Espahangizi has identified a similar dynamic at work in housing policy in Frankfurt, where "the refusal to take measures was primarily based on the view this would boost self-organized entry and create further housing grievances," "Urban Transformations," 192.

60. BArch B 119/5135 September 5, 1973, letter from Bayerische Staatsministerium für Landesentwicklung und Umweltfragen to Bayerische Staatsministerium für Arbeit und Sozialordnung.

61. BArch B 119/5131, Referat Ia7 Ia7-5761, "Betr.: Arbeitskreis für Fragen der Beschäftigung ausländischer Arbeitnehmer; hier: Sitzung am 30. August 1972," virtually identical phrasing appears in August 16, 1972, report preparing for the meeting with the Confederation of German Employers' Associations.

62. LA-B, DST, 4/44-49, Nr. 7115, March 19, 1973, memorandum, and BArch B B 119/5132, March 1973, memorandum. In November 1976, one Labor Ministry official tried to avoid the "Nazi" comparison by describing "police state measures" as "Swiss conditions." LA-B, DST, 4/44-49, Nr. 7118, Wolfgang Bodenbender of the BMA "Zwischenbilanz der Ausländerpolitik."

63. BArch B 119/4150, May 24, 1972, "Ergebnisprotokoll."

64. BArch B 119/5131-5134, see especially BArch B 119/5131, "Betr.: Arbeitskreis für Fragen der Beschäftigung ausländischer Arbeitnehmer; hier: Sitzung am 30. August 1972."

65. The subject line shifts over the course of BArch B 119/5135.

66. Ulrich Herbert and Karin Hunn, "Gastarbeiter und Gastarbeiterpolitik in der Bundesrepublik. Vom Beginn der offiziellen Anwerbestopp (1955–1973)," in *Dynamische Zeiten: Die 60er Jahre in den beiden deutschen Gesellschaften,* ed. Axel Schildt, Detlef Siegfried, and Karl Christian Lammers (Hamburg: Christians, 2000); Marcel Berlinghoff, *Das Ende der 'Gastarbeit.' Europäische Anwerbestopps 1970–1974* (Paderborn: Ferdinand Schöningh, 2013); and Jennifer Miller, "Her Fight Is Your Fight: 'Guest Worker' Labor Activism in the Early 1970s West Germany," *International Labor and Working-Class History* 84 (Fall 2013): 225–247.

67. BArch B 149/59839, November 26, 1973, Abteilung II to Herrn Staatssekretär, and correspondence in BArch B 149/59840.

68. Officials writing about foreign workers tend to assume that to be "single" is a permanent status rather than one that might change during the period of employment. BArch B 119/5136, June 11, 1974 BMA to other ministries.

69. Stuttgart is the most prominent example of a region that did not want to be forced to exclude foreigners but that had no choice. The mayor of Stuttgart argued to no avail that the measure

could be "catastrophic" for his city. The Schwarzwald-Baar Kreis, also in Baden-Württemberg, also objected to the measure. Both regions boasted a strong manufacturing base and low unemployment. LA-B, DST, 4/44-49 Ausländische Arbeitnehmer, Nr. 7117, January 8, 1975, Bürgermeisteramt Stuttgart to BMA and BMI.

70. Ausländerkomittee Berlin (West), *Gleiches Wohnrecht für alle!*, 16. The Foreigners' Committee of West Berlin was initially formed in order to protest a deportation and later grew into a lobby group for foreigners in the city, for example, collecting information about the impact of the housing ban. Arson attacks on its headquarters in 1978 and 1981 presumably destroyed this archive—a reminder that racist violence shapes the histories that are accessible to us. Author's interview with Hans Günter Kleff and DOMiD, FL 00425—"Rassisten schlugen zu."

71. The EEC exemption was confirmed in October 1975, when the ECJ ruled in a case about restricting movement of EEC citizens in France: *Roland Rutili v. Minister of the Interior*.

72. Sybille Münch found only a single *Die Zeit* article about the measure and no article in *Der Spiegel*. *Integration durch Wohnungspolitik? Zum Umgang mit ethnischer Segregation im europäischen Vergleich* (Wiesbaden: VS Verlag, 2010), 299.

73. BArch B 149/121720, March 23, 1976, Türkischen Arbeitnehmer der Adam Opel AG to Bundeskanzler Helmut Schimdt.

74. BArch B 149/121720,March 31, 1976, BMA reply.

75. Letters from several industry pressure groups available in BArch B 149/83759.

76. LA-B, DST, 4/44-49/8, August 29, 1975, "Ergebnisse einer Umfrage des Deutschen Städtetages."

77. LA-B, DST, 4/44-49/8, September 11, 1975, Stadt Nürnberg Referat für Rechts- und Ordnungsverwaltung to DST.

78. LA-B, DST, 4/44-49/8, August 29, 1975, and April 15, 1976, "Zusammenstellung der Ergebnisse von Umfragen des Deutschen Städtetages," and April 23, 1976, München Referat für Kreisverwaltung und öffentliche Ordnung to DST.

79. Responses from the Interior Ministries of the Länder collected in BArch B 149/121721.

80. LA-B, DST, 4/44-49/8, February 25, 1977, BMA to Mitglieder der Bund-Länder-Kommission.

81. Stefanie Eisenhuth argues for treating West Berlin as a "third Germany" in *Die Schutzmacht. Die Amerikaner in Berlin 1945–1994* (Göttingen: Wallstein Verlag, 2018).

82. Rüdiger Hütte, "Berlin and the European Communities," *Yearbook of European Law* 3 (1983): 1–23.

83. Lauren Stokes, "Racial Profiling on the U-Bahn: Policing the 'Berlin Gap' in the Schönefeld Airport Refugee Crisis," article draft in progress.

84. BArch B 149/59841. For a longer exploration of the specific politics surrounding Kreuzberg, see Carla Elizabeth MacDougall, "Cold War Capital: Contested Urbanity in West Berlin, 1963–1989" (PhD diss., Rutgers University, 2011), 175–208. For an in-depth study of everyday life for Turks in Wedding, see Vierra, *Turkish Germans*.

85. Abgeordnetenhaus von Berlin, Ausschuß für Ausländerfragen, Wort-Protokoll, 9. Wahlperiode, 22. Sitzung, 28. Januar 1983, 61.

86. "Eine Beratungsstelle für Ausländer: Die Gruppe 'Wohnen und Leben,'" *Südost Express*, July/August 1978, 11.

87. Fritz Franz, "'Überlastetes Siedlungsgebiet' Berlin?" *Juristische Rundschau* 4 (1976): 148.

88. LA-B, B Rep 002 Nr. 17349, November 20, 1975, "Ergebnisprotokoll."

89. Ausländerkomittee Berlin (West), *Gleiches Wohnrecht für Alle!*, 26.

90. Arın, "Housing Market," 206, and LA-B, B Rep. 002, Nr. 14390, Abgeordnetenhaus von Berlin Drucksache 7/1306, Mitteilungen des Präsidenten Nr. 157, June 23, 1978.

91. LA-B, B Rep. 004, Nr. 1861, April 28, 1980, Bezirksbürgermeister Neukölln to Vorsitzenden des Sonderausschusses für Ausländerfragen, B Rep 002, Nr. 17830, April 26, 1982, Kleine Anfrage Nr. 621, and B Rep 002, Nr. 17351, February 3, 1983, "Ergebnisprotokoll." Also Kreuzberg Museum, SO 36 Archival Collection, Inv. Nr. 2010/12, "Wohnungspolitische Tage AG-4 Wohnmisere der Arbeitsimmigranten und ihrer Familien. Diskussionsvorlage," undated, likely December 1981. There is also an extensive discussion about the possibility of extending the ban to Neukölln in Abgeordnetenhaus von Berlin, Ausschuß für Ausländerfragen, Wort-Protokoll, 9. Wahlperiode, 22. Sitzung, 28. Januar 1983.

92. Staatsarchiv Hamburg [SA H] 445-1, Nr. 833: July 7, 1976, "Entwurf... Leitlinien für die hamburgische Ausländerpolitik," and SA H 131-21, Nr. 3209, April 14, 1977, Senator für Inneres Staak to Bürgermeister Hans-Ulrich Klose.
93. SA H 131-21, Nr. 3209, July 6, 1977, Bürgerinitative ausländische Arbeitnehmer e.V. Haus Rudolfstrasse to the mayor, and November 7, 1977, letter signed by seventeen groups.
94. BArch B 106/81070, August 22, 1971, Laurenz Sohn to Bundestag representative Wilhelm Dröscher, Ausländerkomitee Berlin (West), *Gleiches Wohnrecht für Alle!*, 13, and Abgeordnetenhaus von Berlin, Ausschuß für Ausländerfragen, Wort-Protokoll, 9. Wahlperiode, 22. Sitzung, 28. Januar 1983, 61.
95. Deniz Camlikbeli, "Die bestehenden Wohnverhältnisse stabilisieren die Unterdrückung der Frau und Arbeitsemigrantin," in *Treff- und Informationsort für Frauen aus der Türkei (TIO). Lebenssituation von Frauen aus der Türkei und Möglichkeiten der Sozial- und Gemeinwesenarbeit* (Berlin: Berlin-Verlag, 1982), 82.
96. Ausländerkomitee Berlin (West), *Gleiches Wohnrecht für alle!*, 7.
97. Archiv Grünes Gedächtnis [AGG] C Berlin I.1, Alternative Liste 1978–1992, Signatur 196, November 20, 1981 report by Cihan Arın, "Wohnungsmisere von Arbeitsimmigranten."
98. LA-B, B Rep. 004, Nr. 1147, June 25, 1981, open letter from the Freundeskreis Türkisches Kulturzentrum.
99. Arın, "Housing Market," 208.
100. LA B, B Rep 004, Nr. 3209, VG IV A 241.75.
101. LA B, B Rep 004, Nr. 3209, December 20, 1976, memorandum on "Urteil des Verwaltungsgerichts Berlin vom 28.7.1976." This case is also featured in Ausländerkomitee Berlin (West), *Gleiches Wohnrecht für Alle!*, 22.
102. LA B, B Rep 004, Nr. 3209, OVG I B 119.77, July 12, 1979.
103. LA B, B Rep 004, Nr. 3209, June 30, 1978, memorandum and July 12, 1979, OVG I B 119.77.
104. LA B, B Rep 004, Nr. 3209, February 24, 1978, I A 5 to Abteilung III, and June 30, 1978, memorandum.
105. LA B, B Rep 004, Nr. 3209, July 12, 1979, OVG I B 119.77.
106. LA B, B Rep 004, Nr. 3209, July 12, 1979, OVG I B 119.77.
107. LA B, B Rep 002, Nr. 17180, July 13, 1979, press release "Peter Ulrich: Zuzugssperre-Urteil bedarf intensiver Prüfung," and contents of B Rep. 004, Nr. 1860.
108. Serhat Karakayali, "Across Bockenheimer Landstrasse," *diskus* no. 2/00 (2000), http://www.copyriot.com/diskus/2_00/a.htm; and Azozomox and Duygu Gürsel, "The untold struggles of migrant women squatters and the occupations of Kottbusser Straße 8 and Forster Straße 16/17, Berlin-Kreuzberg," in *Migration, Squatting, and Radical Autonomy*, ed. Pierpaolo Mudu and Sutapa Chattopadhyay (London: Routledge, 2017), 104–117"; and Akcan, *Open Architecture*.
109. Horst Grimminger, "Hausbesetzungen in Frankfurt: Chronik eines Konflikts, seine politischen und ökonomischen Hintergründe und Konsequenzen," *Beiträge zur Konfliktforschung* 6, no. 3 (1976). The rent strikes are also briefly discussed in Espahangazi, "Urban Transformations"; and Führer, *Immobilienspekulation*. Thank you to Sarah Jacobson for allowing me to read draft chapters of "Squatting to Make Ends Meet: Southern Italian Migrants and the Right to a Home in 1970s Italy and West Germany" (PhD diss., Michigan State University, 2021) and an early draft of "Reformulating Urban Citizenship: Italian Migrants and Housing Occupations in 1970s Frankfurt," *Yearbook of Transnational History* vol. 5 (2022).
110. Rainer Molling, Dorothea Reinig, and Horst Schäfer, *Hippie Okul. Bericht über ein außerschulisches Projekt mit türkischen Kindern in Frankfurt-Bockenheim* (Frankfurt: Verlag Jugend und Politik, 1975), 24.
111. Unione inquilini, *Recht auf die Wohnung* (Frankfurt: self-published, 1973), 11.

A 1965 East German children's book intended to "raise awareness of the problems of guest worker children in the FRG" describes Italian communists bringing collective action to the working class in the FRG. The Weismann Press published the book in seven different languages and recorded the Turkish-language version on cassette tapes in 1983. Günther Feustel, *Kinderstreik in Santa Nicole: Keine Oliven für Don Camale* (Munich: Weismann Verlag, 1970).

112. Espahangizi, "Urban Transformations," 203; and Azozomox and Gürsel, "Migrant Women Squatters," 107–111.
113. Häuserrat Frankfurt, *Wohnungskampf in Frankfurt*, 142.
114. Molling, Reinig, and Schäfer, *Hippie Okul*, 20.
115. Molling, Reinig, and Schäfer, *Hippie Okul*, 79, 64.
116. Molling, Reinig, and Schäfer, *Hippie Okul*, 62, and Azozomox and Gürsel, "Migrant Women Squatters," 111–115.
117. For Wolfsburg: Prontera, *Partire, Tornare, Restare?*, 269–270. For Berlin: "1979: Das Jahr des Kindes," *Südost Express*; January 1979, "Kinderspielplatz statt Schrotthändler!" *Südost Express*; April 1979, Kreuzberg Museum, SO 36 Archival Collection, Inv. Nr. 2010/95, Lfd. Nr. 97; and Akcan, *Open Architecture*, 234. For Frankfurt: Häuserrat Frankfurt, *Wohnungskampf in Frankfurt*, 130.
118. Flyer reproduced in Häuserrat Frankfurt, *Wohnungskampf in Frankfurt*, 128.
119. "Gastarbeiterkinder verunglücken häufiger," *Informationsdienst zur Ausländerarbeit*, 1983, no. 1, p. 2.
120. Kreuzberg Museum, Inv. Nr. 2010/13, March 1, 1988, Ergebnisprotokoll.
121. Erika Fekete, *Eine Chance für Fatma. Jeder von uns könnte mit türkischen Kindern arbeiten* (Hamburg: Rowohlt Taschenbuch, 1982), 100–101.
122. "Türkische Kinder im NKZ," *KiezDepesche* Nr. 3, Januar 1983, p. 11.
123. Gert von Bassewitz, *morgens Deutschland. abends Türkei* (Berlin: Verlag Frölich und Kaufmann, 1981), 257–258.
124. Berlinghoff, *Das Ende der 'Gastarbeit'*, 46–47.
125. Ger Mik, "Housing Segregation and Policy in the Dutch Metropolitan Environment," in *Urban Housing Segregation of Minorities in Western Europe and the United States*, ed. Elizabeth D. Huttman (Durham, NC: Duke University Press, 1991), 183.
126. Jozefien De Bock, *Parallel Lives Revisited: Mediterranean Guest Workers and Their Families at Work and in the Neighborhood, 1960–1980* (New York: Berghahn, 2018), 122–125; and Annette Groth, "Ausländerforschung und Ausländerpolitik im europäischen Vergleich," in *Der gläserne Fremde. Bilanz und Kritik der Gastarbeiterforschung und der Ausländerpädagogik*, ed. Hartmut Griese (Opladen: Leske und Budrich, 1984).

Chapter 3

1. English and German speakers will also recognize the tune as "Twinkle, Twinkle, Little Star." For more on the Turkish Workers' Choir, see Edda Brandes, Dieter Hauer, and Marcella Hoffmann, "Der Türkische Arbeiterchor in West-Berlin (1979)," in Max Peter Baumann, ed., *Musik der Türken in Deutschland*, ed. Max Peter Baumann (Kassel: Yvonne Landeck, 1985), 81–92.
2. My translation of the Turkish lyrics is recorded from the single German translation of lyrics also printed in Werkkreis Literatur der Arbeitswelt, ed., *Mein Vaterland ist international: Texte zur Solidarität* (Frankfurt am Main: Fischer Taschenbuch Verlag, 1976), 136–138.
3. For a comprehensive account of the reform that does not focus on the consequences for foreign workers, see Kuller, *Familienpolitik*, 214–222.
4. Moeller, *Protecting Motherhood*, 109–141, quote from Jakob, *Familienbilder*, 129.
5. Kuller, *Familienpolitik*, 160. For accounts of the establishment of child allowances in West Germany, also see Dagmar Nelleßen-Strauch, *Der Kampf um das Kindergeld: Grundanschauungen, Konzeptionen und Gesetzgebung 1949–1964* (Düsseldorf: Droste Verlag, 2003); Merith Niehuss, "French and German Family Policy 1945–60," *Contemporary European History* 4, no. 3 (1995): 293–313: and Moeller, *Protecting Motherhood*, 109–141.
6. Lyons, *Algerian Families*, 94–98, 147–150.
7. Niehuss, "French and German Family Policy," 310–311: and Comte, *European Migration Regime*, 63–66.
8. PAAA B 85/886, December 10, 1955, BMA to Bundeskanzleramt.
9. BArch B 149/22628, January 3, 1963, Bundesanstalt für Arbeit to BMA, March 26, 1963, memorandum, and July 8, 1964, "Abkommen vom 15. Mai 1964 zur Änderung des Abkommens vom 29. Oktober 1959."

10. Ursula Münch, "Familien-, Jugend- und Altenpolitik," in *Geschichte der Sozialpolitik in Deutschland seit 1945. Band 4*, ed. Michael Ruck and Marcel Boldorf (Baden–Baden: Nomos Verlag, 2007), 574.

11. BArch B 149/46772, undated "Niederschrift über die Besprechung . . . am 11. September 1964 im BMA."

12. BArch B 149/22628, June 27, 1968, memorandum.

13. BArch B 149/47271, May 10, 1968, minutes.

14. Mattes, *"Gastarbeiterinnen,"* 53.

15. BArch B 149/22638, August 30, 1967, "Jugoslavien/Kindergeld." For more on the Moroccan workers in West Germany, see Brittany Lehman, "West German-Moroccan Relations and Politics of Labour Migration, 1958–1972," *Journal of Migration History* 5 (2019): 103–133.

16. PAAA B 85/1269, April 5, 1977, BMA to BMF, AA, BMI.

17. PAAA B 85/886, May 7, 1956, memorandum. Manuela Naldini describes this as the "family/ kinship solidarity model" in *The Family in the Mediterranean Welfare States* (London: Frank Cass, 2003).

18. BArch B 149/46775, October 29, 1971, Bundesanstalt to BMA.

19. *Lettere degli Emigrati* (Frankfurt am Main: Editrice Federeuropa, 1967), 60.

20. BArch B 149/22557, February 5, 1954, memorandum and BArch B 149/22628, June 28, 1961, cable from Spanish Embassy.

21. Kuller, *Familienpolitik*, 214–222.

22. Kuller, *Familienpolitik*, 216.

23. BArch B 149/46813, October 1, 1973, memorandum.

24. BArch B 149/46811, February 22, 1972, Abteilung VI to Abteilung II.

25. BArch B 149/46809, September 15, 1971, memorandum and BArch B 149/46811, February 22, 1972, memorandum.

26. BArch B 149/46815, April 1, 1974, Abteilung II to Herr Minister.

27. BArchB 149/46809, September 23, 1971, BMJFG to BMI and BMJ, October 21, 1971, BMI to BMJFG, BMA, and BMJ, and BArch B 149/46810, December 20, 1971, BMJ to BMJFG and BMA.

28. BArchB 149/46811, April 26, 1972, memorandum.

29. BArch B 149/46813, October 17, 1973, memorandum.

30. Lyons, *Algerian Families*, 94.

31. BArch B 149/46815, February 8, 1974, Bundesanstalt für Arbeit to BMA.

32. PAAA B 85/1131, April 23, 1974, AA to BMA.

33. Hartmut Leder, "Für Ausländer weniger?," *Bundesarbeitsblatt* no. 1 (1975): 38 and PAAA B 85/1131, July 8, 1974, "Argumentationskatalog."

34. BArch B 149/46811, February 22, 1972, Abteilung VI to Abteilung II.

35. Leder, "Für Ausländer weniger?," 37.

36. Poll and related correspondence available in BArch B 149/96248.

37. Katharina Focke, "Keine Diskriminierung ausländischer Arbeitnehmer," *Welt der Arbeit*, July 19, 1974, ADW, PB 940, November 26, 1974, Werner Steinjan to Helmut Class.

38. Margret Kuhn, "Kindergeld, Entwicklungshilfe und Bevölkerungsexplosion," *Sozialer Fortschritt* 22, no. 6 (1973): 132–133; and "Kindergeld für Gastarbeiter—ein ernstes Problem," *Sozialer Fortschritt* 24, no. 3 (1975): 59.

39. Leder, "Für Ausländer weniger?," 38.

40. PAAA B 85/1131, May 1974 memorandum.

41. BArch B 149/47272, July 28, 1974, memorandum.

42. BArch B 149/46818, June 20, 1974, Katholischer Arbeitskreis für Fragen Ausländischer Arbeitnehmer to AA and BMA.

43. Leder, "Für Ausländer weniger?," 33.

44. PAAA B 85/1381, July 17, 1974, telegram German Embassy in Belgrade to AA.

45. BArch B 149/96205, December 4, 1979, "Entschließung aus der Personalversammlung für jugoslawische Arbeiter beim Bahnhof Hamburg Süd."

46. Molnar, "Imagining Yugoslavs."

47. PAAA B 85/1381, July 24, 1974, memorandum and "Sprechzettel für die Kabinettsitzung am 31. Juli 1974."

48. PAAA B 85/1383, October 11, 1974, German Embassy in Ankara to AA.
49. Emphasis mine. PAAA B 85/1383, October 11, 1974, German Embassy in Ankara to AA.
50. DOMiD, FL0115—"Esta Medida Del Kindergeld es un Puro Abuso y nada mas."
51. Jose Sanchez, "Kindergeld ¡Discriminacion!," *Carta a los Padres*, December 1974, and "Alemania. Frankfurt: Una Leccion de Provecho," *Lucha Obrera* 24 (1975), 7.
52. Spanisches Zentrum, Essen, *Spanien ist Anders* (Munich: Trikont Verlag, 1974).
53. Qtd. from Alexander Clarkson, *Fragmented Fatherland. Immigration and Cold War Conflict in the Federal Republic of Germany 1945–1980* (New York: Berghahn Books, 2013) 100; and Simon Goeke, *"Wir sind alle Fremdarbeiter!" Gewerkschaften, migrantische Kämpfe und soziale Bewegungen in der Bundesrepublik Deutschland der 1960er und 1970er Jahre* (Paderborn: Ferdinand Schöningh, 2020), 260–269.
54. DOMiD FL0050, "Alle zur Nationalen Kindergelddemo!" and SA H 136-3, Nr. 8, October 30, 1974, "El 17 De Noviembre en Frankfurt/El Sindicato Nos Dejo en La Estacada!" The multinational character of the Spanish-organized demonstration is also particularly stressed by "3 Bin yabancı işçi Çocuk Parası için Frankfurt'ta yürüyüş yaptı," *Tercüman*, 19 November 1974.
55. DOMiD, FL0115, "Esta Medida Del Kindergeld es un Puro Abuso y nada mas," and DOMiD, FL0050, "Alle zur Nationalen Kindergelddemo!" from 1974.
56. BArch B 149/46817, July 1, 1974, memorandum, and Clarkson, *Fragmented Fatherland*, 96.
57. Leder, "Für Ausländer weniger?," 36.
58. Archiv des Deutsche Gewerkschaftsbundes im Archiv der Sozialen Demokratie [DGB Archive] 5/DGAZ 624, July 19, 1974, DGB Landesbezirk Niedersachsen to DGB Abt. AA, and HHW, Abt. 502/7396, Spanisches Kindergeldkomittee Frankfurt, December 1974.
59. "3 Bin yabancı işçi Çocuk Parası için Frankfurt'ta yürüyüş yaptı," *Tercüman*, November 19, 1974, and "Gastarbeiter protestieren gegen die geplante Kindergeldregelung," *General-Anzeiger* July 1, 1974.
60. Manuel Rojas, "Heute das Kindergeld, morgen vielleicht die Rente," *Carta a los Padres,* February 1979.
61. "Wiesbadener Kindergeld-Komittees," *IAF-Informationen* 4/1980, 14.
62. "3 Bin yabancı işçi Çocuk Parası için Frankfurt'ta yürüyüş yaptı," *Tercüman*, 19 November 1974.
63. BArch B 149/46817, June 24, 1974, "Kurze Information" by "Organisationskomitee Ausländerkindergeld Bonn-Bad Godesberg."
64. BArch B 149/46819, July 24, 1974, Abg. Gerhard Braun to Par. Staatssekretär BMJFG.
65. Archiv des Deutschen Liberalismus [ADL] Mischnick A38-168, July 22, 1974, Ausländerbeirat Nürnberg to Wolfgang Mischnick, "Feliz Navidad—solo con nuestros hijos?," *Carta a los Padres*, December 1974, and "Tambien a las Duras, Señor Schmidt!," *Carta a los Padres*, May 1975.
66. Leder, "Für Ausländer weniger?," 37.
67. These arguments found in PAAA B 85/1381, July 25, 1974, telegram from German Embassy in Lisbon to AA, DOMiD FL0115, "Esta Medida Del Kindergeld es un Puro Abuso y nada mas," and LA B-W, Bestand J 152 B III b Nr. 62, flyer by Comité PRO-KINDERGELD Stuttgart/Sindelfingen.
68. "Probleme mit Kindergeld," *Südost Express* (June 1980), 5.
69. Kreuzberg Museum, SO 36 Archival Collection, Inv. Nr. 131, Lfd. Nr. 137, March 2, 1986, TISPJG letter.
70. SA H 136-3, Nr. 8, October 30, 1974, "El 17 De Noviembre en Frankfurt/El Sindicato Nos Dejo en La Estacada!"
71. Goeke, *"Wir sind alle Fremdarbeiter!,"* 212.
72. DOMiD FL0094, "Patronlarin Yeni Bir Oyunu," and "Alemania. Frankfurt: Una Leccion de Provecho," *Lucha Obrera* no. 24 (1975), 7.
73. DOMiD FL0018, "Kindergeld" flyer by "Operai Emigrati."
74. DOMiD FL0115, "Esta Medida Del Kindergeld es un Puro Abuso y nada mas."
75. BArch B 149/46819, July 15, 1974, IG Chemie-Papier-Keramik to BMA. Similar observations in DGB Archive 5/DGAZ624, June 8, 1974, Abt. AA to Bundesvorstand DGB, and IG Metall-Archiv 5/IGMA260013, November 6, 1974 minutes. For more discussion of union reactions to child allowances, also see Oliver Trede, *Zwischen Misstrauen, Regulation und*

Integration. Gewerkschaften und Arbeitsmigration in der Bundesrepublik und in Großbritannien in den 1960er und 70er Jahren (Paderborn: Ferdinand Schöningh, 2015), 278–281.

76. Deutscher Gewerkschaftsbund, *Protokoll 10. Ordentlicher Bundeskongress Hamburg, 25. bis 30. Mai 1975* (Düsseldorf: Deutscher Gewerschaftsbund, 1975), 376–378.
77. SA H 361-9, Nr. 4634, October 4, 1974, Schule Chemitzstrasse Volksschule to Behörde für Schule.
78. "Por no hacernos caso," *El Noticiero*, May 1975, 2.
79. LA-B, DST 4/44-49 Nr. 7120, March 30, 1979, "Gemeinsame Stellungnahme der spanischen Sozialberater und der spanischen Seelsorger in der Bundesrepublik Deutschland zur Neuregelung des Bundeskindergeldgesetzes," and March 1, 1979, Initiativausschuss "Ausländische Mitbürger in Hannover" to Deutsche Städtetag.
80. Karamouzi, *The Second Enlargement*, 150, 155–156, 165, 177, 179–180.
81. BArch B 149/46776, November 13, 1975, Dr. Leder to Herrn Minister.
82. Karamouzi, *The Second Enlargement*, 150.
83. Karamouzi, *The Second Enlargement*, 179–180.
84. Karamouzi, *The Second Enlargement*, 179–180; and Comte, *European Migration Regime*, 113–114, 117.
85. PAAA B 85/1479, October 30, 1978, memorandum.
86. AGG B.II.1, Die Grünen im Bundestag 1983–1990, Signatur 3481, TISPJG broschure "Für Steuergerechtigkeit."
87. AGG, B.II.1, Die Grünen im Bundestag 1983–1990, Signatur 3481, "Für Steuergerechtigkeit," p. 26.
88. Christian Schneider, "Eine Invasion von Gastarbeiterkindern? Eine Einsparung, die teuer werden kann," *Süddeutsche Zeitung* November 8, 1974, trans. Allison Brown, http://german historydocs.ghi-dc.org/docpage.cfm?docpage_id=1517 (last visited December 12, 2018).
89. 'Der Kindergeld-Türke in der Schule,' *Frankfurter Allgemeine Zeitung*, December 17, 1974.
90. 'Billige Kinder,' *Der Spiegel*, October 7, 1974.
91. Jakob, *Familienbilder*, 56.
92. For the longer history of state interest in fertility, see Annette F. Timm, *The Politics of Fertility in Twentieth-Century Berlin* (Cambridge: Cambridge University Press, 2010).
93. BArch B 106/45157, 23 April 1971, Ministerialdirigent Dr. Schiffer memorandum.
94. "Die Kinder wollen keine Kinder mehr," *Der Spiegel*, March 24, 1975.
95. Ruth Lindenberg, 'Bei Ausländerkindern "tickt eine Zeitbombe,"' *Kölnische Rundschau*, 15. April 1976.
96. SA H 131-21, Nr. 3209, April 25, 1977 memorandum, and LA NRW NW 670, Nr. 95, January 27, 1982 memorandum.
97. HHW, Abt. 502/7396, Spanisches Kindergeldkomittee Frankfurt, December 1974.
98. For summaries of the Yugoslavian and Portuguese press, see PAAA B 85/1381, July 17, 1974, telegram from German Embassy in Belgrade to AA, and July 25, 1974, telegram from German Embassy in Lisbon to AA.
99. "Türkiye'den Çocuk Akını Başlıyor!," *Tercüman*, November 4, 1974, and "Türkiye'den Almanya'ya çocuk akını devam ediyor," *Tercüman*, November 27, 1974.
100. Burhan Felek, "Almanya'daki işçilerin çocukları," *Milliyet*, October 12, 1974.
101. BArchB 149/96398, January 20, 1975, Abteilung II MR Dr. Leder to Parl. Staatssekretär.
102. BArch B 149/46819, October 8, 1974, Abteilung II memorandum.
103. Although I was unfortunately unable to locate the press packet itself, I did locate a report from the German Embassy in Ankara on the packet's impact on media coverage in Turkey. BArch B 149/46820, December 27, 1974, Abteilung II to Herr Minister.
104. PAAA B 85/1383, January 15, 1975, German Embassy in Ankara to AA.
105. Gülten Dayioğlu, "Çocuk Parası için Çocuklar Almanya'ya götürülürse durum daha kötü olacak," *Milliyet*, December 12, 1974.
106. Gülten Dayioğlu, *Atil hat Heimweh [Yurdumu özledim]*, trans. Feridun Altuna (Berlin: ikoo Verlag, 1985), 194.
107. For more on Turkish state fears of losing children to the nation, see Brian Joseph-Keysor Miller, "Reshaping the Turkish Nation-State: The Turkish-German Guest Working Program and Planned Development" (PhD diss., University of Iowa, 2015), chapter 4.

108. Gülten Dayioğlu, *Rückkehr zwischen zwei Grenzen: Gespräche und Erzählungen*, trans. Feridun Altuna (Berlin: ikoo Verlag 1986), 128.
109. BArch B 149/47275, January 10, 1979, memorandum, also present in BArch B 149/83935, September 15, 1981.
110. LAB B Rep 002/17830, *Tercüman* clipping with title missing, March 30, 1983.
111. Amparo González-Ferrer, "The Process of Family Reunification Among Original Guest-Workers in Germany," *Zeitschrift für Familienforschung* 19, no. 1 (2007): 10–33; and Ulrich Herbert and Karin Hunn, "Beschäftigung, soziale Sicherung und soziale Integration von Ausländern," in *Geschichte der Sozialpolitik in Deutschland seit 1945, Band 6*, ed. M. Geyer (Baden-Baden: Nomos Verlag, 2008), 755.
112. BArch B 149/47279, December 13, 1976, German Embassy in Ankara to AA memorandum.
113. BArch B 106/85171, December 23, 1974, Grenzschutzdirektion to BMI; March 12, 1975, Grenzschutzdirektion to BMI; and BArch B 106/85172, November 14, 1975, BMI to Grenzschutzdirektion.
114. ADW, PB 941 April 23, 1975, minutes.
115. BArch B 106/85171, November 22, 1974, Stadt Bielefeld Einwohnermeldeamt to Bundestagsabgeordneten Vogelsang.
116. BArch B 149/47277, March 20, 1975, Embassy in Ankara to AA.
117. DGB Archive, 5/DGAZ 624, "Interview im Mittagsmagazin am 19.10.1974."
118. DGB Archive, 5/DGAZ 624, December 23, 1974, Heinz Richter to Karl Schwab.
119. "1068 Gastarbeiterkinder fehlen in der Schule—wo sind sie?," *BILD* October 15, 1975.
120. BArch B 149/47278, April 7, 1976, Bundesanstalt to BMA.
121. For the history of debates over compulsory school attendance for guest worker children, see Brittany Lehman, *Teaching Migrant Children in West Germany and Europe, 1949–1992* (Cham: Palgrave Macmillan, 2019), chapters 2 and 3.
122. "Kindergeld und Schulbesuch," *Informationen für Sozialbetreuer Ausländischer Arbeitnehmer* 51 (1977).
123. Documentation about this case in DGB Archive, 5/DGAZ 625.
124. LA-B, B Rep. 002, Nr. 15643, May 30, 1985, BMI to Herr Bundesverfassungsrichter Prof. Dr. Steinberger als Berichterstatter des Zweiten Senats des Bundesverfassungsgerichts.
125. BArch B 106/117675, December 6, 1982, memorandum.
126. BArch B 106/117679, November 30, 1981, Referat VII1 memorandum.
127. LA-NRW, NW 80, October 1981 memorandum.
128. Biebricher and Vogelmann, "Introduction," 9.
129. ADL, IF-Kommission Ausländerpolitik #4238, April 27, 1982, "Wichtigste Ergebnisse der infas-Ausländer-Studie."
130. LA-NRW, NW 583 Nr. 1753, "Bis zu Sechs Jahren," *FAZ* clipping December 14, 1982.

Chapter 4

1. Gülay Töksöz, *"Ja, sie kämpfen—und sogar mehr als die Männer." Immigrantinnen—Fabrikarbeit und gewerkschaftliche Interessenvertretung* (Berlin: Nozizwe, 1991), 161.
2. Eleonore Kofman, "Female 'Birds of Passage.'"
3. Heather Booth provides detailed analysis of these "dependent migration" statistics in *The Migration Process in Britain and West Germany. Two Demographic Studies of Migrant Populations* (Aldershot, UK: Avebury, 1992), 122–136, 177–178.
4. BArch B 149/121733, February 13, 1979, memorandum.
5. Schönwälder, *Einwanderung und ethnische Pluralität*.
6. Lutz Raphael, *Jenseits von Kohle und Stahl: Eine Gesellschaftsgeschichte Westeuropas nach dem Boom* (Berlin: Suhrkamp, 2019), 47.
7. Thomas Raithel, *Jugendarbeitslosigkeit in der Bundesrepublik. Entwicklung und Auseinandersetzung während der 1970er und 1980er Jahre* (Munich: Oldenbourg Verlag, 2012), 11–13.
8. Goeke, *"Wir sind alle Fremdarbeiter!,"* 230–238.
9. Sarah Haßdenteufel, *Neue Armut, Exklusion, Prekarität: Debatten um Armut in Frankreich und der Bundesrepublik Deutschland, 1970–1990* (Berlin: Walter de Gruyter, 2019), 109–118.

10. Heiner Geißler, *Die Neue Soziale Frage. Analysen und Dokumente* (Freiburg im Briesgau: Herderbücherei, 1980 [original 1976]), 96–97.

11. Mehrländer, *Repräsentativuntersuchung '80*, 574.

12. It is difficult to find data on unauthorized labor market participation by foreigners. Sociologist Ali Uçar offers compelling evidence that it was a widespread phenomenon in *Illegale Beschäftigung und Ausländerpolitik: die Praxis der Ausländerpolitik und die illegale Beschäftigung der ausländischen Arbeiter in der Bundesrepublik Deutschland* (Berlin [West]: EXpress Edition, 1983). Sociologist Serhat Karakayali also offers preliminary thoughts about the extent of illegal labor in *Gespenster der Migration*, especially 165–168.

13. Philipp Ther, *Europe Since 1989: A History*, trans. Charlotte Hughes-Kreutzmiller (Princeton, NJ: Princeton University Press, 2016 [original 2014]), 264–272; and Anke Hassel and Christof Schiller, *Der Fall Hartz IV: Wie es zur Agenda 2010 kam und wie es weitergeht* (Frankfurt: Campus Verlag, 2010).

14. "Integration" became what West German social theorist Ulrich Beck might have called the "biographical solution of systemic contradictions." See *Risk Society: Towards a New Modernity*, trans. Mark Ritter (London: Sage, 1992 [1986]), 137.

15. BArch B 149/121735, "Dokumentation und Resolution zum 'Stichtag' für ausländische Jugendliche," and April 7, 1978, BMA reply to Klaus Siepmann. At coalition discussions in 1976, the SPD and FDP disagreed over the best way to treat family migrants but did not see it as an obstacle to forming a coalition. ADL, Baum N60-631, December 1, 1976, minutes.

16. Woesthoff, "Ambiguities of Anti-Racism," 115, and BArch B 149/54628, June 19, 1974, Embassy Ankara to AA. On "bogus divorce" in the Dutch context, see van Walsum, *Dutch Family Migration Policies*, 108.

17. Erdoğmuş, "Bericht eines 'Illegalen,' " 70, 72.

18. BArch B 106/60276, clipping from December 17, 1970, *Süddeutsche Zeitung*, Karl Heinz Eckert, "Dunkle Geschäfte mit Türken," and BArch B 106/60275, translation from April 17, 1969, *Yeni Gazete*, "Wenn der Arbeiter seine Arbeit nicht verkaufen kann."

19. The grandfather was unfortunately cut from the final version of the episode. The author of the episode, Peter Stripp, worked with noted "guest worker literature" author Aras Ören and with the Berlin police to develop the characters for the episode. Sender Freies Berlin Archive [SFB Archive], Binder 6988/8, HA Fernsehspiele TOD IM U-BAHNSCHACHT von Peter Stripp and "57. Tatort—Tod im U-Bahnschacht," YouTube video, from a program produced by Sender Freies Berlin and aired on ARD on November 9, 1975, posted on June 6, 2012, https://www.youtube.com/watch?v=OXxfoL-lKlQ.

20. LA-B-W, EA 2/303, Bü 276, August 18, 1971, Innenminister S-H to BMI and IM der Länder.

21. Erica Carter, *How German Is She? Postwar West German Reconstruction and the Consuming Woman* (Ann Arbor: University of Michigan Press, 1997).

22. LA B-W, EA 2/303, Bü 276, August 26, 1971, Berlin Senator für Inneres to BMI and Innenministerien.

23. In the Netherlands, this policy was *explicitly* gendered: male workers could bring over family members starting in 1963, while women could not do the same until 1974. van Walsum, *Dutch Family Migration Policies*, 124, 149–150.

24. LA-B-W, EA 2/303, Bü 276, September 3, 1971, Bayer. Staatsministerium des Innern to Innenminister S-H, IM der Länder, BMI.

25. LA-B-W, EA 2/303, Bü 276, January 18, 1972, Innenministerium B-W to Regierungspräsidien.

26. LA-BW, EA 2/303, Bü 276, April 18, 1972, Regierungspräsidium Sudwürttemberg-Hohenzollern memorandum with attached November 25, 1971, decision VG XI A 200.70.

27. BArch B 119/4728, May 23–24, 1973, minutes of meeting.

28. BArch B 119/4728, May 23–24, 1973, minutes of meeting.

29. LA-B-W, EA 2/303, Bü 284, January 12, 1976, Bayerisches Staatsministerium des Innern circular.

30. BArch B 106/85171, November 11, 1974, Referat VII6 to Herrn Minister.

31. The circular is reprinted in LA B B Rep 002, Nr. 17668, Initiativkreis zur Abschaffung des Stichtages, "Dokumentation und Resolution zum 'Stichtag' für ausländische Jugendliche," dated April 1, 1978.

32. LA B B Rep 002, Nr. 17668, Initiativkreis zur Abschaffung des Stichtages, "Dokumentation und Resolution zum 'Stichtag' für ausländische Jugendliche."

33. BArch B 149/54451, *Spiegel*, January 1975 clipping "Grundsätzlich nicht sinnvoll," and January 23, 1975, Abteilung II to Herrn Staatssekretär.

34. BArch B 149/54451, August 21, 1975, BMA memorandum.

35. "Entwurf von Thesen zur Ausländerpolitik," October 23, 1975, reprinted in *epd Dokumentation* 5/76, 4–10.

36. ADW, PB 941, November 28, 1975, Lohmeyer Vermerk für Dr. Schober.

37. ADW, PB 941, December 10, 1975, Diakonische Werk Innere Mission und Hilfswerk memorandum and ADW, PB 942, December 3, 1975, Diakonie and Caritas open letter to Helmut Schmidt.

38. Jan Schneider, *Modernes Regieren und Konsens: Kommissionen und Beratungsregime in der deutschen Migrationspolitik* (Wiesbaden: VS Verlag für Sozialwissenschaften, 2010), 125–126.

39. BArch B 106/81038, January 18, 1977, BMI VII6 to Herrn Parl. Staatssekretär Baum.

40. PAAA B 85/1282, April 26, 1977, Referat 513 memorandum.

41. PAAA B 85/1283, December 17, 1976, "Bericht über die Beratungen der Bund-Länder-Arbeitsgruppe zur Fortentwicklung einer umfassenden Konzeption der Ausländerbeschäfti gungspolitik."

42. Ebd.

43. Ebd.

44. Ebd.

45. BArch B 106/81038, December 2, 1976, Referat VII6 to Herr Minister.

46. BArch B 106/81038, January 18, 1977, BMI VII6 to Herrn Parl. Staatssekretär Baum.

47. BArch B 106/69850, October 8, 1976, Referat VII6 to Herrn Minister.

48. PAAA B 85/1283, December 17, 1976, "Bericht über die Beratungen der Bund-Länder-Arbeitsgruppe zur Fortentwicklung einer umfassenden Konzeption der Ausländerbeschäfti gungspolitik," pp. 56–57.

49. The Interior Ministry's position against restriction was supported by the BMI, BMJFG, BMBW, IM Berlin, Bremen, Hamburg, Hessen, NRW, AM Berlin, Bremen, Hamburg, Hessen, DST, Deutscher Städte und Gemeindebund, while restriction for teenagers was supported by BMWi, IM B-W Bayern, Niedersachsen, R-P Saarland, S-H, AM B-W, Bayern, Niedersachsen, NRW, R-P, Saarland, S-H, Deutscher Landkreistag, and Sozialpartner. The Labor Ministry abstained. BArch B 106/81038, February 17, 1977, Referat VII6 to Herr Minister memorandum.

50. PAAA B 85/1459, February 28, 1977, "Vorschläge der Bund-Länder-Kommission zur Fortentwicklung einer umfassenden Konzeption der Ausländerbeschäftigungspolitik."

51. The new circular, dated June 14, 1977, is reprinted in LA B B Rep 002, Nr. 17668, Initiativkreis zur Abschaffung des Stichtages, "Dokumentation und Resolution zum 'Stichtag' für ausländische Jugendliche," dated April 1, 1978.

52. BArch B 149/54467, June 19, 1978, memorandum.

53. BArch B 106/81039, "Ein neues Subproletariat entsteht," FAZ clipping with notes from February 8, 1978.

54. BArch B 149/59884, July 13, 1978, Referent Dr. Fendrich to Herr Minister.

55. Quote from ADW, PB 943, November 3, 1978, Diakonie to Herbert Ehrenberg at the BMA, also see October 25, 1978, minutes and November 29, 1978, memorandum.

56. BArch B 149/121735, Initiativkreis zur Abschaffung des Stichtages, "Dokumentation und Resolution zum 'Stichtag' für ausländische Jugendliche," dated April 1, 1978, and following correspondence.

57. Peter-Alexis Albrecht and Christian Pfeiffer, *Die Kriminalisierung junger Ausländer. Befunde und Reaktionen sozialer Kontrollinstanzen* (Munich: Juventa Verlag, 1979), 7.

58. Albrecht and Pfeiffer, *Kriminalisierung junger Ausländer*, 42, 50, 119.

59. Emphasis in the original. Hamburger, Seus, and Wolter, *Zur Delinquenz ausländischer Jugendlicher*, 18.

60. "Gençler 'Sınırsız' çalışma izni istiyor," *Hürriyet*, March 12, 1979.

61. Hamburger, Seus, and Wolter, *Zur Delinquenz ausländischer Jugendlicher*, 177.

62. BArch B 149/54468, October 6, 1978, memorandum.

63. Ulrich Geißler, "Armut in Deutschland—eine Neue Soziale Frage? Ist die Sozialpolitik falschprogrammiert? Zu der Dokumentation von Minister Dr. H. Geißler," *Sozialer Fortschritt* 25, no. 3 (1976).

64. Bertold Huber, "Rechtmäßigkeit der Stichtagsregelung im Arbeitserlaubnisverfahren?" *Neue Juristische Wochenschrift* 32, no. 10 (1979): 465; and LSG Hamburg, V ARBf 4/78, *Neue Juristische Wochenschrift* 32, no. 10 (1979): 511.

65. Huber, "Rechtmäßigkeit der Stichtagsregelung," 465; and LSG Essen, L 12 Ar 6/78, *Neue Juristische Wochenschrift* 32, no. 10 (1979), 512. This particular case offers strong support for Serhat Karakayali's argument in *Gespenster der Migration* that "rule by exception" preserves the most flexible possible labor market for German employers.

66. The solution is first described as a kind of "dynamisierter Stichtag" in BArch B 149/54468, October 6, 1978, memorandum.

67. BArch B 149/54468, October 6, 1978, memorandum.

68. Deutscher Bundestag, Drucksache 8/2369, December 8, 1978, "Antrag: Arbeitserlaubnis für die Kinder ausländischer Arbeitnehmer."

69. Deutscher Bundestag, Drucksache 8/2538, February 7, 1979, "Antrag: Arbeitserlaubnis für Ehegatten und Kinder ausländischer Arbeitnehmer."

70. Deutscher Bundestag, Plenarprotokoll 8/139, February 16, 1979, 11040.

71. Deutscher Bundestag, Plenarprotokoll 8/161, June 21, 1979, 12884.

72. Deutscher Bundestag, Plenarprotokoll 8/139, February 16, 1979, 11045.

73. Deutscher Bundestag, Plenarprotokoll 8/139, February 16, 1979, 11043.

74. Dieter Düding, *Heinz Kühn 1912-1992. Eine politische Biographie* (Essen: Klartext-Verlag, 2002), 312.

75. Heinz Kühn, *Stand und Weiterentwicklung der Integration der ausländischen Arbeitnehmer und ihrer Familien in der Bundesrepublik Deutschland: Memorandum der Beauftragten der Bundesregierung,* (Bonn: Bundesminister für Arbeit, 1979), 12.

76. Some examples: Bernd Geiß, "Die Ausländerbeauftragten der Bundesregierung in der ausländerpolitischen Diskussion," in *Deutschland—ein Einwanderungsland? Rückblick, Bilanz und neue Fragen,* ed. Edda Currle and Tanja Wunderlich (Stuttgart: Lucius and Lucius, 2001); Simon Green, *The Politics of Exclusion: Institutions and Immigration Policy in Contemporary Germany* (Manchester: Manchester University Press, 2004), 96–97; Chin, *The Guest Worker Question,* 104–105; and Herbert and Hunn, "Soziale Integration von Ausländern," 776.

77. This point is also made by Zölls, *Regieren der Migration,* 197–198.

78. BArch B 119/6685, September 13, 1979, memorandum.

79. Kühn, *Memorandum der Beauftragten der Bundesregierung,* 12.

80. BArch B 119/6685, November 19, 1979, memorandum, and BArch B 149/83929, November 7, 1979, "Bericht zum Memorandum des Beauftragten der Bundesregierung."

81. BArch B 149/83928, May 10, 1979, memorandum, and BArch B 149/83931, November 19, 1979, memorandum.

82. ADW, PB 945, February 29, 1980, minutes, and March 5, 1980, Kirchliches Ausssenamt to Vorsitzenden des Rates der EKD.

83. BArch B 149/83933, December 8, 1980, memorandum.

84. BArch B 149/83935, January 5, 1981, Liselotte Funcke to Helmut Schmidt, January 16, 1981, Zentralabteilung to Herrn Staatssekretär, and January 26, 1981, Referat 43 über Herrn Abteilungsleiter 4 Herrn Chef des Bundeskanzleramtes memorandum.

85. BArch B 149/54471, September 18, 1980, Abteilung IIa 5 to Herrn Minister.

86. Emphasis in original. BArch B 149/121734, undated memo, "Wartezeit vor Erteilung der Arbeitserlaubnis an Familienangehörige türkischer Arbeitnehmer."

87. BArch B 149/121734, July 14, 1980, memorandum.

88. BArch B 149/121734, December 3, 1979, memorandum.

89. BArch B 149/54471, September 18, 1980, Abteilung IIa 5 to Herrn Minister.

90. For more on the perception of asylum as a cover for economic motives, see Lauren Stokes, "The Permanent Refugee Crisis in the Federal Republic of Germany, 1949–," *Central European History* 52, no. 1 (2019): 19–44.

91. Simone Klausmeier, *Asylbewerber zum "Scheinasylanten": Asylrecht und Asylpolitik in der Bundesrepublik Deutschland seit 1973* (Berlin: EXpress Edition, 1984), 119.

92. Tim Szatkowski, *Die Bundesrepublik Deutschland und die Türkei 1978 bis 1983* (Berlin: Walter de Gruyter, 2016), 32.
93. BArch B 149/67170, Bundesrat Plenarprotokoll 499, May 8, 1981, 121–122.
94. BArch B 149/54404, March 23, 1981, Liselotte Funcke to BMA.
95. Multiple drafts consulted in BArch B 149/54404 and 67170.
96. Deutscher Bundestag, Plenarprotokoll 9/37, May 14, 1981, 1949.
97. Franz Brandt, *Situationsanalyse Nichterwerbstätiger Ehefrauen Ausländischer Arbeitnehmer in der Bundesrepublik Deutschland* (Bonn: BMJFG, 1977), i.
98. Max Rheinstein and Mary Ann Glendon, "West German Marriage and Family Law Reform," *University of Chicago Law Review* 45, no. 3 (Spring 1978): 524.
99. Brandt, *Nichterwerbstätiger Ehefrauen*, 141–142; Summers, "Reconciling Family and Work," 32–33.
100. Brandt, *Nichterwerbstätiger Ehefrauen*, 33, 29.
101. Brandt, *Nichterwerbstätiger Ehefrauen*, 53–59.
102. Brandt, *Nichterwerbstätiger Ehefrauen*, 46.
103. Goodman, "The Decision Makers."
104. Brandt, *Nichterwerbstätiger Ehefrauen*, 111.
105. Kristina Schulz, *Der lange Atem der Provokation: Die Frauenbewegung in der Bundesrepublik und in Frankreich 1968–1976* (Frankfurt: Campus Verlag, 2002), 203; and Sarah E. Summers, "Finding Feminism: Rethinking Activism in the West German New Woman's Movement of the 1970s and 1980s," in *Gendering Post-1945 German History: Entanglements*, ed. Karen Hagemann, Donna Harsch, and Friederike Brühöfener (New York: Berghahn, 2019), 184–206.
106. Brandt, *Nichterwerbstätiger Ehefrauen*, 118.
107. Brandt, *Nichterwerbstätiger Ehefrauen*, 198.
108. Brandt, *Nichterwerbstätiger Ehefrauen*, 201, 209.
109. Brandt, *Nichterwerbstätiger Ehefrauen*, 199.
110. There are several cases of women who have work permits while their husbands are unable to get one, in Humanistischen Union Landesverband Berlin and Jugendverband der Türkei, *Dokumentation über die Aussperrung Jugendlicher Ausländer vom Berliner Arbeitsmarkt* (Berlin: self-published, 1976).
111. BArch B 149/54467, April 25, 1978, letter from Frau K to Herbert Ehrenberg.
112. BArch B 149/54469, June 30, 1980, letter from Frau A to Arbeitsministerium and July 9, 1980, reply.
113. BArch B 149/54469, July 9, 1980, BMA to Frau A and BArch B 149/54471, April 11, 1980, letter from BMA to Dr. M and Herr H.
114. Töksöz, *Immigrantinnen*, 82.
115. Töksöz, *Immigrantinnen*, 194.
116. BArch B 106/81041, February 11, 1980, BMJFG to BMA and BMBildung.
117. Qtd. in Angelika Schmidt-Koddenberg, *Ausländerinnen im Gespräch: Maßnahmen zur Verbesserung der Lebenssituation ausländischer Frauen* (Düsseldorf: Minister für Arbeit, Gesundheit und Soziales des Landes Nordrhein-Westfalen, 1984), 22.
118. Mehrländer, *Repräsentativuntersuchung '80*, 602.
119. Mehrländer, *Repräsentativuntersuchung '80*, 598.
120. Mehrländer, *Repräsentativuntersuchung '80*, 604–606.
121. The "Mediterranean woman" in these texts might be productively compared to the "third world woman," a monolithic subject criticized by Chandra Talpade Mohanty, "Under Western Eyes: Feminist Scholarship and Colonial Discourses," in *Feminism Without Borders: Decolonizing Theory, Practicing Solidarity* (Durham, NC: Duke University Press, 2003), 17–42.
122. For more on the problem of unemployment in the West German context, see Thomas Raithel and Thomas Schlemmer, eds., *Die Rückkehr der Arbeitslosigkeit. Die Bundesrepublik Deutschland im europäischen Kontext 1973 bis 1989* (Munich: Oldenbourg Verlag, 2009). The book does not include any mention of foreigner unemployment. Raithel discusses the unemployment of foreign youth without mentioning the *Stichtag*, in *Jugendarbeitslosigkeit in der Bundesrepublik*, 35–39.

123. Katherine Pratt Ewing, *Stolen Honor: Stigmatizing Muslim Men in Berlin* (Stanford, CA: Stanford University Press, 2008), 52–93.

Chapter 5

1. Hunn, *"Nächstes Jahr,"* 517; Ali Gitmez and Czarina Wilpert, "A Micro-Society or an Ethnic Community? Social Organization and Ethnicity Amongst Turkish Migrants in Berlin," in *Immigrant Associations in Europe*, ed. John Rex, Daniele Joly, and Czarina Wilpert (Aldershot: Gower, 1987).

2. Otto Jörg Weis, "Der 'Lummer-Blitz' hat die Ausländer voll getroffen," *Frankfurter Rundschau*, December 4, 1981, 3; and "20,000 gegen Berliner Ausländererlaß, 'Ohne uns kein Kebab,'" *Tageszeitung*, November 11, 1981.

3. One handbill for the demonstration lists Rita Kantemir of the Alternative List as the contact person, https://archive.org/details/LummerAuslndererlass (last accessed June 24, 2021). For the history of the party, see Keith Duane Alexander, "From Red to Green in the Island City: The *Alternative Liste West Berlin* and the Evolution of the West German Left, 1945–1990" (PhD diss., University of Maryland, 2003).

4. AGG C Berlin I.1, Alternative Liste 1978–1992, Signatur 14 (1/2), Delegiertenrat-Infos 1981, November 24, 1981, press release.

5. AGG C Berlin I.1, Alternative Liste 1978–1992, Signatur 14 (1/2), November 27, 1981, letter from Michel R. Lang, and November 28, 1981, letter from Erika Wilde,

6. Michael Rothberg and Yasemin Yildiz, "Memory Citizenship: Migrant Archives of Holocaust Remembrance in Contemporary Germany," *Parallax* 17, no. 4 (2011): 32–48. On racist jokes in the Federal Republic, see Lauren Stokes, "Türkenwitz. Jüdenwitz. Auschwitz," article draft in progress.

7. Frank Bösch, *Zeitenwende 1979: Als die Welt von Heute begann* (Munich: C. H. Beck, 2019).

8. Jacob S. Eder, *Holocaust Angst: The Federal Republic of Germany and American Holocaust Memory Since the 1970s* (New York: Oxford University Press, 2016).

9. Jonathan Olsen, *Nature and Nationalism: Right-Wing Ecology and the Politics of Identity in Contemporary Germany* (New York: St. Martin's Press, 1999), 104–105.

10. Olsen, *Nature and Nationalism*, 87–91.

11. Cem Özdemir, *Ich bin Inländer: Ein anatolischer Schwabe im Bundestag* (Munich: Deutscher Taschenbuch Verlag, 1997), 55.

12. There were similar anxieties about teenage migration in the Netherlands. The Dutch labor party raised the possibility of restricting migration to under-sixteen-year-olds in 1982, although the Dutch state did not ultimately choose to restrict teenage migrants until 2005. Van Walsum, *Dutch Family Migration Policies*, 153–157.

13. Both agreements published in *Official Journal of the European Communities* 16, No C 113 (December 24, 1973). Also see Berdal Aral, "The Case of Free Movement for Workers Between Turkey and the European Union," *Turkish Yearbook of International Relations* (1997): 1–11.

14. BArch B 136/17999, draft letter from January 29, 1974, Labor Minister to Dr. Patrick J. Hillery, VP of the Kommission der EG, and June 2, 1976, Referat 211 memorandum.

15. BArch B 136/31036, October 31, 1986, Gruppe 41 to Chef des BKA.

16. Günter Buchstab and Hans-Otto Kleinmann, eds., *Helmut Kohl: Berichte zur Lage 1982–1989. Der Kanzler und Parteivorsitzende im Bundesvorstand der CDU Deutschlands* (Düsseldorf: Droste, 2014), 162.

17. Bösch, *Zeitenwende 1979*, 54; and Vierra, *Turkish Germans*, 163–192.

18. BArch B 149/67473, October 21, 1980, Grenzschutzdirektion to BMI.

19. BArch B 149/47280, January 23, 1981, telegram from Botschaft Ankara to AA.

20. BArch B 149/67473, February 19, 1981, BMI to BMJ, AA, BMA.

21. BArch B 149/47280, January 15, 1981, Unterteilung IIb to IIa.

22. Press clippings in BArch B 149/67474, including April 7, 1981, *General-Anzeiger* clipping.

23. BArch B 149/67474, May 12, 1981, BMI to BMA and BMJ.

24. Landtag von Baden-Württemberg, Drucksache 8/3206, November 2, 1982, 9.

25. Evan Smith and Marinella Marmo, *Race, Gender and the Body in British Immigration Control. Subject to Examination* (London: Palgrave Macmillan, 2014), 117–127.

26. Landtag von Baden-Württemberg, Drucksache 8/3206, November 2, 1982, 9, and LA-B-W EA 2/303 Bü 209, June 20, 1982, Staatsministerium B-W to IM B-W. For more on the Society for Threatened Peoples, see Lora Wildenthal, "Imagining Threatened Peoples: The Society for Threatened Peoples (*Gesellschaft für bedrohte Völker*) in 1970s West Germany," in *Imagining Human Rights*, ed. Susanne Kaul and David Kim (Berlin: deGruyter, 2015): 101–117.

27. LA-B-W EA 2/303 Bü 209, June 7, 1983, BMI to Innenministerien.

28. A group of doctors founded the Study Group on Forensic Age Diagnostics in Berlin in 2000 after changes to both asylum and visa law in the 1990s increased the consequences that age could have for an individual migrant and thus the number of age verification requests. Lauren Stokes, "Adult Until Proven Innocent? 'Suspiciously Young Turks,' Age Verification, and Child Migration in West Germany," paper presented at the American Historical Association, January 2017.

29. BArch B 106/81039, November 8, 1978, Baum to Ehrenberg.

30. "Basic Law for the Federal Republic of Germany," trans. Christian Tomuschat, David P. Currie, and Donald P. Kommers, https://www.bundestag.de/blob/284870/ce0d03414 872b427e57fccb703634dcd/basic_law-data.pdf.

31. Till van Rahden, *Demokratie: Eine gefährdete Lebensform* (Frankfurt: Campus Verlag, 2019), 126; and Christiane Kuller, "Soziale Sicherung von Frauen," 229. For illegitimacy law specifically, see Buske, *Unehelichkeit in Deutschland*.

32. Helmut Rittstieg, "Zur Rechtslage junger Ausländer," *Zeitschrift für Rechtspolitik* 12, no. 1 (January 1979): 16.

33. Rittstieg, "Zur Rechtslage junger Ausländer," 17.

34. Gerhart Rudolf Baum, "Aktuelle Probleme der Ausländerpolitik," *Zeitschrift für Ausländerrecht und Ausländerpolitik* 1, no. 1 (1981): 8.

35. Baum, "Aktuelle Probleme," 8.

36. Baum, "Aktuelle Probleme," 9.

37. Baum, "Aktuelle Probleme," 8.

38. BArch B 106/117675, November 20, 1981, Referat VI2 memorandum.

39. BArch B 106/117679, November 26, 1981, Referat VII2 memorandum.

40. BArch B 106/117674, November 19, 1981, Referat VII2 to Herrn Minister.

41. BArch B 106/117674, November 3, 1981, Referat VII2 to Herrn Minister.

42. LA B, B Rep 002, Nr. 41201, November 12, 1981 circular.

43. Puzzo, "British and French Immigration Policy," 82.

44. PAAA B 85/1612, August 19, 1982, memorandum.

45. Emphasis in original. LA B, B Rep 002, Nr. 17825, November 20, 1981, press release.

46. BArch B 149/59886, September 17, 1980, memorandum.

47. Institut für Stadtgeschichte Gelsenkirchen [ISG Gelsenkirchen], 1343, March 19, 1981, Ausländerbeirat minutes and July 16, 1981, Ausländerbeirat minutes. Also see "Gelsenkirchen: 80 Türken mit 18 zurück nach hause. Ausländeramt beruft sich auf schriftliche 'Erklärungen.' " *Westdeutsche Allgemeine Zeitung* July 9, 1981; and "80 Türk gencini Alman vali kurtardi," *Hürriyet* August 3, 1981.

48. Ausländerkomitee Berlin (West), *"Wir sind keine befristeten Menschen" Der Berliner Ausländererlaß von 1981–1982 und seine Auswirkungen* (Berlin (West): self-published, 1983), 18–19. Also see DOMiD FL 0166, FL0332 and FL0465.

49. Ausländerkomitee Berlin (West), *"keine befristeten Menschen,"* 22–23.

50. Ausländerkomitee Berlin (West), *"keine befristeten Menschen,"* 32.

51. Ausländerkomitee Berlin (West), *"keine befristeten Menschen,"* 24.

52. Uçar, *Illegale Beschäftigung*, 50.

53. LA B, B Rep 002, Nr. 17825, November 24, 1981, memorandum.

54. Ausländerkomitee Berlin (West), *"keine befristeten Menschen,"* 3–4.

55. BArch B 149/59886, October 2, 1981, Landespolizeipräsidium to the Regierungspräsidien in B-W.

56. ISG Gelsenkirchen 1314 January 21, 1982, Ausländerbeirat minutes. The Turkish representative and Italian representative both worry that the policy will prevent children from finishing

their schooling in their home country, and the Italian representative worries that children who have been apart from their families while finishing their schooling may have "psychic disturbances" as a result. The Yugoslavian representative compares the policy to the child allowance reform.

57. BArch B 106/117674, December 2, 1981, telegram from Ankara Embassy to AA; and BArch B 106/117679, January 13, 1982, Belgrade Embassy to AA.

58. BArch B 149/59888, November 26, 1981, Abteilung IIa6 RD Dr. Fendrich to the Herrn Staatssekretär.

59. BArch B 149/59889, November 30, 1981, draft speech.

60. Adam McKeown, *Melancholy Order: Asian Migration and the Globalization of Borders* (New York: Columbia University Press, 2008).

61. Elspeth Guild, Kees Groenendijk, and Sergio Carrera, "Understanding the Contest of Community: Illiberal Practices in the EU?," in *Illiberal Liberal States. Immigration, Citizenship and Integration in the EU* (Farnham, UK: Ashgate, 2009).

62. Jakob, *Familienbilder*, 247-334.

63. Van Rahden, *Demokratie*, 103-127.

64. Peter O'Brien, "The Paradoxical Paradigm: Turkish Migrants and German Policies" (PhD diss., University of Wisconsin-Madison, 1988), 132-133. Hartmut Griese offers a scathing critique of "second generation" research shaped by economic imperatives in *Der gläserne Fremde. Bilanz und Kritik der Gastarbeiterforschung und der Ausländerpädagogik* (Opladen: Leske und Budrich, 1984).

65. Achim Schrader, Bruno W. Nikles, and Hartmut M. Griese, *Die Zweite Generation. Sozialisation und Akkulturation ausländischer Kinder in der Bundesrepublik* (Kronberg: Athenäum Verlag, 1976), 187.

66. Schrader, Nikles, and Griese, *Zweite Generation*, 192.

67. Schrader, Nikles, and Griese, *Zweite Generation*, 194.

68. Philosopher Linda Alcoff writes that when racialized subjects find themselves judged by their "visual identity," it is "as if one finds oneself in the world ahead of oneself, the space one occupies as already occupied. One's lived self is effectively dislodged when an already outlined but very different self appears to be operating in the same exact location." Alcoff, *Visible Identities*, 193.

69. Schrader, Nikles, and Griese, *Zweite Generation*, 206.

70. Bernhard Nauck, *Arbeitsmigration und Familienstruktur. Eine Analyse der mikrosozialen Folgen von Migrationsprozessen* (Frankfurt: Campus Verlag, 1985), 181; and Georg Auernheimer, *Der sogenannte Kulturkonflikt. Orientierungsprobleme ausländischer Jugendlicher* (Frankfurt: Campus Verlag, 1988), 40.

71. Griese, *Der gläserne Fremde*, 212.

72. Chelmis, *Betreuung ausländischer Kleinkinder*, 12.

73. Petra Zemlin, *Erziehung in türkischen Familien* (Munich: DJI Verlag, 1981), 60.

74. Anneliese Ude-Pestel, *Ahmet. Geschichte einer Kindertherapie* (Munich: Deutscher Taschenbuch Verlag, 1983).

75. Van Rahden, *Demokratie*, 120-124.

76. For the Iranian Revolution, also see Vierra, *Turkish Germans*, chapter 5.

77. Christoph Elsas, *Einflüsse der islamischen Religion auf die Integrationsfähigkeit der Ausländischen Arbeitnehmer und ihrer Familienangehörigen* (Berlin: Senatskanzlei Planungsleitstelle, 1980), 85.

78. Elsas, *Einflüsse der islamischen Religion*, 87. More recent ethnographic research has suggested that by the 2000s, Turkish women seemed to be responsible for the transmission of gender roles, and Turkish men more responsible for the transmission of national identity. Esin Bozkurt, *Conceptualising "Home": The Question of Belonging Among Turkish Families in Germany* (Frankfurt: Campus Verlag, 2009).

79. Zemlin, *Erziehung in türkischen Familien*, 9.

80. Zemlin, *Erziehung in türkischen Familien*, 34.

81. Zemlin, *Erziehung in türkischen Familien*, 34-35.

82. Zemlin, *Erziehung in türkischen Familien*, 35.

83. Hanns Thomä-Venske, *Islam und Integration. Zur Bedeutung des Islam im Prozeß der Integration türkischer Arbeiterfamilien in die Gesellschaft der Bundesrepublik* (Hamburg: E. B. Verlag Rissen, 1981), 133.

84. Thomä-Venske, *Islam und Integration*, 138.

85. For more on this dynamic in French history, see Naomi Davidson, *Only Muslim: Embodying Islam in Twentieth-Century France* (Ithaca, NY: Cornell University Press, 2012).

86. Hans D. Walz and Arbeitsgruppe Modellprogram für ausländische Kinder und Jugendliche, *Zur Situation von jugendlichen Gastarbeitern in Familie, Freizeit, Schule und Beruf* (Munich: Deutsches Jugendinstitut, 1980), 16.

87. Walz and Arbeitsgruppe, *Zur Situation von jugendlichen Gastarbeitern*, 121–122. The pedagogues concerned with "artists of adaptation" echo the nationalists of the late nineteenth and early twentieth centuries, who criticized "national hermaphrodites" who treated their national identity as a resource rather than an ascribed fact. See Tara Zahra, "Imagined Noncommunities: National Indifference as a Category of Analysis," *Slavic Review* 69, no. 1 (2010). On the "recent history" of monolingualism, Yasemin Yildiz, *Beyond the Mother Tongue. The Postmonolingual Condition* (New York: Fordham University Press, 2012).

88. Schönwälder, *Einwanderung und Pluralität*, 563–564. The fear of the "Germanization" accusation influenced the rejection of Heinz Kühn's 1979 proposal for liberalized citizenship access for the second generation. The reform would wait another twenty years. BArch B 149/83928, May 10, 1979, Referent 43 memorandum. Also LA-B, DST, 4/44-49, Nr. 7121, November 27, 1979, DST memorandum.

89. Tara Zahra, *The Lost Children: Reconstructing Europe's Families After World War II* (Cambridge, MA: Harvard University Press, 2011), 126.

90. Ude-Pestel, *Ahmet*, 98.

91. Ude-Pestel, *Ahmet*, 212.

92. Barbara von Breitenbach, *Italiener und Spanier als Arbeitnehmer in der Bundesrepublik Deutschland. Eine vergleichende Untersuchung zur europäischen Arbeitsmigration* (Munich: Kaiser, 1982), 28–29. Von Breitenbach also compares Italian migrants in the FRG to Italian migrants in Switzerland. Italians living in Switzerland did not enjoy freedom of movement, and they were also much more likely to stay put at their jobs and in Switzerland. In other words, their behavior was much more comparable to non-European behavior in the FRG. It was not culturally, but legally determined.

93. von Breitenbach, *Italiener und Spanier*, 87.

94. Lehman, *Teaching Migrant Children*, 176.

95. Compare to the utility of border-crossing in Zahra, "National Indifference," 114.

96. O'Brien, "Paradoxical Paradigm," 169–170.

97. Andrés López-Blasco, "Tendenzen der Integrationspolitik in der Bundesrepublik Deutschland," in *Ausländerpolitik und Integrationsforschung in der Bundesrepublik Deutschland: eine Darstellung wichtigster Ergebnisse mit Auswahlbiographie* (Munich: DJI Verlag, 1982).

98. S. Jonathan Wiesen, "Miracles for Sale," in *Consuming Germany in the Cold War*, ed. David F. Crew (Oxford: Berg, 2003), 164.

99. LA-B, DST, 4/44-49/7, Nr. 7127, May 3, 1977, minutes.

100. Aktion Gemeinsinn, *Ausländische Kinder: Fremde oder Freunde? Es liegt an uns: gehen wir auf sie zu* (Bonn: Aktion Gemeinsinn), 5.

101. The editorializing about the father's reasons is also demonstrably wrong because Italians did not have their *Kindergeld* cut in the 1974 reform. Aktion Gemeinsinn, *Ausländische Kinder*, 12.

102. Aktion Gemeinsinn, *Ausländische Kinder*, 8–9.

103. Institut für Demoskopie Allensbach, "Ausländische Kinder—Unsere Freunde. Eine Kampagne der Aktion Gemeinsinn," May 1980. Author's correspondence with Aktion Gemeinsinn.

104. BArch B 106/117675, November 20, 1981, Referat VI2 memorandum.

105. BArch B 106/117550, June 25, 1982, BMI V II 2 proposal and September 1, 1982, Referat V II 2 memorandum.

106. BArch B 106/117550, June 21, 1982, Herrn Minister memorandum.

107. BArch B 149/83847, August 14, 1982, memorandum about discussion between Horst Ehmke, Klaus von Dohnanyi, and Chancellor Schmidt.

108. Zimmermann was well aware that he was repeating arguments previously elaborated by the SPD, frequently pointing this out in debates to defend himself from criticism. Deutscher Bundestag, Plenarprotokoll 10/89, October 5, 1984, 6579.

109. "Regierungserklärung des Bundeskanzlers vor dem Deutschen Bundestag, 14. Oktober 1982," http://www.1000dokumente.de/index.html?c=dokument_de&dokument=0144_koh&object=facsimile&l=de.

110. Proceedings of this commission are in BArch B 149/83806, 83807, 83808, 83809, 83810, 83811, 121742, 121743.

111. BArch B 149/121743, January 31, 1983, report of the "Familienzusammenführung" commission.

112. Kahn, "Foreign at Home," chapter 3.

113. BArch B 106/117675, March 18, 1983, BMI to Liselotte Funcke.

114. BArch B 106/93422, July 5, 1983, interview between Dieter Jepsen-Föge and Dr. Friedrich Zimmermann.

115. ADW, PB 948: June 30, 1983, speech by BMI Parlamentarischen Staatssekretärs Carl-Dieter Spranger.

116. BArch B 149/84848, January 7, 1983, press release from BMJFG about interview with Dr. Heiner Geißler.

117. "Aus der Asche," Der Spiegel, October 8, 1984, 49.

118. BArch B 106/139221, Fritz Ossenbühl, May 1983 legal opinion, Helmut Quaritsch, May 11, 1983, legal opinion, and Josef Isensee, September 20, 1983, legal opinion.

119. Quaritsch explicitly drew on the work of Nazi jurist Carl Schmitt in order to ground his position. In 1985 he wrote a book criticizing German courts for interpreting the right to asylum overly generously. Bernd Grzeszick, "Helmut Quaritsch (1930–2011)," in Staatsrechtslehrer des 20. Jahrhunderts: Deutschland-Österreich-Schweiz, ed. Peter Häberle (Berlin: De Gruyter, 2018), 982–991.

120. BArch B 106/139221, Helmut Quaritsch, May 11, 1983, legal opinion.

121. Helmut Quaritsch, "Kindernachzug und Art. 6 GG," Neue Juristische Wochenschrift 37, no. 48 (1984): 2733–2734.

122. Quaritsch, "Kindernachzug," 2734.

123. Quaritsch, "Kindernachzug," 2736.

124. Fritz Franz, "Der Nachzug ausländischer Familienangehöriger im Lichte der Verfassung," Neue Juritische Wochenschrift 37, no. 10 (1984): 531.

125. Bertold Huber, "Familiennachzug und Grundgesetz," Informationsbrief Ausländerrecht (1982): 1–5, 5.

126. BArch B 149/83848, November 30, 1982, expert opinion of Kommissariat der Deutschen Bischöfe, and Woesthoff, "Ambiguities of Anti-Racism," 174–175.

127. DOMiD, Interview with Herbert Leuninger on April 29, 2004.

128. BArch B 149/83848, undated Forschungsgruppe ALFA report.

129. DGB Archive, 5/DGAZ 1009, March 21, 1983, Abt. AA memorandum.

130. Lehman, Teaching Migrant Children, 52.

131. Lehman, Teaching Migrant Children, 180.

132. BArch B 149/83809, December 14, 1982, letter from Project "Außerschulische Arbeit mit ausländischen Kindern und Jugendlichen" an der Fachhochschule Münster to Bundeskanzler Helmut Kohl.

133. Sonja G. Ostrow, "Intersecting Aims, Divergent Paths: The Allensbach Institute, the Institute for Social Research, and the Making of Public Opinion Research in 1950s West Germany," Journal of the History of the Behavioral Sciences (2020): 1–19. Nermin Abadan, perhaps the most important Turkish social scientist to work with Turks in the FRG, had also learned to use surveys as a pedagogical tool in her earlier training in Turkey. Begüm Adalet, Hotels and Highways: The Construction of Modernization Theory in Cold War Turkey (Stanford, CA: Stanford University Press, 2018), 75.

134. DGB Archive, 5/DGAZ 444, August 12, 1983, Allensbacher Berichte 1983 Nr. 16 "Nachzugsalter von Ausländerkindern auf 6 Jahre beschränken?"

135. HHW Abt. 502, Nr. 7411, September 7, 1984, Eduard Stöcker to Holger Börner, *Der Spiegel* September 10, 1984, "Präsident Mustafa."
136. HHW Abt. 502, Nr. 7409, March 17, 1982, *Frankfurter Rundschau* clipping "Im Wortlaut: 'Grenzen rigoros gegen Zustrom von weiteren Ausländern schließen."
137. HHW Abt. 2016/1, Nr. 758, October 25, 1984, *Wiesbadener Tageblatt* clipping "Jentsch: Erlaß gesetzeswidrig. Wiesbaden will sich nicht an neues Ausländerrecht halten."
138. HHW Abt. 502, Nr. 7413, January 25, 1985, *Pressemitteilung des Hessischen Innenministers.*
139. DGB Archive, 5/DGAZ 1033, July 13, 1984, Hessische Minister des Innern to Regierungspräsidenten, and August 9, 1984, BMI to Hessisches Minister des Innern and IM der Länder.
140. DGB Archive, 5/DGAZ 1033, September 4, 1987, Hessische Minister des Innern Kabinettvorlage.
141. PAAA B 85/1610, December 22, 1981, untitled memo.
142. PAAA B 85/1612, August 6, 1982, telegram Ankara Embassy to AA.
143. PAAA BRU-EEU/15020, May 4, 1980, memorandum.
144. PAAA B 201/131106, June 18, 1984, memorandum, PAAA B 201/131107, August 27, 1984, memorandum, and PAAA B 201/131105 memorandum.
145. "Aus der Asche," *Der Spiegel*, October 8, 1984.
146. BArch B 149/83937, March 1984 memorandum.
147. ADL, Liselotte Funcke ÜP 58/2012–100.
148. BArch B 106/139111, February 25, 1988, telegram from ImVbu to BMI.
149. BArch B 149/83942, June 6, 1986, Abteilung II to Herrn Staatssekretär, and June 24, 1986, BMI to BKA.
150. BArch B 189/26095, May 5, 1987, May 13, 1987, and July 10, 1987, memoranda.
151. BArch B 189/26095, July 23, 1987, BMI to BMJFG, and August 11, 1987, BMA to BMJFFG.
152. Funcke describes herself as playing an "alibi-function" in ADL, Liselotte Funcke ÜP 58/2012–100, December 13, 1983, Funcke to Genscher.
153. Hüseyin Yiğit, *Was soll aus uns werden? [Sonumuz ne olacak?],* trans. Herbert Soffel and Hikmet Atilla (Frankfurt: Dağyeli Verlag, 1986), 20.
154. Green, *The Politics of Exclusion,* 120–125.
155. Simon Green, "Divergent Traditions, Converging Responses: Immigration and Integration Policy in the UK and Germany," *German Politics* 16, no. 1 (2007): 106.
156. "Denmark's response to the Commission Green Paper on the Right to Family Reunification of Third-Country Nationals Living in the European Union," March 14, 2012, http://ec.eur opa.eu/dgs/home-affairs/what-is-new/public-consultation/2012/pdf/0023/famreun/memberstatesnationalgovernments/denmark_en.pdf.

Chapter 6

1. This fear would not have been unfounded, as there had been cases of families finding their residence permits shortened by the state after the birth of a child. Budzinski and Schirmer, "Ausländerbehörden," 17.
2. LA-NRW, NW 670, Nr. 95, January 27, 1982, memorandum.
3. Pro Familia studied this topic in 1981. In their sample of seventy-eight Turkish women, sixty of them were using a form of contraception. Claudia Roesch, "Love Without Fear: Knowledge Networks and Family Planning Initiatives for Immigrant Families in West Germany and the United States," *GHI Bulletin* 64 (Spring 2019): 93–113, 109–110.
4. Before it was found in the phone booth, an even more extreme version of the manifesto had circulated in right-wing periodicals as well as in the book *Ausländerstopp: Handbuch gegen Überfremdung.* Andreas Wagner, "Das 'Heidelberger Manifest' von 1981. Deutsche Professoren warnen vor 'Überfremdung des deutschen Volkes,'" in *Manifeste. Geschichte und Gegenwart des politischen Appells,* ed. Johanna Klatt and Robert Lorenz (Bielefeld: transcript Verlag, 2010), 285–313. See the more extreme version in Günter Deckert, *Ausländerstopp: Handbuch gegen Überfremdung* (Kiel: Arndt, 1981), 32–34. Arndt Verlag is a publisher that specializes in revisionist history and Holocaust denial.
5. "Heidelberg Manifesto," trans. Tes Howell, in *Germany in Transit,* 111–113.

6. BArch B 106/117681, July 8, 1983, Abteilungsleiter V to Herrn Minister memorandum.

7. Chin, *Guest Worker Question*, chapter 3, and Chin, *Crisis of Multiculturalism in Europe*. Also see Lutz and Huth-Hildebrandt, "Geschlecht im Migrationsdiskurs. Neue Gedanken über ein altes Thema"; Rostock and Berghahn, "The Ambivalent Role of Gender"; and Rottmann and Marx Ferree, "Citizenship and Intersectionality."

8. Sarah van Walsum makes a similar argument in the Dutch context. *Dutch Family Migration Policies*, 187.

9. BArch B 149/59887, November 13, 1981, BMA proposal for "Sozialverantwortliche Begrenzung des Familiennachzugs von Ausländern aus Nicht-EG-Staaten."

10. BArch B 149/59887, November 19, 1981, Abteilung IIa6 to Herrn Minister.

11. This observation is made, among other places, in AGG B.II.1, Die Grünen im Bundestag 1983–1990, Signatur 4276, Ausländerinnen in der BRD, 1984–1989, September 24, 1984, press release Nr. 489/84, in ADL Baum N60-45, November 22, 1983, Ausländerbeirat Nürnberg to Gerhart Baum, and in Bayerischer Arbeitskreis gegen Familientrennung, ed., *Dokumentation zur Familientrennung* (Nürnberg: self-published, 1986).

12. BArch B 149/83806, undated "Diskussionsunterlage zum Familiennachzug."

13. LA B, B Rep 002, Nr. 17356, February 24, 1983 report of the "Kommission 'Ausländerpolitik.' "

14. Rose Cuison Villazor, "The 1965 Immigration Act: Family Unification and Nondiscrimination Fifty Years Later," in *The Immigration and Nationality Act of 1965: Legislating a New America*, ed. Gabriel J. Chin and Rose Cuison Villazor (Cambridge: Cambridge University Press, 2015): 197–231.

15. In late December 1982, the Foreign Ministry requested reports from every European embassy and the embassy in Washington, DC, about how the other states regulated family migration. The author of the report about the United States praised the quota system but warned that the United States continued to have a problem with ethnically undesirable illegal immigration. BArch B 149/83808, December 6, 1982, Botschaft Washington to AA.

16. BArch B 149/83806, November 24, 1982, report and BArch B 149/83807, December 17, 1982, report.

17. Doris Urbanek, "Forced Marriage vs. Family Reunification: Nationality, Gender and Ethnicity in German Migration Policy," *Journal of Intercultural Studies* 33, no. 3 (2012). For the gendered effects of these policies, see Can M. Aybek, "Time Matters: Temporal Aspects of Transnational Intimate Relationships and Marriage Migration Processes from Turkey to Germany," *Journal of Family Issues* 36, no. 11 (2015).

18. LA B, B Rep 002, Nr. 17356, February 24, 1983, report of the "Kommission 'Ausländerpolitik.' "

19. BArch B 149/83807, December 6, 1982, IM B-W draft proposal.

20. BArch B 149/83806, July 14, 1982, memorandum.

21. BArch B 149/83807, December 6, 1982, IM B-W draft proposal.

22. BArch B 149/83809, December 20, 1982, BMI to other ministries, and December 12, 1982, report.

23. BArch B 106/117678, November 20, 1981, Referat VIII to Abteilungsleiter V.

24. Smith and Marmo, *Subject to Examination*, 170. For a contemporaneous discussion: The Women, Immigration, and Nationality Group, *Worlds Apart. Women Under Immigration and Nationality Law* (London: Pluto Press, 1985).

25. IG Metall-Archiv, ZWA00971 April 7, 1983, *Frankfurter Rundschau* clipping, "Schutz der Ehe hat Grenzen. Gerichtshof bestätigt Abschiebung einer türkischen Frau."

26. LA-NRW, NW 583, Nr. 1752, September 14, 1983, DPA clipping, Jutta Hartlieb, "Schicksal einer jungen Türkin und ihres Babies erregt Gemüter."

27. StadtAN E 52, Nr. 298 Ausländerbeirat, "Info-Blatt des Ausländerbeirates," November 1985, and Bayerischer Arbeitskreis gegen Familientrennung, *Dokumentation zur Familientrennung*.

28. Bayerischer Arbeitskreis gegen Familientrennung, *Dokumentation zur Familientrennung*, 45–51.

29. Reports on this specific case in Terre des Femmes Archive, *Rundbrief* September 1983 and *Rundbrief* January 1984; for similar cases, see *Rundbrief* May 1983, September 1983, and December 1984. For more on Terre des Femmes, see Lora Wildenthal, *The Language of Human Rights in West Germany* (Philadelphia: University of Pennsylvania Press, 2013).

30. LA-NRW, NW 583, Nr. 1753, August 24, 1982, *Westfalenpost* clipping, "Der Ehefrau eines amputierten Türken droht die Ausweisung. Verwaltungsgericht Arnsberg vor einer schwierigen Entscheidung."

31. Bayerischer Arbeitskreis gegen Familientrennung, *Dokumentation zur Familientrennung*, 13, 19.

32. I do not know the final outcome of this case. AGG, C NRW I—LaVo/LGSt Signatur 417 Landesarbeitsgemeinschaft Ausländer Bd. 2, 1983–1985, October 25, 1984, letter from Landesarbeitsgemeinschaft Immigranten und Asyl Die Grünen NRW to IM NRW.

33. LAB, B Rep 002, Nr. 15643, July 5, 1985, Ausländerbeauftragte report.

34. LAB, B Rep 002, Nr. 15643, August 1985 SenInn to BMI. Lummer was also hostile to issuing individual stays of deportation for asylum seekers. Julia Kleinschmidt, "Streit um das 'kleine Asyl': 'De-Facto-Flüchtlinge' und Proteste gegen Abschiebungen als gesellschaftspolitische Herausforderung für Bund und Länder während der 1980er Jahre," in *Den Protest regieren: staatlcihes Handeln, neue sozialen Bewegungen und linke Organisationen in den 1970er und 1980er Jahren*, ed. Alexandra Jaeger, Julia Kleinschmidt, and David Templin (Essen: Klartext Verlag, 2018): 231–258, 242–243.

35. LAB, B Rep 002, Nr. 15644, August 6, 1985, III C 12—0345/341 report.

36. LAB, B Rep 002, Nr. 15644, September 9, 1985, III C S109/01 report.

37. PAAA 190526, July 15, 1986, IM NRW to BM Hans-Dietrich Genscher and BM Friedrich Zimmermann; Barbara John, "Zur rechtlichen Situation ausländischer Frauen und Mädchen," in *Hearing zur Situation ausländischer Frauen und Mädchen aus den Anwerbestaaten. Kurzfassung der Dokumentation* (Bonn: Der Bundesminister für Jugend, Familie, Frauen und Gesundheit: 1988), 45.

38. John, "Zur rechtlichen Situation," 45. Also see Papiertiger Archiv, Binder MigrantInnen/Flüchtlinge Kämpfe, Soliaktionen Inis . . . ab Mai 90–Nov 90 IV, undated flyer "Gegen Nationalismus und Frauenfeindlichkeit Vorsicht Katholikentag!"

39. LAB, B Rep 002, Nr. 15643, May 22, 1985, Consulate Istanbul to AA.

40. BArch B 106/139225, June 7, 1985, BMI to IM NRW and IM der Länder.

41. BArch B 106/139225, October 1985 correspondence between BMI and IM der Länder.

42. BArch B 106/139225, March 27, 1987, Referat V II 2 to Herrn Minister.

43. BArch B 106/139225, December 23, 1985, Staatssekretär im BMI to Staatssekretär des AA, and 28 April 1987, BMI to IM NRW and IM der Länder.

44. John, "Zur rechtlichen Situation," 44.

45. LAB, B Rep 002, Nr. 15643, May 30, 1985, BMI to Herr Bundesverfassungsrichter Prof. Dr. Steinberger als Berichterstatter des Zweiten Senats des Bundesverfassungsgerichts.

46. BVerfGE 76, 1, in *Decisions of the Bundesverfassungsgericht, Volume 5*, trans. Federal Constitutional Court (Baden-Baden: Nomos Verlagsgesellschaft, 2013), 245.

47. BVerfGE 76, 1, in *Decisions of the Bundesverfassungsgericht*, trans. Federal Constitutional Court (Baden-Baden: Nomos Verlagsgesellschaft, 2013), 277.

48. Christian Joppke, "Why Liberal States Accept Unwanted Immigration," *World Politics* 50, no. 2 (1998): 285.

49. Most foreign women were leaving foreign men, and most German women were leaving German men, but 12 percent of German women were abused by foreign men and 30 percent of foreign women were abused by German men. Carol Hagemann-White, *Hilfen für mißhandelte Frauen. Abschlußbericht der wissenschaftlichen Begleitung des Modellprojekts Frauenhaus Berlin* (Stuttgart: Verlag W. Kohlhammer, 1981), 36–37.

50. Traude Ratsch, "Interview mit Ulrike Palmert und Sadiye Kaygun-Dohmeyer, Mitarbeiterinnen des 2. Berliner Frauenhauses," in *Sind wir uns denn so fremd? Ausländische und deutsche Frauen im Gespräch*, ed. Arbeitsgruppe Frauenkongress (Berlin: sub rosa Frauenverlag, 1985).

51. Hagemann-White, *Frauenhaus Berlin*, 170–174.

52. "Frau A" describes a similar dynamic in *Frauen aus der Türkei kommen in die Bundesrepublik. Zum Problem der Hausfrauisierung*, ed. Veronika Bennholdt-Thomsen et al. (Bremen: Ed. Con, 1987), 165–179.

53. Case in LAB, B Rep 002, Nr. 14982. All identifying details, including the woman's name, have been changed.

54. LAB, B Rep 002, Nr. 14982, December 20, 1982, letter from "Yaprak."
55. LAB, B Rep 002, Nr. 14982, May 11, 1983, Rita Kantemir to Weizsäcker.
56. LAB, B Rep 002, Nr. 1498, June 8, 1983, Senator für Inneres to Vorsitzender des Petitionausschusses des Abgeordnetenhauses von Berlin.
57. Drucksache 9/1470 from Abgeordnetenhaus von Berlin, Nr. 500, November 17, 1983.
58. LAB, B Rep 002, Nr. 14982, December 23, 1983, Rita Kantemir to Weizsäcker.
59. Drucksache 10/1919, Niedersächsische Landtag, November 29, 1983, and Drucksache 10/2127, Niedersächsische Landtag, January 17, 1984.
60. LAB, B Rep 002, Nr. 14982, January 19, 1984, press release from Niedersächsische Minister des Innern.
61. Drucksache 9/1470 from Abgeordnetenhaus von Berlin, Nr. 500, November 17, 1983.
62. Sara R. Farris, *In the Name of Women's Rights: The Rise of Femonationalism* (Durham, NC: Duke University Press, 2017); El-Tayeb, *European Others*; El-Tayeb, "Queer Muslims"; Haritaworn, "Queer Injuries"; and Partridge, *Hypersexuality and Headscarves*.
63. Nausi Schirilla, "Diskussion in der Arbeitsgruppe," in *Sind wir uns denn so fremd?*, 111, 114.
64. Traude Ratsch, "Wir fordern ein eigenständiges Aufenthaltsrecht für ausländische Frauen," in *Sind wir uns denn so fremd?*, 46.
65. Qtd. in Chin, *Guest Worker Question*, 167.
66. Franger, *Türkische Frauen*, 42.
67. Töksöz, *Immigrantinnen*, 238.
68. Gaby Straßburger, *Offene Grenzen für Remigranten: Wiederkehrwünsche türkischer Remigrantinnen und das deutsche Ausländerrecht* (Berlin: Verlag für Wissenschaft und Bildung, 1992), 78.
69. Atilla Yakut, *Zwischen Elternhaus und Arbeitsamt: türkische Jugendliche suchen einen Beruf* (Berlin: EXpress Verlag, 1986), 448–449.
70. Jannis Panagiotidis, *The Unchosen Ones: Diaspora, Nation, and Migration in Israel and Germany* (Bloomington: Indiana University Press, 2019), 93.
71. Eli Nathans, *The Politics of Citizenship in Germany: Ethnicity, Utility, and Nationalism* (Oxford: Berg, 2004), 181–184, and Miriam Rürup, "Das Geschlecht der Staatenlosen. Staatenlosigkeit in der Bundesrepublik Deutschland nach 1945," *Journal of Modern European History* 14, no. 3 (2016): 411–430, 414.
72. Rürup, "Das Geschlecht der Staatenlosen," 418–420. Although the FRG incorporated the Convention into domestic law in 1957, it did not enter the UN as a full member until 1973 and thus did not ratify the UN Convention until 1974.
73. LA-NRW, NW 760, Nr. 171, November 28, 1957, BMI to Innenminister der Länder. The change did lead to a more gender-neutral practice in the *Aussiedler* bureaucracy, as after 1959 officials examining ethnic German petitions were instructed to discover which partner—regardless of gender—had decisively influenced the culture of the family. Panagiotidis, *Unchosen Ones*, 94.
74. LA-NRW, NW 760, Nr. 171, September 6, 1965, IM S-H to BMI and Innenminister der Länder.
75. LA-NRW, NW 760, Nr. 171, September 23, 1965, IM Bayern to BMI and Innenminister der Länder.
76. LA-NRW, NW 760, Nr. 171, October 8, 1965, RP IM to BMI and Innenministerien der Länder, October 8, 1965, Senator für Inneres Berlin to BMI and Innenministerien der Länder.
77. Case printed in *Deutsche Verwaltungsblatt*, May 1, 1971, 364–365.
78. LA-NRW, NW 760, Nr. 171, October 7, 1970, Bayer. Staatsministerium des Innern to Regierung von Oberbayern.
79. Bavaria also leaned heavily on this argument in its appeal of the case with the Iraqi husband. LA-NRW, NW 760, Nr. 171, April 25, 1971, Bayer. Staatsministerium des Innern to Staatsanwaltschaft beim Verwaltungsgericht Münschen.
80. BArch B 106/69852, Band 1, Januar 7, 1970, "Frau J." to Petitionsausschuß des Landestages Schleswig-Holstein.
81. BArch B 106/69852, Band 2, February 25, 1971, Niedersächsische Minister des Innern to BMI.
82. BArch B 106/69852, Band 2, April 2, 1970, Hessische Minister des Innern memorandum.

83. BArch B 106/36021, March 1, 1972, "Frau G" to Bundeskanzleramt.
84. BArch B 106/36021, Band 1, March 12, 1972, "Frau K" to BMI.
85. BArch B 106/81050, Band 5, December 30, 1971, Innenminister Schleswig-Holstein to BMI.
86. LA-NRW, NW 760, Nr. 171, April 28, 1971, BMI memorandum.
87. BArch B 106/36022, August 29, 1972, "Frau W" to BMI.
88. BArch B 106/81050, June 18, 1971, Senator für Inneres Berlin to BMI.
89. BArch B 106/81050, 17 Dezember 1971, Bayer. Staatsministerium des Innern to BMI.
90. BArch B 106/36021, 16.5.1973, Frau "D" to Abg. Liselotte Funke.
91. BArch B 106/81050, September 11, 1973, Frau "B" letter to SPD Landessekretariat Prof. Emke.
92. BArch B 106/90136, Allgemeine Verwaltungsvorschrift zur Änderung der allgemeinen Verwaltungsvorschrift zur Durchführung des Ausländergesetzes, Drucksache 210/72, May 10, 1972, and BArch B 106/69852, Band 2, December 15, 1970, BMI to Innenminister der Länder.
93. Julia Woesthoff provides an excellent account of some of the internal conflicts within the IAF in "'Foreigners and Women Have the Same Problems': Binational Marriages, Grassroots Organizing, and the Quest for Legal Equality in Post-1968 Germany," *Journal of Family History* 38, no. 4 (2013): 422–442. Her article includes an account of how the IAF came to include foreign men as well as foreign women.
94. Clarkson, *Fragmented Fatherland*; and Molnar, *Yugoslav Migrations to Postwar Germany.*
95. BArch B 106/36022, IAF September 27, 1972, "Grundsatzerklärung."
96. BArch B 106/81051, Band 7, September 2, 1973, BMI report.
97. BArch B 106/36022, January 14, 1976, "Frau K." to Bundestages Petitionsausschuß, and the case in LA-NRW, NW 538, Nr. 12.
98. BArch B 106/36022, August 29, 1972, "Frau W." to BMI.
99. BArch B 106/36022, Band 2, "Frau K." to BMI, January 28, 1975, and BMI to "Frau K." February 19, 1975.
100. Nathans, *Politics of Citizenship*, 238–239.
101. Although this problem received special attention when men from Islamic countries abducted their children, this was not a problem that was limited to a single ethnic group. In a February 1982 survey of Interior Ministries, several officials reported that they knew of cases where children had been abducted to Turkey, Morocco, and Syria, but also to France, Canada, and the United States, with one American soldier even abducting his child while the mother was at a doctor's appointment. The survey is in LA B-W, EA 2/303, Bü 159.

    The IAF published two pamphlets about this problem. The first offered practical advice for families in this situation: Rosi Wolf-Almanasreh, *Kindesmitnahme durch ein Elternteil— Ursachen, Lösungsmöglichkeiten und Prävention. Bestandsaufnahme nach fünfzehnjähriger Beratungsarbeit mit bi-nationalen Familien* (Frankfurt: self-published, 1988). The second was published after the success of Betty Mahmoody's memoir *Not Without My Daughter*, which had sold over 3 million copies in Germany by 1991. The IAF's book attempted to give a more objective and less sensationalistic account of the phenomenon. Interessengemeinschaft der mit Ausländern verheirateten Frauen, *Hätte Betty uns gefragt...* (Frankfurt: self-published, 1991).
102. Interessengemeinschaft der mit Ausländern verheirateten Frauen, *Über die Lage der Ausländerfrauen. "Tribunal" zum deutchen Internationalen Privatrecht* (Frankfurt: self-published, 1977), 32–34.
103. IAF, *Über die Lage der Ausländerfrauen*, 39.
104. LA-B, B Rep 002/17179, September 7, 1977, "Was Kostet eine Deutsche Frau oder Wie Man als Ausländer durch eine Scheinehe auf Dauer in Deutschland leben und arbeiten kann."
105. BArch B 106/81051, Band 8., November 22, 1977, IAF to BMI.
106. Klaus-Peter Wolf, *Die Abschiebung oder Wer tötete Mahmut Perver?* (Munich: Die Schatzkiste, 2002 [original 1984]).
107. BArch B 149/83807, December 2, 1982, Bayerische Staatsministerium des Innern memorandum.
108. LA-NRW, NW 760, Nr. 173, August 4, 1981, Standesbeamte in Köln to Staatliche Aufsichtsbehörde für Personenstandsangelegenheiten.

109. BArch B 149/83807, December 2, 1982, Bayerische Staatsministerium des Innern memo-randum and Interessengemeinschaft der mit Ausländern verheirateten Frauen, *Scheinehen in der Bundesrepublik?* (Berlin: self-published, 1985), 21.

110. See the remarks of Frau B. in LA-B, B Rep 002, Nr. 17828, "Inhalts-Protokoll. Ausschuß für Ausländerfragen. 7. Sitzung 5. Februar 1982."

111. BArch B 149/83807, December 2, 1982, Bayerische Staatsministerium des Innern memorandum.

112. "Eine Ehe 'aus Berechnung' zahlt sich nicht aus . . ." *IAF-Informationen* 1/81.

113. LA-B, B Rep 002/17829, March 5, 1982, SenInn Berlin memorandum. For a larger per-spective on "denunciation" in German history, see Robert Gellately, "Denunciations in Twentieth-Century Germany: Aspects of Self-Policing in the Third Reich and the German Democratic Republic," *Journal of Modern History* 68, no. 4 (1996).

114. The IAF newsletter often published hate mail and graffiti in the form of ordinary "reader letters." For one example, see *IAF-Informationen* 4/78–1/79, where four very positive letters sit next to an anonymous letter consisting only of "Schweinerei mit den Rassenmischungen, die Ihr treibt!"

115. LA-B, B Rep 002, Nr. 17828, "Inhalts-Protokoll. Ausschuß für Ausländerfragen. 7. Sitzung 5. Februar 1982."

116. LA-B, B Rep 002, Nr. 17828, "Inhalts-Protokoll. Ausschuß für Ausländerfragen. 7. Sitzung 5. Februar 1982."

117. IAF, *Scheinehen in der Bundesrepublik?* 6. LA-B, B Rep 002, Nr. 17829, March 5, 1982, memorandum.

118. ADL, Baum N60-167, July 1, 1985, Mannheim Oberbürgermeister to members of the Gemeinderat.

119. Peter Finger, "Scheinehen und Praxis der Standesbeamten," *Das Standesamt* 37, no. 4 (1984): 91.

120. BArch B 106/81051, November 11, 1977, IAF "Stellungnahme zur Report-Sendung des Bayrischen Fernsehens am Montag, den 7. November 1977." More such material is collected in IAF, *Scheinehen in der Bundesrepublik?*

121. "Der Druck des Ausländerrechts auf familiäre Entscheidungen," *IAF-Informationen* 3/86, pp. 16–18.

122. Institut für Stadtgeschichte Frankfurt [ISG Frankfurt], Verband binationaler Familien und Partnerschaften, V86/23, correspondence from multiple chapters.

123. ISG Frankfurt, Verband binationaler Familien und Partnerschaften, V86/23, January 29, 1989, letter from Bochum chapter, January 1989, "Stellungnahme zum Entwurf des Grundsatzprogramms von der IAF-Gruppe Duisburg."

124. ISG Frankfurt, Verband binationaler Familien und Partnerschaften, V86/23, January 1989 "Stellungnahme zum Entwurf des Grundsatzprogramms von der IAF-Gruppe Duisburg."

125. "IAF als Selbsthilfeorganisation und Hort von Selbsthilfegruppen. Risiken und Perspektiven," *IAF-Information*, 4/1983, pp. 22–24. ISG Frankfurt, Verband binationaler Familien und Partnerschaften, V86/31, "Protokoll vom 12.6.79" and "Gespraech mit der Rosi am 18.11.74."

126. This case is discussed in more detail in Quinn Slobodian, "The Borders of the *Rechtsstaat* in the Arab Autumn: Deportation and Law in West Germany, 1972/73," *German History* 31, no. 2 (2013): 204–224.

127. Inge El-Himoud, "Eheberatung," *IAF-Informationen* 3/1979, p. 36.

128. Sarah van Walsum makes a similar observation in the Dutch case. *Dutch Family Migration Policies*, 271–272.

129. Damani Partidge conducted anthropological fieldwork with Black men in Germany in the 1990s and 2000s. Many of his informants state that the German wife's power to grant and revoke residency creates an uneven power dynamic that can quickly turn abusive. "'We Were Dancing in the Club, Not on the Berlin Wall': Black Bodies, Street Bureaucrats, and Exclusionary Incorporation into the New Europe," *Cultural Anthropology* 23, no. 4 (2008): 668.

130. PAAA B 85/1602, January 28, 1982, draft proposal. The reference is to the biblical account of Herod the Great having ordered a slaughter of children. Herod heard from the Magi that there was a newborn King of the Jews and ordered that all young boys near Bethlehem be killed, an event known as the "Massacre of the Innocents."
131. This equivalence is made frequently in Klaus J. Bade, Pieter C. Emmer, Leo Lucassen, and Jochen Oltmer, eds., *The Encyclopedia of Migration and Minorities in Europe: From the 17th Century to the Present* (Cambridge: Cambridge University Press, 2011).
132. Jessica Autumn Brown, "Citizenship of the Heart and Mind: Educating Germany's Immigrants in the Ideological, Emotional, and Practical Components of Belongingness" (PhD diss., University of Wisconsin-Madison, 2010), 112–134.
133. Wendy Brown, *States of Injury: Power and Freedom in Late Modernity* (Princeton, NJ: Princeton University Press, 1995), 27.

Chapter 7

1. Peter Giesers, "Nirgendwo ist Heimat," *Kölner Stadt-Anzeiger*, October 27, 1987, reprinted in *Mitteilungen der Beauftragten der Bundesregierung für die Integration der ausländischen Arbeitnehmer und ihrer Familienangehörigen. Wiederkehroption für ausländische Jugendliche* (October 1988), 33.
2. Details about the case taken from *Wiederkehroption*, 27–28 and 33–37, and Straßburger, *Offene Grenzen für Remigranten*, vii–viii.
3. See Triadafilos Triadafilopoulos, "Introduction. Assessing the Consequences of the 1999 German Citizenship Act," *German Politics and Society* 30, no. 1 (2012), and the rest of the special issue on the citizenship reform, especially the article by Andreas Fahrmeir, "Coming to Terms with a Misinterpreted Past? Rethinking the Historical Antecedents of Germany's 1999 Citizenship Reform," *German Politics and Society* 30, no. 1 (2012).
4. Edgar Wolfrum discusses citizenship reform in *Rot-Grün an der Macht: Deutschland 1998–2005* (Munich: C. H. Beck, 2013), 176–181, 185–187.
5. Norbert Frei, Franka Maubach, Christina Morina, and Maik Tändler, *Zur Rechten Zeit: Wider die Rückkehr des Nationalismus*, Berlin: Ullstein, 2019.
6. Patrice G. Poutrus, *Umkämpftes Asyl. Vom Nachkriegsdeutschland bis in die Gegenwart* (Berlin: Ch. Links Verlag, 2019), 168–177, and Ronja Oltmanns "'Wer die Mißbräuche des Asylrechts nicht bekämpft, der fördert [. . .] Ausländerfeindlichkeit.' Die Instrumentalisierung der rassistischen Anschläge und Pogrome Anfang der 1990er Jahre für die faktische Abschaffung des Grundrechts auf Asyl," *Sozial.Geschichte Online* 27 (2020): 1–38.
7. BArch B 136/17999, June 2, 1976, Referat 211 memorandum and April 27, 1979, Gruppe 41 memorandum.
8. BArch B 136/17999, May 9, 1979, Gruppe 41 memorandum.
9. Szatkowski, *Die Bundesrepublik Deutschland und die Türkei*, 106–107.
10. BArch B 136/17999, April 27, 1982, Gruppe 41 memorandum.
11. BArch B 136/31036, October 31, 1986, Gruppe 41 to Chef des BKA, and November 13, 1986, memorandum.
12. "Don't Call Us," *The Economist*, November 29, 1986, 66. Also see *Akten zur Auswärtigen Politik der Bundesrepublik Deutschland. 1986*, ed. Matthias Peter and Daniela Taschler (Berlin: Walter de Gruyter, 2017), Dokument 368, 17.12, Aufzeichnung des Referats 411, pp. 1919–1922.
13. BArch B 136/31036, November 13, 1986, Gruppe 41 to Chef des BKA.
14. BArch B 136/31036, November 24, 1986, Referat 211 memorandum.
15. BArch B 136/31036, December 12, 1986, "The Statement of the Turkish Government Concerning Free Movement of Workers."
16. Kerem Öktem, *Angry Nation: Turkey Since 1989* (London: Zed Books, 2011), 77–78.
17. *AAPD 1986*, Dokument 180, 30.06, Aufzeichnung des Ministerialdirigenten Trumpf, pp. 943–948.
18. European Court of Justice, *Demirel v. Stadt Schwäbisch Gmünd*, September 30, 1987, http://curia.europa.eu/juris/liste.jsf?language=en&num=C-12/86.

19. For more details on family members in the Ankara Agreement, see Nicola Rogers, *A Practitioner's Guide to the EC-Turkey Association Agreement* (The Hague: Kluwer Law International, 2000), 33–39.

20. Deutscher Bundestag, Plenarprotokoll 10/33, November 10, 1983, 2222.

21. Elmar Hönnekopp, "Ausländische Jugendliche nach der 'Rückkehr'—wieder ein Seiteneinsteiger-Problem?" *Mitteilungen aus der Arbeitsmarkt und Berufsforchung* 4/87, pp. 479–489, here 484.

22. Hönnekopp, "Ausländische Jugendliche nach der 'Rückkehr,'" 486–487.

23. Hönnekopp, "Ausländische Jugendliche nach der 'Rückkehr,'" 487.

24. Kahn, "Foreign at Home," chapter 5.

25. DGB Archive, 5/DGAZ Nr. 602, 26 Juli 1988, Abt. AA to Sekretäre der Abt. AA.

26. Deutscher Bundestag, Drucksache 11/1931, March 3, 1988, "Entwurf eines Gesetzes über die Wiederkehrerlaubnis für in der Bundesrepublik Deutschland aufgewachsense Ausländer."

27. *Wiederkehroption*, 4.

28. *Wiederkehroption*, 16–17.

29. BArch B 106/139111, September 14, 1987, press release, "Ausländerbeauftragte schlägt Wiederkehroption für in Deutschland aufgewachsene ausländische Jugendliche vor."

30. Deutscher Bundestag, Plenarprotokoll 11/113, December 1, 1988, 8203.

31. Kreuzberg Museum, SO 36 Archival Material, Inv. Nr. 2013/117, Lfd. Nr. 149, May 2, 1988, "Gewalt in Kreuzberg" letter from AG Kreuzberg Dr. Uwe Lehmann-Brauns.

32. Straßburger, *Offene Grenzen für Remigranten*, 10.

33. Straßburger, *Offene Grenzen für Remigranten*, 94–98.

34. Straßburger, *Offene Grenzen für Remigranten*, 100.

35. Straßburger, *Offene Grenzen für Remigranten*, 18.

36. IG Metall-Archiv, ZWA004246, BMI, September 16, 1983, "Konzeption des BMI für das neue Ausländergesetz."

37. IG Metall-Archiv, ZWA004246, BMI, September 16, 1983, "Konzeption des BMI für das neue Ausländergesetz."

38. DGB Archive, 5/DGAZ000611, BMI January 8, 1988, proposal.

39. "Bis an die Grenzen," *Der Spiegel*, November 28, 1988, 38.

40. Green, *The Politics of Exclusion*, 61.

41. DGB Archive, 5/DGAZ 605, September 23, 1988, Wolfgang Pahle of DGB Landesbezirk R-P to Abt. AA.

42. "Recht absonderlich," *Der Spiegel*, May 2, 1988, 52.

43. ADL, Liselotte Funcke ÜP 58/2012–101, Funcke to Kohl on April 2, 1988, and April 12, 1988.

44. Klaus J. Bade, "Ausländer- und Asylpolitik in der Bundesrepublik Deutschland: Grundprobleme und Entwicklungslinien," in *Einwanderungsland Deutschland: bisherige Ausländer- und Asylpolitik; Vergleich mit anderen europäischen Ländern* (Bonn: Friedrich-Ebert Stiftung, 1992), 58.

45. Deutscher Bundestag, Drucksache 11/6955, April 24, 1990, "Beschlußempfehlung des Innenausschusses (4. Ausschuß)."

46. Nathans, *Politics of Citizenship*, 248.

47. Stefan Senders, "Laws of Belonging: Legal Dimensions of National Inclusion in Germany," *New German Critique* 67 (Winter 1996): 154.

48. Helmut Rittstieg, "Einwanderung von Aus- und Übersiedlern—Verdrängung von Inländern fremder Staatsangehörigkeit: Stellungnahme zum Regierungsentwurf für ein neues Ausländergesetz," *Zeitschrift für Rechtspolitik* 23, no. 4 (1990): 131.

49. Mandel, *Cosmopolitan Anxieties*, 31. Also see Can Candan, *Duvarlar—Mauern—Walls*, http://www.onlinefilm.org/en_EN/film/55435.

50. Deutscher Bundestag, Plenarprotokoll 11/195, February 9, 1990, 15024.

51. Deutscher Bundestag, Drucksache 11/90, January 5, 1990, "Entwurf für ein Gesetz zur Neuregelung des Ausländerrechts," 42.

52. Deutscher Bundestag, Plenarprotokoll 11/195, February 9, 1990, 15046.

53. Deutscher Bundestag, Plenarprotokoll 11/195, February 9, 1990, 15048.

54. Green, *Politics of Exclusion*, 72.

55. Deutscher Bundestag, Plenarprotokoll 11/207, April 26, 1990, 16286, and Papiertiger Archive, Binder MigrantInnen/Flüchtlinge Kämpfe, Soliaktionen Inis ... ab Mai 90–Nov 90 IV, undated flyer, "Gegen Nationalismus und Frauenfeindlichkeit Vorsicht Katholikentag!"
56. Deutscher Bundestag, Plenarprotokoll 11/207, April 26, 1990, 16277.
57. Qtd. in Christine Morgenstern, *Rassismus—Konturen einer Ideologie. Einwanderung im politischen Diskurs der Bundesrepublik Deutschland* (Hamburg: Argument Verlag, 2002), 227–228.
58. Deutscher Bundestag, Plenarprotokoll 11/207, April 26, 1990, 16289, 16295.
59. BArch B 106/117567, October 11, 1982, Bayer. Staatsministerium des Innern to BMI and IM der Länder, and December 10, 1982, BMI to Bayer. Staatsministerium des Innern and IM der Länder.
60. BArch B 106/117567, particularly August 18, 1988, memorandum.
61. BArch B 106/117567, May 9, 1988, BMI an den Vorsitzendes des Innenausschusses des Deutschen Bundestages.
62. BArch B 106/117569, June 30, 1989, Oberstadtdirektor Essen to BMI.
63. BArch B 106/117567, November 19, 1988, "Frau E" to Rita Süssmuth and following correspondence.
64. BArch B 106/117568, April 21, 1989 *FAZ* clipping, "Anne Frank konnte nicht mehr flüchten ..."
65. BArch B 106/117568, February 28, 1989, BMA to BMI, and March 1, 1989, AA to BMI.
66. BArch B 106/117568, March 14, 1989, Staatssekretär Neusel to Herrn Minister, and March 6, 1989, Ankara Embassy to AA.
67. Deutscher Bundestag, Plenarprotokoll 13/152, January 17, 1997, 13745–13755, and "Reine Luftnummer," *Der Spiegel*, January 20, 1997, 76–77.
68. AGG, C NRW III—KV Köln Signatur 5, "4.3.97: Bundesweiter Aktionstag gegen die Visumspflicht für Kinder. Hand in Hand für unsere Kinder—Kanther, jetzt reicht's!"
69. "'Mehr Druck aus der Gesellschaft nötig,'" *Der Spiegel*, March 17, 1997, 17.
70. Simon Green, "Between Ideology and Pragmatism: The Politics of Dual Nationality in Germany," *International Migration Review* 39, no. 4 (Winter 2005): 921–952, 925.
71. Anita Böcker and Dietrich Thränhardt, "Multiple Citizenship and Naturalization: An Evaluation of German and Dutch Policies," *Journal of International Migration and Integration* 7, no. 1 (Winter 2006): 71–94, 76–77.
72. Zeynep Kadırbeyroğlu, "National Transnationalism: Dual Citizenship in Turkey," in *Dual Citizenship in Europe: From Nationhood to Societal Integration*, ed. Thomas Faist (Aldershot, UK: Ashgate, 2007), 135.
73. For more on this debate, see Ingo von Münch, *Die deutsche Staatsangehörigkeit. Vergangenheit—Gegenwart—Zukunft* (Berlin: De Gruyter, 2007), 132–135.
74. Deutscher Bundestag, Plenarprotokoll 14/28, March 19, 1999, 2294.
75. Deutscher Bundestag, Plenarprotokoll 14/28, March 19, 1999, 2288.
76. Deutscher Bundestag, Plenarprotokoll 14/28, March 19, 1999, 2291.
77. Deutscher Bundestag, Plenarprotokoll 14/28, March 19, 1999, 2288, and Deutscher Bundestag, Plenarprotokoll 14/40, May 7, 1999, 3426, 3430.
78. Deutscher Bundestag, Plenarprotokoll 14/40, May 7, 1999, 3432.
79. Deutscher Bundestag, Plenarprotokoll 14/40, May 7, 1999, 3449.
80. Deutscher Bundestag, Plenarprotokoll 14/40, May 7, 1999, 3447.
81. Deutscher Bundestag, Plenarprotokoll 14/40, May 7, 1999, 3459.
82. Bundesrat, Plenarprotokoll 738, May 21, 1999, 182.
83. Deutscher Bundestag, Plenarprotokoll 14/40, May 7, 1999, 3455.
84. Deutscher Bundestag, Plenarprotokoll 14/40, May 7, 1999, 3457.
85. I did not locate any discussion explaining why January 1, 1990, became the cutoff date, although it may well exist in closed archives. Deutscher Bundestag, Drucksache 14/3913, July 21, 2000, and Deutscher Bundestag, Plenarprotokoll 14/157, March 14, 2001, 15357–15358.
86. Simon Green, "Much Ado About Not-Very-Much? Assessing Ten Years of German Citizenship Reform," *Citizenship Studies* 16, no. 2 (2012): 175–176.

87. Çetin Çelik, "'Having a German Passport Will Not Make Me German': Reactive Ethnicity and Oppositional Identity Among Disadvantaged Male Turkish Second-Generation Youth in Germany," *Ethnic and Racial Studies* 38, no. 9 (2015) 1653–1654.

88. Sandra Bucerius, "'What Do You Expect? That We All Dance and Be Happy?' Second-Generation Immigrants and Germany's 1999 Citizenship Reform," *German Politics and Society* 30, no. 1 (2012): 77.

89. Jessica Autumn Brown, "Citizenship of the Heart and Mind." "'We Must Demonstrate Intolerance toward the Intolerant': Boundary Liberalism in Citizenship Education for Immigrants in Germany," *Critical Sociology* 42, no. 3 (2016).

90. Brown shows that the standardized citizenship test obfuscates the multiplicity of German identity and history in other ways. For example, one question on the test is "Which religion has influenced European and German culture? a) Hinduism, b) Christianity, c) Buddhism, or d) Islam." The "correct answer" for the test is "Christianity," an answer that erases many faiths within Europe, not least Judaism. "Boundary Liberalism," 467.

91. Green, *The Politics of Exclusion,* 178; and Sandra Bucerius, *Unwanted—Muslim Immigrants, Dignity, and Drug Dealing* (New York: Oxford University Press, 2014).

92. For more on the argument that these restrictions would protect women from forced marriage, see Urbanek, "Forced Marriage vs. Family Reunification."
    Sociologist Can Aybek has found that these new requirements for spousal migration are having gendered effects: he found that women migrating to Germany as spouses tended to already be married before taking the language course, while men migrating to Germany as spouses often put the wedding off until they had passed the language course and exam, something that was done by the women already living in Germany. He also found that the language exam created stress and delay and threatened the stability of the relationship for many couples. Aybek, "Time Matters."

93. Deutscher Bundestag, Plenarprotokoll 17/242, June 5, 2013, 30597–30598.

94. Deutscher Bundestag, Plenarprotokoll 17/242, June 5, 2013, 30599.

95. Deutscher Bundestag, Plenarprotokoll 17/242, June 5, 2013, 30602.

96. Deutscher Bundestag, Plenarprotokoll 17/242, June 5, 2013, 30610.

97. Elke Winter, Annkathrin Diehl, and Anke Patzelt, "Ethnic Nation No More? Making Sense of Germany's New Stance on Dual Citizenship by Birth," *Review of European and Russian Affairs* 9, no. 1 (2015): 8.

Chapter 8

1. Letters in DOMIT Tuncer, Enver 001.

2. Michael Meng, "Silences About Sarrazin's Racism in Contemporary Germany," *Journal of Modern History* 87, no. 1 (March 2015): 102–135, p. 109.

3. Laura Block and Saskia Bonjour, "Fortress Europe or Europe of Rights? The Europeanisation of Family Migration Policies in France, Germany and the Netherlands," *European Journal of Migration and Law* 15 (2013): 212.

4. Block and Bonjour, "The Europeanisation of Family Migration Policies."

5. Block and Bonjour, "The Europeanisation of Family Migration Policies," 223.

6. Anne Staver, "From Right to Earned Privilege? The Development of Stricter Family Immigration Rules in Denmark, Norway and the United Kingdom" (PhD diss., University of Toronto, 2014).

7. Farris, *Rise of Femonationalism.*

8. Deutscher Bundestag, 18 Wahlperiode, 156. Sitzung, 19. February 2016, 15368.

9. Deutscher Bundestag, 18 Wahlperiode, 156. Sitzung, 19. February 2016, 15357.

10. Deutscher Bundestag, 18 Wahlperiode, 199. Sitzung, 10. November 2016, 19793.

11. Deutscher Bundestag, 18 Wahlperiode, 199. Sitzung, 10. November 2016, 19788.

12. Deutscher Bundestag, 18 Wahlperiode, 156. Sitzung, 19. February 2016, 15357.

13. Deutscher Bundestag, 18. Wahlperiode, 237. Sitzung, 1. Juni 2017, 24162.

14. Deutscher Bundestag, 19. Wahlperiode, 40. Sitzung, 15. Juni 2018, 3952.

15. Deutscher Bundestag, 19. Wahlperiode, 36. Sitzung, 7. Juni 2018, 3351, and 19. Wahlperiode, 8. Sitzung, 19. Januar 2018, 637.

16. Deutscher Bundestag, 19. Wahlperiode, 36. Sitzung, 7. Juni 2018, 3344.
17. Deutscher Bundestag, 10. Wahlperiode, 33. Sitzung, 10. November 1983, 2236–2238.
18. Deutscher Bundestag, 19. Wahlperiode, 8. Sitzung, 19. Januar 2018, 631.
19. Deutscher Bundestag, 19. Wahlperiode, 11. Sitzung, 1. Februar 2018, 778.
20. Deutscher Bundestag, 19. Wahlperiode, 11. Sitzung, 1. Februar 2018, 792.
21. Deutscher Bundestag, 19. Wahlperiode, 36. Sitzung, 7. Juni 2018, 3345.
22. Deutscher Bundestag, 19. Wahlperiode, 11. Sitzung, 1. Februar 2018, 784.
23. Deutscher Bundestag, 19. Wahlperiode, 40. Sitzung, 15. Juni 2018, 3948.

BIBLIOGRAPHY

Archives Used

Archiv des Deutsche Gewerkschaftsbundes im Archiv der Sozialen Demokratie, Bonn [DGB Archive]
Archiv des Deutschen Caritasverbands, Freiburg [A-DCV]
Archiv des Deutschen Liberalismus, Gummersbach [ADL]
Archiv des Diakonischen Werkes der EKD, Berlin [ADW]
Archiv der Sozialen Bewegungen Freiburg [ASB Freiburg]
Archiv Grünes Gedächtnis, Berlin [AGG]
Bundesarchiv, Koblenz [BArch]
Deutsches Rundfunkarchiv, Frankfurt [DRFA]
Dokumentationszentrum über die Migration in Deutschland, Cologne [DOMiD]
Hessisches Hauptstaatsarchiv, Wiesbaden [HHW]
Historical Archives of the European Union, Florence [HA-EU]
IG Metall Archiv im Archiv der sozialen Demokratie, Bonn [IG Metall Archiv]
Institut für Stadtgeschichte Frankfurt [ISG Frankfurt]
Institut für Stadtgeschichte Gelsenkirchen [ISG Gelsenkirchen]
Kreuzberg Museum, SO 36 Archival Collection, Berlin
Landesarchiv Berlin [LA-B]
Landesarchiv Berlin, Deutsche Städtetag Collection [LA B, DST]
Landesarchiv Baden-Württemberg, Stuttgart [LA-BW]
Landesarchiv Nord Rhine Westphalen, Düsseldorf/Duisburg [LA-NRW]
Papiertiger Archive, Berlin
Politisches Archiv des Auswärtigen Amts, Berlin [PAAA]
Robert Havemann Gesellschaft, Archiv der DDR-Opposition, Berlin (Archiv der DDR-Opposition)
Sender Freies Berlin Archive, Berlin [SFB Archive]
Staatsarchiv Hamburg [SA H]
Stadtarchiv Nürnberg [StadtAN]
Terre des Femmes Archive, Berlin

Selected Primary Sources

Aktion Gemeinsinn. *Ausländische Kinder: Fremde oder Freunde? Es liegt an uns: gehen wir auf sie zu.* Bonn: Aktion Gemeinsinn, 1980.
Albrecht, Peter-Alexis, and Christian Pfeiffer. *Die Kriminalisierung junger Ausländer. Befunde und Reaktionen sozialer Kontrollinstanzen.* Munich: Juventa Verlag, 1979.

Arbeitsgruppe Frauenkongreß. *Sind wir uns denn so fremd? Ausländische und deutsche Frauen im Gespräch.* 2nd ed. Berlin: sub rosa Frauenverlag, 1985.

Arın, Cihan, Sigmar Gude, and Hermann Wurtinger. *Auf der Schattenseite des Wohnungsmarkts: Kinderreiche Immigrantenfamilien. Analyse mit Verbesserungsvorschlägen in Wohnungsbelegung, Erneuerung, Selbsthilfe und Eigentum. Studie im Auftrag der Internationalen Bauausstellung Berlin 1987.* Basel: Birkhäuser Verlag, 1985.

Auernheimer, Georg. *Der sogenannte Kulturkonflikt. Orientierungsprobleme ausländischer Jugendlicher.* Frankfurt: Campus Verlag, 1988.

Ausländerkomitee Berlin (West). *Gleiches Wohnrecht für Alle! Dokumentation zur Zuzugssperre für Ausländische Arbeiter.* Berlin (West): self-published, 1978.

Ausländerkomitee Berlin (West). *"Wir sind keine befristeten Menschen"* Der Berliner Ausländererlaß von 1981–1982 und seine Auswirkungen. Berlin (West): self-published, 1983.

Baum, Gerhart Rudolf. "Aktuelle Probleme der Ausländerpolitik." *Zeitschrift für Ausländerrecht und Ausländerpolitik* 1, no. 1 (1981): 7–12.

Bayerischer Arbeitskreis gegen Familientrennung, ed. *Dokumentation zur Familientrennung.* Nürnberg: self-published, 1986.

Becker, Walter. *Ehen mit Ausländern.* Münster: Aktion Jugendschutz, 1966.

Bingemeier, Karl, Edeltrud Meistermann-Seeger, and Edgar Neubert. *Leben als Gastarbeiter. Geglückte und mißglückte Integration.* Cologne: Westdeutscher Verlag, 1970.

Brandt, Franz. *Situationsanalyse Nichterwerbstätiger Ehefrauen Ausländischer Arbeitnehmer in der Bundesrepublik Deutschland.* Bonn: BMJFG, 1977.

Budzinski, Manfred, and Mechthild Schirmer. "Wirkungen der Beschränkung des Familiennachzugs für Ausländer." *Evangelischer Pressedienst Dokumentation* 5a (January 1983).

Budzinski, Manfred, and Mechthild Schirmer. "Wie Ausländerbehörden mit Ausländerfamilien umgehen." *Evangelischer Pressedienst Dokumentation* 43a (October 1983).

Beauftragte der Bundesregierung für die Integration der ausländischen Arbeitnehmer und ihrer Familienangehörigen. *Wiederkehroption für ausländische Jugendliche* (October 1988).

Chelmis, Sabine. *Die Betreuung ausländischer Kleinkinder in Krippen, Tagespflegestellen und bei Verwandten.* Munich: DJI Verlag, 1982.

Dayioğlu, Gülten. *Atil hat Heimweh.* Translated by Feridun Altuna. Berlin: ikoo Verlag, 1985.

Dayioğlu, Gülten. *Rückkehr zwischen zwei Grenzen: Gespräche und Erzählungen.* Translated by Feridun Altuna. Berlin: ikoo Verlag, 1986.

Deckert, Günter. *Ausländerstopp: Handbuch gegen Überfremdung.* Kiel: Arndt, 1981.

Dominguez, Javier. *El hombre como mercancia: españoles en Alemania.* Bilbao: Desclée de Brouwer, 1976.

Elsas, Christoph. *Einflüsse der islamischen Religion auf die Integrationsfähigkeit der Ausländischen Arbeitnehmer und ihrer Familienangehörigen.* Berlin: Senatskanzlei Planungsleitstelle, 1980.

Erdoğmuş, Feride. "'Am Großmarkt wartet schon die Polizei.' Bericht eines 'Illegalen' aus der Türkei." In *Ausländer, die verfemten Gäste,* edited by Christian Habbe, 69–78. Reinbek bei Hamburg: SPIEGEL-Verlag, 1983.

Franger, Gaby. *Wir haben es uns anders vorgestellt. Türkische Frauen in der Bundesrepublik.* Frankfurt: Fischer Taschenbuch Verlag, 1984.

Franz, Fritz. "Der Nachzug ausländischer Familienangehöriger im Lichte der Verfassung." *Neue Juritische Wochenschrift* 37, no. 10 (1984): 530–533.

Geißler, Ulrich. "Armut in Deutschland—eine Neue Soziale Frage? Ist die Sozialpolitik falschprogrammiert? Zu der Dokumentation von Minister Dr. H. Geißler." *Sozialer Fortschritt* 25, no. 3 (1976): 49–54.

Geißler, Heiner. *Die Neue Soziale Frage. Analysen und Dokumente.* Freiburg im Briesgau: Herderbücherei, 1980 [original 1976].

Griese, Hartmut. *Der gläserne Fremde. Bilanz und Kritik der Gastarbeiterforschung und der Ausländerpädagogik.* Opladen: Leske und Budrich, 1984.

Hagemann-White, Carol. *Hilfen für mißhandelte Frauen. Abschlußbericht der wissenschaftlichen Begleitung des Modellprojekts Frauenhaus Berlin.* Stuttgart: Verlag W. Kohlhammer, 1981.

Hamburger, Franz, Lydia Seus, and Otto Wolter. *Zur Delinquenz ausländischer Jugendlicher. Bedingungen der Entstehung und Prozesse der Verfestigung.* Wiesbaden: Bundeskriminalamt, 1981.

Häuserrat Frankfurt. *Wohnungskampf in Frankfurt.* Munich: Trikont-Verlag, 1974.

Hess, Henner, and Achim Melcher. *Ghetto ohne Mauern. Ein Bericht aus der Unterschicht.* Frankfurt am Main: Suhrkamp Verlag, 1973.

Hessisches Institut für Betriebswirtschaft, ed. *Ausländische Arbeitskräfte in Deutschland.* Düsseldorf: Econ-Verlag, 1961.

Hönnekopp, Elmar. "Ausländische Jugendliche nach der 'Rückkehr'—wieder ein Seiteneinsteiger-Problem?" *Mitteilungen aus der Arbeitsmarkt und Berufsforchung* 4, no. 87 (1987): 479–489.

Huber, Bertold. "Rechtmäßigkeit der Stichtagsregelung im Arbeitserlaubnisverfahren?" *Neue Juristische Wochenschrift* 32, no. 10 (1979): 463–466.

Huber, Bertold. "Familiennachzug und Grundgesetz." *Informationsbrief Ausländerrecht* 4 (1982): 1–5.

Humanistischen Union Landesverband Berlin and Jugendverband der Türkei. *Dokumentation über die Aussperrung Jugendlicher Ausländer vom Berliner Arbeitsmarkt.* Berlin: self-published, 1976.

Interessengemeinschaft der mit Ausländern verheirateten Frauen. *Über die Lage der Ausländerfrauen. "Tribunal" zum deutchen Internationalen Privatrecht.* Frankfurt: self-published, 1977.

Interessengemeinschaft der mit Ausländern verheirateten Frauen. *Scheinehen in der Bundesrepublik?* Berlin: self-published, 1985.

Interessengemeinschaft der mit Ausländern verheirateten Frauen. *Hätte Betty uns gefragt . . .* Frankfurt: self-published, 1991.

Interessengemeinschaft der mit Ausländern verheirateten Frauen. *Ratgeber für die Selbsthilfearbeit. Eine Bestandsaufnahme über die Selbsthilfe in der IAF als Anleitung zum Weitermachen.* Frankfurt: self-published, 1987.

John, Barbara. "Zur rechtlichen Situation ausländischer Frauen und Mädchen." In *Hearing zur Situation ausländischer Frauen und Mädchen aus den Anwerbestaaten. Kurzfassung der Dokumentation,* 41–56. Bonn: BMJFFG, 1989.

Kuhn, Margret. "Kindergeld, Entwicklungshilfe und Bevölkerungsexplosion." *Sozialer Fortschritt* 22, no. 6 (1973): 132–133.

Kuhn, Margret. "Kindergeld für Gastarbeiter—ein ernstes Problem." *Sozialer Fortschritt* 24, no. 3 (1975): 59.

Kühn, Heinz. *Stand und Weiterentwicklung der Integration der ausländischen Arbeitnehmer und ihrer Familien in der Bundesrepublik Deutschland: Memorandum der Beauftragten der Bundesregierung.* Bonn: Bundesminister für Arbeit, 1979.

Kurz, Ursula. "Partielle Anpassung und Kulturkonflikt. Gruppenstruktur und Anpassungsdispositionen in einem italienischen Gastarbeiter-Lager." *Kölner Zeitschrift für Soziologie und Sozialpsychologie* 17 (1965): 814–832.

Leder, Hartmut. "Für Ausländer weniger?" *Bundesarbeitsblatt* 1 (1975): 33–38.

López-Blasco, Andrés. "Tendenzen der Integrationspolitik in der Bundesrepublik Deutschland." In *Ausländerpolitik und Integrationsforschung in der Bundesrepublik Deutschland: eine Darstellung wichtigster Ergebnisse mit Auswahlbiographie,* edited by Andrés López-Blasco and Alois Weidacher, 7–21. Munich: DJI Verlag, 1982.

Maturi, Giacomo. *Hallo Günther! Der Ausländische Arbeiter Spricht zu Seinem Deutschen Kollegen.* Heidelberg: Curt Haefner Verlag, 1966.

Mehrländer, Ursula. *Situation der ausländischen Arbeitnehmer und ihrer Familienangehörigen in der Bundesrepublik Deutschland. Repräsentativuntersuchung '80.* Bonn: Forschungsbericht im Auftrag des Bundesministers für Arbeit und Sozialforschung, 1981.

Noel, Camillo. *Kommunalpolitische Aspekte des wachsenden ausländischen Bevölkerungsanteils in München. Problemstudie.* Munich: Stadtentwicklungsreferat, 1972.

Özdemir, Cem. *Ich bin Inländer: Ein anatolischer Schwabe im Bundestag.* Munich: Deutscher Taschenbuch Verlag, 1997.

Peter, Matthias, and Daniela Taschler, eds. *Akten zur Auswärtigen Politik der Bundesrepublik Deutschland. 1986.* Berlin: Walter de Gruyter, 2017.

Quaritsch, Helmut. "Kindernachzug und Art. 6 GG." *Neue Juristische Wochenschrift* 37, no. 48 (1984): 2731–2736.

Ridolfi, Silvano, and Gianfranco Barberini, eds. *Lettere degli Emigrati*. Frankfurt am Main: Editrice Federeuropa, 1967.

Rittstieg, Helmut. "Zur Rechtslage junger Ausländer." *Zeitschrift für Rechtspolitik* 12, no. 1 (January 1979): 13–18.

Rittstieg, Helmut. "Einwanderung von Aus- und Übersiedlern—Verdrängung von Inländern fremder Staatsangehörigkeit: Stellungnahme zum Regierungsentwurf für ein neues Ausländergesetz." *Zeitschrift für Rechtspolitik* 23, no. 4 (1990): 129–132.

Schmidt-Koddenberg, Angelika. *Ausländerinnen im Gespräch: Maßnahmen zur Verbesserung der Lebenssituation ausländischer Frauen*. Düsseldorf: Minister für Arbeit, Gesundheit und Soziales des Landes Nordrhein-Westfalen, 1984.

Schrader, Achim, Bruno W. Nikles, and Hartmut M. Griese. *Die Zweite Generation. Sozialisation und Akkulturation ausländischer Kinder in der Bundesrepublik*. Kronberg: Athenäum Verlag, 1976.

Spanisches Zentrum, Essen. *Spanien ist Anders*. Munich: Trikont Verlag, 1974.

Steuer, W., and K. Schramm. "Ehen zwischen deutschen und ausländischen Arbeitnehmern." *Das öffentliche Gesundheitsdienst* 1, no. 27 (1965): 487–493.

Thomä-Venske, Hanns. *Islam und Integration. Zur Bedeutung des Islam im Prozeß der Integration türkischer Arbeiterfamilien in die Gesellschaft der Bundesrepublik*. Hamburg: E. B. Verlag Rissen, 1981.

Ude-Pestel, Anneliese. *Ahmet. Geschichte einer Kindertherapie*. Munich: Deutscher Taschenbuch Verlag, 1983.

Walz, Hans D., and Arbeitsgruppe Modellprogram für ausländische Kinder und Jugendliche. *Zur Situation von jugendlichen Gastarbeitern in Familie, Freizeit, Schule und Beruf*. Munich: Deutsches Jugendinstitut, 1980.

Werkkreis Literatur der Arbeitswelt, ed. *Mein Vaterland ist international: Texte zur Solidarität* (Frankfurt am Main: Fischer Taschenbuch Verlag, 1976).

Wolf, Klaus-Peter. *Die Abschiebung oder Wer tötete Mahmut Perver?* Munich: Die Schatzkiste, 2002 [original 1984].

Wolf-Almanasreh, Rosi. *Kindesmitnahme durch ein Elternteil—Ursachen, Lösungsmöglichkeiten und Prävention. Bestandsaufnahme nach fünfzehnjähriger Beratungsarbeit mit bi-nationalen Familien*. Frankfurt: self-published, 1988.

Yakut, Atilla. *Zwischen Elternhaus und Arbeitsamt: türkische Jugendliche suchen einen Beruf*. Berlin: EXpress Verlag, 1986.

Yiğit, Hüseyin. *Was soll aus uns werden?* Translated by Herbert Soffel and Hikmet Atilla. Frankfurt: Dağyeli Verlag, 1986.

Zemlin, Petra. *Erziehung in türkischen Familien*. Munich: DJI Verlag, 1981.

Selected Secondary Sources

Adalet, Begüm. *Hotels and Highways: The Construction of Modernization Theory in Cold War Turkey*. Stanford, CA: Stanford University Press, 2018.

Adelson, Leslie. *The Turkish Turn in Contemporary German Literature: Toward a New Critical Grammar of Migration*. New York: Palgrave Macmillan, 2005.

Ahmed, Sara. *Willful Subjects*. Durham, NC: Duke University Press, 2014.

Akcan, Esra. *Open Architecture: Migration, Citizenship, and the Urban Renewal of Berlin-Kreuzberg by IBA-1984/87*. Basel: Birkhäuser, 2018.

Akgündüz, Ahmet. *Labour Migration from Turkey to Western Europe, 1960–1974: A Multidisciplinary Analysis*. Aldershot, UK: Ashgate, 2008.

Alcoff, Linda. *Visible Identities: Race, Gender, and the Self*. New York: Oxford University Press, 2006.

Alexander, Keith Duane. "From Red to Green in the Island City: The *Alternative Liste West Berlin* and the Evolution of the West German Left, 1945–1990." PhD diss., University of Maryland, 2003.

Alexopoulou, Maria. "Vom Nationalen zum Lokalen und zurück? Zur Geschichtsschreibung in der Einwanderungsgesellschaft Deutschland." *Archiv für Sozialgeschichte* 56 (2016): 463–484.

Alexopoulou, Maria. "'*Ausländer*'—A Racialized Concept? 'Race' as an Analytical Concept in Contemporary German Immigration History." In *Who Can Speak and Who Is Heard/Hurt? Facing Problems of Race, Racism, and Ethnic Diversity in the Humanities in Germany*, edited by Mahmoud Arghavan, Nicole Hirschfelder, Luvena Kopp, and Katharina Motyl, 45–67. Bielefeld: transcript, 2019.

Aral, Berdal. "The Case of Free Movement for Workers Between Turkey and the European Union." *Turkish Yearbook of International Relations* 17 (1997): 1–11.

Arın, Cihan. "The Housing Market and Housing Policies for the Migrant Labor Population in West Berlin." In *Urban Housing Segregation of Minorities in Western Europe and the United States*, edited by Elizabeth D. Huttman, 199–214. Durham, NC: Duke University Press, 1991.

Aybek, Can M. "Time Matters: Temporal Aspects of Transnational Intimate Relationships and Marriage Migration Processes from Turkey to Germany." *Journal of Family Issues* 36, no. 11 (2015): 1529–1549.

Bade, Klaus J. "Ausländer- und Asylpolitik in der Bundesrepublik Deutschland: Grundprobleme und Entwicklungslinien." In *Einwanderungsland Deutschland: bisherige Ausländer- und Asylpolitik; Vergleich mit anderen europäischen Ländern*, 51–68. Bonn: Friedrich-Ebert Stiftung, 1992.

Bade, Klaus J., Pieter C. Emmer, Leo Lucassen, and Jochen Oltmer, eds. *The Encyclopedia of Migration and Minorities in Europe: From the 17th Century to the Present*. Cambridge: Cambridge University Press, 2011.

Bailkin, Jordanna. *The Afterlife of Empire*. Berkeley: University of California Press, 2012.

Barnett, Michael N. "Introduction." In *Paternalism Beyond Borders*, edited by Michael N. Barnett, 1–43. Cambridge: Cambridge University Press, 2017.

Beck, Ulrich. *Risk Society: Towards a New Modernity*. Translated by Mark Ritter. London: Sage Publications, 1992.

Bennholdt-Thomsen Veronika et al., eds. *Frauen aus der Türkei kommen in die Bundesrepublik. Zum Problem der Hausfrauisierung*. Bremen: Ed. Con, 1987.

Berlinghoff, Marcel. *Das Ende der 'Gastarbeit.' Europäische Anwerbestopps 1970-1974*. Paderborn: Ferdinand Schöningh, 2013.

Biebricher, Thomas, and Frieder Vogelmann. "Introduction." In *The Birth of Austerity: German Ordoliberalism and Contemporary Neoliberalism*, edited by Thomas Biebricher and Frieder Vogelmann, 1–22. London: Rowman & Littlefield, 2017.

Biess, Frank. *Republik der Angst: Eine andere Geschichte der Bundesrepublik*. Reinbek bei Hamburg: Rowohlt, 2019.

Block, Laura, and Saskia Bonjour. "Fortress Europe or Europe of Rights? The Europeanisation of Family Migration Policies in France, Germany and the Netherlands." *European Journal of Migration and Law* 15, no. 2 (2013): 203–224.

Block, Laura. *Policy Frames on Spousal Migration in Germany: Regulating Membership, Regulating the Family*. Wiesbaden: Springer, 2016.

Böcker, Anita, and Dietrich Thränhardt. "Multiple Citizenship and Naturalization: An Evaluation of German and Dutch Policies." *Journal of International Migration and Integration* 7, no. 1 (Winter 2006): 71–94.

Bojadžijev, Manuela. *Die windige Internationale: Rassismus und Kämpfe der Migration*. Münster: Westfälisches Dampfboot, 2008.

Booth, Heather. *The Migration Process in Britain and West Germany. Two Demographic Studies of Migrant Populations*. Aldershot, UK: Avebury, 1992.

Bösch, Frank. *Zeitenwende 1979: Als die Welt von Heute begann*. Munich: C. H. Beck, 2019.

Bozkurt, Esin. *Conceptualising "Home": The Question of Belonging Among Turkish Families in Germany*. Frankfurt: Campus Verlag, 2009.

Brandes, Edda, Dieter Hauer, and Marcella Hoffmann. "Der Türkische Arbeiterchor in West-Berlin (1979)." In *Musik der Türken in Deutschland*, edited by Max Peter Baumann, 81–92. Kassel: Yvonne Landeck, 1985.

Von Breitenbach, Barbara. *Italiener und Spanier als Arbeitnehmer in der Bundesrepublik Deutschland. Eine vergleichende Untersuchung zur europäischen Arbeitsmigration*. Munich: Kaiser, 1982.

Briggs, Laura. *How All Politics Became Reproductive Politics: From Welfare Reform to Foreclosure to Trump*. Berkeley: University of California Press, 2017.

Brown, Jessica Autumn. "Citizenship of the Heart and Mind: Educating Germany's Immigrants in the Ideological, Emotional, and Practical Components of Belongingness." PhD diss., University of Wisconsin-Madison, 2010.

Brown, Jessica Autumn. "'We Must Demonstrate Intolerance Toward the Intolerant': Boundary Liberalism in Citizenship Education for Immigrants in Germany." *Critical Sociology* 42, no. 3 (2016): 455–471.

Brown, Wendy. *States of Injury: Power and Freedom in Late Modernity*. Princeton, NJ: Princeton University Press, 1995.

Bucerius, Sandra. "What Do You Expect? That We All Dance and Be Happy?' Second-Generation Immigrants and Germany's 1999 Citizenship Reform." *German Politics and Society* 30, no. 1 (2012): 71–85.

Bucerius, Sandra. *Unwanted—Muslim Immigrants, Dignity, and Drug Dealing*. New York: Oxford University Press, 2014.

Buchstab, Günter, and Hans-Otto Kleinmann, eds. *Helmut Kohl: Berichte zur Lage 1982–1989. Der Kanzler und Parteivorsitzende im Bundesvorstand der CDU Deutschlands*. Düsseldorf: Droste, 2014.

Buske, Sybille. "'Fräulein Mutter' vor dem Richterstuhl: Der Wandel der öffentlichen Wahrnehmung und rechtlichen Stellung lediger Mütter in der Bundesrepublik 1948 bis 1970." *WerkstattGeschichte* 27 (2000): 48–67.

Buske, Sybille. *Fräulein Mutter und ihr Bastard: Eine Geschichte der Unehelichkeit in Deutschland, 1900–1970*. Göttingen: Wallstein Verlag, 2004.

Campt, Tina. *Other Germans: Black Germans and the Politics of Race, Gender, and Memory in the Third Reich*. Ann Arbor: University of Michigan Press, 2004.

Candan, Can, dir. *Duvarlar—Mauern—Walls*, 2000; Turkey and USA: self-published, DVD.

Carter, Erica. *How German Is She? Postwar West German Reconstruction and the Consuming Woman*. Ann Arbor: University of Michigan Press, 1997.

Cazorla Sánchez, Antonio. *Fear and Progress: Ordinary Lives in Franco's Spain, 1939–1975*. Oxford: Wiley-Blackwell, 2010.

Çelik, Çetin. "'Having a German Passport Will Not Make Me German': Reactive Ethnicity and Oppositional Identity Among Disadvantaged Male Turkish Second-Generation Youth in Germany." *Ethnic and Racial Studies* 38, no. 9 (2015): 1642–1662.

Chappel, James. "Nuclear Families in a Nuclear Age: Theorising the Family in 1950s West Germany." *Contemporary European History* 26, no. 1 (2017): 85–109.

Chappel, James. *Catholic Modern: The Challenge of Totalitarianism and the Remaking of the Church*. Cambridge, MA: Harvard University Press, 2018.

Chin, Rita. *The Guest Worker Question in Postwar Germany*. Cambridge: Cambridge University Press, 2007.

Chin, Rita, Heide Fehrenbach, Geoff Eley, and Atina Grossmann. *After the Nazi Racial State: Difference and Democracy in Germany and Europe*. Ann Arbor: University of Michigan Press, 2009.

Chin, Rita. "Turkish Women, West German Feminists, and the Gendered Discourse on Muslim Cultural Difference." *Public Culture* 22, no. 3 (2010): 557–581.

Chin, Rita. *The Crisis of Multiculturalism in Europe: A History*. Princeton, NJ: Princeton University Press, 2017.

Çil, Hasan. *Anfänge einer EPOCHE. Ehemalige türkische Gastarbeiter erzählen/bir DÖNEMin başlangıçları. Bir zamanların konuk işçileri anlatıyor*. Berlin: Verlag Hans Schiler, 2003.

Clarkson, Alexander. *Fragmented Fatherland. Immigration and Cold War Conflict in the Federal Republic of Germany 1945–1980*. New York: Berghahn Books, 2013.

Cohen, Deborah. *Braceros: Migrant Citizens and Transnational Subjects in the Postwar United States and Mexico*. Chapel Hill: University of North Carolina Press, 2011.

Comte, Emmanuel. *The History of the European Migration Regime: Germany's Strategic Hegemony*. New York: Routledge, 2018.

Cooper, Melinda. *Family Values: Between Neoliberalism and the New Social Conservatism*. New York: Zone Books, 2017.

Cuison Villazor, Rose. "The 1965 Immigration Act: Family Unification and Nondiscrimination Fifty Years Later." In *The Immigration and Nationality Act of 1965: Legislating a New America*, edited by Gabriel J. Chin and Rose Cuison Villazor, 197–231. Cambridge: Cambridge University Press, 2015.

Davidson, Naomi. *Only Muslim: Embodying Islam in Twentieth-Century France*. Ithaca, NY: Cornell University Press, 2012.

Dikeç, Mustafa. *Badlands of the Republic: Space, Politics and Urban Policy*. Hoboken, NJ: Wiley-Blackwell, 2007.

Düdung, Dieter. *Heinz Kühn 1912–1992. Eine politische Biographie*. Essen: Klartext-Verlag, 2002.

Eder, Jacob S. *Holocaust Angst: The Federal Republic of Germany and American Holocaust Memory Since the 1970s*. New York: Oxford University Press, 2016.

Eggers, Maureen Maisha, Grada Kilomba, Peggy Piesche, and Susan Arndt, eds. *Mythen, Masken und Subjekte: Kritische Weißseinsforschung in Deutschland*. Münster: UNRAST-Verlag, 2005.

El-Tayeb, Fatima. "Dangerous Liaisons. Race, Nation, and German Identity." In *Not so Plain as Black and White. Afro-German Culture and History, 1890–2000*, edited by Patricia Mazón and Reinhild Steingröver, 27–60. Rochester, NY: University of Rochester Press, 2005.

El-Tayeb, Fatima. *European Others: Queering Ethnicity in Postnational Europe*. Minneapolis: University of Minnesota Press, 2011.

El-Tayeb, Fatima. "'Gays Who Cannot Properly Be Gay': Queer Muslims in the Neoliberal European City." *European Journal of Women's Studies* 19, no. 1 (2012): 79–95.

El-Tayeb, Fatima. *Undeutsch: Die Konstruktion des Anderen in der Postmigrantischen Gesellschaft*. Bielefeld: transcript, 2016.

Espahangizi, Raika. "Migration and Urban Transformations: Frankfurt in the 1960s and 1970s." *Journal of Contemporary History* 49, no. 1 (2014): 183–208.

Ewing, Christopher. "The Color of Desire: Contradictions of Race, Sex, and Gay Rights in the Federal Republic of Germany." PhD diss., City University of New York, 2018.

Ewing, Katherine Pratt. *Stolen Honor: Stigmatizing Muslim Men in Berlin*. Stanford, CA: Stanford University Press, 2008.

Fahrmeir, Andreas. "Coming to Terms with a Misinterpreted Past? Rethinking the Historical Antecedents of Germany's 1999 Citizenship Reform." *German Politics and Society* 30, no. 1 (2012): 17–38.

Farris, R. *In the Name of Women's Rights: The Rise of Femonationalism*. Durham, NC: Duke University Press, 2017.

Fehrenbach, Heide. *Race after Hitler: Black Occupation Children in Postwar Germany and America*. Princeton, NJ: Princeton University Press, 2005.

Findlay, Eileen J. Suárez. *We Are Left Without a Father Here: Masculinity, Domesticity, and Migration in Postwar Puerto Rico*. Durham, NC: Duke University Press, 2014.

Foucault, Michel. *The Birth of Biopolitics. Lectures at the Collège de France 1978–1979*. Edited by Arnold I. Davidson. Translated by Graham Burchell. New York: Picador, 2008.

Frei, Norbert, Franka Maubach, Christina Morina, and Maik Tändler. *Zur Rechten Zeit: Wider die Rückkehr des Nationalismus*. Berlin: Ullstein, 2019.

Frisch, Max, "Vorwort." In *Siamo Italiani/Die Italiener: Gespräche mit italienischen Arbeitern in der Schweiz*, edited by Alexander J. Seiler, 7–11. Zürich: EVZ-Verlag, 1965.

Frohman, Larry. "'Only Sheep Let Themselves Be Counted': Privacy, Political Culture, and the 1983/87 West German Census Boycotts." *Archiv für Sozialgeschichte* 52 (2012): 335–378.

Führer, Karl Christian. *Die Stadt, das Geld und der Markt: Immobilienspekulation in der Bundesrepublik 1960–1985.* Berlin: Walter de Gruyter, 2016

Geiß, Bernd. "Die Ausländerbeauftragten der Bundesregierung in der ausländerpolitischen Diskussion." In *Deutschland—ein Einwanderungsland? Rückblick, Bilanz und neue Fragen,* edited by Edda Currle and Tanja Wunderlich, 127–140. Stuttgart: Lucius and Lucius, 2001.

Gellately, Robert. "Denunciations in Twentieth-Century Germany: Aspects of Self-Policing in the Third Reich and the German Democratic Republic." *Journal of Modern History* 68, no. 4 (1996): 931–967.

Gitmez, Ali, and Czarina Wilpert. "A Micro-Society or an Ethnic Community? Social Organization and Ethnicity amongst Turkish Migrants in Berlin." In *Immigrant Associations in Europe,* edited by John Rex, Daniele Joly, and Czarina Wilpert, 86–125. Aldershot: Gower, 1987.

Goeke, Simon. *"Wir sind alle Fremdarbeiter!" Gewerkschaften, migrantische Kämpfe und soziale Bewegungen in der Bundesrepublik Deutschland der 1960er und 1970er Jahre.* Paderborn: Ferdinand Schöningh, 2020.

González-Ferrer, Amparo. "The Process of Family Reunification Among Original Guest-Workers in Germany." *Zeitschrift für Familienforschung* 19, no. 1 (2007): 10–33.

Goodman, Charity. "The Decision Makers: Spanish Migrant Women in West Germany." PhD diss., Rutgers, 1984.

Göktürk, Deniz, David Gramling, and Anton Kaes, eds. *Germany in Transit: Nation and Migration, 1955–2005.* Berkeley: University of California Press, 2007.

Green, Simon. *The Politics of Exclusion: Institutions and Immigration Policy in Contemporary Germany.* Manchester: Manchester University Press, 2004.

Green, Simon. "Between Ideology and Pragmatism: The Politics of Dual Nationality in Germany." *International Migration Review* 39, no. 4 (Winter 2005): 921–952.

Green, Simon. "Divergent Traditions, Converging Responses: Immigration and Integration Policy in the UK and Germany." *German Politics* 16, no. 1 (2007): 95–115.

Green, Simon. "Much Ado About Not-Very-Much? Assessing Ten Years of German Citizenship Reform." *Citizenship Studies* 16, no. 2 (2012): 173–188.

Grzeszick, Bernd. "Helmut Quaritsch (1930–2011)." In *Staatsrechtslehrer des 20. Jahrhunderts: Deutschland-Österreich-Schweiz,* edited by Peter Häberle, 982–991. Berlin: De Gruyter, 2018.

Guild, Elspeth, Kees Groenendijk, and Sergio Carrera. "Understanding the Contest of Community: Illiberal Practices in the EU?" In *Illiberal Liberal States. Immigration, Citizenship and Integration in the EU,* edited by Elspeth Guild, Kees Groenendij and Sergio Carrera, 1–25. Farnham: Ashgate, 2009.

Haderer, Margaret. "'Economic Policies Are the Best Social Policies': West German Neoliberalism and the Housing Question After 1945." *American Journal of Economics and Sociology* 77, no. 1 (January 2018): 149–167.

Hagemann, Karen. "Between Ideology and Economy: The 'Time Politics' of Child Care and Public Education in the Two Germanys." *Social Politics* 13, no. 2 (2006): 217–260.

Hagemann, Karen. "A West German 'Sonderweg'? Family, Work, and the Half-Day Time Policy of Childcare and Schooling." In *Children, Families, and States. Time Policies of Childcare, Preschool, and Primary Education in Europe,* edited by Karen Hagemann, Konrad H. Jarausch, and Cristina Allemann-Ghionda, 275–300. New York: Berghahn Books, 2011.

Hahamovitch, Cindy. *No Man's Land: Jamaican Guestworkers in America and the Global History of Deportable Labor.* Princeton, NJ: Princeton University Press, 2011.

Hannah, Matthew G. *Dark Territory in the Information Age. Learning from the West German Census Controversies of the 1980s.* Farnham, UK: Ashgate, 2010.

Haritaworn, Jin. "Queer Injuries: The Racial Politics of 'Homophobic Hate Crime' in Germany." *Social Justice* 37, no. 1 (2010): 69–89.

Haritaworn, Jin. *Queer Lovers and Hateful Others: Regenerating Violent Times and Places.* London: Pluto Press, 2015.

Haßdenteufel, Sarah. *Neue Armut, Exklusion, Prekarität: Debatten um Armut in Frankreich und der Bundesrepublik Deutschland, 1970–1990*. Berlin: Walter de Gruyter, 2019.

Hassel, Anke, and Christof Schiller. *Der Fall Hartz IV: Wie es zur Agenda 2010 kam und wie es weitergeht*. Frankfurt: Campus Verlag, 2010.

Hausen, Karin. "Frauenerwerbstätigkeit und erwerbstätige Frauen. Anmerkung zur historischen Forschung." In *Frauen arbeiten: weibliche Erwerbstätigkeit in Ost- und Westdeutschland nach 1945*, edited by Gunilla-Friederike Budde, 19–45. Göttingen: Vandenhoeck and Ruprecht, 1997.

Heineman, Elizabeth D. *What Difference Does a Husband Make? Women and Marital Status in Nazi and Postwar Germany*. Berkeley: University of California Press, 1999.

Herbert, Ulrich. *Hitler's Foreign Workers: Enforced Foreign Labor in Germany Under the Third Reich*. Translated by William Templer. Cambridge: Cambridge University Press, 1997.

Herbert, Ulrich, and Karin Hunn. "Gastarbeiter und Gastarbeiterpolitik in der Bundesrepublik. Vom Beginn der offiziellen Anwerbestopp (1955–1973)." In *Dynamische Zeiten: Die 60er Jahre in den beiden deutschen Gesellschaften*, edited by Axel Schildt, Detlef Siegfried, and Karl Christian Lammers, 273–310. Hamburg: Christians, 2000.

Herbert, Ulrich, and Karin Hunn. "Beschäftigung, soziale Sicherung und soziale Integration von Ausländern." In *Geschichte der Sozialpolitik in Deutschland seit 1945, Band 6*, edited by Martin H. Geyer, 751–778. Baden-Baden: Nomos Verlag, 2008.

Höhn, Maria. *GIs and Fräuleins: The German-American Encounter in 1950s West Germany*. Chapel Hill: University of North Carolina Press, 2002.

van Hook, James C. *Rebuilding Germany: The Creation of the Social Market Economy, 1945–1957*. Cambridge: Cambridge University Press, 2004.

Hunn, Karin. *"Nächstes Jahr kehren wir zurück . . ." Die Geschichte der türkischen 'Gastarbeiter' in der Bundesrepublik*. Göttingen: Wallstein Verlag, 2005.

Jakob, Mark. *Familienbilder: Sozialer Wandel, Wissenschaft und Familienpolitik in der BRD 1954–1982*. Wiesbaden: Springer VS, 2019.

Jamin, Mathilde. "Fremde Heimat: Zur Geschichte der Arbeitsmigration aus der Türkei." In *50 Jahre Bundesrepublik—50 Jahre Einwanderung: Nachkriegsgeschichte als Migrationsgeschichte*, edited by Jan Motte, Rainer Ohliger, and Anne von Oswald, 145–164. Frankfurt: Campus Verlag, 1999.

Janz, Oliver, and Roberto Sala, eds. *Dolce Vita? Das Bild der italienischen Migranten in Deutschland*. Frankfurt: Campus Verlag, 2011.

Jarausch, Konrad. *After Hitler: Recivilizing Germans, 1945–1995*. Translated by Brandon Hunziker. New York: Oxford University Press, 2006.

Jessen, Ralph. "Bewältigte Vergangenheit—blockierte Zukunft? Ein prospektiver Blick auf die bundesrepublikanische Gesellschaft am Ende der Nachkriegszeit." In *Das Ende der Zuversicht? Die siebziger Jahre als Geschichte*, edited by Konrad Jarausch, 177–195. Göttingen: Vandenhoeck & Ruprecht, 2008.

Joppke, Christian. "Why Liberal States Accept Unwanted Immigration." *World Politics* 50, no. 2 (1998): 266–293.

Kadırbeyoğlu, Zeynep. "National Transnationalism: Dual Citizenship in Turkey." In *Dual Citizenship in Europe: From Nationhood to Societal Integration*, edited by Thomas Faist, 127–146. Aldershot, UK: Ashgate, 2007.

Kahn, Michelle Lynn. "Foreign at Home: Turkish German Migrants and the Boundaries of Europea, 1961–1990." PhD diss., Stanford University, 2018.

Kane, Thomas T. *Streams of Change. Fertility, Nuptiality, and Assimilation of Guestworker Populations in the Federal Republic of Germany*. New York: Garland, 1989.

Karakayali, Serhat. *Gespenster der Migration. Zur Genealogie illegaler Einwanderung in der Bundesrepublik Deutschland*. Bielefeld: transcript Verlag, 2008.

Karamouzi, Eirini. *Greece, the EEC and the Cold War 1974–1979: The Second Enlargement*. New York: Palgrave Macmillan, 2014.

Klausmeier, Simone. *Asylbewerber zum "Scheinasylanten": Asylrecht und Asylpolitik in der Bundesrepublik Deutschland seit 1973*. Berlin: EXpress Edition, 1984.

Kleinschmidt, Julia. "Streit um das 'kleine Asyl': 'De-Facto-Flüchtlinge' und Proteste gegen Abschiebungen als gesellschaftspolitische Herausforderung für Bund und Länder während der 1980er Jahre." In *Den Protest regieren: staatlcihes Handeln, neue sozialen Bewegungen und linke Organisationen in den 1970er und 1980er Jahren*, edited by Alexandra Jaeger, Julia Kleinschmidt, and David Templin, 231–258. Essen: Klartext Verlag, 2018.

Knortz, Heike. *Diplomatische Tauschgeschäfte: 'Gastarbeiter' in der westdeutschen Diplomatie und Beschäftigungspolitik 1953–1973*. Köln: Bohlau, 2008.

Kofman, Eleonore. "Female 'Birds of Passage' a Decade Later: Gender and Immigration in the European Union." *International Migration Review* 33, No. 2 (Summer 1999): 269–299.

Kofman, Eleonore. "Family-Related Migration: A Critical Review of European Studies." *Journal of Ethnic and Migration Studies* 30, no. 2 (March 2004): 243–262.

Kolbe, Wiebke. "Gender and Parenthood in West German Family Politics from the 1960s to the 1980s." In *State Policy and Gender System in the Two German States and Sweden 1945–1989*, edited by Rolf Torstendahl, 133–167. Uppsala: Uppsala University Press, 1999.

Kuller, Christiane. *Familienpolitik im föderativen Sozialstaat: Die Formierung eines Politikfeldes in der Bundesrepublik 1949–1975*. Munich: R. Oldenbourg Verlag, 2004.

Kuller, Christiane. "Soziale Sicherung von Frauen—ein ungelöstes Strukturproblem im männlichen Wohlfahrtsstaat. Die Bundesrepublik im europäischen Vergleich." *Archiv für Sozialgeschichte* 47 (2007): 199–236.

Lehman, Brittany. "West German-Moroccan Relations and Politics of Labour Migration, 1958–1972." *Journal of Migration History* 5 (2019): 103–133.

Lehman, Brittany. *Teaching Migrant Children in West Germany and Europe, 1949–1992*. Cham: Palgrave Macmillan, 2019.

Loza, Mireya. *Defiant Braceros: How Migrant Workers Fought for Racial, Sexual, and Political Freedom*. Chapel Hill: University of North Carolina Press, 2016.

Lüdtke, Alf, ed. *The History of Everyday Life: Reconstructing Historical Experiences and Ways of Life*. Translated by William Templer. Princeton, NJ: Princeton University Press, 1995.

Lutz, Helma. *Welten verbinden. Türkische Sozialarbeiterinnen in den Niederlanden und der Bundesrepublik Deutschland*. Frankfurt: Verlag für Interkulturelle Kommunikation, 1991.

Lutz, Helma, and Christine Huth-Hildebrand. "Geschlecht im Migrationsdiskurs. Neue Gedanken über ein altes Thema." *Das Argument* 40, no. 224 (1998): 159–173.

Lyons, Amelia H. *The Civilizing Mission in the Metropole: Algerian Families and the French Welfare State During Decolonization*. Stanford: Stanford University Press, 2013.

Mandel, Ruth. *Cosmopolitan Anxieties. Turkish Challenges to Citizenship and Belonging in Germany*. Durham, NC: Duke University Press, 2008.

Mattes, Monika. *"Gastarbeiterinnen" in der Bundesrepublik: Anwerbepolitik, Migration und Geschlecht in den 50er bis 70er Jahren*. Frankfurt: Campus Verlag, 2005.

McKeown, Adam. *Melancholy Order: Asian Migration and the Globalization of Borders*. New York: Columbia University Press, 2008.

Meng, Michael. "Silences About Sarrazin's Racism in Contemporary Germany." *Journal of Modern History* 87, no. 1 (March 2015): 102–135.

Miller, Jennifer A. "On Track for West Germany: Turkish 'Guest-Worker' Rail Transportation to West Germany in the Postwar Period." *German History* 30, no. 4 (2012): 550–573.

Miller, Jennifer A. "Her Fight Is Your Fight: 'Guest Worker' Labor Activism in the Early 1970s West Germany." *International Labor and Working-Class History* 84 (Fall 2013): 225–247.

Miller, Jennifer A. *Turkish Guest Workers in Germany: Hidden Lives and Contested Borders, 1960s–1980s*. Toronto: University of Toronto Press, 2018.

Miller, Brian Joseph-Keysor. "Reshaping the Turkish Nation-State: The Turkish-German Guest Working Program and Planned Development." PhD diss., University of Iowa, 2015.

Mierzejewski, Alfred C. *Ludwig Erhard: A Biography*. Chapel Hill: University of North Carolina Press, 2004.

Minian, Ana Raquel. *Undocumented Lives: The Untold Story of Mexican Migration*. Cambridge, MA: Harvard University Press, 2018.

Mitchell, Maria D. *The Origins of Christian Democracy: Politics and Confession in Modern Germany.* Ann Arbor: University of Michigan Press, 2012.

Moeller, Robert G. *Protecting Motherhood: Women and the Family in the Politics of Postwar West Germany*. Berkeley: University of California Press, 1993.

Moeller, Robert G. "The Elephant in the Living Room: Or Why the History of Twentieth-Century Germany Should Be a Family Affair." In *Gendering Modern German History: Rewriting Historiography*, edited by Karen Hagemann and Jean H. Quataert, 228–249. New York: Berghahn, 2007.

Mohanty, Chandra Talpade. "Under Western Eyes: Feminist Scholarship and Colonial Discourses." In *Feminism Without Borders: Decolonizing Theory, Practicing Solidarity*, 17–42. Durham, NC: Duke University Press, 2003.

Molnar, Christopher A. "Imagining Yugoslavs: Migration and the Cold War in Postwar West Germany." *Central European History* 47, no. 1 (2014): 138–169.

Molnar, Christopher A. *Memory, Politics, and Yugoslav Migrations to Postwar Germany*. Bloomington: Indiana University Press, 2018.

Morcillo, Aurora G. *True Catholic Womanhood: Gender Ideology in Franco's Spain*. DeKalb: Northern Illinois University Press, 2000.

Morgenstern, Christine. *Rassismus—Konturen einer Ideologie. Einwanderung im politischen Diskurs der Bundesrepublik Deutschland*. Hamburg: Argument Verlag, 2002.

von Münch, Ingo. *Die deutsche Staatsangehörigkeit. Vergangenheit—Gegenwart—Zukunft*. Berlin: De Gruyter, 2007.

Münch, Ursula. "Familien-, Jugend- und Altenpolitik." In *Geschichte der Sozialpolitik in Deutschland seit 1945. Band 4*, edited by Michael Ruck and Marcel Boldorf, 549–610. Baden Baden: Nomos Verlag, 2007.

Naldini, Manuela. *The Family in the Mediterranean Welfare States*. London: Frank Cass, 2003.

Nasiali, Minayo. *Native to the Republic. Empire, Social Citizenship, and Everyday Life in Marseille Since 1945*. Ithaca, NY: Cornell University Press, 2016.

Nathans, Eli. *The Politics of Citizenship in Germany: Ethnicity, Utility, and Nationalism*. Oxford: Berg, 2004.

Nauck, Bernhard. *Arbeitsmigration und Familienstruktur. Eine Analyse der mikrosozialen Folgen von Migrationsprozessen*. Frankfurt: Campus Verlag, 1985.

Nelleßen-Strauch, Dagmar. *Der Kampf um das Kindergeld: Grundanschauungen, Konzeptionen und Gesetzgebung 1949-1964*. Düsseldorf: Droste Verlag, 2003.

Nicholls, Anthony J. *Freedom with Responsibility: The Social Market Economy in Germany, 1918–1963*. New York: Oxford University Press, 1994.

Niehuss, Merith. "French and German Family Policy 1945-60." *Contemporary European History* 4, no. 3 (1995): 293–313.

Nocera, Lea. *Cercasi Mani Piccole E Abili: La Migrazione Turca in Germania Occidentale in una Prospettiva di Genere 1961-1984*. Istanbul: Edizione Isis, 2012.

Nolan, Mary. *Visions of Modernity: American Business and the Modernization of Germany*. New York: Oxford University Press, 1994.

O'Brien, Peter. "The Paradoxical Paradigm: Turkish Migrants and German Policies." PhD diss., University of Wisconsin-Madison, 1988.

Öktem, Kerem. *Angry Nation: Turkey Since 1989*. London: Zed Books, 2011.

von Oertzen, Christine. *Teilzeitarbeit und die Lust am Zuverdienen. Geschlechterpolitik und gesellschaftlicher Wandel in Westdeutschland 1948-1969*. Göttingen: Vandenhoeck & Ruprecht, 1999.

Olsen, Jonathan. *Nature and Nationalism: Right-Wing Ecology and the Politics of Identity in Contemporary Germany*. New York: St. Martin's Press, 1999.

Oltmanns, Ronja. "'Wer die Mißbräuche des Asylrechts nicht bekämpft, der fördert [. . .] Ausländerfeindlichkeit.' Die Instrumentalisierung der rassistischen Anschläge und Pogrome

Anfang der 1990er Jahre für die faktische Abschaffung des Grundrechts auf Asyl." *Sozial. Geschichte Online* 27 (2020): 1–38.

Omi, Michael, and Howard Winant. *Racial Formation in the United States. From the 1960s to the 1990s.* 2nd ed. New York: Routledge, 1994.

Ostrow, Sonja G. "Intersecting Aims, Divergent Paths: The Allensbach Institute, the Institute for Social Research, and the Making of Public Opinion Research in 1950s West Germany." *Journal of the History of the Behavioral Sciences* 57, no. 2 (2021): 130–148.

von Oswald, Anne, and Barbara Schmidt. " 'Nach Schichtende sind sie immer in ihr Lager zurückgekehrt . . .' Leben in 'Gastarbeiter'-Unterkünften in den sechziger und siebziger Jahren." In *50 Jahre Bundesrepublik—50 Jahre Einwanderung: Nachkriegsgeschichte als Migrationsgeschichte,* edited by Jan Motte, Rainer Ohliger, and Anne von Oswald, 184–214. Frankfurt: Campus Verlag, 1999.

Oulios, Miltiadis. *Blackbox Abschiebung. Geschichte, Theorie und Praxis der deutschen Migrationspolitik.* 2nd ed. Berlin: Suhrkamp Verlag, 2015.

Panagiotidis, Jannis. *The Unchosen Ones: Diaspora, Nation, and Migration in Israel and Germany.* Bloomington: Indiana University Press, 2019.

Partridge, Damani. " 'We Were Dancing in the Club, Not on the Berlin Wall': Black Bodies, Street Bureaucrats, and Exclusionary Incorporation into the New Europe." *Cultural Anthropology* 23, no. 4 (2008): 660–687.

Partridge, Damani. *Hypersexuality and Headscarves: Race, Sex, and Citizenship in the New Germany.* Bloomington: Indiana University Press, 2012.

Poutrus, Patrice G. *Umkämpftes Asyl. Vom Nachkriegsdeutschland bis in die Gegenwart.* Berlin: Ch. Links Verlag, 2019.

Prontera, Grazia. "The Migration Experience of Italian Workers in the Federal Republic of Germany in the Postwar Years." In *Postwar Mediterranean Migration to Western Europe: Legal and Political Frameworks, Sociability and Memory Cultures,* edited by Clelia Caruso, Jenny Pleinen, and Lutz Raphael, 151–170. Frankfurt: Peter Lang, 2008.

Prontera, Grazia. *Partire, Tornare, Restare? L'esperienza migratoria dei lavoratori italiani nella Repubblica Federale Tedesca nel secondo dopoguerra.* Milan: Guerini e Associati, 2009.

Ptak, Ralf. *Vom Ordoliberalismus zur Sozialen Marktwirtschaft. Stationen des Neoliberalismus in Deutschland.* Wiesbaden: VS. Verlag für Sozialwissenschaften, 2004.

Ptak, Ralf. "Neoliberalism in Germany: Revisiting the Ordoliberal Foundations of the Social Market Economy." In *The Road from Mont Pelerin: The Making of the Neoliberal Thought Collective,* edited by Philip Mirowksi and Dieter Plehwe, 98–138. Cambridge, MA: Harvard University Press, 2009.

Puzzo, Catherine. "British and French Immigration Policy in the 1970s: A Comparative Analysis." *Contemporary European History* 12, no. 1 (2003): 71–92.

van Rahden, Till. *Demokratie: Eine gefährdete Lebensform.* Frankfurt: Campus Verlag, 2019.

Raithel, Thomas, and Thomas Schlemmer, eds. *Die Rückkehr der Arbeitslosigkeit. Die Bundesrepublik Deutschland im europäischen Kontext 1973 bis 1989.* Munich: Oldenbourg Verlag, 2009.

Raithel, Thomas. *Jugendarbeitslosigkeit in der Bundesrepublik. Entwicklung und Auseinandersetzung während der 1970er und 1980er Jahre.* Munich: Oldenbourg Verlag, 2012.

Raphael, Lutz. *Jenseits von Kohle und Stahl: Eine Gesellschaftsgeschichte Westeuropas nach dem Boom.* Berlin: Suhrkamp, 2019.

Rass, Christoph, and Melanie Ulk. "Armando Rodrigues de Sá revisited. Bildwissenschaftliche und historische Analysen im Dialog." In *Migration ein Bild geben: Visuelle Aushandlungen von Diversität,* edited by Christoph Rass and Melanie Ulk, 419–446. Wiesbaden: Springer, 2018.

Rheinstein, Max, and Mary Ann Glendon. "West German Marriage and Family Law Reform." *University of Chicago Law Review* 45, no. 3 (Spring 1978): 519–552.

Rieker, Yvonne. "Südländer, Ostagente oder Westeuropäer? Die Politik der Bundesregierung und das Bild der italienischen Gastarbeiter 1955-1970." *Archiv für Sozialgeschichte* 40 (2000): 231–258.

Rieker, Yvonne. *"Ein Stück Heimat findet man ja immer." Die italienische Einwanderung in die Bundesrepublik.* Essen: Klartext Verlag, 2003.

Roesch, Claudia. "Love Without Fear: Knowledge Networks and Family Planning Initiatives for Immigrant Families in West Germany and the United States." *GHI Bulletin* 64 (Spring 2019): 93–113.

Rogers, Nicola. *A Practitioner's Guide to the EC-Turkey Association Agreement.* The Hague: Kluwer Law International, 2000.

Rölli-Alkemper, Lukas. *Familie im Wiederaufbau: Katholizismus und bürgerliches Familienideal in der Bundesrepublik Deutschland 1945–1965.* Paderborn: Schöningh, 2000.

Rostock, Petra, and Sabine Berghahn. "The Ambivalent Role of Gender in Redefining the German Nation." *Ethnicities* 8, no. 3 (2008): 345–364.

Rothberg, Michael, and Yasemin Yildiz. "Memory Citizenship: Migrant Archives of Holocaust Remembrance in Contemporary Germany." *Parallax* 17, no. 4 (2011): 32–48.

Rottmann, Susan B., and Myra Marx Ferree. "Citizenship and Intersectionality: German Feminist Debates About Headscarf and Antidiscrimination Laws." *Social Politics* 15, no. 4 (2008): 481–513.

Ruble, Alexandria N. "Creating Postfascist Families: Reforming Family Law and Gender Roles in Postwar East and West Germany." *Central European History* 53, no. 2 (2020): 414–431.

Rürup, Miriam. "Das Geschlecht der Staatenlosen. Staatenlosigkeit in der Bundesrepublik Deutschland nach 1945." *Journal of Modern European History* 14, no. 3 (2016): 411–430.

Sala, Roberto. *Fremde Worte: Medien für 'Gastarbeiter' in der Bundesrepublik im Spannungsfeld von Aussen- und Sozialpolitik.* Paderborn: Ferdinand Schöningh, 2011.

Schiller, Kay, and Christopher Young. *The 1972 Munich Olympics and the Making of Modern Germany.* Berkeley: University of California Press, 2010.

Schneider, Jan. *Modernes Regieren und Konsens: Kommissionen und Beratungsregime in der deutschen Migrationspolitik.* Wiesbaden: VS Verlag für Sozialwissenschaften, 2010.

Schönwälder, Karen. "'Ist nur Liberalisierung Fortschritt?' Zur Entstehung des ersten Ausländergesetzes der Bundesrepublik." In *50 Jahre Bundesrepublik—50 Jahre Einwanderung: Nachkriegsgeschichte als Migrationsgeschichte*, edited by Jan Motte, Rainer Ohliger, Anne von Oswald, 127–144. Frankfurt: Campus Verlag, 1999.

Schönwälder, Karen. *Einwanderung und ethnische Pluralität. Politische Entscheidungen und öffentliche Debatten in Großbritannien und der Bundesrepublik von den 1950er bis zu den 1970er Jahren.* Essen: Klartext-Verlag, 2001.

Schulz, Kristina. *Der lange Atem der Provokation: Die Frauenbewegung in der Bundesrepublik und in Frankreich 1968-1976.* Frankfurt: Campus Verlag, 2002.

Senders, Stefan. "Laws of Belonging: Legal Dimensions of National Inclusion in Germany." *New German Critique* 67 (Winter 1996): 147–176.

Shonick, Kaja. "Émigrés, Guest Workers, and Refugees: Yugoslav Migrants in the Federal Republic of Germany, 1945-1995." PhD diss., University of Washington, 2008.

Silverman, Maxim. *Deconstructing the Nation. Immigration, Racism and Citizenship in Modern France.* London: Routledge, 1992.

Slobodian, Quinn. "The Borders of the *Rechtsstaat* in the Arab Autumn: Deportation and Law in West Germany, 1972/73." *German History* 31, no. 2 (2013): 204–224.

Slobodian, Quinn. *Globalists: The End of Empire and the Birth of Neoliberalism.* Cambridge, MA: Harvard University Press, 2018.

Smith, Evan, and Marinella Marmo. *Race, Gender and the Body in British Immigration Control. Subject to Examination.* London: Palgrave Macmillan, 2014.

Spicka, Mark E. "City Policy and Guest Workers in Stuttgart, 1955–1973." *German History* 31, No. 3 (2013): 345–365.

Staver, Anne. "From Right to Earned Privilege? The Development of Stricter Family Immigration Rules in Denmark, Norway and the United Kingdom." PhD diss., University of Toronto, 2014.

Stehle, Maria. "Narrating the Ghetto, Narrating Europe: From Berlin, Kreuzberg to the *Banlieues* of Paris." *Westminster Papers in Communication and Culture* 3, no. 3 (2006): 48–70.

Stokes, Lauren. "The Permanent Refugee Crisis in the Federal Republic of Germany, 1949–." *Central European History* 52, no. 1 (2019): 19–44.

Straßburger, Gaby. *Offene Grenzen für Remigranten: Wiederkehrwünsche türkischer Remigrantinnen und das deutsche Ausländerrecht.* Berlin: Verlag für Wissenschaft und Bildung, 1992.

Summers, Sarah E. "Reconciling Family and Work: The West German Gendered Division of Labor and Women's Emancipation, 1960s to 1980s." PhD diss., Chapel Hill, 2012.

Summers, Sarah E. "Finding Feminism: Rethinking Activism in the West German New Woman's Movement of the 1970s and 1980s." In *Gendering Post-1945 German History: Entanglements,* edited by Karen Hagemann, Donna Harsch, and Friederike Brühöfener, 184–206. New York: Berghahn, 2019.

Szatkowski, Tim. *Die Bundesrepublik Deutschland und die Türkei 1978 bis 1983.* Berlin: Walter de Gruyter, 2016.

Taylor, Paul C. *Race: A Philosophical Introduction.* Cambridge: Polity Press, 2004

Ther, Philipp. *Europe Since 1989: A History.* Translated by Charlotte Hughes-Kreutzmiller. Princeton, NJ: Princeton University Press, 2016.

Timm, Annette F. *The Politics of Fertility in Twentieth-Century Berlin.* Cambridge: Cambridge University Press, 2010.

Töksöz, Gülay. *"Ja, sie kämpfen—und sogar mehr als die Männer." Immigrantinnen—Fabrikarbeit und gewerkschaftliche Interessenvertretung.* Berlin: Nozizwe, 1991.

Trede, Oliver. *Zwischen Misstrauen, Regulation und Integration. Gewerkschaften und Arbeitsmigration in der Bundesrepublik und in Großbritannien in den 1960er und 70er Jahren.* Paderborn: Ferdinand Schöningh, 2015.

Triadafilopoulos, Triadafilos. "Introduction. Assessing the Consequences of the 1999 German Citizenship Act." *German Politics and Society* 30, no. 1 (2012): 1–16.

Uçar, Ali. *Die soziale Lage der türkischen Migrantenfamilien. Mit einer empirischen Untersuchung unter besonderer Berücksichtigung der arbeits- und sozialrechtlichen Fragen.* Berlin (West): EXpress Edition, 1982.

Uçar, Ali. *Illegale Beschäftigung und Ausländerpolitik: die Praxis der Ausländerpolitik und die illegale Beschäftigung der ausländischen Arbeiter in der Bundesrepublik Deutschland.* Berlin (West): EXpress Edition, 1983.

Urbanek, Doris. "Forced Marriage vs. Family Reunification: Nationality, Gender and Ethnicity in German Migration Policy." *Journal of Intercultural Studies* 33, no. 3 (2012): 333–345.

Varsori, Antonio. "The EEC and Greece's Application to Join the Community, 1959–1976." In *Institutions and Dynamics of the European Community, 1973–1983,* edited by Johnny Laursen, 202–220. Baden-Baden: Nomos, 2015.

Vierra, Sarah Thomsen. *Turkish Germans in the Federal Republic of Germany: Immigration, Space, and Belonging, 1961–1990.* Cambridge: Cambridge University Press, 2018.

Wagner, Andreas. "Das 'Heidelberger Manifest' von 1981. Deutsche Professoren warnen vor 'Überfremdung des deutschen Volkes." In *Manifeste. Geschichte und Gegenwart des politischen Appells,* edited by Johanna Klatt and Robert Lorenz, 285–313. Bielefeld: transcript Verlag, 2010.

van Walsum, Sarah. *The Family and the Nation: Dutch Family Migration Policies in the ontext of Changing Family Norms.* Newcastle: Cambridge Scholars, 2009.

Wiesen, S. Jonathan. "Miracles for Sale: Consumer Displays and Advertising in Postwar Germany." In *Consuming Germany in the Cold War,* edited by David F. Crew, 151–178. Oxford: Berg, 2003.

Wildenthal, Lora. *The Language of Human Rights in West Germany.* Philadelphia: University of Pennsylvania Press, 2013.

Wildenthal, Lora. "Imagining Threatened Peoples: The Society for Threatened Peoples (*Gesellschaft für bedrohte Völker*) in 1970s West Germany." In *Imagining Human Rights,* edited by Susanne Kaul and David Kim, 101–117. Berlin: deGruyter, 2015.

Winter, Elke, Annkathrin Diehl, and Anke Patzelt. "Ethnic Nation No More? Making Sense of Germany's New Stance on Dual Citizenship by Birth." *Review of European and Russian Affairs* 9, no. 1 (2015): 1–19.

Woesthoff, Julia. "Ambiguities of Anti-Racism: Representations of Foreign Laborers and the West German Media, 1955–1990." PhD diss., Michigan State University, 2004.

Woesthoff, Julia. "'When I Marry a Mohammedan': Migration and the Challenges of Interethnic Marriages in Post-War Germany." *Contemporary European History*, 22, no. 2 (2013): 199–231.

Woesthoff, Julia. "'Foreigners and Women Have the Same Problems': Binational Marriages, Grassroots Organizing, and the Quest for Legal Equality in Post-1968 Germany." *Journal of Family History* 38, no. 4 (2013): 422–442.

Wolbert, Barbara. *Der getötete Paß: Rückkehr in die Türkei: Eine ethnologische Migrationsstudie.* Berlin: Akademie Verlag, 1995.

Wolfrum, Edgar. *Rot-Grün an der Macht: Deutschland 1998–2005.* Munich: C. H. Beck, 2013.

The Women, Immigration, and Nationality Group. *Worlds Apart. Women Under Immigration and Nationality Law.* London: Pluto Press, 1985.

Wong, Aliza S. *Race and the Nation in Liberal Italy, 1861–1911: Meridionalism, Empire, and Diaspora.* New York: Palgrave Macmillan, 2006.

Wray, Helena. "An Ideal Husband? Marriages of Convenience, Moral Gate-keeping and Immigration to the UK." *European Journal of Migration and Law* 8, no. 3 (2006): 303–320.

Yildiz, Yasemin. *Beyond the Mother Tongue. The Postmonolingual Condition.* New York: Fordham University Press, 2012.

Zahra, Tara. "Imagined Noncommunities: National Indifference as a Category of Analysis." *Slavic Review* 69, no. 1 (2010): 93–113.

Zahra, Tara. *The Lost Children: Reconstructing Europe's Families after World War II.* Cambridge, MA: Harvard University Press, 2011.

Zimmerman, Andrew. *Alabama in Africa: Booker T. Washington, the German Empire, and the Globalization of the New South.* Princeton, NJ: Princeton University Press, 2012.

Zölls, Philip. *Regieren der Migration. Von Einwanderungsprozessen und Staatlichen Regulierungspolitikern.* München: Allitera Verlag, 2019.

INDEX

For the benefit of digital users, indexed terms that span two pages (e.g., 52–53) may, on occasion, appear on only one of those pages.

Tables and figures are indicated by t and f following the page number.